DECADES NEVER START ON TIME
A RICHARD ROUD ANTHOLOGY

edited by
MICHAEL TEMPLE & **KAREN SMOLENS**

A BFI book published by Palgrave Macmillan

First published in 2014 by
PALGRAVE MACMILLAN

on behalf of the

BRITISH FILM INSTITUTE
21 Stephen Street, London W1T 1LN
www.bfi.org.uk

There's more to discover about film and television through the BFI.
Our world-renowned archive, cinemas, festivals, films, publications and learning resources are here to inspire you.

Palgrave Macmillan in the UK is an imprint of Macmillan Publishers Limited, registered in England, company number 785998, of Houndmills, Basingstoke, Hampshire RG21 6XS. Palgrave Macmillan in the US is a division of St Martin's Press LLC, 175 Fifth Avenue, New York, NY 10010. Palgrave Macmillan is the global academic imprint of the above companies and has companies and representatives throughout the world. Palgrave® and Macmillan® are registered trademarks in the United States, the United Kingdom, Europe and other countries.

Cover images: (front) © couch; (back) © Helaine Messer
Designed and set by couch
Printed in China

This book is printed on paper suitable for recycling and made from fully managed and sustained forest sources. Logging, pulping and manufacturing processes are expected to conform to the environmental regulations of the country of origin.

British Library Cataloguing-in-Publication Data
A catalogue record for this book is available from the British Library
A catalog record for this book is available from the Library of Congress

ISBN 978-1–84457–625–8 (pb)
ISBN 978-1–84457–626–5 (hb)

CONTENTS

ACKNOWLEDGMENTS

We would like to thank the following people and institutions for their help with this project. For their editorial support, Rebecca Barden (formerly of BFI Publishing, now at Bloomsbury Publishing), Jenni Burnell and Sophia Contento of Palgrave Macmillan and BFI Publishing.

For granting us permission to reproduce material from its Richard Roud Collection, the Howard Gotlieb Archival Research Center, Mugar Memorial Library, Boston University.

For his help in the archive, Ryan Hendrickson of the Howard Gotlieb Archival Research Center.

For permission to reproduce material written by Richard Roud: Karen and Edith Smolens, *The Guardian*, *Sight & Sound*, Phillip Nobile and Macmillan Publishing, the British Film Institute, the Film Society of Lincoln Center, the Museum of Modern Art (New York).

For permission to reproduce their photographs, Paula Court, Helaine Messer and Alain Resnais.

For its financial contributions to travel expenses and transcription costs, Birkbeck, University of London.

For his help with research into sources and references, and for constant moral support, Bob McCarthy. For his encouragement and advice, Lee Shostak.

For their assistance with the transcription of articles and documents, and with the preparation of the indexes, Dana Knight and Muriel Temple.

Finally, we would like to dedicate this book to Edith and Irving Smolens, as well as to Lucie and Paul Temple.

PREFACE

DAVID THOMSON

He could be imperious, but then he darted towards mischief if he felt too much pomp was showing. He had a temper and did not enjoy the community of fools, but he was candid and rueful about the chump he could be. There he was – living in England and doing a lot to change London – but he was American, with a voice that had something of Boston, plenty of Paris, a cutting edge from too many cigarettes and his own unexpected shyness. He was like an explorer who had come ashore and seen that there was a job to be done in Britain, or on the South Bank. So he went about it like Walter Burns in *His Girl Friday*. Not that there was such a girl. Richard was gay at a time when that was not the easiest thing to be. His friendships remained discreet and, as with so many characters from American comedy of the *His Girl Friday* era, Richard's gayness gave him licence to talk to women freely, personally and cheekily. They adored him as he delighted in being mystified by them.

What did he do for London? Well, as Michael Temple suggests in his rich Introduction, he sensed he was lucky to be there at that time, as the French New Wave broke on the shore and as it became possible to re-examine Hollywood movies. The National Film Theatre and the London Film Festival had been in existence before Richard appeared, but he whipped them into shape and guessed there was a community of young people who needed to be exposed to a range of cinema. So he defined the Film Festival as a highly selective gathering of the best films (not more than twenty-five for a year) and he was lucky because in those early 1960s the cinema was exploding. But he reorganized our thoughts on the past, too. Large seasons were ushered in – the long survey of French film was vital, and it had a profound effect on the understanding of Renoir and of how the New Wave directors were nourished by their past.

In London in the late 1950s, a controversy had been building at *Sight & Sound*. It was an estimable magazine, only a quarterly then, but irritated by the way young writers in *Cahiers du Cinéma* and *Positif* were going into raptures on American directors: not just Howard Hawks and Alfred Hitchcock, but Edgar G. Ulmer, Samuel Fuller, Nicholas Ray, Douglas Sirk and so on. Many of the films by those directors were not known or not respectable in Britain. *Cahiers* thought they were raw gold in the stream, and a few young Brits were reading *Cahiers* and wondering. Richard was the natural translator and enabler for that mood. He never burnt his bridges with *Sight & Sound* (and he tended to have an incendiary attitude to bridges), but at the NFT he began to do surveys of American film, too: a great Hawks season, recognition of Fritz Lang, Joseph Losey and Nick Ray.

Nineteen-sixty was the moment for this English wave. There were critical disputes over what cinema was, and the NFT was the place where the materials were aired out for the battles. It was a heady time. In 1960, I had entered the London School of Film Technique (that was its name then) because it was the only site of higher education in film in Britain. So I went to the NFT as if it was a university. In time, Richard became film critic of the

Manchester Guardian and he seemed to be writing all over the place. Moreover, the London Film Festival was such a success that New York invited him to come and do the same trick at the Lincoln Center. He did it, but, as he said, with the films of the late 1960s and early 70s, how could anyone fail?

Well, failure was easier to find than you might have thought. By the mid-1980s, the films were not as good (we have to admit it) and Richard and the system at the Lincoln Center were often at odds. Eventually, he was fired, and I can't say that his temper and his casual attitude to paperwork were not at fault. But he was writing – articles and then books. The firing was ugly, decisive in many ways and a sign that film had been taken over not just by academia but by bureaucracy and its power groupings.

So it's important to know that Richard was not simply brilliant, eloquent and right most of the time. He was a brusque version of Octave in *La Règle du jeu*. He was on the fringes of the party, introducing people, bubbly with pleasure, and as much at ease with a Godard as with a Minnelli, a Truffaut or a Losey. It's high time that the world had a good anthology of his work, and I am delighted to be able to read the draft of his Truffaut book. But you should know that in London, New York, Paris and Cannes, you wanted to be sitting at Richard's table. He knew so much, and yet he was a pretender of genius when his knowledge ran short. He was witty, rude (Richard Rude was heard sometimes), amusing and easily amused. He had dark moods and grievances, too (like Octave), but they didn't seem to last too long. When I was on the selection committee of the New York Film Festival with Roud and Richard Corliss, Molly Haskell and Andrew Sarris, Jim Hoberman and Dave Kehr, we had to see an impossible number of films, and it was Richard who devised the scheme whereby if two people had had enough we'd turn a film off and move on. But then after a film had been killed, if one of us went to him privately and said he or she really loved the film, it had another chance. If one person was passionate for a film, then Richard kept the door open. He might tease the picture, and his own kindness, but he seldom ignored commitment. It's understandable that he felt lucky in his timing, but so many of us were lucky to ride on his wave.

Richard Roud at the National Film Theatre, London, early 1960s. Photograph by Alain Resnais

INTRODUCTION

MICHAEL TEMPLE

> He combined acute intelligence with a passion for the best the cinema could do. And he
> was able to communicate his enthusiasm.
>
> Roud, 'Face to face: James Agee'

This book was born from a shared passion for the films of Jean-Luc Godard. When BFI
Publishing decided to reissue Richard Roud's classic monograph on the film-maker as part
of its BFI Silver collection, I was asked to write a foreword to the new edition. The aim of
my preface was modest in scale and scholarly in nature. Since Roud's study had originally
been published in 1967, my brief was to contextualise and evaluate his discussion of
Godard, first, in relation to the vast body of Godard-related criticism and scholarship that
had emerged in the intervening forty or so years and, second, in response to the extraordinarily rich and multifarious paths that the film-maker's career had taken – and continues
to take – since his 1960s heyday. Apart from the sheer pleasure of rereading Roud's book,
for me it was a revelation to discover how well his *Jean-Luc Godard* had stood the test of
time. Partly this was due to the book's intrinsic merits, for example Roud's lively, engaging
style; his passionate commitment to Godard's work and to the cause of art cinema in the
1960s; and his subtle ability to combine close critical readings of the films with a sophisticated sense of their social and cultural context. But I was also struck by two external factors that have only become apparent with the passing years.

The first is what I would call Roud's historical good fortune. In other words, the simple
fact that when he wrote his study of Godard at the end of the 1960s (an updated second
edition of the book had appeared in 1968 and a revised third edition in 1970), it was possible for Roud to grasp at that point in film history the entire Godardian oeuvre in both
hands, and to look at it critically as a coherent body of work: complex, multifaceted,
uneven, mercurial, but apprehensible as an organic whole from the individual viewpoint of
a suitably well-informed and lucid observer. Moreover, in his twin role as film critic and film
programmer, Roud had been able to follow the evolution of that work as a truly contemporary witness, from film to film, as each new work contradicted or complemented his perception of Godard's cinema and, in the course of that prolific and inventive decade, no
doubt his very understanding of cinema itself. Looking at Godard's vast and diverse catalogue of works today, no individual critic or scholar would now feel so fortunate or privileged as Roud was in the late 1960s. Few observers would pretend to know the whole
corpus in all its periods, dimensions, and formats; even fewer could claim to have lived
through its evolution from the late 1950s to the present. There is a second factor, however, that sets Roud and his *Godard* book apart, but it is more a question of philosophical
or spiritual attitude than a matter of historical opportunity. Writing in 1967, in the first edition of his study, Roud had stated very honestly that: 'No book on Godard can hope to be
up to date for very long.' A mere two years later, trying to come to terms not only with the

impact of *La Chinoise* (1967) and *Week End* (1967), but also with the events of May 1968 and the dramatic personal and artistic changes that Godard had experienced at that time, Roud went a little further in stating his critical philosophy: 'Godard's future development is impossible to predict.' The wisdom of this phrase struck me as being even more pertinent in the 2010s than it had been some forty years earlier. It helped me to understand that today Godard's future development remains as wonderfully impossible to predict as ever, and that those of us who feel inspired rather than intimidated by that uncertainty are still the richer and happier for it …

My encounter with Roud via Godard in 2010 was, of course, more of a rediscovery than a revelation, since I knew Roud's *Godard* already and, without really making the connection between his other books, I was also aware of his study of Jean-Marie Straub and Danièle Huillet, just as I had explored his *Cinema: A Critical Dictionary*, and had likewise greatly enjoyed his biography of Henri Langlois. But the writing of the preface did act as a catalyst, insofar as I discovered therein my deep admiration for Roud as a writer, and a certain intellectual complicity in our understanding of Godard, of cinema – and of the limits of knowing anything about either Godard or cinema at all. On a more practical level, I was inspired to find out more about Richard Roud's life and career in the film culture of the post-war period. For although there was no brief from the BFI to write biographically about Roud himself in the foreword, my professional curiosity led me to try to piece together the different elements of his work, and the available information about his life, into some sort of primitive portrait. This is what I wrote:

Critic, programmer, and author, Roud combined these three complementary strands of his 'passion for films' from the late 1950s up to his death from a heart attack in 1989. Throughout this dynamic and polyvalent career, he moved essentially between three cultures and three cities: Paris, London, and New York. Born in Boston, USA, in 1929, Roud had come to Europe in the 1950s to study on a Fulbright scholarship, first in Montpellier, France, then in Birmingham, England. Having initially earned his living by teaching English to US soldiers based in the UK (which would make a nice topic for a sketch by Godard), Roud was to find more rewarding employment when his friend Alain Tanner, the young Swiss film-maker, suggested that he try his luck at the BFI, which was then situated in Dean Street in London's Soho. It was Penelope Houston, editor of *Sight & Sound*, who gave him a chance to write film criticism for the organ of the BFI, his first articles appearing in 1956. By 1959, Roud had made himself sufficiently appreciated within the BFI to become programme officer at the National Film Theatre on London's South Bank; and the following year he was put in charge of the London Film Festival, which was then still in its infancy. In 1962, the founders of the New York Film Festival persuaded the BFI to allow Roud to work simultaneously for their new project, which was largely inspired by the London model. Roud duly served as programme director and chairman of the programme committee in New York from 1963 to 1970, when he was named festival director, a post that he held until his controversial resignation in 1987. Between 1963 and 1969, Roud combined running the two festivals, along with his programming role at the NFT; in addition to which he was working as chief film critic for the *Guardian*, while continuing to write regularly for *Sight & Sound* and other film journals. At the end of the 1960s, he gave up the London Film Festival and *Guardian* jobs (although he still wrote for the latter as a 'roving arts correspondent'), ostensibly in order to focus on the New York Film Festival. However, Roud remained a multi-tasking, transatlantic servant of the *cinéphile* cause, throughout the next two decades. In France, notably, he had always enjoyed close contact with many key figures of Parisian film culture, such as Henri Langlois, the legendary director of the Cinémathèque Française, and with film-makers such as Alain Resnais, Agnès Varda, Jacques Rivette, and most especially François Truffaut, whose biography Roud was working on at the time of his death.[1]

It was this unfinished biography of Truffaut that would become the link between my preface to the Godard book and the current collection of Roud's known and unknown writings. Having read about the Truffaut book repeatedly in almost all the obituaries and celebratory articles written about Roud, I necessarily wondered whether such a biography had ever really existed, or whether it was one of these unverified pieces of information that, once attached to a name or a reputation, gets uncritically repeated from source to source until it has acquired the status of fact. Via BFI Publishing, who had been dealing with Roud's estate regarding rights to the *Godard* re-edition, I was put in contact with Karen Smolens, the daughter of Edith Smolens (née Roud), Richard's sister. When I enquired about the existence of the Truffaut manuscript, I was delighted to hear from Karen that not only did it really exist, but also that she would immediately send me a copy of it by post. Thus began a collaboration and eventually a friendship that together have driven this project along over the last few years.

The Truffaut biography turned out to be a very substantial document indeed. It ran to some 115 pages, typewritten in single spacing, and amounting to something like 50,000 words. Moreover, I was delighted to discover that whereas the phrase 'unfinished project' had led me to expect a fragmented or incomplete manuscript, what I read was very much a full draft of a well-written and thoroughly researched study of Truffaut's life and films. Nonetheless, in response to Karen's initial request that I should let her know whether or not I thought it was worth publishing as it stood, I suggested that from an academic point of view too much time had probably now passed for Roud's text still to seem fresh and up to date. Notably, I pointed out that the market in Truffaut biographies had pretty much been cornered by the very thorough and successful study written by Antoine de Baecque and Serge Toubiana, first published in 1996 and then translated into English in 2000. Apart from their talent and experience, the French authors had also benefited from access to all sorts of documents and information that were simply unavailable to Roud when he was working on his Truffaut project in the 1980s. Given the historical interest and critical value of Roud's text, however, two options seemed possible. One would be to present extracts from it as part of an archival piece for a scholarly journal such as *Film History* or *1895, revue d'histoire du cinéma*; the other would be to include it as an important unknown document in the context of a 'reader' of Roud's journalistic and critical writings. When I put the latter idea to Karen, she responded enthusiastically that she had always dreamt of putting together just such a collection as a tribute to her uncle's life and work. She also revealed that there existed a considerable further amount of unpublished material, including a partially drafted manuscript for an autobiography or memoir entitled by Roud − rather curiously − 'Decades Never Start On Time'. Up to this point, I had seen my role simply as tying up some loose ends in relation to the *Godard* preface, and offering some academic advice about a hypothetical publication. However, this new evidence of unknown material, as well as the happy coincidence of Karen's long-cherished project with my own idea of a collected volume, encouraged me to look for possible publishers who might be interested in this kind of proposal. To my surprise, BFI Publishing replied almost immediately that they would be very willing to take the project forward themselves, partly as a natural extension of the *Godard* re-edition, but also as a contribution to the developing fields of the history of film culture in general, and the history of film criticism in particular. With a provisional agreement in place, my first priority for the project was to establish with Karen's help a sense of the range of sources from which we would select the material for our collection. Once that was done, we would need to decide on what basis we would either select or exclude material and, finally, how we would then organise and present the selected materials in the book itself.

Let us first look at the question of sources. These are best represented in the following five categories: *Sight & Sound*; the *Guardian*; other criticism and journalism; books; and archives.

First, *Sight & Sound* is such an important source because it was the publication with which Roud had the longest working relationship. His earliest contribution dates from 1956, a review of *The Man in the Grey Flannel Suit* (1956), and his last piece from 1989, a study of four films by Louis Malle.[2] There are about 100 items in total, written over a period of thirty-three years. Some of these texts are relatively short film reviews written for *Sight & Sound* and for the *Monthly Film Bulletin*, which was the sister publication of *Sight & Sound* until the early 1990s, when the BFI decided to merge the quarterly journal and the film bulletin into a single monthly magazine.[3] In addition, Roud contributes to *Sight & Sound* a good number of film festival reports from Cannes, Berlin, or Rotterdam, in other words quite journalistic pieces giving Roud's accounts of some of the films he has seen and perhaps indicating the general mood of the festival in question; there are also occasional interviews with film-makers and book reviews. In terms of sheer quantity, then, roughly one hundred pieces in thirty-three years may not seem a great deal. But this would be to misjudge the importance of *Sight & Sound* for Roud's career and to misunderstand the enduring value of his writing for that publication. As we have seen, Roud started out at the BFI, as a writer for *Sight & Sound* and the *Monthly Film Bulletin*, and as a programmer for the National Film Theatre and the London Film Festival. Without that early encouragement from Penelope Houston, it is possible that Roud's extraordinary journey through international cinema in the 1960s and 70s might never have happened at all. In return, Roud remained a faithful and regular contributor to the BFI's publishing activities throughout his career, and in terms of quality it is fair to say that he did some of his best writing for *Sight & Sound*. As a quarterly publication, the format gave Roud the opportunity to write for an informed public the kind of reflective essays that would have been more difficult to publish in a generalist magazine or daily newspaper. This is why we have retained a fairly high proportion of pieces from this source, focusing especially on Roud's longer, analytical essays about individual films or film-makers, for example 'Rondo Galant: the world of Jacques Demy' (1964) and 'Going between [about *The Go-Between*]' (1971). We have also included several of Roud's substantial discussion-pieces about more general questions in film culture, for example film criticism in 'Face to face: James Agee' (1959), or film festivals in 'London and New York' (1981).

The second major source for our collection is the *Guardian*. As in the case of *Sight & Sound*, Roud's relationship with one of the UK's best-known quality newspapers is a truly long-term affair. Having served as the *Guardian*'s principal film critic from 1963 to 1969, Roud took on a more broadly defined role in the 1970s and 80s, writing freely about art, theatre, music, opera, dance, architecture – as well as cinema, of course – as he moved around the world, between New York, London, Paris and the various films festivals and other artistic events that he attended in the course of his busy but no doubt very enjoyable schedule. In quantitative terms, it should therefore be no surprise that Roud wrote more articles for the *Guardian* than he did for any other publication. We have retained about thirty articles from a total of more than 700, in other words about one in twenty. That still represents a very substantial sample, particularly as we have chosen articles across the full span of Roud's employment at the newspaper from 1963 to 1989. Compared to much of his work for *Sight & Sound* – the best of which is often written with a certain critical distance from the flow of events – Roud's journalism for the *Guardian* is more typically the product of the daily or weekly pressures of producing a certain amount of copy, about a certain cultural topic or series of cultural objects, in time for a certain deadline. This does not mean, however, that the quality of Roud's journalistic writing is weaker than his feature writing, or that the value of his insights is uneven. On the contrary, Roud had a natural gift for prose that makes his writing always clear, engaging and elegant. At the same time, his critical appetite for cinema and the arts in general seems insatiable, as does his desire to communicate his thoughts and feelings to his readers, and to inspire in them a critical consciousness or simply a sense of wonderment.

Apart from his regular contributions to *Sight & Sound* and the *Guardian*, Roud wrote occasional criticism and journalism for a number of newspapers and magazines that were more or less specialised in film and cultural matters. Among the specialised film journals, the best known are *Film Comment* (the journal of the Film Society of Lincoln Center, New York), *Films and Filming* (for many years the independent British alternative to the publicly funded *Sight & Sound*), *Film Culture* (the magazine founded by New York experimental film-makers Adolfas and Jonas Mekas) and *Cahiers du Cinéma* (the most prestigious of French film journals, at least during the 1950s and 60s).[4] Among the non-specialised newspapers and magazines for which Roud wrote at one time or another, we can note *The Saturday Review*, *The Village Voice*, *Encounter*, *The Tatler*, *Tribune* and *The Sunday Times*. For our purposes, however, these occasional sources have provided a relatively low proportion of the material included in the current collection, the most important of them being *Film Comment*, to which Roud contributed a variety of articles over the years, including the series of 'diary' pieces that he and other film critics – such as Jonathan Rosenbaum – wrote from London, Paris and other locations around the world in the 1970s.[5] In addition to writing for magazines and newspapers, Roud composed numerous texts for specific film occasions (e.g. the piece about the tenth anniversary of the NFT, or the text for the Film Society of Lincoln Center's tribute to Fred Astaire), or for multi-authored film books (e.g., the piece about Jean Renoir's *La Règle du jeu* in a volume about the 'favourite movies' of various film critics). A very special case in this category would be the long introduction that Roud composed for the catalogue accompanying 'Rediscovering French Film', the retrospective season organised by the Museum of Modern Art, New York, in 1983. This text is both a perceptive survey of French cinema from its origins to the 1950s, one that any film student could still very profitably read today, and an engaging first-person account of the importance of French films in Roud's intellectual life and personal development.

The fourth source of material is Roud's impressive corpus of work as an author of books, i.e. as distinct from his writing as film critic or journalist. For it is not the least of his achievements that in the midst of all his other activities Roud somehow found the creative energy to write several important works, among which, of course, his monograph on

Godard is the best known. In 1958, he produced the relatively modest but still useful *Max Ophüls: An Index* for the BFI, the research for which led indirectly to the beginning of his friendship with Mary Meerson and Henri Langlois. In 1971, he wrote his aforementioned *Straub*, a ground-breaking study of the films of Jean-Marie Straub and Danièle Huillet; less well known than his *Godard*, but a beautifully crafted and essential text on the subject. There followed in 1980 the two-volume *Cinema: A Critical Dictionary: The Major Filmmakers*, with Roud acting as general editor of this 1,000-page reference book, as well as contributing several substantial entries on individual film-makers. Finally, in 1983 he wrote for Viking Press *A Passion for Films*, which is both a brilliant biography of Langlois and an institutional history of the Cinémathèque Française. Since Roud's books are now mostly out of print, with the exception of the *Godard*, reissued in 2010, we have chosen to include in this anthology sample extracts from those that are currently unavailable. Together they should demonstrate to a new readership that Roud's work as a film author and historian remains pertinent in terms of scholarly content and inspiring in terms of style and intellectual range. To put it very simply, anyone teaching a course on Ophüls or Godard or Straub and Huillet would still use Roud's books today; his entries on individual film-makers in the *Critical Dictionary* remain models of lucid and rigorous auteur criticism for specialists and students alike; and the Langlois portrait is certainly better than either the French biography by Georges Langlois and Glenn Myrent or the hagiographic film by Jacques Richard, and provides a perfect complement to Laurent Mannoni's more recent *Histoire de la Cinémathèque française* (Gallimard, 2006).[6]

The final source for the texts and documents chosen for this book is the Richard Roud collection at the Howard Gotlieb Archival Research Center, which is housed within the Mugar Memorial Library, Boston University. The collection consists of about thirty 'Paige' archival boxes, whose diverse contents the library catalogue divides into eight categories: manuscripts, correspondence, photographs, printed matter, scripts, scrapbooks, audiovisual and personal memorabilia. For our purposes we can simplify these categories into three more general types: visual, written and audio. The visual materials are mainly Roud's collection of film photographs, of which there are several thousand in total. Some of these are film stills that Roud must have collected for research and illustration purposes in relation to his book projects and articles. Much of the rest is the kind of publicity material that is distributed to journalists as part of the general promotional drive for the release of a film. In addition, there are some personal photographs of Roud himself or of people and places related to his working life, some of which we have been able to use in this book.

Among the written materials, which constitute the majority of the archive collection, there are a number of significant documents that we are publishing here for the first time. To give a few examples of this unique material, we can highlight 'How to see a movie (in the USA)' (1959), a brilliant text about the geography and technology of film-spectatorship in the age of the specialist art house and films-on-TV; this seems to have been written for *Sight & Sound*, but was never published, at least not in the journal itself. Another unpublished piece is a highly lucid and entertaining talk on 'Film criticism in the UK', which must have been Roud's contribution to a public debate about the practice of film criticism in different countries, seemingly organised at Cannes in 1967. A third example, written in 1976 in the context of a broader institutional discussion within the Lincoln Center about the operation of the NYFF, is the document entitled 'Memorandum on processes of prospection and selection [of films for the New York Film Festival]', which provides a fascinating insight into the workings of a major film festival. There are several other pieces that in the end we decided not to include here, although they remain important documents for further research. In 1964, for example, Roud co-authored with Amos Vogel a long and detailed report entitled 'Proposal for a Lincoln Center Film Institute', in which the authors set out an ambitious and even visionary project for a New York Cinémathèque, including a film archive, a film library and a film school – all in all, a significant investment in the preservation and study of the moving image, to be established alongside the nascent New York Film Festival. A similar type of policy document – which we decided not to include in the final selection of material – is 'Cable TV and the arts', a substantial report that Roud authored for the Sloan Commission on Cable Communications in 1971. These two documents show an important dimension to Roud's profile, one that we could easily forget within the flux of different activities that constituted his career – that is, the role of public intellectual, conscious of his responsibilities towards the wider community, beyond the narrow confines of the film world and its inward-looking tribal mentality.

In addition to these more or less finished but unpublished documents, we find in the archive a great number of drafts and preparatory notes for the wide range of texts that Roud wrote throughout his career. For example, we find draft versions of film programmes for the National Film Theatre, London Film Festival and New York Film Festival, as well as Roud's preparatory notes towards his literary output *per se*: his newspaper reviews and magazine articles and, of course, his books. These draft materials show us the extreme care and attention that Roud invested in his writing, despite the tight deadlines and unpredictable circumstances in which he must have produced most of his critical and journalistic work. Likewise, these materials allow us to appreciate the considerable amount of background research that Roud conducted in preparation for his writing. We find, for example, hundreds of newspaper and magazine articles on film and other related topics; as well as countless film programmes, festival catalogues, press books and other types of informational material. There are even entire film scripts, some in their published version and others in the form of working documents presumably given to Roud by the film-maker or production company in question. Finally, in terms of the written documents in the archive, there is Roud's personal and professional correspondence, which provides useful information about certain major projects (e.g., the Langlois book, the Truffaut biography, the Cinema dictionary) and key working relationships (e.g., the complexities of the NYFF, contract negotiations with the *Guardian* and Roud's publishers). On a personal note, I found it both enlightening and moving to read through some of the letters and telegrams that he received from film-makers such as Bernardo Bertolucci, Jacques Demy, Rainer Werner Fassbinder, Jean-Luc Godard, Pier Paolo Pasolini, Alain Resnais, François Truffaut and Agnès Varda. This was not so much for the precise information that they contain, as for the general taste that they give us of the cultural climate in which Roud worked. I was particularly struck by the friendly and intimate tone in which these luminaries of post-war cinema culture address Roud, even when the prime reason for writing to him is clearly professional – for example, a visit to New York for the film festival. He is clearly on very close terms with many of these important figures, and his relationship with them appears to have been truly an exchange between equals, rather than the kind of functional or self-serving dialogue one might normally expect to exist between a famous film-maker and a journalist or programmer.

The audiovisual material is potentially one of the great treasures of the Boston archive, although in relation to the current book of Roud's critical *writings* there is little or no material that it would have made sense to include here. This is nothing to do with the intrinsic quality or interest of these recordings; it is just that the audio tapes are essentially interviews that Roud conducted in preparing some of his journalistic writing and, in particular, three of his books: the study of Straub, the Langlois biography and the unpublished book about Truffaut. Although these recordings are therefore very genuine and often original sources of information about the people and topics discussed, we cannot consider them as samples of Roud's critical writing as such – or even, if we were to stretch a point, as examples of his general critical thinking – not least because as an interviewer Roud remains relatively discreet and sticks to asking questions or putting those questions into some kind of a context. To give a few examples, we can note that for the *Straub* monograph there are several lengthy, informative and surprisingly good-humoured interviews with Jean-Marie Straub and Danièle Huillet. In the context of the Langlois project, there are numerous interviews featuring, among others, Kenneth Anger, Pierre Braunberger, Louise Brooks, Freddie Buache, Lotte Eisner, Georges Franju, Jean-Luc Godard, Georges Langlois, Serge Losique, Jacques Rivette and Jean Rouch. Given the stellar cast of interviewees, these recordings form a significant block of potential research material, not just in relation to Langlois but also in more general film historical terms. Regarding the Truffaut project, Roud conducted interviews, for example, with Nestor Almendros, Fanny Ardant, Janine Bazin, Catherine Deneuve, Claude de Givray and Robert Lachenay; there are also several lengthy transcripts of interviews with Truffaut himself. In addition to the recordings related to these three book projects, there are substantial interviews with Bernardo Bertolucci, Joseph Losey and Alain Resnais; in the case of Losey, one of these pieces is a fascinating four-way discussion about *The Go-Between* involving Losey, L. P. Hartley, Harold Pinter and Roud himself. Finally, the audiotapes confirm the impression given by the written correspondence – that is, the sense of complicity, of a friendly exchange between equals, which informs Roud's working relationship with key figures of modern film culture.

Having discussed the origins of this project, and the sources on which the collection draws, I shall now focus on the selection and organisation of the material, as well as commenting briefly on some examples of texts that show the evolution of Roud as a critic and commentator. I confess that, given the sheer quantity of consistently great critical writing by Roud, it was a very difficult task to choose which texts to keep and which to leave out (see Bibliography for details of those texts mentioned here but not retained in the final selection). One of the first editorial decisions that I took was to include only texts and documents about cinema, thus excluding everything that Roud wrote about the visual and performing arts in general. This is not to say that his writing about these topics is not worth reading; nor that it could not be anthologised in some other collection at another time. For Roud was clearly a very cultivated man, and his genuine interest in the arts covered the full range of traditional highbrow culture. This included literature, of course, which is probably his most constant source of reference and comparison when he is writing about film. For the purposes of this book, however, it was clear to me that a decision about using material unrelated to cinema had to be made, and I made my decision on the basis of two firmly held beliefs. The first is that however much Roud appreciated art in general, and followed various art forms with great attention and even connoisseurship, his real love, his true love was cinema; and the course of his life was determined by that 'passion for films' to such a degree that it puts all other considerations in the shade. With cinema, Roud was someone special, and he gave us something special; without cinema he would perhaps have become a good cultural journalist, or maybe he would have done something else entirely with his life. Second, the most significant aspect of Roud's writing is its contribution to film culture, both for its intrinsic value as a very fine body of film criticism and for its symbolic function as a representation of a certain moment in film history. For Roud lived through an exceptional time of change and innovation, of extraordinarily beautiful films by a generation of risk-taking film-makers working both within the commercial mainstream and around its visible margins. It is his ability to talk to us about those times both as a critic and as a participant that makes his writing so valuable today: a chronicle of the modern art film's coming of age.

For these two reasons, I have only included texts about cinema. Having made that decision, I then decided that the collection had to include samples of the full range of types of writing that Roud practised in his career. It was immediately clear to me that the writing from *Sight & Sound* would occupy a significant place in the book; likewise the texts for the *Guardian*, although the proportion of material retained would obviously be a lot lower in this latter case. Among the other sources of criticism and journalism, I was purely motivated by the quality of the writing – a very personal criterion of judgment, I confess – and by the abiding interest of the topics or films discussed for audiences today. Regarding the books, I felt it was necessary to have something from each of them, with the exception of the *Godard*, so I focused on chapters or extracts that seemed to me to work effectively even when separated from the context of the books as complete works. In the case of the Langlois book, for example, I chose the most personal of Roud's chapters, where the author relates as a first-person narrative his working relationship with Langlois and describes how this evolved over the years that they knew each other. For the *Straub* I chose the opening chapters, which present the film-maker's cultural background and the early years of his career with Danièle Huillet, rather than selecting the more detailed analysis of films that Roud deploys in later sections of the book. Finally, in relation to the archive source, it seemed to me vital to include as high a proportion of this rare material as was practically possible – for example, almost half of the drafts for 'Decades Never Start On Time' and about a fifth of the Truffaut manuscript.

In terms of organisation, I was sure that it would be a mistake to divide the book into different types of writing, whether that division was to be a question of generic differences or in relation to the sources of the material. For me the only way to present the material was to be linear and heterogeneous at the same time. In other words, to arrange it along very clear chronological lines, while mixing all the various materials together. Reflective essay, film review, book extract and archive document, all produced by the intense flow of Roud's personal creative energies, and yet all caught up in the same historical movement forward through time. Having laid out the material in this fashion, I decided to create five blocks of time, partly in order to make the book more accessible and manageable for the reader, and partly in order to show the changes in Roud's work through the different stages of his career. These five periods are as follows: 1956–62; 1963–9; 1970–6; 1977–83; 1984–9. As these periods are purely an editorial invention on my part, I shall briefly explain why I have done it this way and illustrate my points with a few select examples of material.

The most striking thing about the first period, 1956–62, is the confidence and ambition of Roud's writing from the very start of his career. He was born into criticism already equipped with a distinctive voice and an intellectual personality, operating at a very high level of performance as a film writer and essayist, as well as a regular film critic. For a young man in his late twenties and early thirties, Roud already shows us that combination of sharp style and critical intelligence which was to make him such a key player in the film culture of this period. Thus, we find a series of very substantial, thoughtful and well-informed essays on topics that demand both a strong intellectual grasp of film culture and a good general knowledge of film history. Several of these texts deal with key questions of film aesthetics: 'The empty streets' (1957), on the adaptation of successful plays; 'Two cents on the rouble' (1957), on films based on great novels; and 'Novel novel; fable fable?' (1962), on film's relationship to modernist trends in narrative fiction (only the last of these has been included in the anthology). Three pieces are concerned with the conditions and culture of movie-going: 'Britain in America' (1956), on the distribution and appreciation of British cinema in the USA; the aforementioned 'How to see a movie (in the USA)' (1959); and 'NFT: the first ten years' (1962), a reflection on the institutional dimension of film culture. One text in particular points the way towards those new trends in European cinema which were to define Roud's film journey for the next ten years: 'The Left Bank' (1962), although in this regard we could also have included the earlier 'Five films [by Antonioni]' (1960). And, finally, there are two very lucid pieces about the history and practice of film criticism itself: the aforementioned 'Face to face: James Agee' (1959), followed by 'Face to face: André Bazin' (1959), a beautifully judged assessment of these two great critics operating in very different cultural contexts (to which we could have added 'The French Line' (1960), a nicely balanced evaluation of the seductive appeal and rhetorical excesses of 'la politique des auteurs' in Parisian film criticism). Finally, we should note that there were two high-quality articles that in the end we excluded from the final selection of material, because Roud reused the material in the context of his *Cinema: A Critical Dictionary* and we have preferred to retain the later version. These are 'The early work of Robert Bresson' and 'The naturalness of Renoir', both from 1959, which – along with his short book about Max Ophüls – show Roud's spiritual allegiance to certain key influential artists whose work would always remain an important point of reference for his aesthetic values.[7]

The second period, 1963–9, is the most intense seven years of Roud's career, insofar as he was simultaneously maintaining three areas of professional activity each of which would probably have been sufficient for a normal human being: programming at the NFT in London, co-directing the NYFF across the Atlantic (Roud never flew, incidentally, he always took the boat back to the USA) and writing for the *Guardian* his regular articles about the week's film releases in London as well as festival reports and other topical film items. In terms of Roud's writing style for the *Guardian*, he maintains a very high standard, despite the reduced format of the newspaper articles and the accelerated rhythm of their production. The voice is always clear and elegant and the critical personality immediately recognisable. He knows that he is speaking from a highly privileged position, in terms of his personal access and exposure to new films from around the world, but he is never patronising towards his audience. He never loses sight of the fact that for many people cinema is primarily a form of weekly entertainment. Nor does he fail to recognise that the practical realities of distribution, censorship and economics will inevitably limit the range of innovative films that his readership is likely to be able to experience at first hand. Yet one does get a sense of a mission, lucid and measured, but a mission nonetheless. For what Roud is trying to do in his *Guardian* pieces in particular is to communicate to a general readership – beyond the film-lovers of the NFT and *Sight & Sound* – his enthusiasm for the new film-makers of French, Italian and European cinema generally who, taken together, were effectively transforming film as an art form during this period. Thanks in part to critical voices such as Roud's – although there are many other cultural, economic and political factors that we cannot discuss here – these innovative and in some cases downright revolutionary film-makers were able to gain a strategic foothold in the mainstream of film culture, and even the film industry, while producing films that broke with virtually all the conventions of classical Hollywood cinema such as the film world had known it, since the coming of sound.

During this second period we can see Roud establishing a critical dialogue that is always a dynamic three-way exchange between himself, his readership and the new visions and voices – to take the Italian example – of Michelangelo Antonioni, Pier Paolo Pasolini, Marco Bellocchio, Mario Comencini, Ermanno Olmi, Bernardo Bertolucci; or from France the so-called New Wave of François Truffaut, Jacques Rivette, Claude Chabrol, Alain Resnais, Agnès Varda, Chris Marker, Jacques Demy and, of course, Jean-Luc Godard. While Roud is obviously aware of other new developments in cinemas across the world at this time, especially given his presence at all the key film festivals and his curatorial responsibilities in London and New York, it is clear to me that in the 1960s his cinephile heart always beats just a little faster for the new Italian and French films of this period. It is not that he does not know or care about what is happening in Spain, Germany, Czechoslovakia, Poland, Argentina or Japan; or for that matter the UK and the USA. It is just that with Antonioni and Bertolucci, as with Resnais, Truffaut and Godard, Roud is forging almost spiritual as much as aesthetic bonds with artists who have changed his way of seeing cinema and the world. Of all these figures, it is Godard who stands out even from this very distinguished group. We have retained a good number of Roud's articles about key Godard films of the 1960s: *Le Mépris* (1963), *Une Femme mariée* (1964), *Pierrot le fou* (1965), *Alphaville* (1966), *Masculin féminin* (1966), *Caméra-oeil* (1967), *Week End* (1967), and *Le Gai Savoir* (1969).[8] These articles allow us to trace Roud's fascination with Godard throughout the decade, an intense admiration for the artist which never becomes mere hero-worship, since the critic is always able to keep some kind of distance from the film-maker's status as the Picasso-like genius of contemporary cinema. The numerous texts on Godard also function in our collection as a stand-in for Roud's 1967 monograph, for which these articles were in creative terms a long series of sketches and preparatory essays. Finally, to speak of cinema in the 1960s, especially in relation to the rapidly evolving work of Godard during that time, is also inevitably to speak of politics and May 1968. This is why we have included Roud's article on the 'Langlois affair' in early 1968, and some examples of his series of reports about the derailment and eventual closing down of the Cannes Film Festival in May, as well as the continuing atmosphere of confusion, protest and repression that hung over the festivals of Pesaro, Karlovy Vary and Berlin that year.

In professional terms, it was 1969 that was, in fact, the turning point for Roud. Whether by choice or by necessity, Roud at the age of forty accepted some changes in the organisation of his complicated working life. In addition to redefining his job at the *Guardian*, he gave up being programme director of the London Film Festival (which he had been since 1960, as well as being programme director of the NFT from 1959 to 1967), a role that for several years he had been combining with the direction of the New York Film Festival (in collaboration with Amos Vogel up until 1968). He also gave up his membership of the editorial board of *Sight & Sound* and *Monthly Film Bulletin*. Taken together, these changes represented a certain lightening of Roud's workload, as well as a shifting of focus away from London towards New York and Paris. Without having any secret access to the inner workings of Roud's mind, I would guess that he may have begun to get bored with the weekly routine of writing film criticism in London, and the new disposition that he arranged with the *Guardian* gave him a steady income while allowing him to move around the globe, from festival to festival, spend more time in France and focus his curatorial energies on the needs of the NYFF and the internal politics of the Lincoln Center. In terms of his writing in the period 1970–6, Roud seems like a man who is reinvigorated by his new working conditions. In contrast to the often sombre general mood in left-leaning cultural circles post-1968, for example, he writes with great freedom and confidence about the ideologically sensitive subject of film and politics, for example in his article on Costa Gavras's *L'Aveu* versus Claude Chabrol's *Le Boucher* (July 1970), in a general discussion of 'political cinema' (October 1970) and in his piece about *Le Chagrin et la pitié* (May 1971). In this crucial middle period of his career, Roud appears to be taking stock of the great harvest of new films and film-makers that he witnessed in the preceding decade, while at the same time remaining alert to emerging trends in the next generation of artists, most of whom would typically be at least ten to fifteen years younger than himself (whereas he was more or less the same age as Chabrol, Godard, Rivette, Truffaut and so on). Thus, Roud in the early 1970s continues and even extends his dialogue with the work of Straub and Huillet, his monograph appearing in 1971, along with several articles and interviews throughout this period. Likewise his existing critical relationships with Rivette (e.g., the piece on *Out 1: Spectre*, July 1973), with Antonioni (e.g., the analysis of *The Passenger* in the summer of 1975), with Pasolini (e.g., the discussion of *Salò*, January 1976) and with Buñuel (e.g., reviews of *The Discreet Charm of the Bourgeoisie*, November 1972, and *The Phantom of Liberty*, September 1974) are all taken to new degrees of admiration and interrogation.[9]

At the same time, Roud engages enthusiastically with the renaissance of US cinema in his perceptive discussions of films such as Peter Bogdanovich's *The Last Picture Show* (1971), George Lucas's *American Graffiti* (1973), Martin Scorsese's *Mean Streets* (1973) and Terence Malick's *Badlands* (1973).[10] And he is very much aware of the strength of the New German cinema, whose progress he had tracked from its beginnings in film reviews and festival reports about the emergence of Werner Herzog (e.g., *Signs of Life* in the report on Berlin festival, July 1968) and Wim Wenders (e.g., the article on *The Goalkeeper's Fear of the Penalty*, March 1972), among others.[11] In particular, Roud starts an intense critical conversation with the films of Rainer Werner Fassbinder, whom he sees as the most original and profound of the new German film-makers, and whose work he will follow closely right up to Fassbinder's death in 1982 (see 'Biter bit', Summer 1982). Perhaps the most important shift in Roud's thinking and sensibilities in this period, however, is his clear realignment from Godard to Bertolucci. Whereas pre-1968 it was Godard who was the benchmark for Roud in relation to the current state of cinema, there is a clear sense of distancing that takes place in the early 1970s, with the younger Bertolucci emerging as the critic's most admired contemporary film-maker. Between 1969 and 1972, Roud seems to have lost Godard – as did many film enthusiasts – and even though he welcomes the return to something like 'cinema' with *Tout va bien* in 1972 (see 'Godard is dead, long live Godard-Gorin', Summer 1972), the tone of his pieces about the Sonimage venture (July 1975) and *Numéro deux* (January 1976) is more polite curiosity than wholehearted critical engagement.[12] By contrast, Bertolucci – who likewise distanced himself quite dramatically from Godard during this time – becomes the new model of the complex and daring director who can combine formal brilliance and artistic creativity with a sense of narrative spectacle. For Roud, the Italian is still committed to involving the audience

Decades Never Start On Time

dramatically and emotionally in his work, whereas Godard appears bound by a moral imperative to expose the ideologically pernicious nature of artistic illusion and filmic story-telling (see, for example, the discussion of *The Conformist* in 'Fathers and sons', Spring 1971, and *Last Tango in Paris* in November 1972).

The final two chronological periods, 1977–83 and 1984–9, have much in common in terms of their tone and content. In truth, I have divided them into two periods less for the-matic or narrative reasons than in the interests of manageability, since they both contain lengthy extracts of material from several books or book projects by Roud, and would thus be somewhat unwieldy as one long section. What they seem to share is a turn towards the past, both in terms of Roud's increasing role as a film historian rather than as a film critic, and also in more personal terms as he begins to look back on his own past, and to pass in review what I have called his journey through cinema. This shift from being a commen-tator of film's present to a chronicler of cinema's past can be situated in 1977. To be pre-cise, we can date it as 13 January 1977, the date of Henri Langlois's death, although I am not suggesting that Roud was so personally affected by Langlois's passing that his work changed radically as a result. I am rather saying that with hindsight there appears to be a shift in the manner and meaning of Roud's output from that date. It is a sense of an end-ing, the end of that modern movement in film history beginning with Italian neo-realism in the mid-1940s, then flowing through the various and successive 'new waves' of European and world cinema in the 1950s and 60s, before finally losing the historical initiative to the resurgent Hollywood mainstream of the mid-70s, notably in the form of the high-concept movie – for example, the release of *Jaws* in 1975. In terms of the evolution of Roud's work, it is striking that, from the elegiac obituary that he writes for Henri Langlois in early 1977, there is henceforth almost nothing really new that he writes about with great enthusiasm, no entirely new film phenomenon that will change his understanding of what cinema is, no ground-breaking new film-maker whose next film he will be looking forward to review. The writing does not become noticeably sadder, or more nostalgic, nor does Roud just become a grumpy old critic complaining about how films used to be better in the past, 'they don't make them like they used to', etc. Likewise, it is very difficult to imagine Roud grandly the-orising about the 'death of cinema', without a degree of irony or just plain modesty helping him to keep things in perspective. His discussion of what he calls 'popcorn movies' such as Steven Spielberg's triumphant series of films in the late 1970s and early 80s – *Jaws* (1975), *E.T.* (1982), *Raiders of the Lost Ark* (1981), *Close Encounters of the Third Kind* (1977) – is never condescending or reactionary. For all Roud's intellectual sophistication and love of Antonioni, Bertolucci, Godard, Resnais and company, he still understands the basic pleasure of cinema as pure escapist entertainment and its irrefutable status as one of the cultural miracles of the twentieth century. And yet when we read his writings of these final years, it is clear that something has changed, and in my view it is fundamental, and irreversible, like the slow, natural movement towards death.

The obituary of Langlois is the first of several such pieces that Roud was called upon to write during this time. In our collection it is followed by the obituaries of Chaplin (December 1977), of Fassbinder (Autumn 1982), of Lotte Eisner (Summer 1984) and of Joseph Losey (Winter 1984). Apart from the text for Chaplin, all of these obituaries are written very much from the heart, with Roud drawing explicitly on his personal relation-ships with his subjects. In other words, death becomes a source of literary inspiration and philosophical reflection. Thus, it is the death of Langlois that inspires Roud to write *A Passion for Films*, just as the death of Truffaut in October 1984 is the inspiration for

Roud's unpublished study of the film-maker's life and works. It is worth noting that evidence from Roud's correspondence suggests that he was likewise thinking of writing a biography of Losey, immediately after the latter's death, also in 1984. In addition to these texts arising from the death of a film personality, there is a powerfully retrospective vein running through much of what Roud wrote during the last ten years of his life. The *Critical Dictionary*, for example, is in some ways a summation of Roud's vision and knowledge of cinema, and his own entries for the dictionary become the occasion for him to return to a particular film-maker who has meant a great deal to him and to think about the evolution of his critical relationship to the works of Bresson, Renoir, or Resnais over several decades. The same spirit of reflection informs 'The Left Bank revisited' (Summer 1977), insofar as Roud is situating himself as a critic of a certain standing, and as a man of a certain age, in relation to a whole generation of film-makers whose life and work has run more or less in parallel to his own: Alain Resnais, Chris Marker, Agnès Varda and Marguerite Duras.[13] Finally, this reflective and retrospective tone is clearly tangible in the comparative discussion of the London and New York film festivals (Autumn 1981) and the fortieth anniversary of the Cannes Film Festival (May 1986).[14] And the role of the film festival in Roud's personal itinerary as well as in the history of post-war cinema is, of course, both the chief narrative device and the key thematic figure of 'Decades Never Start On Time', the unfinished first-person memoir whose title we have borrowed for our collection.

As a literary genre, the autobiography is traditionally preoccupied as much with death as with life. Sensing the end approaching, the author projects himself 'beyond the grave' and tells his own story from that impossible vantage point. At the same time, the writing subject becomes the imaginary object of his own story, like the painter staring into the mirror to capture his self-portrait. In Roud's case, the strategy of 'Decades Never Start On Time' would have no doubt been part autobiography and part self-portrait, showing him at work as a critic in a variety of locations and situations, and inscribing his own story as a film critic and *festivalier* within the broader historical canvas of post-war film culture. We know from the correspondence in the archive that Viking Press rejected Roud's project in 1984 and there is no sign that he proposed it to any other publishers. Did he just decide to drop the whole idea? Or did he merely put it on hold? After all, he must have been aware that the model of the film memoir – that is, 'my life in cinema and cinema's role in my life' – was very much in the cultural mood of the times for cinephiles of his generation. He can hardly have failed to notice that a critic such as Jonathan Rosenbaum, for example, had been able to publish to some acclaim his *Moving Places: A Life at the Movies* in 1980.[15] Likewise, much of French critic Serge Daney's celebrated writing of the 1980s experimented with a first-person mode of film criticism that weaves personal experience and political subjectivity into the history of post-war cinema. And finally, given Roud's close connections to the inner circles of French film culture, he must have heard that Godard's much talked about *Histoire(s) du cinéma* project was, in essence, based on a similar idea of self-examination in the mirror of film history. So it is not illegitimate to speculate that Roud might one day have been persuaded to return to his own film memoir, perhaps even fashioning it into something more historically substantial, a critical autobiography, so to speak, recounting his life in film criticism and reflecting on how the history of cinema had conversely 'written' his life. We will never know, of course, because death – real, not symbolic or imagined – intervened most brutally in February 1989 and brought Roud's dynamic and productive existence to a sudden end, at the age of fifty-nine. Let us hope that this collection of texts and documents will go some way to allowing Roud to tell his story in his own words, for a new generation of readers who will be able to enjoy his film criticism for its style and passion and intelligence, and also for the critical light that it casts on a period of film history that still has the power to fascinate cinephiles and inspire young film-makers today.

Notes

1. Michael Temple, 'Foreword to the third edition', Richard Roud, *Jean-Luc Godard* (London: BFI/Palgrave Macmillan, 2010), viii–ix.
2. '*The Man in the Grey Flannel Suit*', *Sight & Sound*, 26.2, Autumn 1956, 97; 'Malle X 4', *Sight & Sound*, 58.2, Spring 1989, 125–7.
3. For a history of *Sight & Sound* see Geoffrey Nowell-Smith, 'The *Sight & Sound* story, 1932–1992', in Christophe Dupin and Geoffrey Nowell-Smith (eds), *The British Film Institute, the Government and Film Culture, 1933–2000* (Manchester: Manchester University Press, 2012), 237–51. See also the digital archive of *Sight & Sound*, which the BFI has now made available online.
4. Regarding Roud's collaboration with the *Cahiers du Cinéma*, we have in fact been able to find just one article, a 'letter from London' about Joseph Losey's *The Servant* (1963), published in 1964. In the archive, however, there is a draft of a second 'lettre de Londres', this time about Stanley Kubrick's *Dr. Strangelove* (1964). In both cases it would appear that Roud has written the French text himself, rather than have it translated.
5. See Bibliography for details of these *Film Comment* texts, which we have not been able to include in this anthology for want of space.
6. Georges Langlois, Glenn Myrent, *Henri Langlois, premier citoyen du cinéma* (Paris: Editions Denoël, 1986); Jacques Richard, *Le Fantôme d'Henri Langlois* (2004).
7. For the Bresson piece, see *Film Culture*, 20, 1959, 44–52; for Renoir, see William Whitebait (ed.), *International Film Annual*, 3 (London: John Calder, 1959), 105–15.
8. See 2.2 'End of Bardolotry' about *Le Mépris*; 2.7 'Object lesson' about *Une Femme mariée*; 2.9 'New films' about *Pierrot le fou*; 2.8 'Anguish: Alphaville'; 2.11 'Masculin féminin'; 2.12 'Far from Vietnam' about *Caméra-oeil*; 2.14 'Weekend in Paris' about *Weekend*; and 2.19 'Le Gai Savoir'.
9. See Bibliography for references to those articles not included in the anthology.
10. For the discussion of *The Last Picture Show*, see 'Citizen Bogdanovich', *Guardian*, 6 November 1971, 10.
11. See Bibliography for references to these two articles about early Herzog and Wenders films.
12. The pieces about Godard's post-1968 work are not included here; see Bibliography.
13. Although not included here, Roud's texts on Truffaut's *La Chambre verte* (1978), Resnais's *Mon oncle d'Amérique* (1980) and Rivette's *Pont du Nord* (1981) can likewise be read very much like extracts from longstanding conversations between old friends; see Bibliography for references.
14. The second of these texts, 'Freedom of the city forty years on' (*Guardian*, 15 May 1986, 13) is not included here.
15. In the archive there is evidence that Roud had started thinking about 'Decades Never Start On Time' as early as April 1977. Likewise, in a letter dated 23 August 1977, Jonathan Rosenbaum told Roud that he was going to start working on 'a critical autobiography or memoir involving movies'. It is interesting to note how this new genre in film writing was beginning to emerge in the cultural atmosphere of the time.

Roud at Cannes Film Festival, 1988. (© Paula Court 1988)

RICHARD ROUD: A CHRONOLOGY

KAREN SMOLENS

1929
- 6 July, Richard Stanley Roud is born in Boston, Massachusetts, to Charles Roud and Mabel Baker Roud; one sibling, Edith Louise, born 3 July 1927. Father is an engineer and industrialist; partner of Laminated Sheet Products Corporation in Boston.

1934
- Richard sees his first film at age five.

1940
- Mother, Mabel, dies after long illness at age forty-six, when Richard is eleven.

1944
- Sees his first foreign-language film, Sacha Guitry's *Les Perles de la couronne* (1937), with his father and sister.

1946
- Graduates from Brookline High School, Brookline, Massachusetts. Yearbook quote: 'Ambition: To see the world – All of it.'

1950
- Wins first prize, University of Wisconsin's Annual Vilas Essay Prize Contest for his essay 'Aspects of Donne'.
- Graduates from University of Wisconsin, Madison, AB cum laude in English.
- Fulbright Scholarship – Université de Montpellier, France.
- Father, Charles, dies of heart attack at age fifty-six.

1951–3
- Moves to England to attend University of Birmingham, Shakespeare Institute; begins postgraduate work towards PhD in English Literature.

1954–5
- New York University Reading Institute, Instructor in English and remedial reading.

1956–8
- Instructor in English, University of Maryland Overseas Division, at American airbases in East Anglia, England.

1956
- Meets Penelope Houston, Editor of *Sight & Sound*.
- 'Ionesco, the opposite of sameness' is published in *Encore* in 1956; republished in *The Encore Reader* in 1965.

1956
- First film review in *Sight & Sound* – Nunnally Johnson's *The Man in the Grey Flannel Suit* (1956).
- Arranges and chairs symposium on 'Trends in Contemporary Theatre' at Institute of Contemporary Art, London.

1957
- Starts contributing to the *Monthly Film Bulletin* of the British Film Institute.

1958
- Begins contributing film reviews to *Films and Filming*.
- Article 'The theatre on trial. Three drama critics and their verdicts and what they said' is published in *Encounter*, edited by Stephen Spender and Irving Kristol.
- Two Eugene Ionesco plays, *The Chairs* and *The Lesson* are produced in London with English translations by Donald Watson and Richard Roud.
- Contributes programme notes for the twenty-fifth anniversary brochure of the British Film Institute.
- First meeting with Henri Langlois and Mary Meerson at the Cinémathèque Française when Roud is researching films of Max Ophüls.
- *Max Ophüls: An Index* is published by the British Film Institute.
- First film programming responsibilities for the National Film Theatre's 'Free Cinema' programme. In a tense deadline situation, because he is fluent in French, Roud is called upon to obtain early New Wave films (Truffaut's *Les Mistons* [1958] and Chabrol's *Le Beau Serge* [1958]) for the Festival. This is his first encounter with the French New Wave.

1959
- Article 'The early works of Bresson' is published in *Film Culture* and reprinted the following year in *Film and Filming*.
- Appointed Programme Director, National Film Theatre, a position he will hold until 1966. First full programme planned for the National Film Theatre is 'The French Season'. Meets and acts as tour guide for François Truffaut when Truffaut makes his first visit to London for screening of *Les Quatre Cents Coups* (1959) at the London Film Festival.

1960
- 'The French Season', planned by Richard Roud, presented by Leslie Hardcastle, begins 1 March.
- Appointed Programme Director, London Film Festival, a position he will hold until 1969.

- Attends Cannes Film Festival for the first time where he sees Jean-Luc Godard's *À bout de souffle* (1960).
- Joseph Losey requests a meeting following a positive review of Losey's film, *The Criminal* (1960) (also known as *Concrete Jungle*).

1961
- Attends Venice Film Festival and meets Alain Resnais, who will win the grand prize that year for *L'Année dernière à Marienbad* (1961).
- Meets Agnès Varda and Jacques Demy when they arrive in London for Demy's screening of *Lola* (1961) at London Film Festival.
- Roud uses the term 'Left Bank group' in *Sight & Sound* article to distinguish a group of directors working in Paris led by Alain Resnais, Agnès Varda and Chris Marker from those of the '*Cahiers du Cinéma* group' including Godard, Truffaut and Chabrol.
- Appointed member Editorial Board, *Sight & Sound*.
- Writes 'The NFT: the first ten years' for the National Film Theatre's tenth anniversary.

1962
- Appears on BBC's *The Cinema Today* on 14 February, introducing Michelangelo Antonioni and his films.
- In the spring, writes letter to William Schuman, President of the Lincoln Center for the Performing Arts, at the suggestion of *New York Times* film critic, Eugene Archer, offering assistance in the development of a film festival in New York City.
- Meets with William Schuman in London, at which time plans for 'twinning' New York and London Film Festivals begin. While the formal appointment will not be made at this meeting, Roud's American citizenship is a significant factor in the decision to work with the British Film Institute.
- First meeting of significance with Godard in London when Godard's film, *Vivre sa vie* (1962), is selected to be shown at the London Film Festival.
- Screens Bernardo Bertolucci's first film, *La commare secca* (1962) at the London Film Festival, where he and Roud will meet for the first time.

1962–5
- Appointed to Editorial Staff Committee, *Sight & Sound*.

1962–7
- Contributes 'Films of the year' to *Encyclopaedia Britannica Yearbooks*.

1963
- Visits New York in January to discuss arrangements for New York Film Festival at Lincoln Center and is appointed its Programme Director. At that meeting he recommends Amos Vogel, founder of the Cinema 16 Film Society, as Festival Organiser in New York.

- In January, Roud is hired as film critic for the *Manchester Guardian*. First film review (of the collective sketch film *RoGoPaG* [1963]) appears on 28 March.
- 25 August, fills in as guest columnist for Judith Crist in the *New York Herald Tribune*. 'Film art's new frame', introduces the First New York Film Festival and the art of film as part of the programming of the Lincoln Center for the Performing Arts.
- 10 September, the first New York Film Festival opens in collaboration with the British Film Institute and the Museum of Modern Art. Opening night film: Luis Buñuel's *El ángel exterminador* (1962).
- Joseph Losey, Adolfas Mekas, Amos Vogel and Richard Roud appear on *Camera Three*, an American television programme broadcast on CBS, dedicated to the arts, discussing Losey's *The Servant* (1963) and Mekas's *Hallelujah the Hills* (1963), both screened at the inaugural New York Film Festival.

1965
- Appointment to the Critics' Circle in London for his work as film critic for the *Guardian*.

1967
- Becomes Director of English/French Press Conferences at the Cannes Film Festival.
- Named Chairman, Programme Committee of the New York Film Festival. He will remain Programme Committee Chair until 1987.
- *Jean-Luc Godard* is published by the British Film Institute as the first book in its Cinema One Series.

1968
- William Schuman resigns as President of the Performing Arts at Lincoln Center. The Film Society of Lincoln Center is created under the aegis of Lincoln Center to maintain the annual film festival and undertake other programmes related to film.
- Guest Director and Lecturer for three-week programme on the films of Jean-Luc Godard at the Museum of Modern Art, New York.
- Contacted by Howard Gotlieb, Chief of Special Collections at Boston University, inviting him to donate his papers to the newly formed archives devoted to the study of contemporary arts and literature.

1969
- Begins work as Managing Editor of *Cinema: A Critical Dictionary*, with anticipated publication dates of 1973–4.
- Film Society of Lincoln Center is founded. Amos Vogel resigns as Festival Organiser.
- Leaves position as Programme Director of the London Film Festival.
- Becomes Roving Arts Reporter for the *Guardian* on 27 December. *The Guardian* announces: 'Richard Roud has been appointed Special Arts Correspondent. He will be reporting on significant arts events in Europe and America as well as Britain.'

• Guest Director and Lecturer of three-week programme on 'Alain Resnais, his Predecessors and Contemporaries' at the Museum of Modern Art, New York.

1970
• *Jean-Marie Straub* is published by the British Film Institute in its Cinema One Series.
• *Jean-Luc Godard* is revised and expanded for publication by the British Film Institute.

1971
• Named co-director of New Directors/New Films Series at its inception, presented by the New York Film Society and the Department of Film, Museum of Modern Art, New York. He will remain co-director and member of the selection committee until the autumn of 1987.
• Named Director, New York Film Festival.
• Writes commissioned study for the Alfred P. Sloan Foundation, 'Cable Television and the Arts', the conclusions of which are incorporated in the Foundation's published reports.

1972
• Writes introduction for *Godard on Godard*, edited by Tom Milne, published by Secker and Warburg.
• Contributes introduction for *Alphaville: A Film by Jean Luc-Godard*, English translation of screenplay by Peter Whitehead, published by Lorrimer Press.
• *Last Tango in Paris* (1972) has world premiere on closing night of the New York Film Festival. Compared by one critic to the premiere of Stravinsky's *The Rite of Spring*, in Paris, 1913.

1973
• Begins contributing to *Film Comment*.

1976
• Purchases apartment in Paris and henceforth divides his time between Paris, London and New York.

1977
• *About the Arts*, an American television arts programme produced by WNYC, New York, is broadcast, with host Barbarelee Diamonstein-Spielvoge, Roud and Wim Wenders discussing the Film Festival and *The American Friend* (1977), shown at the 1977 New York Film Festival.
• Roud conducts François Truffaut's first American television interview for the CBS programme, *Camera Three*.

1978
• Made Chevalier, Légion d'honneur, France.

1980
• *Cinema: A Critical Dictionary* is published, after years of delays and missed deadlines, by Secker and Warburg, London, and The Viking Press, New York.

1981
• Organises 'British Film Week' in New York in conjunction with the Museum of Modern Art.

1983
• *Rediscovering French Film*, edited by Mary Lea Bandy, with an introduction and contributing essays by Richard Roud, is published by the Museum of Modern Art in New York, to accompany its French film exhibition.
• *A Passion for Films: Henri Langlois and the Cinémathèque Française*, is published by The Viking Press, New York.

1984
• Receives Theatre Library Association of America award for *A Passion for Films: Henri Langlois and the Cinémathèque Française* as 'an outstanding contribution to the literature of recorded performance'.
• Deaths of Joseph Losey and François Truffaut.
• Richard is named in Truffaut's will as a member of a committee in the USA to assist his daughter, Laura Truffaut-Wong, with 'making decisions regarding any release of books, montage films, TV films or videotapes' concerning her father's life or work. A second committee is named in France, headed by his daughter, Eva.
• Signs a contract in November with Alfred A. Knopf to begin work on a biography of François Truffaut.

1985
• Made Chevalier, L'Ordre des Arts et des Lettres, France.

1986
• Suffers serious heart attack en route to New York in early summer.

1987
• The Film Society of Lincoln Center's Board of Directors forces Roud's resignation as Director of the New York Film Festival, after much publicised political in-fighting with FSLC administration. This announcement was made immediately following the well-received twentieth-fifth festival. The international film community expresses public outrage and support for Roud at the time of his dismissal and following his departure.
• Roud's removal from his post as Director leads to the resignations of Richard Corliss and David Denby from the NYFF's Programme Committee in protest.
• Roud accepts appointment as film consultant for the Film Society of Lincoln Center.

1988

- Becomes Director Emeritus, New York Film Festival.
- Receives Special Citation from the National Society of Film Critics. The citation reads: 'The National Society of Film Critics is pleased to honour Richard Roud for his invaluable contributions to the New York Film Festival and his vital role in introducing international cinema to the American audience.'
- Begins programming for a French Film Retrospective at Lincoln Center, 'Thirty Years of the French New Wave', to be shown in New York in August, 1989. This programme will be dedicated to Richard following his death.
- Completes first draft of Truffaut biography.
- Accepts position as Director of Sarasota French Film Festival, Sarasota, Florida in November.

1989

- 15 January, Roud suffers a massive heart attack while on vacation in Nîmes, France, and will never regain consciousness.
- 13 February, Richard Roud dies at age fifty-nine, after remaining in a coma for one month. His ashes are returned to the US for burial in Everett, Massachusetts, with other members of his family.
- 28 February, a memorial service is held in New York City. Speakers include Nestor Almendros, John Ashbery, Vincent Canby, Molly Haskell, Andrew Sarris, Susan Sontag, Martin Scorsese, Harvey Gram, Richard Corliss; by telephone, Bernardo Bertolucci and by letter, Jack Lang, French Minister of Culture.

1990

- Richard Roud papers are donated by his family to the Howard Gotlieb Archival Research Center, Mugar Library at Boston University, Boston, Massachusetts.

1999

- *A Passion for Films: Henri Langlois and the Cinémathèque Française* is republished by Johns Hopkins Press.

2009

- 23 January, at the Lincoln Center's Walter Reade Theater, screenings of Max Ophüls *La Ronde* and Jean-Marie Straub and Danièle Huillet's *Chronicle of Anna Magdalena Bach* commemorate the twentieth anniversary of Roud's death.

2010

- *Jean-Luc Godard*, with new introduction by Michael Temple, is republished by the British Film Institute.

The Thirty-Nine Steps (1935)

PART 1 1956–62

1.1 'BRITAIN IN AMERICA'

The recent crowds at the National Film Theatre for the festival of Rank films would have surprised an American filmgoer. Indeed, a festival of British films on these lines would have been unthinkable at the Museum of Modern Art, the Film Theatre's New York counterpart. (If they ran a festival of British films, they would have shown pictures like *Shooting Stars*, *The Robber Symphony* and *Drifters*.) Not that *The Lady Vanishes*, *On Approval* or *Blithe Spirit* would be unappreciated by an American audience. It is simply that hardly a week goes by in New York when one cannot see most of these films at any-one of the small 'art' cinemas, or on television. It is not generally realised in English film circles that the double bill made up of *The Lady Vanishes* and *The 39 Steps* is the *Aida* of the American art cinema: whenever the receipts fall because the current offering is not a success, it is taken off and the Hitchcock bill is announced for a two-week season 'by popular demand'. Even a film that was not perhaps wildly popular in England – such as *Saraband for Dead Lovers* – will turn up on 42nd Street about three times a year, generally coupled, it is true, with a dubbed Italian sex-film. Moreover, certain films are probably *more* popular in America than in England; *The Ladykillers*, for instance, or *To Paris with Love*.

It is not easy to obtain statistics about the money British films have earned in America, but a lot has surely been made. There are three major British companies distributing films in America, Rank, Associated British-Pathé and British Lion,[1] and if we consider their greatest successes, and their failures, we can perhaps get some idea of what kind of British film appeals to the American public, before considering what sort of public this is.

To begin with the Rank Organisation. Their most successful films in America over the past few years, *Hamlet* and *The Red Shoes*, are atypical cases, in that they were generally released on what is known as a road-show basis: two performances a day only, and with prices approaching those of theatre tickets. Furthermore they were 'cultural' films, and as such were seen by people who do not usually or frequently attend the cinema. Schoolchildren and students flocked or were dragged, to *Hamlet;* schoolgirls and balletomanes mustered for *The Red Shoes*. (I am not attempting to disparage these films – although as films they certainly left something to be desired – only trying to suggest the kind of audience to which they appealed.) Rank's other successes, in order of popularity, have been as follows: *The Purple Plain**, *The Million Pound Note**, *Where No Vultures Fly**, *Doctor in the House**, *The Cruel Sea**, *Genevieve*, *To Paris with Love*, *The Ladykillers*, *The Lavender Hill Mob*, *The Man in the White Suit*, *The Planter's Wife**, *West of Zanzibar**, *The Card* and *Christopher Columbus**.[2]

Bearing in mind that, except for the art houses, exhibitors generally choose a film on the basis of its press-book, its title and, most important of all, its stars, we must subtract from the above list all those films having American stars, if we are to assess the pictures that did well solely on their intrinsic merit. Naturally the exhibitor would buy and could sell to his audience any film with Gregory Peck (*The Purple Plain*, *Million Pound Note*), Claudette Colbert (*The Planter's Wife*) or Fredric March (*Christopher Columbus*). We might also subtract *The Cruel Sea*, which was sold largely on the tremendous popularity of the book in America. It is now possible to make a second, and more meaningful, list of those Rank all-British films that were most popular with American audiences: *Doctor in the House*, *Genevieve*, *To Paris with Love*, *The Ladykillers*, *The Lavender Hill Mob*, *The Man in the White Suit*, *The Card*, *Where No Vultures Fly* and *West of Zanzibar*.

All but two of these films are comedies, five of them starring Alec Guinness. In short, what many English critics have long suspected, is true: American audiences like their British films British. They do not, generally speaking, take to British films deliberately designed to suit the American market, unless these have American stars. The two obvious exceptions are *Where No Vultures Fly* and its sequel *West of Zanzibar*, but the Rank Organisation have confided that, although these films did extremely well financially, the higher production costs, the expense of colour prints, etc., resulted in profits no greater than those for the more economical *Lavender Hill Mob*. Furthermore, bearing in mind the enormous costs involved in wide-circuit distribution, Rank have found that a film like *Genevieve*, which ran 17 weeks at the Sutton Theatre (600 seats) in New York, can do nearly as well as the picture that makes a limited circuit run.

So much for the successes. What about the films that have *not* done well in America – the 'disappointments', as they are euphemistically termed in the industry? Film organisations are, naturally enough, reluctant to discuss their failures, but the Rank Organisation have been kind enough to tell me of the two films that most 'disappointed' them: *Scott of the Antarctic* and *The Blue Lamp*. To understand why these films were not well received in America, it is worth considering the reasons for their British popularity. *Scott* was certainly well received here, but as Mr Jympson Harman commented, 'What you got out of it depended a lot on what you put into it.' And what was put in? According to the reviewer in the *Sunday Dispatch*, 'Such a film as *Scott* is welcomed at a time when other races speak disparagingly of our "crumbling empire" and our lack of spirit … [This film] makes us believe again that ours is the finest breed of men on earth. And so we are.' Naturally, American audiences could not be expected to react in quite the same way, and they therefore felt all the more strongly the film's 'kind of flatness' (*Evening News*), its 'snowbound humour … [and the fact that it came out] as just another adventure story, more monotonous than most' (*Daily Telegraph*). For American audiences, the upper lips were too stiff, the behaviour too gentlemanly; they felt too that 'high-mindedness, like patriotism, is not enough' (*News Chronicle*).

As for *The Blue Lamp*, a typical British reaction was perhaps that of the *Sunday Graphic's* critic, who described it as, 'Nothing more than a competent and workmanlike film about the Metropolitan Police. It hasn't the skill, the wit or the tension of *Naked City…* its nearest American counterpart.' On the other hand, this reviewer went on, 'because it has some well-photographed and authentic London backgrounds, because the police have co-operated to some effect with the producers, and because it makes an honest effort to show what a good job of work is done daily by the London policeman, most people will like it very much indeed.' And so they did; but in America, where even the concept of the unarmed policeman is incredible, it was found rather bland when compared with *Naked City* and other American 'realistic' thrillers. Again the stiff upper lip was too much in evidence: Americans, rightly or wrongly, find this much more congenial when it is on the point of breaking out into a broad grin, as in the firing squad scene of *The Captain's Paradise.* I do not think that they doubt the historical truth of British heroism, but, like many people here, they are not taken in by what Richard Winnington called 'Huggetry' – the naive mixture of coyness, patronage and sentimentality that runs through many British working-class films.

I said earlier that it is impossible to get any exact figures about how well or how badly British films have done in America. The reason is not difficult to understand. Barring an abortive attempt shortly after the war to distribute films in the US themselves, the Rank Organisation have generally sold their films to American distributors for a flat sum. And the re-distributor has never been very willing to divulge figures of subsequent receipts, perhaps fearing that if Rank knew just how well some of their films had done they might be inclined to raise the flat-rate price. This has been an unsatisfactory state of affairs, and Rank, fresh from their success in South America, have now decided to form their own distribution set-up in the United States.

The Rank Organisation makes about twenty films a year, but just what percentage of these will be deemed 'suitable' for the American market is not yet known. In any case, they are also prepared to distribute films produced by other British companies. (Whether other companies will in fact avail themselves of this offer also remains uncertain, and in some cases appears more than doubtful.) Rank feel that British films have not yet been given a fair opportunity in the American market, and to remedy this situation the organisation is pre-pared to acquire several theatres in New York and elsewhere. As a start, they have taken a lease on the Sutton Theatre, a 600-seat luxury art house in the fashionable East 50s. The first films they expect to release there are *Reach for the Sky*, *The Battle of the River Plate* and *The Spanish Gardener.* More cinemas will be acquired if there is any difficulty in getting adequate outlets, but these will be considered only on 'economic' terms. Rank intend to go very slowly, to avoid being caught out as they were in their first American venture.

On the question of whether American artists will be used in forthcoming productions, Rank have gone on record as saying that there will be no change in the existing produc-tion policy. Since Rank have already made a fair number of films with American stars, this answer seems slightly ambiguous.

Not all Rank films, however, will be distributed by their American organisation, since their contract with Universal is still in force, and has 'many more years' to run. Under the present system, Rank divide the twenty films made each year into two groups of ten (each group of equal value), with Rank taking one group and Universal having the right to take any that it chooses from its ten. The 'split', as it is called, is made in London, on the basis of titles, stories and stars only, and Universal are not shown the actual film. This system may, of course, result in direct competition between two British films in the same American city at the same time – one distributed by Rank, one by Universal. But Rank welcome such competition as a means of keeping their American outfit on its toes. Rank also believe that when they have made a little progress they may get further help from the American motion picture industry. The new plan actually goes into operation about Easter, 1957.

At Lion International, the picture is somewhat different. They were organised a year ago, and to date have distributed only three films in America: *Private's Progress*, *Geordie* and

I Am a Camera. All have been successes. As before, we may set aside *I Am a Camera*, which has been sold on the strength of its popularity as a stage play and on the presence of Julie Harris in the leading part. *Geordie*, to be more accurate, is *going* to be a success: it is at present only in its third week at the Little Carnegie in New York, but if the review in *Time* is any indication it should certainly be popular. (And, as a matter of fact, while I was at Lion International, a cable arrived stating: 'Circuit break possible, send fifteen more prints!') *Private's Progress*, in any case, is an undoubted hit, and since this film was made essentially for the home market its world-wide success has left its producers slightly astonished. So, once more, a British film made with no eye to the American market is doing very well there and perhaps for precisely that reason. Wisely, I think, Lion are more or less banking on a Guinness-like American career for Ian Carmichael; and since, like Guinness, he is not a British version of Gregory Peck or Jerry Lewis or any Hollywood type, his films will probably cover their costs in the United States alone. Imitations never really do well on a free market; the American exhibitor presented with a choice between Marilyn Monroe and Diana Dors is always likely to take Monroe.

It is interesting to note that one of British Lion's next films will be *Under the Influence*, produced by the Boulting Brothers in collaboration with the American distributing firm Robert Dowling-Ilya Lopert.[3] Although the Dowling-Lopert interest will be substantial, there will be, it is claimed, 'no concessions to the American market'. Actually, Lopert has agreed with Boulting that the genuinely British film stands a better chance with the growing American audience than those pictures consciously slanted for commercial success on the other side of the Atlantic. On the other hand, and this may be typical of a certain tendency in the industry to 'hedge their bets', Lion will also distribute a film called *Manuela*, which, according to their hand-out, is 'strong film fare'. 'Designed for the international market, with an international cast, it pulls no punches, and is probably the most adult approach to a passionate love story to go into production in Britain for a long time.' One can only wish them luck!

The last of the three major distributing companies is Associated British-Pathé, whose most popular films in America have been: *Mr Potts Goes to Moscow*, *Last Holiday*, *South of Algiers*, *Happy Ever After*, *Happy Go Lovely*, *Duel in the Jungle* and *The Dam Busters*.

Subtracting from this list the films featuring American stars, we are left with only three pictures – *Mr Potts Goes to Moscow* (*Top Secret* in the USA), *Last Holiday* and *The Dam Busters*. *Dam Busters* comes as something of a surprise, since the film was vouchsafed only a Brooklyn premiere and was not reviewed in most of the metropolitan dailies. When I asked whether these circumstances had not impeded the film's career in the United States, I was told that the company did not care to discuss the matter. So we must presumably leave it at that. The other two films are, as might be expected, comedies of a very British type. Nevertheless, A.B.-Pathé express somewhat different opinions from the other organisations, claiming that there is no proof that Americans like their British films to be specifically British.

As to distribution methods, A.B.-Pathé have always premiered their films at the art houses, since they believe that the publicity attendant on a successful New York art house showing soon filters down to the small exhibitor in the hinterlands. Considering that this method is also being increasingly used for American pictures (*Marty* and *Lili*, for instance), the company foresee no change in their policy. They have great hopes for their new version of *The Good Companions*, to be released sometime this year. [...][4]

SOURCE: 'BRITAIN IN AMERICA', *SIGHT & SOUND*, 26.3, WINTER 1956–7, 119–23

Decades Never Start On Time

1.2 MAX OPHÜLS

In England and America Max Ophüls occupies a very special place, that of the beloved minor master. In France, although he had made six or seven films there between 1934 and 1940, Ophüls was almost unknown until 1950. If he was mentioned in French histories of the cinema, it was as the 'Austrian' director of *Liebelei* – and sometimes not even as that. Bardèche and Brasillach, for instance, pretend that he was not the real director of that film. But with *La Ronde*, and more especially *Madame de ...*, his stock began to go up. His reputation reached its zenith with *Lola Montès*; and Ophüls is now considered by many French critics to be one of the cinema's greatest directors.

What has brought about this change in their evaluation of Max Ophüls? The quality of his last four films has a good deal to do with it, of course, but there are other reasons too. There are at present two overlapping groups of critics with a particular interest in Ophüls. The first group might be

MAX OPHULS

AN INDEX | RICHARD ROUD

British Film Institute · 3/6

Roud's study of Max Ophüls, 1958

called the 'Neo-Christians'. Their leader is Henri Agel and their organ the magazine *Téle-Ciné* (although many of the contributors to *Cahiers du Cinéma* and *Cinéma 58* also belong to this group). The starting-point was *Télé-Ciné*'s *fiche* for *La Ronde*. The film, we were told, was only superficially a frivolous picture of immorality; beneath, it was a demonstration of the vanity of the flesh and the absurdity of life without faith. It was *Lola Montès*, however, that really offered these Grail-seekers scope: Lola is a 'saint' (François Truffaut). She is 'a daughter of Eve, inheritor of Original Sin, still dizzy from the Fall'; the ring-master is 'messianic'; and 'Ophüls brings us to the very foot of the Cross' (Dominique Delouche). 'If he paints Hell [in *Lola*] it is to bring us a glimpse of God' (Claude Beylie).

The second group is more catholic and less Catholic. There has been a strong movement in France during recent years against the classic theory that editing (*montage*) was the fundamental element in the cinema. Many writers in France (and elsewhere) now hold that camera movement within a sequence is much more important than the movement from shot to shot. This idea has been especially developed by Henri Agel, Alexandre Astruc, André Bazin, and others. And, of course, if there is one thing particularly characteristic of Ophüls it is his preference for camera movement over *montage*.

Another characteristic of some French critics and directors today is their disdain for the traditional story-telling film. They are much more interested in presenting a state of mind, an idea, a climate of feeling, than in straightforward narrative. Of course stories are still used, but as a pretext – something to hang the film on to. And again, although Ophüls's films tell stories, in many cases – particularly in *Lola Montès*, but also in such works as *La signora di tutti* – the story is not the main element in the film.

Then again, most French critics of the younger generation had not seen any of Ophüls's pre-1950 films until the recent retrospective programmes at the Cinémathèque Française. Therefore, they saw all his earlier productions with *Lola Montès* in mind. Just as each incident of Lola's life was given meaning in the film by our knowledge of the end of her life, so each film of Ophüls was judged according to whether or not it was a prefiguration of one or other of the elements in *Lola Montès*. But hindsight can lead to a falsification of judgment; and the fact that Ophüls died after making *Lola Montès* contributed further to the confusion: to these critics, *Lola* appears as the culmination of his life's work – his 'Sistine Chapel', according to Claude Beylie. *La signora di tutti* is a fine film, but not because Gaby Doriot is a prefiguration of Lola Montès; and *Werther* is still a bad film whether or not it is an 'astonishing sketch' for *Madame de…*.

Finally, the admirers of Ophüls are partly influenced by the current anti-classical, pro-baroque and rococo mood in France. To be sure, after Versailles, Salzburg makes a pleasant change. And, compared with the 'classical' technique of René Clair in *Porte des Lilas*, *Lola Montès* does seem like a breath of fresh air. Moreover, France is really only now discovering certain aspects of German-Austrian culture to which England and America were introduced through the many refugees of the 1930s. For example, a work like *Ariadne auf Naxos* is still known only to the happy few in France; and Bavarian and Austrian rococo architecture, the plays of Schnitzler, and so on, have all the charm of novelty.

All these reasons, however, are hardly likely to influence the Anglo-Saxon filmgoer. They are either remote from our preoccupations, or they are irrelevant. For us, Ophüls remains a little master, but a very remarkable one.

Perhaps the most astonishing thing about Ophüls's work is its sense of continuity. He made 21 full-length films in five countries over a period of 25 years, and yet they are all of a piece. First, it must be remembered that this sense of continuity stems partly from the fact that he generally worked with the same people. Most of his films were photographed by Eugène Schüfftan, Franz Planer or Christian Matras. His production director (Ralph Baum), his set designer (Jean d'Eaubonne), his script writer (Jacques Natanson) followed him from film to film, and sometimes from country to country. Yet, unlike William Wyler, whose dependence on the camerawork of Gregg Toland was so cruelly revealed after Toland's death, Max Ophüls is ultimately the only one responsible for his films. He has a style; the fact that he often worked with the same team only brought this out the more.

The most obvious characteristic of Ophüls's style is its incredible fluidity. The trade-mark of an Ophüls film is, of course, the tracking shot. As James Mason explained in his little poem:

> I think I know the reason why
> Producers tend to make him cry.
> Inevitably they demand
> Some stationary set-ups, and
> A shot that does not call for tracks
> Is agony for poor dear Max,
> Who, separated from his dolly,
> Is wrapped in deepest melancholy.
> Once, when they took away his crane,
> I thought he'd never smile again …

Ophüls relied more than most directors on tracking shots, crane shots, pan shots. He made relatively little use of the close-up, or static compositions, or the classic *montage* procedure. His technique had its disadvantages. Tracking-for-tracking's sake could lead to such ridiculous scenes as the opening of the *Maison Tellier* episode in *Le Plaisir*. Also, excessive movement can defeat its own purpose: instead of engendering a feeling of excitement, it can become simply boring. On the other hand, Ophüls's fluid style can be terribly intoxicating, as in the circus scene of *Lola Montès*, the café scene in *Liebelei*, or the ball episode in *La signora di tutti*.

The musical element in his films is not less important, if harder to define. Firstly, the musical score plays a major part in his films. In *La signora di tutti*, the motif of the waltz at Gaby's first ball plays an important dramatic role in the film. The same is true of the songs in *Lola Montès* and *La Ronde*. But Ophüls also used words, phrases, images musically – the recurring leitmotif of 'Vergogna' in *La signora di tutti*; 'Ça va aller' in *Lola Montès*; 'Quarante francs par jour' in *Divine*. These phrases are used almost operatically: they identify characters, they denote themes, they mark transitions.

Ophüls's narrative technique must also be briefly mentioned. In relatively few of his films does he tell his story straight-forwardly. In *La Tendre Ennemie*, *La signora di tutti* and *Lola Montès*, particularly, he invented a method of narration whose ingenuity perfectly suits the story he has to tell.

Finally, there is Ophüls's passion for decor: cages, mirrors, staircases (there are sixty shots of staircases in *Madame de …*), laces, gauzes, hangings, chandeliers. This heavily-charged decorative style is not to everyone's taste, and there are films in which one gets the impression that everything is being seen through yards of *tulle*. But it *is* a style, and a style in most cases in keeping with his subject.

What are Ophüls's subjects? The simplest answer is: women. More specifically: women in love. Most often, women who are unhappily in love, or to whom love brings misfortune of one kind or another. The surroundings in which they live are usually luxurious; in any event, they generally manage at least one performance at the opera and one ball during the course of the film. They usually live between 1880–1900: J'aime le passé. C'est telle-ment plus reposant que le présent – et plus sûr que l'avenir' (['I like the past. It is more restful than the present – and more certain than the future'] Anton Walbrook in *La Ronde*). The setting is usually 'Vienna'; sometimes it is actually Vienna. Either way, though, it is not the real *fin-de-siècle* Vienna but rather an ideal Vienna – the city of operetta and Strauss waltzes.

In his choice of subject-matter, Ophüls often came close to trashiness and occasionally overstepped the boundary. But for most of the time he managed to keep his balance. His subjects in themselves may be of little interest to many people, and it is not for a creative interpretation of reality as most people know it that we go to Max Ophüls. His good films, or many of them, are examples of the triumph of form over content. 'He is a director who rarely moves out of a minor key, and who, within self-imposed limitations, has achieved a real personal style; his films may be unimportant, but they are never trivial' (Penelope Houston).

SOURCE: *MAX OPHÜLS: AN INDEX* (LONDON: BFI, 1958), 3–6

1.3 FACE TO FACE: JAMES AGEE

The publishers of *Agee on Film* have printed as preface a letter written by W. H. Auden to the editor of *The Nation*:

> I do not care for movies very much, and I rarely see them … I am all the more surprised, therefore, to find myself not only reading Mr Agee before I read anyone else in *The Nation* but also consciously looking forward all week to reading him again … What he says is of such profound interest, expressed with such extraordinary wit and felicity, and so tran-scends its ostensible – to me, rather unimportant – subject, that his articles belong in that very select class … of newspaper work which has permanent literary value.

This was surely meant as the highest of tributes. Yet it posits an idea of the function of the film critic which is not so very different from that of the editor of one famous London newspaper – who is said to ask of his movie critics only that they provide enough of the plot and enough amusing remarks to furnish those who have not seen the film with a reasonable supply of cocktail chatter. In a sense, of course, this idea of the film review is but a debased continuation of the genteel tradition of the irresponsible, whimsical and impressionistic essayist.

Auden was not James Agee's only admirer. A considerable Agee cult grew up during the years of his *Nation* reviews. One heard – at least, the late George Barbarow heard – 'many a happy moron proclaim that he would rather read an Agee review than see the pic-ture' (*Partisan Review*). Naturally, the cult provoked an answering reaction. Agee was dep-recated for his habit of occasionally spending more space on bad films than on good ones, because the bad gave him more opportunities to write amusingly. His style sometimes ran away with him, as in the following breathless excerpt from his notice on a film called *Carnival in Costa Rica*:

> If this sort of un-American propaganda takes decent hold in Hollywood, the day will come when the husband of a high-bridged daughter of the Confederacy will shag into the scuppernong arbour playing ootchmagootch to a slice of watermelon and reciting *Ballad for Americans*, between spat seeds, in an Oxford accent.

Agee was no funnier than Otis Ferguson (see Ferguson's description of how to make a 'montage film' in *Garbo and the Nightwatchmen*). He was occasionally less incisive than Robert Warshaw (compare their reviews of *The Best Years of Our Lives*). He was less interestingly 'offbeat' than Manny Farber. But he was America's best film critic, because he combined acute intelligence with a passion for the best the cinema could do. And he was able to communicate his enthusiasm.

James Agee was born in 1910 in Knoxville, Tennessee. Educated at Harvard, he began life as a writer. In the 1930s he published a book of poems, *Permit Me Voyage*, and a study of Southern sharecroppers, *Let Us Now Praise Famous Men*. But his interest in the cin-ema went back to his childhood: in his novel *A Death in the Family*, he movingly describes his father and himself (mother didn't approve) going off to see Chaplin and Mack Sennett at the local movie house. One of his finest essays, 'Comedy's Greatest Era' (first published in *Life*), lovingly evokes the peculiar pleasure that Lloyd, Langdon, Keaton and Chaplin were capable of giving. It is a very nostalgic but careful analysis of exactly how during those years slapstick attained the greatness of art:

> The early silent comedians never strove for or consciously thought of anything which could be called artistic 'form', but they achieved it … Leo McCarey once devoted almost the whole of a Laurel and Hardy two-reeler to pie-throwing. The first pies were thrown thoughtfully almost philosophically. Then innocent bystanders began to get caught into the vortex. At full pitch it was Armageddon. But everything was calculated so nicely that until late in the picture, when havoc took over, every pie made its special kind of point and piled on its special kind of laugh.

James Agee began to review films regularly for *Time* in 1941, and for *The Nation* (vaguely equivalent to *The New Statesman*) in 1942. *The Nation* allowed him greater freedom and an opportunity for a more personal expression of his views. In his first column, he set forth his basic creed:

> I can begin by describing my condition as a would-be critic. I suspect that I am, far more than not, in your own situation: deeply interested in moving pictures, considerably experienced from childhood in watching them and thinking and talking about them, and totally, or almost totally, without experience or even much second-hand knowledge of how they are made.

What is fascinating to watch, as one goes through *Agee on Film*, is the way in which the critic became steadily more interested in 'how they are made'. By the time he wrote his essay on John Huston for *Life* (1950), his knowledge and understanding of film technique was explicit:

> The shots are cantilevered, sprung together in electric arcs, rather than buttered together. A given scene is apt to be composed of highly unconventional alternations of rhythm and patterns of exchange between long and medium and close shots and the standing, swinging and dollying camera. The rhythm and contour are very powerful but very irregular, like the rhythm of good prose rather than of good verse; and it is this rangy, leaping, thrusting kind of nervous vitality which binds the whole picture together.

But technique was still only important in a human context. Agee felt very strongly that the cinema was the perfect medium for realism raised to the level of high poetry. He complained that few Americans either behind or in front of the camera gave evidence of any recognition or respect for themselves or one another as human beings. And he judged films against the standards of what he would have called the great humanists of the cinema: Griffith, Chaplin, Eisenstein, Dovzhenko and Vigo. Agee was 'an agnostic in politics', but his comments on *Open City* show his thoroughgoing awareness of the political implications of art:

> I cannot help doubting that the basic and ultimate practising motives of institutional Christianity and leftism can be adequately represented by the most magnanimous individuals of each kind; and in that degree I am afraid that both the religious and the leftist audience – and more particularly the religio-leftists, who must be the key mass in Italy – are being sold something of a bill of goods.

Agee was very much affected by the war. He was keenly aware of his own position as a non-combatant in a New York office, and this may have led him to overrate certain war films because they 'helped to diminish the astronomical abyss which exists between the experienced and the inexperienced in war'. Thus, he could write of *The Story of G.I. Joe*: 'If by any chance this film is not a masterpiece, then however stupid my feeling is, I cannot help resenting those films which are.'

But Agee, like every critic, was also influenced by the public for whom he wrote and the milieu in which he lived. He waged a constant battle against other American critics such as Bosley Crowther (*New York Times*), and against the prevalent American 'middlebrow–highbrow' approach to the cinema. He overrated Rouquier's *Farrebique* (comparing it with Homer, Hesiod and Virgil) partly because he was so angered by Crowther's comment that *Farrebique* 'was lacking in strong dramatic punch ... not even a plain folk triangle'. On the other hand, his reaction against other New York critics prompted Agee's most brilliant piece of sustained critical writing – his courageous and perceptive defence of *Monsieur Verdoux*.

Unfortunately, this necessary running battle against the middlebrow–highbrows took up a great deal of space; and in a column in which he glanced at *Shadow of a Doubt* in six lines, he devoted sixty-three to Dieterle's *Tennessee Johnson*:

> Another of those screen biographies for which thousands of cultivated people will lay aside *Jalna* for an evening because they like to feel benevolent towards a really good movie ... I have given perhaps exorbitant space to *Tennessee Johnson* because it furnishes, for many, the illusion that Hollywood is 'coming of age', and because a lifetime subscription to the *Atlantic Monthly* does not seem to me synonymous with 'coming of age'.[5]

Agee was also bothered by the fact that so many people who thought of themselves as serious-minded and progressive thoroughly disapproved of crime melodramas. They seem not to realise, he said, that for years so much has been forbidden or otherwise made impossible in Hollywood that crime offers one of the few chances of getting any sort of vitality on the screen.

The careful reader will note discrepancies between Agee's reviews of, say, *Henry V* and *Hamlet* in *The Nation* and those in *Time*. For *Time* he wrote 'selling notices', because he thought that both films ought to be seen by as many people as possible. In *The Nation*, with its infinitely smaller circulation, he felt able to express his doubts and reservations more fully. Again, the problems are those which confront any critic in a society not basically disposed to take the cinema seriously.

One must also remember that if Agee wrote somewhat infrequently about European films, it was because his knowledge of them was necessarily limited. European pictures often take a long time to reach America, and Agee never mentioned films like *Une Partie de campagne*, *Douce* or *La Bataille du rail* because they were not shown in New York until after 1948, when he gave up reviewing to go to Hollywood. When *L'Atalante* and *Zéro de conduite* were given their New York premiere (in 1947!), however, he recognised them for the great films they are. On the other hand, too many of the serious American critics are generally contemptuous of American movies. One of Agee's greatest services was to point out that 'most of the really good popular art produced anywhere comes from Hollywood'; and, he added, 'much of it bears John Huston's name.' When Agee left New York, it was to write for Huston the script of *The African Queen*. Huston, however, did not use all of his script; and it was for other directors that Agee was able to do his best creative writing in the cinema: *The Bride Comes to Yellow Sky* (part of *Face to Face*) and *The Night of the Hunter*, one of the most poetic and perceptive films to have come out of Hollywood since the war. From his beginning, as a critic who knew little of the making of films, he had moved steadily towards the creative centre.

James Agee died in 1955. Two years later, his novel *A Death in the Family* was published and won the Pulitzer Prize. On reviewing it, we are told, many critics called for a volume which would bring together his writings on the movies. *Agee on Film* handsomely answers this demand, though it seems a pity the publishers have not taken more trouble in editing Agee's writings. They have reprinted the two essays from *Life*, a selection of the *Time* reviews, two miscellaneous essays, and *The Nation* articles complete including misprints and subsequent apologies for misprints. They have managed to introduce misprints of their own, like 'nymph in thy *prisons* [orisons] be all my sins remembered.' Unkindest cut of all, however, is the reference to *Sight & Sound* as a British magazine 'now defunct'. Nevertheless, they have made Agee's writings on the cinema available to the world; and *Agee on Film* now takes its place among the dozen or so books essential to anyone for whom the cinema is not 'a rather unimportant subject.'

SOURCE: 'FACE TO FACE: JAMES AGEE', *SIGHT & SOUND*, 28.2, SPRING 1959, 98–100

1.4 FACE TO FACE: ANDRÉ BAZIN

NOTE: In conjunction with this article on André Bazin one can usefully read Roud's 'The French line' (Sight & Sound, 29.4, Autumn 1960, 166–71), which discusses French film criticism of the 1950s more broadly, as well as his later 'André Bazin: his fall and rise' (Sight & Sound, 37.2, Spring 1968, 94–6), which returns to Bazin's criticism in the context of the late 1960s.

Writing about James Agee's work in the last issue of *Sight & Sound*, I commented on the way in which film criticism in the Anglo-Saxon countries is biased towards the impressionistic and the chatty, distrustful of theory. Basically, perhaps, critics suffer from the same feelings of inferiority as do teachers: deep in the Anglo-Saxon ethos is embedded the idea that those who can, do; those who can't, teach − or criticise. Furthermore, the cinema is still not generally considered a serious subject. Film critics, with few exceptions, are regarded as entertainers; and since people generally conform sooner or later to the idea society has of them, film critics become entertainers.

In France, the situation is quite different. First of all, criticism in general has always been considered important. The distinction between creative writing (poetry, plays, novels) and critical prose (essays, critiques) has never been as strong as in England and America. In the past fifty years especially, criticism has assumed an ever more important place in French literature. Valéry's collected criticism is ranked by many Frenchmen higher than his poetry, Gide's *Journal* higher than his novels and tales; and did not Gide himself declare that he would find the diary of Flaubert during the period when he wrote *Madame Bovary* more interesting (if it existed) than the novel itself?

It is essential for a proper understanding of French film criticism to realise the enormous prestige attached to philosophical interpretation, aesthetic theorising and formal analysis. During the first years of the cinema in France, it was regarded, as elsewhere, as a *divertissement* for the masses, of little artistic significance. It was not until the end of the First World War that French intellectuals discovered the cinema – generally through the revelation of Charlie Chaplin. The 1920s were the first golden age of French film criticism: almost everyone – artists, writers and *littérateurs* – suddenly discovered that the cinema was an art. Or, rather, that it could be. But they also felt that they had to defend its right to be considered an art rather than simply a method of reproduction. So they fastened on the idea of *montage* as a proof that the cinema was an art form. The image itself, as a photograph of reality, was, they said, only the raw material: it was the arrangement of the succession of images that could make the cinema an art. Furthermore, the cinema acquired extra *cachet* as being the only art that could penetrate the world of dreams and the subconscious mind: this was the apogee of the surrealists, and the period when Freud's discoveries first infiltrated French culture. The important thing was to prove that the cinema was intellectually respectable. And this could only be done by surrounding it with what Anglo-Saxons are likely to consider an exorbitant amount of waffle.

The importance of André Bazin's criticism can best be understood if one sees it in this context of French attitudes towards the cinema. His collected criticism is dedicated to Roger Leenhardt and François Truffaut, the latter his protégé and the former his great predecessor. Leenhardt is known in England chiefly for his film *Les Dernières Vacances*, and for his numerous documentaries. But during the years from 1934 to the war, when he was writing the cinema column for the Christian-Left monthly *Esprit*, his ideas fertilised a whole generation and (to change the metaphor) prepared the way for the critical movement which began during the war and of which Bazin was the uncontested leader and prime mover.

Before Leenhardt, French thinking about the cinema had been dominated by two schools: the group referred to earlier, which believed in 'artistic' cinema – the cinema of soft-focus photography, flashy effects, superimpositions, expressionistic or modernistic sets – and the group which considered the cinema important only as a mass art – like, says Leenhardt, the Marxist historian Georges Sadoul. Until the early 1930s the first group (represented by men like Brasillach, Moussinac and Jean-George Auriol) was the more influential. But the arrival of sound seemed to nullify their theories. They simply refused to accept it, and spent most of their time bewailing the good old days:

> Even today [1935] it is questionable whether it is possible to love the film sincerely unless one knew it in the silent days, in those last years which are inseparable from the days of one's youth … But we who witnessed the birth of an art may possibly also have seen it die. Recalling all that it promised, we are left with the melancholy regret one feels for a thing foredoomed. (Bardèche and Brasillach)

One or two, however, did welcome sound. Benjamin Fondane, for example, thought sound was going to be magnificent – one more element to add to the repertory of symbolic *montage* effects. It would replace superimposition. How wonderful, he said, you can show a man thinking of his broken life and at the same time you will hear the sound of a glass breaking. Or you could show a family row while the sound of waves breaking on the shore was heard!

Roger Leenhardt, though, was neither an aesthete nor a social historian, but a film editor. He welcomed sound because, as he said, it was there and nothing could be done about it. The film critic, he thought, should not have a preconceived idea of what films *ought* to be like: his theories should be constructed on the basis of the films actually being made. He became enthusiastic about Hollywood films because he thought the Americans, with their dynamic empiricism, were the only ones who knew what to do about the invention of sound film: they simply went ahead and made sound movies.

So while the aesthetic critics, prisoners of their theories, appreciated only Marcel L'Herbier, *The Cabinet of Dr. Caligari* and, *à la rigueur*, René Clair, Leenhardt was boosting the American comedies, gangster pictures and films of social protest. He was also the first to appreciate the films of Jean Renoir – their lack of formalism, or carefully composed and consciously beautiful images, and their non-reliance on the classic elements of *montage*. Strongly influenced by Leenhardt's ideas, André Bazin carried them a few steps further; and Leenhardt, as he himself admits, gave up writing about the cinema because Bazin was his logical and accomplished successor.

André Bazin was born in Angers in 1918. From early childhood he had always wanted to become a teacher, and he went through the prescribed course of study at the Ecole Normale. Although he passed his examinations brilliantly, he was refused a teaching post because of his stutter. Then came the war. Mobilised, Bazin spent the phoney war vegetating in a barracks at Bordeaux. His interest in the cinema had first been awakened by Roger Leenhardt's articles in *Esprit*; and now the enforced inactivity of barracks life, and the prompting of a fellow-soldier whose parents owned a whole chain of cinemas in Bordeaux, led him to spend all his free time at the movies. After the *débâcle*, Bazin returned to civilian life and became friendly with Pierre-Aimé Touchard, one of the editors of *Esprit*, whose Leftish and Catholic viewpoint was sympathetic to him. When Touchard was put in charge of the Maison des Lettres, a kind of students' cultural association, he asked Bazin to direct the cinema section.

All Bazin's friends (Touchard, Claude Roy, and Leenhardt himself) tell us that when they first knew him he was somewhat overfond of philosophical terms and abstract terminology. Touchard thinks that this was due to Bazin's bitterness about his lack of university training, and was an attempt to prove that he was not inferior to those who had more education than himself. But this interest in philosophy was also perhaps an attempt to provide himself with a solid basis for his critical work: a need which would not be felt in England or America, but would seem imperative in France. Furthermore, Bazin belonged to the generation which discovered and embraced existentialism. In his attempt to discover the essence of the cinema, he used the phenomenological approach of Sartre and Merleau-Ponty: he derived the essence of the cinema from experience of its existence. From this return to the source, this consideration of the ontology of the cinema, came his most important contribution to film aesthetics: the re-evaluation of *montage*.

Struck by certain resemblances between the silent films of Stroheim, for example, and the sound films of Renoir and Welles, Bazin argued that the traditional idea of a schism between the silent and the sound film was false. More important was the distinction between those directors who believed in the image and those, such as Stroheim, who believed in reality. By the image, Bazin implies everything art can add to the representation of reality: composition, stylisation of decor, lighting and acting, and, the most important element, *montage*. In his sense, *montage* can be defined as the creation – by cutting, juxtaposition, etc. – of a meaning which the individual images did not possess. The *montage* films of Eisenstein, Kuleshov and Abel Gance did not show an event: they evoked it. The meaning of their films remained rather in the organisation of the elements of reality than in those elements themselves.

The other school of directors – Stroheim, Murnau, Dreyer and Flaherty – did not use *montage* except in a purely negative way, to eliminate unnecessary elements. In *Nanook of the North*, for instance, there is a sequence in which Nanook hunts a seal. Rather than show us first Nanook, then the seal, then Nanook, then the seal – building up the impression of Nanook's anxious waiting through a *montage* effect – Flaherty filmed it all in one sequence. He did not suggest tension: he simply showed it to us. And this, Bazin said, is infinitely more moving. Now this kind of cinema could only be enriched by the invention of sound, since sound is an important element of reality. Therefore, concluded Bazin, if *montage*, stylisation and expressionism are not the very essence of cinema, then the coming of sound was not as radical a break as had been assumed. It killed a certain kind of cinema, but not *the* cinema.

The great connecting link between Stroheim, Dreyer, etc., and the 1940s and 1950s was Jean Renoir. He understood their films, and he was able to continue in their tradition. In suppressing *montage*, he sought to maintain their respect for the unity of space which is implied by a non-montage procedure. To do this, he began to experiment in the early 1930s with composition in depth, frequent use of tracking and pan shots, and greater action within the frame. He was thus able to preserve the relationship between his characters and their surroundings; their natural and dramatic unity was not broken.

Although Bazin would have been the last to maintain that no other director of the 1930s made good films, his point was that the direction taken by the cinema since 1940 has been the one pointed out earlier by Renoir. One must always bear in mind that for Bazin film theory was valid only as an explanation of why films are made the way they are. An aesthetic is founded on what *is*. The trend which began with Renoir, towards less and less *montage*, longer and longer sequences, was intensified by Orson Welles and continued by Visconti, Rossellini and the younger French school. It is implied by composition in depth, allowing the director to show action without constant cross-cutting. It also presupposes a kind of lateral 'depth of focus' which has since come to us in the form of CinemaScope. Bazin welcomed CinemaScope because it existed, but also because it seemed to him a logical continuation of the tendency to preserve scenic unity. CinemaScope, no less than Renoir's depth of focus and Visconti's endless tracking and pan shots, permits a director to integrate the real duration of events and the actual relation of characters to dramatic space. Whether every director who uses CinemaScope realises this possibility is, of course, another matter: for Bazin, it was enough that it *could* be used in this way. And two recent French films, *Les Amants* and *Une Vie*, provide examples of how effective it can be. Even before CinemaScope, however, dramatic events formerly achieved by *montage* could be presented more or less simultaneously and, more important, realistically. (An excellent example is the scene in *Citizen Kane* which shows us at the same time and in the same image Susan on the bed in the middle-ground, the fatal glass in the foreground, and Kane entering the room in the background.)

The effect is realistic because the continuity of dramatic space and dramatic time has been respected. Thus, for Bazin, depth of focus was not just one small element of cinematic syntax. It was of capital importance because it brought the spectator's rapport with the image closer to his rapport with reality. *Montage* unduly restricted the meaning of any given scene or event: the possibility of a richer, freer interpretation was the great advantage of the new method.

Bazin also welcomed the Italian neo-realist school because its new content was paralleled by its new form: the absence of all expressionism in the images, lighting, sets, and so on tended to give these films that sense of ambiguity which Bazin found in reality itself. This last concept is perhaps the most difficult to explain. What he meant, I think, is that the significance of objects, people and events depends on one's point of view. The classic *montage* procedure imposed one view, that of the director, to the exclusion of all others. Although the director's point of view will naturally remain clear, the freer system does not prevent one from sensing various meanings – not contradictory, perhaps, but complementary. The film, said Bazin, thereby gains something of the ambiguity, the multiple levels of interpretation and meaning, that have long been the privilege of the novel. The cinema is no longer a spectacle, but a language. Reality is neither evoked nor described: it is graven directly on to the film.

Bazin's reference to the novel is significant. He strongly disapproved of the purist view of the cinema, and the leading article of volume two of his collected criticism, *Qu'est-ce que le cinéma?*, is a defence of film adaptations from plays and novels titled 'Pour un cinéma impur'.

Briefly, he thought that the whole idea of 'spécificité cinématographique' (what we call *using the medium*) was not only out-dated but invalid. Surely, he maintains, adaptations such as *Le Journal d'un curé de campagne*, *Les Parents terribles*, *Une Partie de campagne* and *Greed* can stand comparison with any of the 'pure' film masterpieces. The problem, then, is not whether to adapt but how. And here his main contribution was the insistence that you can make a better film if you respect the form of the original. Cocteau planned a film version of *Les Parents terribles* in 1946, but later abandoned this 'screen treatment' because he realised that the play's theatricality was part of its very essence and must be respected. In other words, Bazin said, Cocteau realised that the function of the camera was not to add, but to *intensify*. Instead of dissolving his play into a film (adding exteriors, transitions, flashbacks, etc.), he used the camera to underline, to sharpen, and to confirm his scenic structure and its psychological implications. The idea that *Les Parents terribles* was an excellent movie but somehow not really a 'film' is madness, Bazin said. One can only agree.

As the stage–screen dichotomy has broken down since the war, so has the wall between the novel and the film – ever since Malraux filmed *L'Espoir* and *then* wrote the novel. Bazin, along with Alexandre Astruc, believed that the time has now come when the novelist can write his novel directly on film: the *caméra-stylo*. Bazin also believed that the art film (Resnais, Emmer, etc.) is one of the most important recent developments in the cinema. Most would part company from him at this point on aesthetic grounds. But one cannot deny the educational value of the art film; and Bazin never lost interest in the power of the cinema as a means of mass education. Nor did he foreswear his concern for social problems. Although he was not particularly interested in the committed cinema (*cinéma engagé*), he maintained that the cinema cannot exist without taking into account the society it mirrors.

From his fairly humble beginnings in organisations like *La Maison des Lettres*, *Jeunesses Cinématographiques*, and *Travail et Culture*, Bazin became the most important French film critic of his time. The volume of words he turned out was almost incredible. He was regular reviewer for a daily newspaper, *Le Parisien Libéré;* he took over Roger Leenhardt's column in the monthly *Esprit;* he wrote weekly for *L'Observateur* (now *France Observateur*) and for *Radio-Cinéma-Télévision;* occasionally for the now-defunct *Revue du Cinéma,* as well as other monthlies. He is best known, however, for his articles in *Cahiers du Cinéma,* of which he was an editor. It is perhaps due to him that this has become one of the most important film magazines in the world; or it might be more accurate to say that *Cahiers du Cinéma* owed a great deal of its vitality and interest to the interaction between Bazin and the younger members of the *Cahiers* team. Although they were all united by their admiration for certain directors (Murnau, Welles, Rossellini, Stroheim, Dreyer, Bresson, etc.), it is nevertheless clear that the young Turks (not so young any more) were often in disagreement with Bazin. The two most notorious examples of this dissension were Bazin's articles attacking *Cahiers'* 'politique des auteurs' and its 'Hitchcocko-Hawksian' bias.

But Bazin's greatest influence may yet be seen in the films of his protégé François Truffaut (whose first feature, *Les 400 Coups,* is dedicated to him) and of the other young French directors who owe so much to the climate of opinion for which he, more than anyone else, was responsible.

Unlike James Agee, Bazin never did any creative work in the cinema. But I am sure that Bazin's contribution to the cinema will ultimately be seen to be more important than that of Agee. Not because Bazin was any more intelligent, nor because he had better taste. Indeed, it is amazing how often they agreed in their assessments. (Except for Welles, of course, whom Agee literally couldn't see.) Nor is it that Bazin was fundamentally any more serious than Agee. It is simply that Bazin had the luck to work in a milieu where art, aesthetics and form are taken far more seriously than they are in Britain and America. To be sure, the French can often overwhelm by an indiscriminate display of culture and erudition, by sheer wordiness and rhetoric and by occasional lunatic flights of fancy – and Bazin was not exempt from these faults. But he wrote for an audience which was passionately interested in the cinema. He did not have to try to entertain people for whom it was 'a rather unimportant subject.' One thing, ultimately, seems clear: the tradition in which Bazin wrote is more fruitful, more valid, and more fundamentally serious than that of Agee.

SOURCE: 'FACE TO FACE: ANDRÉ BAZIN', *SIGHT & SOUND,* 28.3, SUMMER 1959, 176–9

1.5 HOW TO SEE A MOVIE (IN THE U.S.A.)

NOTE: This typewritten text from the archive does not appear ever to have been published, although it reads as though it may have been intended for Sight & Sound, *certainly for a British readership.*

The easiest way is on television. Here in England where FIDO (the Film Industry Defence Organisation)[6] faithfully guards against a deluge of films, it is not widely know that on an average day in New York City, about twenty-five films are shown. For example, on Thursday, June 25th 1959, the day's films began at 9:00 am with *The War against Mrs Hadley* on Channel 3 and *Jam Session* on Channel 7; the last film of the day, *Men of Sherwood Forest,* began at 1:10 am the following morning. During the day almost every kind of film was shown: good films, bad films, unknown films – *What Every Woman Wants*, *Love Crazy*, *In This Our Life*. Some are shown twice in a day, such as *Melody for Two*, seen at 10:00 am and 1:30 pm.[7] There are seven channels visible in New York City; three network stations, the other four are independent. As one might suspect, it is the independents who show the greatest number of films for obvious economic reasons. Indeed, one channel, Channel 9, self-styled 'New York's Movie station', operates what can only be described as a repertory theatre system. It plays the same film five nights a week, twice a night at 7:30 and 10:30 pm with matinees on the weekend. During the week of June 20th the film was *Escape to Burma*, starring Barbara Stanwyck and Robert Ryan. This series is called 'Million Dollar Movie'; presumably the great number of showings is needed to recoup the cost of showing films. A less expensive film, *Catherine the Great*, was shown only once a day at 3:30 pm on Channel 9.

Obviously, smaller cities see fewer films. In a city like Boston (population about two million) there are only four channels, and one of them is 'educational'. Nevertheless, on these three channels are shown on the average of ten movies a day. In a still smaller town like Youngstown, Ohio, only about three films are shown daily – unless of course one goes to the expense of a powerful aerial. Then one can pick up Cleveland, Akron, and Erie stations, and the total number of films goes up to fifteen.

What kinds of films are shown on TV? All kinds. They range from ancient relics like George Arliss's *Richelieu* to Jean Renoir's *The River* – in black and white of course. Foreign films (complete with subtitles) are also shown – *Schweitzer*, *Jungle Doctor*, *The Blue Angel*, *Open City*. And of course, British films: *The Woman in Question*, *Madonna of the Seven Moons*, and *The Square Ring* (billed as starring Kay Kendall and Jack Warner).

Not only feature films are shown: all day long one can see Three Stooges and Ritz Brothers shorts, as well as a never-ending stream of cartoons: in New York there is even a programme called 'The Mighty Mouse Playhouse.'

This may sound like paradise for the movie fan longing to catch up on lost films like *Black Legion*, etc., but unfortunately there is one very big drawback. Most programs do not show films complete. There are station breaks, there are commercials (on the average five to a film), and when a film will not fit into the allotted time, it is simply cut to fit. There is, however, one channel in New York which does show films complete, but only on its Late Show. Even in the provinces, certain 'class' films are shown in two parts on two succeeding days, preceded by the virtuous announcement that not a single foot has been cut from these deathless films: this treatment is reserved for such masterpieces as *If Winter Comes*, *The Cat and the Fiddle* (Jeanette MacDonald and Ramon Novarro), and *My Son, My Son*.

Obviously such a flow of films cannot go on indefinitely. Over periods of six months or so, the same films will inevitably be shown twice or even three times. So far program planners have stopped short at *The Jazz Singer*, but in the ever-growing need for new material, they and the motion picture companies are inexorably going to be forced to use silent film material. Already MGM's top executives are reported to be considering ways and means of adapting Metro's huge back-log of 'non-talkies' (a euphemism?) for TV. Tentative plans, we are told, call for adding sound tracks and cutting the films to 54 minutes running time. 54, so as to allow for 6 minutes, or 10% of the hour, for commercials. One of the first films to be treated is supposed to be King Vidor's *The Big Parade*. What will be done to fit *Intolerance* into 54 minutes is difficult and painful to imagine. Perhaps it will receive the 2 or 3 day *If Winter Comes* treatment.

Failing TV, there are the drive-ins. These of course existed long before the war, but during the '30s they were largely patronised by young couples as a convenient and semi-legal place to neck, or indeed, to copulate. During the war petrol restrictions forced most of them to close down, but since 1945 they have re-opened and many more have been built. Partly as result of pre-war amorous activity, which of course led to a sharp increase in the birth rate, and partly due to the disappearance during the war of the servant class, drive-ins are now largely frequented by couples with children. Rather than leave the children at home alone or with an expensive baby-sitter, they are bundled off in the back seat to the drive-ins. There they can either watch the film or go to sleep. When a film that will appeal specially to children is shown, like *The Shaggy Dog*, the management shows it first for the benefit of the children who, after having seen it, can curl up and sleep through the second feature, in this case *The Hangman*. Generally, of course, the children are put to bed at the end of the show, but one has heard of isolated examples of parents who leave their children to sleep the whole night in the back of the car. Presumably too tender-hearted to wake them on returning home, they prefer to let them spend the night in the garage.

Most drive-ins admit children free, except for films like *The Shaggy Dog*: they declare in their advertisements: 'Children's admission 35 cents this engagement only. A charge for children is economically required under producer's policy at all theatres and drive-ins showing *Shaggy Dog*.' Not only are children generally admitted free of charge: most drive-ins feature 'Giant Playgrounds'. One theatre precedes every advertisement with the statement: 'We love children. Your youngsters are welcome at the __ drive-in. FREE. PLAYGROUND.' But the inducement of free playgrounds and free admission for the children is presumably not enough. Therefore, for adults, amenities are offered which transformed the drive-in into what one imagines to be the equivalent of a Soviet Park of Culture[8] [...]: 9-hole miniature golf courses, free gifts to every car, snack bars, restaurants, even waitress service to your car. The public-spiritedness of the drive-in managers goes even further. During the recent steel strike in America, steel workers were admitted – on producing their union card – at reduced prices for the duration of the strike. Although most drive-ins show double features, some go as far as to offer triple features in an attempt to get people out of the house and away from the television.

If one can resist the comfort of sitting at home, and if one is willing to forget the varied cultural and social advantages of the drive-in, one can of course go to what is now called a 'four-wall theatre.' They still exist, but there are fewer every year. However, the firm of business analysts, Sindlinger and Co., report that the motion picture industry may be heading for its best season in years. During the week of May 30th last, the attendance figures were found to be up 15.4% over the same period the preceding year.

But it still costs a lot of money to see a first-run movie in New York. The average Times Square cinema charges $2.00 a seat (all parts – most US theatres only have one admission price), or 14 shillings. On Saturday night it rises to $2.50 or 17/6. The first-run art houses are not much cheaper: the equivalent of the Academy asks, and gets, $1.75 or 12 shillings.

In the provinces, of course, prices are lower. One can see one first-run film or two second-run films for about 7 shillings. This is still expensive but on the second-run films one gets one's money's worth: *Imitation of Life* and *Gideon's Day* (re-baptised *Gideon of Scotland Yard* and shown in black and white – as a second feature it was not considered economical to make colour prints); *The Sound and the Fury* and *I Want to Live*; or *Auntie*

Mame and *Gigi*. These shows go on for 3 and one half hours, sometimes four. The first-run cinemas in the provinces often have to resort to extraordinary tactics to compete with these monster double bills: accordingly, they offer, apart from the rococo grandeur (sometimes Jewish Renaissance) of the cinema palace itself, stage attractions. On one Saturday morning 'kiddy show' the children were offered not only *Teenagers from Outer Space* and a second horror film, but also a bob-a-loop contest. The bob-a-loop is a rather old game which has recently been revived. A ball with a hole in one end is attached to a peg by a string. The object is to make the ball land on the peg. This contest was to play off the local bob-a-loop champions, but it was further graced by the presence of the state champion.

Back in New York, one interesting development this year has been the Chaplin revival. Chaplin in recent years has suffered from poor distribution in the US. *Monsieur Verdoux* only lasted two weeks on Broadway and did not even play many US cities. *Limelight* fared better, but *A King in New York* has not, I believe, ever been shown commercially at all in America. The most enterprising of the film societies, Cinema 16, organised trips across the Canadian border to see the film. But now this summer both *Modern Times* and *The Gold Rush* are playing to packed houses in New York. This revival was reportedly sparked off by an extraordinary little cinema in the wilds of Queens, the Inwood. This theatre's policy is to alternate bills like *Caroline Chérie* and *The Red Inn* with silent film programmes: *The Phantom of the Opera* (Lon Chaney, Sr) and *The Cabinet of Dr. Caligari*, shown full length with live piano accompaniment – two pianos, even. They began showing Chaplin films (under direct authorisation from Chaplin himself, it appears), and their enormous success tempted other exhibitors to try. After an exclusive engagement at the Plaza theatre, an art house, *Modern Times* will now be shown in a large first-run cinema – apparently an unprecedented occasion.

The most upsetting development in film exploitation in recent years has been in the domain of foreign films. In New York far fewer are shown, and what is shown is not of the quality of 10 years ago. For example, during the week of June 20th, twenty-three foreign films were on show in Manhattan. (In this calculation I do not include the 86th Street Casino, a cinema which shows four German films a week, but without subtitles and is hence patronised exclusively by the German colony: they show mainly films like *Die Prinzessin von St Wolfgang* and *Der Schmied von St Bartholomae*.) Of the 23 films most of them were trash of one sort or another: *Girls of the Night* was playing simultaneously at five cinemas. Four theatres were showing Fernandel films. Four others were showing not very interesting German films. This, by the way, represents a sharp increase over previous years when only a few features from Germany were presented for English-speaking audiences. In the last 18 months 35 Germans films were shown in New York, their main showcase being the 72nd St Playhouse, operated by Bakros films who also release a number of the German imports. About all one could see of value was *Aparajito*, *En cas de malheur*, *Il tetto*, and *Wild Strawberries*. This does not sound too bad, but the catch is that *Aparajito* has been playing for about 10 weeks, and *En cas de malheur* for several months. So the number of good foreign films one can see in New York each year is much smaller than it used to be, both because there are fewer art houses (where are the Beverley, the Elysée, the Irving, and the Avenue of yesteryear?) and because most of them prefer to exploit films for as long as possible.

A further difficulty arises from the re-titling of foreign films. *Amici per la pelle* was called *The Woman in the Painting*; *Muerte de un ciclista*, *Age of Infidelity*; *Calle mayor*, *The Love Maker*, and most peculiarly of all, *Rendez-vous de juillet* becomes *Rendez-vous with Juliet*.

According to the *Saturday Review of Literature* (although this may be a misprint), *Les 400 Coups* is called *The 405 Blows* in America! Not only is this re-titling distasteful, but it also means that the filmgoer must be very determined and very well informed to realise just what films are showing.

Another great annoyance for American film enthusiasts is the time it takes for some foreign films to arrive in New York; four years for *Diary of a Country Priest*, for example, and even then it was cut by about 25 minutes. Other films – *Lola Montès*, *Senso*, *Le amiche*, *Le Rideau cramoisi* – have still not arrived and show no signs of doing so in the near future.

Now of course many foreign films are not shown commercially in Great Britain either, but at least they are seen briefly at the National Film Theatre or at film societies. I mean films of such importance as *Ossessione* and *La terra trema*. The Museum of Modern Art Film Theatre, which is the opposite number of the NFT, largely confines itself to showing the same old films over and over again. This is not entirely their fault: a film can be brought to England from the Continent, kept a few days, and sent back quite cheaply. But when a film crosses the Atlantic, the costs mount astronomically. So only once in a while can the Museum afford the luxury of a big foreign season; when they can, it is only fair to say that they do a pretty good job. The only other source of special foreign films is Cinema 16, but they only have 15 showings a year, and well over half of their programs are devoted to American films.

Looking on the bright side of things, the Rugoff-Baker chain of theatres (5th Avenue, Beekman, Art, 8th Street, Grammercy) go on doing their best to import good new films. They have been so successful commercially that this autumn they have opened a new cinema. The old 34th Street, a former semi-fleapit, has been transformed into a luxurious art house. And the old Thalia cinema goes on with its fantastic summer festivals. The Thalia is probably the worst cinema in the world (Champollion is the runner-up) for projection, sound, and comfort. It is a reconverted night club and architecturally it is not at all suitable for showing films. All these annoyances are outweighed by its programs; e.g., *Les Parents terribles* and *L'Aigle à deux têtes*; *Open City* and *Paisà*. During the summer festival the program is changed daily, so one can really catch up. The only snag is that each summer the programs are virtually the same. Film culture is upheld in the Bronx by the Ascot theatre; sample program: *Umberto D.* and *Ugetsu monogatari*.

Outside New York the foreign film situation is perhaps better than it used to be. Foreign films are reaching smaller and smaller cities. One was staggered to see *Pather Panchali* playing in a steel town in Ohio. True, it was shown 'under the auspices of the Planned Parenthood Association'. Presumably *Pather Panchali* was to serve as the awful example of what could happen if one neglected Malthusian practices. Actually, the point of the sponsorship was that the Association guaranteed the film against loss, and accordingly pushed its members to go to see it, tickets being available at their Clinic as well as at the box-office. This particular theatre showed foreign films about once a month, and always under the auspices of something or other. Nevertheless, whether to the greater glory of contraceptives or not, *Pather Panchali* was seen, and for this much one must be grateful.

Generally speaking in the smaller town it is only Bardot who crashes the language barrier. Or rather the national barrier, for her films are shown in a dubbed version in the smaller cities. Her films are so widely shown that she is now 7th in popularity among movie stars in America, and needless to say, the only foreign star among the top ten, or probably the top 50.

The greatest increase in the showing of continental films has been in the larger provincial cities. Where formerly there were only 2 and one half art houses in Boston, there are now six. One of them goes in largely for sex films, another for American and British classics, but the number of continental films to be seen has greatly increased. This is probably the result of the general cultural levelling out which has been caused by television, as well as of the smaller number of Hollywood films being produced each year. Whereas before film culture (such as it was) was almost entirely concentrated in New York, it has now infiltrated the larger provincial centres.

Perhaps a special word ought to be said here about the status of British films in America. It would seem to have changed somewhat since my article of January 1957, 'Britain in America'. The Exeter in Boston (the doyen of the art houses specialising in British films) still goes on showing *Genevieve* and *Laughter in Paradise*. But the Paris cinema in New York has, logically enough, I suppose, given up Alec Guinness for a time, and gone back to showing French films. The Sutton, leased by Rank as an outlet for British films, has been showing *Gigi* for many a month, and the Little Carnegie has done the same with *En cas de malheur*. Still, British films are being seen, but more and more in ordinary cinemas. This year has seen the triumph of *Room at the Top*. The film was very cleverly exploited with just the right combination, it would seem, of sex and culture. The usual advertisement showed the bedroom scene with beneath it to the right: 'A motion picture so Frankly Physical … so Boldly Unashamed we recommend it for Adult Audience only!' To the left was printed: 'British Film Academy winner 1959, Best Picture of the year, Simone Signoret best foreign actress.'

But obviously it wasn't just clever exploitation that made the success of *Room at the Top*. Nor was it because it was 'so frankly physical.' From what one could make out from people one talked to who had seen it, it was because it was a British picture that was *about* something. Even though it was very strongly set in a British milieu and was made with little or no attempt to 'cater for the international market', it has captured that market because it dealt honestly and dramatically with a theme that was universally understood. It would be nice if one could predict that *Look Back in Anger* will be equally successful, but it seems extremely doubtful. Most important of all, it will be difficult for a mass American audience to identify with Jimmy Porter. The problems he is up against either do not exist in America or are present in a very different form. Frankly, judging from the reception the film got from a ship-board showing to a group of Americans on their way to Europe this summer, its career in the US will be disastrous.

How relevant is the situation of the cinema as it has been described to conditions now and in the future in England? First of all, it would seem that when the third channel comes into being, and when television broadcasting extends its hours (as it has done, and no doubt will go on doing), the pressure of having to find enough material to fill up all those hours will no doubt make for an increase in the number of films shown on television, FIDO notwithstanding. When this happens, some more cinemas are going to close. The only ones that will profit from television are the cinemas showing continental films — for it seems doubtful that there will be any relaxing of the moral standards for television. Indeed, one hears that an important film distributor in Great Britain is already planning to set up a circuit of 35 cinemas in London and the provinces to show nothing but continental films. Many of these films will no doubt be sex dramas and nudist elegiacs, but there will also be films of quality shown as well.

As for the ordinary circuit cinema it is probable (indeed, the trend has already begun) that it will start to show two feature films in an attempt to give the customer a good reason for forsaking the comfort of his home. Lastly, the drive-ins: they, I think, will have to wait until enough people own motor-cars – which may occur in the foreseeable future – and until English weather becomes less treacherous – but this seems doubtful. So the joys of the pleasure garden *cum* Roman Bath[9] will never come to England's green and pleasant land.

SOURCE: 'HOW TO SEE A MOVIE (IN THE USA)', ARCHIVE DOCUMENT, 1959, RICHARD ROUD COLLECTION, HOWARD GOTLIEB ARCHIVAL RESEARCH CENTER, BOSTON, BOX 1, F8, ITEM J.30, 13 PAGES

1.6 NOVEL NOVEL; FABLE FABLE?

Is it still possible to write novels …? The answer, it seems to me, is certainly not yes and perhaps, tentatively, no. I mean real novels – not fairy tales or fables or romances or *contes philosophiques*, and I mean novels of a high order … I ought to make it clear that these distinctions are in no way pejorative. I do not mean 'novel good, fable bad', merely 'novel novel; fable fable'. When people nowadays tell you something is 'not a novel', as they are fond of saying, for instance about *Dr Zhivago*, it is always in a querulous tone, as though someone had tried to put something over on them, sell them the Empire State Building or Trajan's Monument or the Palace of Culture when they know better; they were not born yesterday. That is not my intention … Mary McCarthy (*Partisan Review*, Summer 1960)

The development of the novel and that of the film as art forms are more closely parallel than one might imagine. Over the past sixty years, the cinema has undergone an evolution similar to that of the novel in its history of some 200-odd years. If one takes the mainstream of *narrative* cinema, one can see a development counterpointing that of the novel which can most conveniently be expressed in tabular form:

DEFOE – The primitives of the cinema: they appealed to their audiences in the same way as the early novelists (within their limited technical means of course) by presenting stories purportedly true, or at least events and characters purportedly real.

FIELDING, DICKENS – Griffith and the American cinema of the Twenties: more elaborate fictions, laced with sentimental indulgence and moral uplift, more complicated narrative techniques than those of the primitives (cf. *Bleak House* and *Intolerance*).

BALZAC, DOSTOYEVSKY – Stroheim and Pabst: greater freedom in choice of subject matter; greater psychological daring; greater power and brutality.

ZOLA and THE GONCOURTS – The Italian neo-realist movement.

HENRY JAMES – Antonioni.

Parallels like these are obviously neither tight nor exhaustive. They leave out the un-comparables (Welles and Flaubert) and the non-narrative cinema: Eisenstein (epic, not narrative); Dovzhenko and Vigo (poetry, not narrative); Dreyer and Bresson (allegory or fable).

That the novel and the film should display such connections is not surprising if one considers that their popularity as art forms proceeded largely from the same sources. With the advent of bourgeois culture in the eighteenth century, and with the fillip given to universal education by Protestantism, more and more people began to learn how to read and, equally important, to have time to read. And so literature was faced with a growing audience *capable* of reading but not sophisticated enough to read, say, *Hero and Leander*, *Arcadia* or *Euphues*. For it takes a more educated perception to read a poem or a romance from which the relevant human significance must be deduced than a realistic tale which can always be regarded simply as a story of what happened to real people. Defoe, Richardson or Fielding can be read purely for the narrative: Sidney, Marlowe or Lyly cannot. *Birth of a Nation* can be enjoyed purely as a story: *Hiroshima, mon amour* cannot.

Recent developments in the cinema can best be understood by considering what course the novel has taken since Joyce (or was it Henry James?) killed it. True to that principle of alternation which underlies the history of all the arts, the novel went back to those literary forms which prevailed before its birth. In *Ulysses*, Joyce returned to the epic; in *The Castle*, Kafka returned to the fable, the allegory. Others, according to a no less general principle, turned to non-novelistic forms: Virginia Woolf, in *The Waves*, to the introspective poem; Alain Robbe-Grillet to the world of the painter, the description of appearances.

In the cinema, the move from the novel to the fable goes back, I would say, to Bresson's *Les Dames du Bois de Boulogne* (1945), although I am sure one could find earlier examples – cases might be made out for *La Règle du jeu* and for *L'Atalante*. But *Les Dames du Bois de Boulogne* provides as good a starting point as any other, and consideration of it will help to pinpoint the differences between the novel and the fable. *The novel*, briefly, *means what it is about*. In a good novel, emotion is expressed by finding (to use Eliot's words) a set of objects, a situation, a chain of events, which will be the formula of that particular emotion. Artistic inevitability, says Eliot, lies in the complete adequacy of the external to the emotion. The feeling of dissatisfaction, of something baffling about the film, experienced by critics and audiences at the time *Les Dames* was first shown proceeded, I think, from the fact that the plot of the film and its theme – what Bresson is saying – are *not* objectively correlated. There is an enormous difference between the story (the apparent subject) and the theme (the real subject).

The apparent subject of *Les Dames* is a not very believable intrigue, adapted from Diderot's *Jacques le fataliste*, about how a woman connives to make her former lover marry a prostitute in order to revenge herself on him. The real subject is the triumph of love over hate: love can create, hate can only destroy. Why does Bresson choose such a simple and not very interesting plot to express himself? The answer is, presumably, that he does not want us to get lost in the labyrinth of the well-constructed plot, he does not want us to become so involved with lifelike and identifiable-with characters that we will fail to grasp the more general aspects of his theme. Furthermore, the choice of a deliberately artificial plot allows him to 'eliminate anything which might distract from the interior drama,' as he himself declared. The whole *mise en scène* of the film is not subjugated to an expression of the plot or a pointing up of the story; plot, theme and form are related, but in a much more complex and interesting manner. The whole becomes equal to the multiplication of the parts, not to their sum.

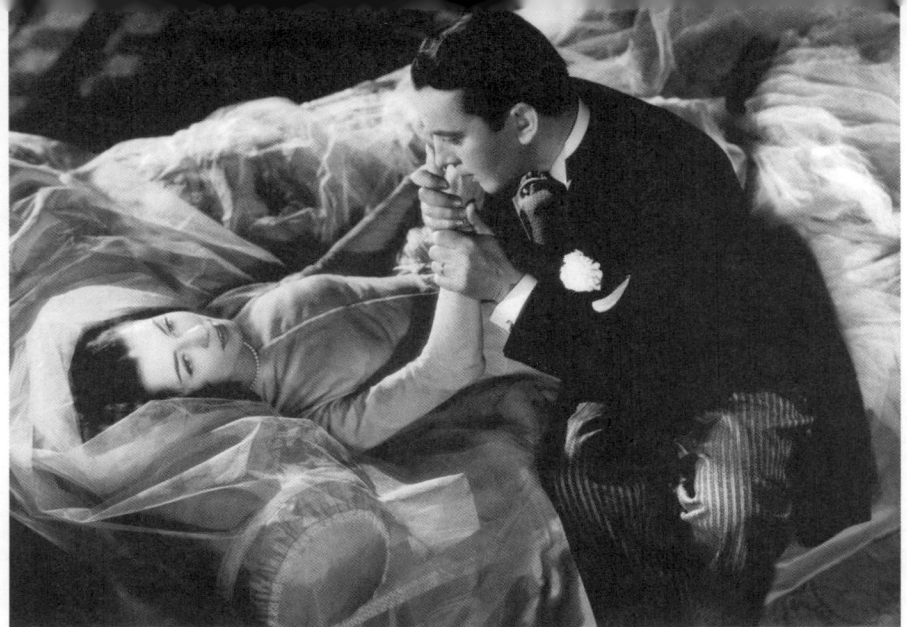

Les Dames du Bois de Boulogne (1945)

Les Dames du Bois de Boulogne is now a 'classic', but Bresson's most recent film, *Pickpocket*, has not been properly appreciated, to my way of thinking, even in the pages of *Sight & Sound*. And this is because it has been judged according to criteria which were based implicitly on the aesthetic of the nineteenth-century novel. But other aesthetics exist; others have existed. Although the novel has dominated our culture for over a hundred years, it is an historical fact whose beginning can be situated and its end posited.

In his review of *Pickpocket* for *Sight & Sound*, Eric Rhode ultimately found himself forced to reject the film because Bresson never made it clear just why the hero, Michel, became a pickpocket:

> What in fact is the weakness which drives him to an adventure in theft for which he was not made? Recent sociological and psycho-analytical knowledge should give us some idea, but Bresson seems indifferent to these findings. Disturbing overtones suggest he isn't conscious of them at all …

If Bresson's film had been an attempt at a novelistic character study, a realistic depiction of people, then this criticism would perhaps be damning (although one doubts whether 'recent psycho-analytical knowledge' is absolutely indispensable to the artist). But Bresson has, I think, made it quite clear that his film is not realistic, that it is, in fact, a non-realistic allegory or fable. As Michel descends into the same (disused) tube station for the tenth time and rides back and forth on the same tube line over and over again in the company of the same extras, he says, 'I always took care to vary my trips, first taking one line and then another.' This seeming inattention to detail in so meticulous an artist as Bresson can only mean that he is not in the least interested in a realistic texture. Nor should he be, given what he has set out to do. He is not interested in psychological realism either. Michel's lines about his two years in London ('I lost all my money on gambling and women') are almost unbelievable coming from those ascetic lips. One might almost say that Bresson needed an excuse to bring Michel back to Paris and any excuse was as good as another.

Properly speaking, Michel is not a character at all. The actor Bresson chose to play him does not even try to act the role; his delivery and his face come as close to anonymity as possible. Like Matisse, who in his chapel at Vence carefully left the faces of the saints blank so that the faithful might read into them anything they wanted or were able, so Bresson has purposely made Michel as vague and as unparticularised as possible. Michel is the sinner, the man who is trying to find salvation and redemption. His friend, Jacques, attempts to help him, but Jacques's way is that of good works, which are not sufficient in Bresson's theology. He offers him sound advice, jobs, bourgeois morality. But these are not enough for Michel – nor even for Jacques, for his way of life does not prevent him from abandoning Jeanne and the child she has had by him. Even Michel's thefts can be interpreted as an attempt to *snatch* salvation: the first and last thefts we are shown take place at race-tracks; Michel is trying to profit by the luck (grace) of those who have won.

But neither Jacques's secular wisdom, nor Michel's efforts to attain grace by stealth, are of avail. Nor are Michel's endeavours at mere respectability, when he returns from England and settles down in a job to support Jeanne and her child. The hound of heaven follows him still, and even he realises that he must be caught before he can be free. And so he *lets* himself be caught. But even penance is not sufficient; Jeanne represents the force of love, and it is only through her that Michel finally achieves grace.

Mr Rhode found *Pickpocket* inferior to *Un Condamné à mort s'est échappé* because in the earlier film a similar theme was treated realistically, 'or enough, anyway, for it to make sense on a literal level.' This is quite true; *Pickpocket* does not make sense on a literal level. Presumably Mr Rhode, deceived by the fact that the screen is (usually) a realistic medium and by the realistic setting of *Pickpocket* (Paris exteriors, no studio work), assumed that Bresson's intentions were realistic. *Pickpocket*, however, has much closer links with *Les Dames du Bois de Boulogne* than with *Un Condamné*. *Les Dames*, as we have seen, is also an allegory; and its plot is hard to take in any literal way. Both films are sufficiently non-realistic and de-personalised for us to be free to interpret the problems they pose in our own terms. What interested Bresson in these films was the road to redemption, not the particular scenery along that road. 'Recent psycho-analytical knowledge' might attempt to tell us that Michel's sin is homosexuality (this idea has been advanced in many quarters), but I think this would be to miss the point. This interpretation is certainly possible, but Bresson leaves us free to substitute *any* temptation to evil. 'The ability to make the necessary connections' is not to be found in *Pickpocket*, to be sure; we must make them ourselves.

The same is certainly true of *L'Année dernière à Marienbad*: we must make the connections. In Resnais's earlier *Hiroshima, mon amour* there was a split between apparent and real subject. But the apparent subject, the plot, was 'interesting' enough and complex enough to make the film more easily palatable to those whose aesthetic bias demands a world of logical relationships. The characters were sufficiently personalised (the heroine at least) for the viewer to be able to take the story straight, even while he may have noticed that there was something else going on in the film besides the account of a rather neurotic young woman of 'doubtful morality' whose unfortunate wartime experiences had branded her for ever.

In *L'Année dernière* Resnais and Robbe-Grillet provide no such crutch. It is difficult (though not impossible) to identify with a woman called 'A' or a man called 'X'. Resnais's treatment of the setting leaves one in no doubt that this is a different world from, say, that of Vicki Baum's *Grand Hotel*. In fact, the deliberate thinness of the plot, the lack of incident, the absence of any explanation of the characters' motivations, or even any placing of the characters, has led some critics to dismiss the film as the triumph of form over content, as a purely abstract (read *cold*) work with nothing to say. *L'Année dernière* was reviewed in the last issue of *Sight & Sound*, so there is no point in going into it at any great length here, except to make the obvious observation that it has gone further than *Les Dames*, *Pickpocket* or *Hiroshima* towards the fable. One now understands just what it was that Resnais saw in Visconti's *White Nights:* with all its flaws, it too was an attempt to capture the sense of wonder, the timelessness of the non-contingent world of the fable. Far from finding *L'Année dernière* trivial or chilly, I think it is one of the most emotional films ever made; but the emotions are stirred not only by the characters or their predicament but also by a total response to the work of art which none the less does have a meaning. Surely love, the interaction of past and present, freedom and bondage are not unimportant as subjects? As important as − unblushingly to use an Aunt Sally − whether a man gets his stolen bicycle back or not.

One need not go on about Robbe-Grillet and the *nouveau roman* to justify Resnais's use of an unrealistic and unmotivated plot. The same thing can be found in a play like Shakespeare's *Winter's Tale*. It is an allegory (actually a restatement of the Persephone myth), an allegory of redemption, like *Pickpocket*. In fact a comparison of certain recent French films with some of Shakespeare's romantic comedies and tragi-comedies is more fruitful than one might at first imagine. The French fascination with America can easily be paralleled by the Elizabethan intoxication with an imagined Italy. Both are equally unrealistic: Italy and America are seen at once as impossibly evil (the Circes of the Nations) and as glamorously alluring. They both provide distance, stimulus and an escape from realism (cf. *Tirez sur le pianiste*, another misunderstood and underrated film).

Resnais and Bresson are important enough directors to be assured at least a modicum of serious attention. Even when a critic dislikes *Pickpocket* or *L'Année dernière*, he is generally respectful enough to couch his rejection in serious terms. But the problem of critics' criteria when confronted with a fable was really brought out at last year's London Film Festival. There were two outstanding 'comedies' in the Festival − *Lola* and *Il posto* (*Une Femme est une femme* belongs to no genre). Both films were well received, but it is enlightening to compare the reactions. By and large, *Il posto* was preferred (even, alas, by the British Film Institute, in awarding the Sutherland Trophy). I submit that this was mainly due to the fact that *Il posto* was the kind of comedy critics tend to treat respectfully because it is satire, because it criticises certain social conditions, and above all, because it is realistic. It had a plot which could be taken seriously. And yet it seems to me that *Lola* lies smack in the middle of the really great tradition of comedy − unrealistic, contrived, yet moving − like *As You Like It*, *Twelfth Night* or the tragi-comedies of Euripides. An important work of art in spite of − although this is begging the question − its plot.

Like Shakespeare's comedies, *Lola* has a basically simple plot. Lola is a dancer in Nantes; her lover left her seven years ago to make his fortune; he returns to marry her, thereby disappointing another young man who has since fallen in love with Lola. This basic story line is delightfully complicated by a number of parallel and subsidiary incidents which have been described by Jacques Siclier in a recent number of *Sight & Sound* as attempts to tell the story of Lola's whole life without using flashbacks: the past and future, as it were, continuously present through the use of parallel situations. I do not really see it this way myself; nor, I am happy to say, does the director, Jacques Demy. For one thing the parallels do not always work. For another, as in poetry, the connections are made metaphorically: they are not precise equivalents but analogues, and hence all the more telling.

Lola is, like *As You Like It*, a fable about the different kinds of love. Just as in *As You Like It* we have the Phoebe/Silvius relationship, that of Touchstone and Audrey, Celia and Oliver, and Rosalind and Orlando, all of them different but complementary views of love, so in *Lola* the subject is love in all its manifestations: Roland/Lola, Lola/Michel, Cécile/Frankie, Frankie/Lola, Roland/Madame Desnoyers, etc.

One of the chief joys of *Lola*, as of most fables, is in watching the mechanism work itself out, slowly, ineluctably, and above all elegantly. Demy has found visual equivalents to the formal pattern of verse in prose in the Shakespearian comedies: 'I will help you if I can, I would love you if I could, I will marry you if ever I marry woman, and I shall be married tomorrow.'

Gracefully and effortlessly, scene balances scene, shot counters shot until the complications are resolved into the most elegant of cotillions. And yet there is nothing fusty or old-fashioned about the style of the film. For all its dedication to Max Ophüls, there is nothing of the gauzy appeal to the past. Lola is resolutely contemporary; the photography by Coutard is bright, sharp, and in the café scenes formal, even approaching the abstract. Except for Lola's nightclub, the El Dorado, the locations are airy, cool and simple. (Here again, as with *Pickpocket*, the realistic trappings of *Lola* led some critics into assuming it was a naturalistic film. This ambivalent approach put off many; to others, it constituted a large part of the film's appeal – the constant tension between real and unreal, a dialectic whose synthesis was achieved by the film itself.) But from the fluid and occasionally audacious camera movements, the welter of chance meetings, resemblances, coincidences, and the elegance of the choreography, there emerges a kind of truth, the most important kind, the truth of the emotions.

I am not saying that *Lola* is as great a work as *Twelfth Night* or *As You Like It*, but only that it is the same *kind* of work. Demy has used a complicated, illogical fable which has allowed him to create a film in which he can treat his subject – love – as fully and as widely as possible. He has also, on his own level, solved an important problem. He has provided an interesting story – everyone loves a good story – and yet he has kept it sufficiently at a distance for him not to become restricted by it in any way.

The principle underlying the basic aesthetic of the nineteenth-century novel was that it should deal realistically with recognisable characters who behaved in a logical manner. A world was created by the novelist, but a world of logical relationships, and one based on rationalist thought, the thought of the novel's greatest period of development. And many still feel that the summit of art is achieved when what the novelist wants to say finds expression through a watertight story – one in which the characters' actions and destinies can be explained by psychological, economic and political reasons. Coincidence can only be allowed if, like garlic, it is used sparingly. As any guide to novel writing will tell you, no character can die unless he has been shown to be dangerously ill, suicidal or addicted to hazardous sports. We can all remember that the greatest objection to *L'avventura* was that Anna, whom one had taken to be the principal character, disappeared after twenty minutes of the film and was never heard from again. As Jung put it, there is no legitimate place in the rationalist world for invisible, arbitrary or so-called supernatural forces. We distinctly resent the idea of these forces, he continues, for it was not so long ago that we made our escape from the frightening world of dreams and superstitions and constructed for ourselves a picture of the cosmos worthy of rational consciousness.

In the past twenty or thirty years, rationalism has undergone a severe testing; world events have shaken the beliefs of many in progress; existentialism (both the Danish and the German as well as the French kind) has insisted on the irrationality of man. England and America have held on the most tenaciously to rationalism, at least on the conscious level, but they are learning that neither tranquillisers nor good old common sense can buy off the Furies. The irrational can only be placated by a just and due recognition of its existence and a modicum of respect. 'The rationalism of the Enlightenment will have to recognise that at the very heart of its light there is also a darkness,' writes William Barrett.

Hence the fable is perhaps the art form most suited to our time. It recognises the irrational elements in life: the importance of coincidence, of chance and the gratuitous, of luck (or, as Bresson would call it, of grace); the ever-present possibility of death (accidental or otherwise); and it is thus more lifelike and more real than that literature which goes under the name of realism.

No less important, however, is the fact that the fable frees the film-maker from the obligations of story-telling as such, just as painters were absolved a hundred years ago by the invention of the camera from the duty of reproducing reality and were able to follow other and more dangerous paths. Of all the films I have discussed, *L'Année dernière* is the best example of what this new freedom can bring. If ever there was an example in the cinema of the completely integrated work of art, this is it. Image, sound, dialogue, music, camera movements, are all autonomous, interacting one with another to create patterns of extreme complexity and brilliance. And this was possible, I submit, because plot was, so to speak, kept in its place. Just as thematic material in music or subject matter in painting never dominates the work as a whole, so Resnais and Robbe-Grillet have never sacrificed to their plot the other elements which make up a film.

I am not trying to say that this is the only way to make a great film. *La notte* is living proof to the contrary – although even there … What I *am* trying to say is that *Ulysses* can no more be judged by the same criteria as *Le Père Goriot* than *L'Année dernière* can be by those applicable to *Greed*, *Toni* or *The Tokyo Story*.

SOURCE: 'NOVEL NOVEL; FABLE FABLE?', *SIGHT & SOUND*, 30.1, SPRING 1962, 84–8

1.7 NATIONAL FILM THEATRE: THE FIRST TEN YEARS

Perhaps the most spectacular development of the British Film Institute since its inception in 1933 was the opening of the National Film Theatre. When one thinks of the long and bitter struggle to establish a National Theatre – not with us even yet – one is all the more astonished that somehow the NFT came into being ten years ago.

Somehow … The idea of a National Film Theatre was one of the dreams of the founders of the BFI. When in 1948 its creation was recommended by the Radcliffe Report, it seemed impossible of fulfilment. But in 1951 a site was located: the Telekinema of the Festival of Britain. At the end of the Festival, the building was destined to be torn down, but by intensive efforts in which the then Director and Secretary of the Institute, Denis Forman and Robert Camplin played leading parts, a stay of execution was achieved and permission to use the building as a National Film Theatre was granted.

And so in October 1952, equipped with the financial assistance of the film industry, the first national film theatre in the world opened its doors under the management of Frank Hazell, who remained General Manager of the theatre until 1958. From the beginning it was established as a club cinema: completely free of censorship, and able to import films without paying duty. This last is important, for while the British Film Institute is supported by a Treasury grant, the NFT has had to be completely self-supporting. And so it has been, thanks to the enthusiasm and support of its members, but also in no less degree thanks to the support of the film trade, both in this country and abroad.

The National Film Theatre has never paid a rental fee for any of the films it has shown, and has thus been able to use all its limited resources to bring in films from all parts of the world and to achieve the standards of presentation demanded by a National film theatre. Silent films are shown with a piano accompaniment; foreign films, if un-subtitled, are provided with an English translation which is relayed over individual earphones; occasionally the theatre finds it necessary to sub-title a film; film directors come from far and near to introduce their films to members; months of research and negotiation are sometimes necessary to put on a three-week season; finally, a staff of five full-time projectionists is needed to cope with the preparation and screening of the 200 or more changes of programme at the Theatre each year — films whose condition may require hours of repair if they are to get through a projector. And yet, in spite of exceptionally heavy presentation costs and low admission prices, the National Film Theatre, whose activities are controlled and coordinated by the Institute's Secretary, Stanley Reed, does manage to break even.

When the Telekinema finally had to be pulled down to make way for the South Bank development scheme, the Institute with the active help and encouragement of the London County Council even managed to build a new theatre. An appeal fund was successfully launched to equip a new building under Waterloo Bridge. And in October 1957, the new theatre was opened by Her Royal Highness, the Princess Margaret, in the presence of Réné Clair, John Ford, Vittorio de Sica, and Akira Kurosawa. Nostalgia for the old theatre's more intimate atmosphere and perfect sightlines was soon forgotten in the enormously extended range of programming made possible by the new theatre: wide screen, Metroscope, Vistavision, RKO-Scope, optical CinemaScope, magnetic CinemaScope, Anamorphic Vistavision; silent films could be shown at 16, 18, 20 and 24 frames per second; 8 millimetre films screened on an arc projector; there were slide-projectors, filmstrip projectors, tape decks, and four-track stereophonic sound equipment.

The National Film Theatre is unique, then, in its standing, its relations with the industry, its technical resources and its method of operating. It is also unique in its programmes.

From the very beginning, the NFT has attempted a two-fold task: to recapture and re-evaluate the past achievements of the cinema, and to bring to its members the best of the new and experimental, the off-beat and the exotic. During its first years, it largely concentrated on the past. With glee the rusty tins were seized from their shelves, and the NFT revived the great American silent comedies, resuscitating Buster Keaton, Harry Langdon and Larry Semon. Indeed, it would be fair to say that had it not been for the work of the NFT (and its counterparts abroad), we would never have seen the commercial re-issues of films like *The General* and Harold Lloyd's *World of Comedy*. The large and enthusiastic NFT audiences proved to the commercial world that the work of the great silent comedians still held enormous appeal for contemporary audiences. The same phenomenon could be observed at work in the Garbo revival of a few years ago.

Momma Don't Allow (1955)

In the early days of the theatre, the spirit of *Sequence* was well to the fore, with pro-gramme planner Karel Reisz organising seasons devoted to the American Musical, Humphrey Jennings, Jacques Becker, Hitchcock, and De Sica. Film-goers of 1954 were reminded of the baroque grandeur of the films of Erich von Stroheim, who again assumed in British eyes his rightful place as one of the great artists of the cinema. 1955 saw two full-dress seasons, one devoted to the work of Buñuel, the other to John Ford. Until the existence of the NFT, it was almost impossible for film critics or students ever to see in the period of a month or so the complete works of any film director, and impossible, there-fore, ever to evaluate properly his achievements. The Buñuel and Ford seasons proved a revelation to many, and seasons devoted to the work of individual directors have since formed an important part of the NFT's work.

Around 1956, the NFT began to turn increasingly towards the present. In January of that year two important seasons were presented: important not only in themselves but as the beginning of a new orientation: *New Activity* and *Free Cinema One*. *New Activity* was the NFT's first attempt to bring London new films from abroad, films which had been neglected by commercial distributors, the 'Cinderellas of the Film Festivals'. There is no need now to explain what *Free Cinema* was – the term has entered film history. But in 1956, it meant Lindsay Anderson's *O Dreamland*, Tony Richardson's and Karel Reisz's *Momma Don't Allow*, and Lorenza Mazzetti's *Together*. Miss Mazzetti retains her interest in cinema despite success as a novelist and Karel Reisz, Tony Richardson, and Lindsay Anderson have, of course, gone on to become three of Britain's leading directors.

Encouraged by the success of this 'New Activity', the NFT went on in the same year to present the British Premiere of *Pather Panchali*, *Free Cinema Two* and a comprehensive Russian Panorama – which included new films as well as old. The year ended with Derek

Prouse's great Italian Season, introducing to Londoners the films of Visconti, Maselli, Rossi and Fellini and, with a comprehensive season devoted to new French shorts, including works by many young directors who have since become world-famous. Actually, in the case of the New Wave, the NFT got in on the ground floor, for in September 1958, David Robinson arranged for the presentation of Truffaut's *Les Mistons* and Chabrol's *Le Beau Serge* in *Free Cinema Five*, this almost a year before the New Wave achieved recognition in France itself.

But of all the NFT's endeavours to discover and present the newest developments in the art of the cinema, none has been more important or more influential than the London Film Festival. James Quinn, who had taken over the Directorship of the Film Institute in 1955, saw the value of a Festival in London in advancing both the work of the Theatre and the wider purposes of the Institute. The first Festival, held in conjunction with the *Sunday Times*, took place in the new theatre in October 1957. It was a tremendous success, as has been each succeeding Festival. Of late the atmosphere at the theatre during the last two weeks of October is redolent of the quasi-religious over-tones of Bayreuth. And not only for Londoners: more than a few people from the country have said that they take their holidays to coincide with the Festival period.

The Festival's aim is to present the best films from all the major festivals of the world, thus reducing the enormous time-lag which used to exist between production and eventual United Kingdom distribution. Its success can be measured not only by the many remarkable films it has introduced to London, but also by the great number which have subsequently received commercial distribution. A list of all the festival films will be found on page 15 [of this booklet]; it speaks for itself.

Screenings of new discoveries in the cinema have not been restricted to the London Film Festival period, however. The NFT is proud of having brought to London works by such important directors as Ozu, Mizoguchi, and Kurosawa (*The Japanese Season*, 1957); Ingmar Bergman (*Swedish Season*, 1959); Jean Rouch (*The Negro World*, 1959) – but actually his films were first presented by the director at the National Film Theatre as early as 1953; Jean-Pierre Melville (*Bob le Flambeur* was shown during the 1960 *French Season*); John Cassavetes (*Shadows* was previewed in the *Beat Square and Cool Season*, 1960); Jacques Rivette and Marcel Hanoun (*Channel Crossing*, 1961); and Michelangelo Antonioni (1961).

Antonioni is perhaps the best example of the influence the National Film Theatre can exert. Before the fifth London Film Festival in 1960, only his *Le amiche* had been shown commercially in Great Britain, and as a second feature at that. But the screening of *L'avventura* at the Festival, the subsequent Sutherland Award, followed two months later by a full-dress season of all his films presented and annotated by Richard Roud, Programmes Officer since 1960, were sufficient to make his almost a household name. This may sound like boasting. It is not so intended. There is nothing more rewarding, after all, than to be able to communicate one's enthusiasm, to make better known the works of a man one admires – and success is naturally very gratifying. But it must never be forgotten that credit for a large part of this success must go to the press. Without the enthusiastic support of London's film critics, one doubts whether the NFT would ever have been able to achieve what it has. One takes their interest for granted, but it is the very lack of an enlightened press in, say, New York, that has made an operation there like the National Film Theatre unthinkable.

Excitement over the new has never led the NFT to forget its other function, that of a 'National Gallery' of the cinema. John Huntley, the Programme Controller, has been indefatigable in the lively presentation of early material on weekly screenings from The National Film Archive and elsewhere, reviving and re-evaluating the past 60 years of film. *British Comedy of the '30s* proved to many that Will Hay was just as funny now as he ever was; our seasons devoted to the films of the great American production companies – MGM, Warners, United Artists, Samuel Goldwyn – proved enormously enjoyable both to those who have never seen the films and to those who were able to confirm their memories.

But one should not think of old films as simply a nostalgic wallowing in a past one either knew or regretted having missed. Screenings at the National Film Theatre of such heretofore little-known masterpieces as Bresson's *Les Dames du Bois de Boulogne*, Renoir's *La Chienne* and the complete version of *La Règle du jeu*, Eisenstein's *Strike*, Ophüls's *La signora di tutti* and the complete *Lola Montès*, Henry King's *Stella Dallas* and Dovzhenko's *Ivan* have proved to be as rewarding aesthetically and emotionally as the best of recent films.

Slowly and in the most non-authoritarian way possible, the National Film Theatre is rewriting film history. Before the NFT existed people had to take what the film books said as gospel; denied a chance of seeing the received list of film classics, and even more important, denied the chance of seeing enough older films to make their *own* list of classics, one had simply to accept the established values. When one considers the list of the top fifteen films as established by *Sight & Sound*'s 1962 poll of film critics (although the poll was international, the majority of critics were English), one finds such films as *Ugetsu monogatari*, *La terra trema*, *L'avventura*, *Pather Panchali*, *Ikiru* and *Nazarin* – all works which the NFT showed in London for the first time. Equally significant, perhaps, is the rise of *La Règle du jeu* from tenth place in 1952 to third in 1962. Renoir is now in third place in the classification by directors; Antonioni, fifth; Mizoguchi, eighth; Buñuel and Visconti tied for tenth place. With all the modesty in the world it is hard to avoid the conclusion that perhaps the National Film Theatre has had something to do with this shift in critical thinking.

A catalogue of past achievement may seem to imply complacency. In fact the Institute is far from satisfied. The National Film Theatre still lacks facilities for the proper study and discussion of cinema which a true national film centre should have. A lecture hall is badly needed and a small theatre where programmes of an exploratory nature in terms of film history and experiment can be put on and where conferences and discussions can take place without interruption to the regular programme pattern of the main auditorium. Similarly, there is a need for ampler and more convenient club premises. There are plans for these improvements, in which both the Treasury and the London County Council have signified interest, but final agreement (in October 1962) has yet to be reached.

Among the other shortcomings of which the Institute is conscious is its almost complete failure to extend the work of the National Film Theatre outside London. Some people object, and with reason, to the use of the words *National* and *British* for what are in effect London operations. The Institute has every sympathy with the feelings of film-lovers outside London whose appetite is whetted, but never satisfied, with each appearance of the National Film Theatre programme booklets. For this problem there seems no ready-made solution, for while it is just possible for the NFT to survive in London without major subsidy, this could not happen in less thickly populated areas. Further, the generosity of the film industry would be sorely strained if they were asked to provide the same free services for a number of provincial centres as they do for the National Film Theatre. Perhaps the best hope lies in one or both of two possibilities. If a small chain of even five or six National Film Theatres could be established the programming costs of each of them might be so proportionately reduced as to allow some viable arrangement with the industry for the supply of films to be entered into. And if local authorities in other areas were willing to assist the establishment of film theatres in their areas, as the London County Council had done – the cost, compared with the subsidy needed by the live theatre, music, ballet or opera, is very modest – this seemingly intractable problem might, after all, be resolved.

SOURCE: 'NFT 10TH ANNIVERSARY: THE FIRST TEN YEARS', BROCHURE, NATIONAL FILM THEATRE, OCTOBER 1962, 8 PAGES

1.8 THE LEFT BANK

Classification is a kind of analogy: it proves nothing and is only valuable if it tells us more about what is being classified. Ever since the New Wave broke upon the world, critics have tried to divide the flood of new young film-makers into smaller and more meaningful groups. The *Cahiers du Cinéma* team would seem to constitute one group. Another is made up of Agnès Varda, Chris Marker and Alain Resnais. Agnès Varda's *oeuvre* is still relatively unknown in this country; Chris Marker's is almost totally so. One hopes that the forthcoming season of their works at the National Film Theatre will help to make them better known and will also demonstrate that they all have something more in common than, as Agnès Varda declared in a recent interview, their love of cats. This article is, in effect, an examination of that 'something more.' A few facts, first.

The average age of Marker, Resnais and Varda is about 37. They were all born and brought up outside of Paris – Resnais in Brittany, Varda in Sète, near Montpellier, Marker, God-knows-where. They all live in Paris on the left bank of the Seine – Montparnasse, Alésia, Val de Grâce. With one or two exceptions their films are all set outside of Paris. They all began to make films long before the New Wave explosion of 1958: Marker in 1953, Varda in 1954, Resnais in 1948. All have made documentaries – and Marker has made *only* documentaries. These, then, are some of the facts. What conclusions can be drawn from them?

The Left Bank, as the saying goes, is not so much an area as a state of mind. It implies a high degree of involvement in literature and the plastic arts. It implies a fondness for a kind of bohemian life, and an impatience with the conformity of the Right Bank. A centre of the avant-garde and a cosmopolitan refuge since the turn of the century, it has also traditionally been frequented by the politically left. The Dôme was not only a rendezvous for Picasso, Joyce and Hemingway; Trotsky and Lenin were also habitués.

This political, artistic and social climate is what presumably attracted all three artists to this neighbourhood; it is also reflected in their work. In a recent interview, Roger Leenhardt characterises the *Cahiers* faction as people who discovered Shakespeare through Orson Welles. This may be an exaggeration, but there is no mistaking the wider cultural background and broader artistic interests of the Left Bank group. One has only to compare the writers Resnais has chosen as his collaborators (Robbe-Grillet, Duras, Cayrol) with the favourites of some of the *Cahiers* group (Roger Vailland, Françoise Sagan, and worse). Then, too, the fact that the Left Bank group have come to the cinema steeped in the tradition of the avant-garde and the literary and artistic preoccupations of recent years, has given them a greater interest in the problems of form.

Decades Never Start On Time

(opposite) Agnès Varda, (top) Alain Resnais,
(bottom right) Chris Marker

The Godard–Truffaut group, on the other hand, have grown up with the cinema. They feel that its essence is in its very rawness, its direct communication of experience – like Hitchcock, like Hawks. Whether this split is due to the difference in ages, whether the Godard–Truffaut group (who are also, let us remember, hostile to Antonioni) is more 'cinematic' or more 'modern', is not for us to say. But the fact remains that there is a basic difference in conception; a difference that has often been covered up by the log-rolling so characteristic of the 'young French cinema.'

Perhaps because of their age-group, Marker, Varda and Resnais also seem to have inherited the legacy of the thirties: a passionate concern about political and social problems and a conviction that these problems have their place in the realm of art. They are, it seems to me, all humanists, although they might very well quarrel with the term.

In an open letter to Armand Gatti (director of *L'Enclos*) printed at the end of his book *Coréennes*, Marker excuses himself for not having treated in the book the Great Problems. There are enough people doing that already, he tells Gatti: just refer to your daily newspaper. It is not my job, he continues, to distribute praise and blame, nor to give lessons. There are plenty of people to do that, too. Marker (and Resnais, and Varda) do not believe that the aim of art is to teach lessons, nor necessarily to draw conclusions. But unlike Truffaut, I would say, and Godard, they do feel that personal problems and emotions should be seen in a social context. Resnais's earlier documentaries (*Guernica*, *Nuit et brouillard* and *Les Statues meurent aussi*, which was co-directed by Marker) all deal more or less directly, if in a highly personal manner, with political and social issues. So, indeed, do all of Marker's films to date. As his work has never been seen in London (with the exception of *Description of a Struggle*), and because he is perhaps the collective conscience, the common denominator of the Left Bank group, it might be well to pause for a moment to describe the completely original and highly significant genre he has created.

Sunday in Peking, *Letter from Siberia*, *Cuba sí*. 'I write to you from a far-off country,' begins the letter from Siberia, and each of Marker's films is a letter, an essay, a declaration. More than any other director, Marker seems to have fulfilled Astruc's famous prophecy of the *caméra-stylo*, writing films as one writes a book. The most remarkable thing about Marker's film-essays is that their fascinating, maddening, highly literary commentaries (Malraux plus Giraudoux divided by x) seem neither to have preceded the shooting of the films nor to have followed it. Image, text and idea seem miraculously to have been created simultaneously. Although the commentaries have been published, they only take on real meaning when one has seen the films. The great episodes – like the parade in *Cuba sí* which transforms itself into a jubilant conga-line, or the parodies of communist–capitalist propaganda in *Letter from Siberia* – scarcely come over on the printed page. And yet Marker has been accused of being precious, literary and over-ingenious. But what hasn't he been accused of! *Cuba sí* is banned in France and in Germany; *Les Statues meurent aussi* is only authorised in a truncated version. His next film *Le joli mai* will certainly be forbidden by the censor, dealing as it does with the less agreeable aspects of life under the Fifth Republic. But one feels that Marker has made his films not so much as propaganda, not so much to convince others, but because he has felt the need to express what he personally thinks about China, Russia, Israel and Cuba. Marker is fairly unorthodox in his political sentiments. 'We will go to the moon. Either from Siberia, or from New Mexico – it doesn't matter much. There is only man.' And if Marker had ever made his *L'Amérique rêve*, we would have seen realised his fascination for America, for its pop art, its comic strips – a fascination that he shares with Resnais, a fascination for the image, in whatever form it appears − Mandrake the Magician or Miró. 'Images, portents, signs.' But Marker's calligraphy is also made up of music, animation, poetry, colour: every technique, every effect is conjugated and the result is a kind of one-man total cinema, a twentieth-century, a 1 to 1.33 Montaigne.

But Resnais, we know, was aiming at opera, not essay. What he sought for a long time was a form which would be able to express both social problems and emotional ones. Something between documentaries such as *Guernica* and his early 16mm efforts like *Ouvert pour cause d'inventaire*, which treats the problems of fear and desire, of a man and a woman who try vainly to come together. The solution to his problem was found by Agnès Varda; and, typically enough, she found her example in literature. Faulkner's *The Wild Palms* is a book made up of two short stories. One, 'The Old Man', is the story of a convict who sacrificed everything to escape from freedom and love; the other, 'The Wild Palms', is the story of a man who sacrificed everything *for* freedom and love and who lost both. The stories are each split into five parts, and printed in alternate chapters.

The effect Faulkner obviously aimed at was a kind of contrast or counterpoint; but it was the success of this form that gave Agnès Varda the hope that she might accomplish something along similar lines. In her first feature, *La Pointe Courte*, independently produced in 1954, she filmed the struggle of a small fishing village in the South of France against the economic domination of the big combines, side by side with the story of a young man from the village who has come home with his Parisian wife in a last attempt to sort out the failure of their marriage. The two stories are told side by side, but the two themes are never intermingled. It was up to the spectator to make the connections between these themes − to compare them, to contrast them. In spite of the brilliance of its conception and its astonishing visual beauty, *La Pointe Courte* is not entirely successful if only because of the pretentious performance of its leading lady. Silvia Montfort was neither an Emmanuelle Riva nor a Delphine Seyrig, and actresses of their stature are necessary for this kind of potentially irritating role. But the idea worked − so well that when Agnès Varda asked Resnais to help her edit the film he was very reluctant to do so, precisely because she had succeeded in doing something he had been aiming at for a long time. He eventually gave in, and it is no exaggeration to see in *La Pointe Courte* the not very distant ancestor of *Hiroshima, mon amour*. *Hiroshima* is more successful, I think, not only because of its greater technical skill (*La Pointe Courte* was Varda's very first attempt at film-making) but also because Resnais succeeded completely in fusing not only past and present but also the girl's personal conflict with the larger problems of war and peace. *Cléo de 5 à 7* also reflects the binary structure of *La Pointe Courte*, at once both objective and subjective − Cléo's odyssey from the Rue de Rivoli to the Salpêtrière Hospital and her spiritual odyssey from ignorance to understanding.

Cléo, however, is further from *Marienbad* than *Hiroshima* was from *La Pointe Courte*. No doubt *Muriel*, the film on which Resnais is now working, and *La Mélangite*, Agnès Varda's next film, will be even farther apart. Marker, as we have seen, has created his own 'thing', as Henry James would have said. But as the new geometry has taught us that parallel lines do sometimes meet, perhaps it would admit that they can also start from a single point − and that point would be somewhere between the Dôme and the Rue Mouffetard, between the Sorbonne and the Rue Jacob, on the left bank of the Seine.

SOURCE: 'THE LEFT BANK: MARKER, VARDA, RESNAIS', *SIGHT & SOUND*, 32.1, WINTER 1962−3, 24−7

Notes

1. Roud's note: Given the differences in methods of distribution, the disparity in the length of time they have been operating, and the amount and quality of the information the companies have made available, the three companies must be treated separately, as any attempt to consider results simultaneously would unavoidably give a false picture of the facts.
2. Roud's note: The asterisked titles refer to films which were not restricted to the art houses, but were able to make limited circuit runs.
3. This adaptation of Geoffrey Kerr's 1953 novel was never made.
4. The second part of this article discusses the 'art house' in the USA, a subject which is covered in the unpublished 'How to See a Movie (in the USA)'.
5. Agee is referring to the series of *Jalna* novels by Canadian author Mazo de la Roche (1879–1961), cited in this context as an archetypal 'middle-brow' cultural product.
6. FIDO, the Film Industry Defence Organisation, was established in 1958, in order to protect the cinema industry, especially the distribution sector, from the threat posed by films being screened on British television.
7. Roud's note: The complete list of films shown this day was as follows: *The War against Mrs Hadley, Jam Session, Melody for Two, Country Parson, Paris after Dark, Cardinal Richelieu, Catherine the Great, What Every Woman Wants, Million Dollar Manhunt, Sing and Be Happy, Roughly Speaking, The Great John L., Escape to Burma, Love Crazy, In This Our Life, T-Men, The Mad Doctor of Market Street, Dakota Lil, I Am a Criminal*, and *Men of Sherwood Forest*. Note that this was a weekday. On the preceding Saturday *thirty-two* films were shown.
8. There appears to be a missing line in the typescript here, although the sentence broadly makes sense as it is.
9. Unclear what the phrase 'the pleasure garden *cum* Roman Bath' means in this context. The city of Bath has both Georgian 'pleasure gardens' and 'Roman baths' but here the combination of the two terms remains obscure in Roud's draft.

PART 2 1963–9

2.1 FESTIVAL AT THE LINCOLN CENTER

When the Lincoln Center for the performing arts announced a few months ago that film was going to be a part of its future programme hardly an eyebrow was raised.[1] Fifteen years ago, of course, you could always get up a lively discussion at almost any American cocktail party about whether movies were an art or not. Only those who claimed they were an art called them films or cinema. Nowadays, in New York at any rate, I don't think, anyone can work up much excitement over the topic. At long last in America, the country which has produced more great films (and more terrible ones) than any other, people have begun to realise that movies are just as important, and just as respectable, as music, ballet, or theatre.

So everyone accepted in principle the inclusion of film at Lincoln Center, that complex of theatres, concert hall, which is to be the best.[2] But when it was announced that the first film event was going to be a film festival it was a different story. 'It'll never work,' they said. A film festival in New York in the second week of September? Why, *everyone* is away. Besides, who in New York would go to see new films which had not yet received the imprimatur of the all-powerful film critics?

Then, too, there is New York's boom-or-bust psychology – a film or a book is either the greatest or the worst ever. This, of course, explains why America is the country of comebacks: nowhere else can you become a has-been so quickly. And when the festival announced it was going to show 21 of the year's great films the reaction was incredulous – everyone knew there weren't more than four or five good films a year anyhow.

Another drawback, they said, was the international make-up of the festival. New Yorkers have grown blasé on the subject of international co-operation – perhaps because their city is the home of the United Nations. Why, they wondered, did Lincoln Center appeal to the British Film Institute to help them to organise their festival? Why was the New York festival modelled on the London Film Festival? And what was the London Film Festival, anyhow? Finally, the idea that the films were going to be, as one critic put it, 'handpicked' seemed very dubious in the land of committee rule and democratic procedure. Unkindest cut of all, the films were going to be handpicked – curious phrase, did they expect a machine to do it? – by a member of the staff of the British Film Festival Institute (me).

These were the initial reactions. People were slightly mollified when they realised that the Museum of Modern Art of New York was also part of the set-up, that the festival was being presented with the active support of the film trade in New York, and that the festival organiser, whatever his affiliations with the British Film Institute, was actually lucky enough to have been born and raised in the land of the free.

THE FIRST NEW YORK
FILM FESTIVAL

September 10-19, 1963

Brochure for the first New York Film Festival, 1963

Well, the festival is over now, and to everyone's surprise it was a tremendous success. All but three of the films were completely sold out; press reactions were on the whole very good; and, most important, audience reactions were even better than those of the press. Musing on the subject, *Variety* actually went so far as to suggest that perhaps business would be better generally if, horrible thought, film critics could be done away with. 'There's nothing wrong with the industry that getting rid of the critics wouldn't cure.'

This is going too far, perhaps, but the festival did prove several things: that there is an audience in New York for the film which has had no advance promotion, no advertising campaign, no rave reviews. That there is an audience for the latest Buñuel, the latest Losey, the latest Resnais. That, although none of his films has even been shown in New York, there are people who know who Chris Marker is. And, finally, that if, as Lincoln Center's president said, the role of the arts is to provide 'enrichment beyond understanding,' then the best films do just that.

SOURCE: 'FESTIVAL AT THE LINCOLN CENTER', *GUARDIAN*, 10 OCTOBER 1963, 8

2.2 END OF BARDOLOTRY

The only sound to be heard up and down the Champs-Elysées these days is a loud and prolonged moan. Business has never been worse, and it's all the fault of the New Wave. Those producers who jumped most eagerly on the New Wave bandwagon a few years ago are, naturally enough, the ones who are complaining the most bitterly.

To be sure they have some reason to be upset. There were reports that when Claude Chabrol's *L'Oeil du malin* was first screened last year there was at least one day when no one turned up at the box-office until the 10 pm show: for eight hours the film ran to the usherettes and to no one else. Chabrol did have some success with *Landru*, but when it was decided to bring out *Ophelia* – to try to cash in on the *Landru* success – the same thing happened as with *L'Oeil du malin*. Alain Resnais's *Muriel* was turned down by the all-powerful Siritsky circuit, which had taken *Marienbad*, and was forced into a less attractive group of halls for its first release. François Truffaut was unable to finance his adaptation of Ray Bradbury's *Fahrenheit 451* and finally had to abandon the project. *Les Carabiniers*, Jean-Luc Godard's last film to be released, lasted for only one week.

Godard's latest film, *Le Mépris*, has had an even more interesting career. *Le Mépris*, an adaptation of the Moravia a novel *Ghost at Noon*, is a large-budget colour film starring

Brigitte Bardot and Jack Palance. Produced by Carlo Ponti and partly financed by the great American impresario Joe Levine, the film was an attempt to create a new image for Mademoiselle Bardot. Her last two films had been terrible flops in France and abroad, and it seemed that something had to be done.

Godard did it all right: not only did he give us a new Brigitte, he also made a remarkable film. But although the film was finished in July it still hasn't been released. When Levine saw the film he decided that the new image was too new and that Brigitte wasn't sexy enough. So now the film is held up pending reshooting of certain scenes and the addition of still others. Both Godard and Levine are intransigent and the future of Le Mépris is highly problematical.

I have gone into the Mépris story at some length because it provides perhaps the key to what has gone wrong in France. The point is that it is not just the New Wave that is in danger: it is the French cinema as a whole. Brigitte Bardot was, after all, the one really absolute guarantee of success at the box-office. You could raise money and get a distribution guarantee on her name alone – without a story, director, or anything. The very fact that Ponti and Levine let her do a film with someone as far out as Godard shows the degree of their desperation – things had come to the point where they would try anything. That they did not like the result is unimportant.

The French film industry has at last come up against the same problems the Americans faced in the early fifties and the British in the late fifties: television and the rise in the standard of living. There is a very revealing graph published in the yearbook number of the leading French trade paper, Le Film Français: it compares the number of spectators from 1950 to 1962 with the number of television sets and private cars. Spectators have fallen from 371 million a year to 310 million. But television sets have risen from three thousand to three million, and private cars from one and three quarter million to six and a quarter million. The rise of cars and television sets was at first gradual, but the big jump came about 1959, and the effect of this is making itself felt now. Saturday night, which used to be the big movie night, is so no longer, especially from April to October: people, are going away for the weekend. It's the same old story.

So when the producers claim it's all the fault of the intellectual New Wave films, one must beg to differ. As a matter of fact the New Wave films were never the big money-makers. Take the standard list of 'best sellers' published by Le Film Français: the only New Wave films in the top twenty-five are Orfeu Negro and Les Amants. Films like Hiroshima, mon amour, Breathless, and Les 400 Coups don't even make the top seventy. This doesn't mean they didn't make money: they did. But it does mean that the New Wave, whatever its faults, is not at the root of the industry's problems.

At the end of an article like this one is supposed to come up with some kind of solution. I'm afraid I don't have one, except the obvious suggestion of making fewer films and selling them better. By selling them better I mean coming to the realisation that there are two film markets today – one for the big spectacular film, and one for the so-called art film. If the producers of films like Muriel would resign themselves to the fact that this film is destined for the art-house circuits and not for the big cinemas, that would already be a step in the right direction. And it is significant that the Film Français annual began last year for the first time to include an evaluation of the smaller specialised houses which, the magazine comments, are now taking an ever-growing share of the whole industry's receipts.

SOURCE: 'END OF BARDOLOTRY', GUARDIAN, 31 OCTOBER 1963, 7

2.3 MURIEL OBSERVED

There are three reasons why *Muriel* (Cameo-Poly) is the most important film in recent years.

First, because of what it says. Resnais and his scriptwriter Jean Cayrol have made the first French film since the war which gives us a really meaningful image of France. The story of *Muriel* is not 'difficult'; or rather, it demands only as much attention as an Agatha Christie novel. Hélène, a widow in her early forties, has invited an old flame to come to visit her in the hope of reviving a romance which dates back to the last war. She lives in Boulogne with her son, a disillusioned veteran of the Algerian war. He is tormented by the contamination of the brutality he was unable to resist during his military service. The Muriel of the title was an Arab girl who was tortured to death by his platoon – while he just stood by. Alphonse, the old flame, arrives, accompanied by a young girl he calls his niece.

So there we have it – in the bombed and rebuilt city of Boulogne, the conflict of two generations and the specific and related malaise of each. The story is perfectly valid in itself, but it does not take too much insight to see what Resnais and Cayrol are getting at. On the one hand, we have the older prewar generation who have never been able to adjust to the changes brought by the war.

Hélène's vain attempt to revive the past is not so different from the General [de Gaulle]'s attempts to revive the glories of a France that no longer exists, a France that can never come again. And after all, Hélène earns her living by selling antiques and fritters it away gambling at the casino. One does not want to push the parallels too far, but it is tempting: for example, Hélène is being courted by a devoted intelligent man, a man in every way more suited to her than Alphonse. He does not live in the past – his job is running a demolition company.

On the other hand, we have the younger generation: Hélène's son brought low by the colonial adventure in Algeria and the heartless, detached 'niece', a representative of that segment of the postwar generation that has taken refuge behind a façade of egotism. Leaving aside any symbolic interpretations, one can see that *Muriel* has a much richer, more complex action than any of Resnais's earlier films. It is also quite different in style.

Which brings us to the second reason why *Muriel* is so important a film: the way in which the story is told, the form of the film. Resnais has forgone all the baroque extravagance of *Marienbad*, the lyricism of *Hiroshima, mon amour*. The style of this film is cool, spare, and tough. None of the exhilaration of his fast forward-tracking shots, no beautiful decors – even though the film is in colour. Using one of the ugliest towns in the world, the hard aniline dyes of cheap clothing, and actors who are not immediately attractive (even the divine Delphine Seyrig of *Marienbad* is disguised here as the 40-year-old, slightly dowdy Hélène), Resnais has nevertheless managed to make a film that is always excitingly beautiful to look at.

Because he is expressing so much, he has been forced to evolve a kind of Hebraic shorthand: he has cut out the vowels, the linking scenes. In *Hiroshima* Resnais began by shortening the transitional scenes (people walking down staircases, etc.). Here they are almost entirely suppressed. No time is wasted, and the film moves with lightning speed. Every shot is essential, and what's more, every shot serves not only to advance the plot or to make a point, but also has its place in a film which is formally as organised as a fugue. *Muriel* is as easy to 'understand' on a first viewing as Beethoven's Ninth, but it is only on a second or third viewing that one begins to appreciate more fully the beauty of the way it is put together.

The third reason why *Muriel* is a truly great film is that Resnais has been able to combine reasons one and two. Because he has proved that a film can be both aesthetically and intellectually satisfying. This was true of *Hiroshima* and *Marienbad*, too, but *Muriel* is an altogether more ambitious and rigorous undertaking. If you see nothing else this year, see *Muriel*.[3] [...]

SOURCE: 'MURIEL OBSERVED', *GUARDIAN*, 20 MARCH 1964, 13

2.4 CANNES HO!

'Off to Cannes? I thought you were serious about films.' Or words to that effect. It seems the starlets and bikini side of festivals has been so well publicised that most people think that that's all there is. Do film festivals have any value apart from the opportunities for a lot of free-loading in the sun? Strange as it may seem, they not only still do, but they always have: at least the big ones, Cannes and Venice – and to a slightly lesser degree Berlin, Karlovy Vary, San Sebastian, and Locarno.

Suppose you're a young film-maker in a country which is not generally considered to be an important film-producing nation. What do you do to get yourself and your film known? Take the case of Leopoldo Torre Nilsson. Until May, 1957, it is safe to say that no more than ten people outside Argentina had ever heard of him. And then, at the Cannes Festival that year, he showed his film *House of the Angel* – and literally overnight he became famous. Which is not surprising when you consider that at a major festival are gathered journalists and critics from all over the world with nothing to do but look at films. I know they spend time on the beach but they still have to see more films at Cannes than they ever would in London, Paris, or Rome.

Torre Nilsson's is not an unique case: in Venice in 1951 there happened to be a film called *Rashomon* – and we know what that one led to. As recently as 1962 a little Polish film turned up in Venice. It wasn't in competition – the Poles seemed to think it wasn't big enough, important enough, to represent them, but they sent it along for what Venice calls the Information Section – films projected in the afternoon to sort of let people know what's going on. No one was more surprised than the Polish representatives when the film won the International Critics' Award and was bought for almost every country in the world. 'You really like it?' they marvelled. The film was *Knife in the Water*.

So it often happens that it is not the films in competition that are the exciting discoveries but the fringe efforts. Venice has long devoted its afternoons to this kind of film, and in the past years Cannes has enlarged its fringe activities, now dignifying them with the name Critics' Section. For in fact an international group of film critics is charged with the task of making sure overlooked films don't get overlooked.

But it isn't always just a question of a film from a small or far-off country. In Venice in 1962 three films were shown in the Information Section – *Accattone*, *Il posto*, and *L'assassino* – which made people realise there were new forces at work in the Italian cinema. Each of the three films helped the other, just as at Cannes in 1959 the New Wave was born – or rather seen to be born – by the combination of *Hiroshima, mon amour*, *Les 400 Coups*, and one or two others.

It isn't only the films out of competition that make the trip to Cannes or Venice worthwhile. Take the case of Antonioni. He had been making films since 1951, but it wasn't until the Cannes festival of 1960, where *L'avventura* was presented, that he suddenly became a world figure. To be sure *L'avventura* was a bigger film than any he had made before, but had it not been for Cannes one wonders if he would have so quickly achieved international fame. Actually, to be honest, if his film had not created such a scandal, if it had not been so hooted and hissed at, it might have even then passed unnoticed. So, even negatively, festivals have their value.

Then, too, a festival like Cannes is, reduced to its lowest terms, a great convenience. For apart from the films in competition and the films out of competition there is also what's called the Film Market. During the day, local cinemas are rented to distributors from all countries to show their latest product to buyers. Strictly commercial, and a lot of the films are trash – but every year a number of films turn up that the critic might never have otherwise seen. At Cannes in 1962 one such film was Wajda's *Siberian Lady Macbeth*. Last year there was Jacques Demy's *La Baie des Anges*. This year, who knows? Maybe nothing, but then again, maybe something.

One of the silliest objections to film festivals is that you see too much. You do. But no matter how many sleepless nights, no matter how much of a hangover, or how many boring Hong Kong films one has sat through, when an unknown film called *Il posto* by an unknown director called by the uncompromising name of Ermanno Olmi comes on – one's back straightens up, one's eyes open wide, one's neck begins to tingle, and one knows that film festivals are a great institution. I left for Cannes yesterday.

SOURCE: 'CANNES HO!', *GUARDIAN*, 30 APRIL 1964, 8

2.5 RONDO GALANT: THE WORLD OF JACQUES DEMY

> Willy and Rose turned out not to be cousins, just how nobody knows, and so they married and had children and sang with them and sometimes singing made Rose cry and sometimes it made Willy get more and more excited and they lived happily ever after and the world just went on being round. (Gertrude Stein, *The World Is Round*, 1939)

Jacques Demy has made three feature films to date. All have been based on original scripts written by him and by him alone. With all the talk about the *politique des auteurs* and the desirability of the director being an *auteur complet*, it may have escaped notice that Demy is the only New Wave director with a considerable body of entirely original work to his credit. The world of his films is a world of his creation. What kind of world is it?

It is a world from which death is absent. And this is rarer than one would think. Even when poor old Aunt Elise of *Les Parapluies de Cherbourg* (1964) finally has to be got rid of, she specifically reassures us, 'I have lived a long time, you know. I can leave this world without regrets.' In fact, not only do Demy's characters not die, they are even transferred from one film to the next, thus conferring on them another life. Roland, the disappointed lover of *Lola* (1961), finally finds a kind of happiness in *Les Parapluies de Cherbourg*. And we have been assured by Demy of the imminent return of Lola and Cécile in one of his next films. Actually, they have both returned already, but in a different guise.

Lola, for example, is paralleled in *Les Parapluies* by Madeleine: both girls patiently await the return of their lovers – Lola's Michel from his seven years in the Tropics, Madeleine's Guy from his two years in Algeria as well as from his infatuation with another girl. Roland

Lola (1961)

himself has in a sense become the Michel of *Lola*, returning rich to Cherbourg as Michel to Nantes. This doubling of characters also goes on in the same film – the young Cécile in *Lola* is also another younger version of Lola, just as her American sailor is the younger Michel.

All of Demy's films are built on a circular motion. *Lola* begins with the entrance of Michel into Nantes in his big white car and ends with his departure, this time accompanied by the faithful Lola. *La Baie des Anges* (Demy's second film, 1963), once the prologue is over, starts with Jackie (Jeanne Moreau) and Jean (Claude Mann) entering the Nice casino, and the film ends with their exit. *Les Parapluies* opens in one Esso garage and ends in another. Like some fantastic cotillion, the characters and themes move in complicated variations but always in circular motion. And this is one reason why death is absent, for death would break the circle, destroy the pattern, stop the dance.

But it is not only death that is absent. So is evil. Demy does not deny the existence of evil; he just isn't interested. He feels that even without evil, there are enough problems in this world. He is interested in love, and that is sufficiently complicated as it is.

Lola deals with almost every kind of love: disappointed love with Roland and Lola; triumphant love with Lola and Michel; puppy love with Cécile and Frankie; sexual attraction with Frankie and Lola; tentatively genteel love with Roland and Cécile's mother. *Les Parapluies* is a bit more complex, if less complicated. Geneviève and Guy are both 18. When he is sent off to do his military service in Algeria, they swear undying love. Almost in spite of themselves, they both gradually realise – she first – that their love is not strong enough to stand separation. So when she has the chance to marry another, older, man who will give her child by Guy a name, she accepts. Guy returns to Cherbourg, and although he has grown apart from her, his ego cannot at first let him accept the fact that she has betrayed him. But maturity comes, even to Guy, and he marries Madeleine, the patient Griselda who has always loved him.

La Baie des Anges is Demy's most subtle statement about love. Its apparent subject is the story of a young bank employee who becomes fascinated by gambling and the woman he meets in the casinos. She (Jeanne Moreau) has left her husband and child and wanders from Enghien to Nice, from Deauville to Monte Carlo. At first she treats Jean as a kind of mascot – he seems to bring her luck. By the end of the film, however, in spite of the difference in their ages and characters and the apparent impossibility of their remaining long together, they miraculously decide to have a go. At least he knows her weakness.

For gambling is but the ostensible subject of the film; it is only a metaphor. Jackie is the kind of woman who has to be reassured *daily* that luck is with her, that God is on her side, and, most important, that she is still sexually attractive. It is only when one considers her passion for daily sorties to the casinos in this light that the film takes on its full meaning and that it can be seen, not as an interruption to the Demy saga, but as an integral part of it. And Jean gets her in the end because he has passed the test, he has accepted her as she is.

'Passes the test': this is a recurring element in Demy's films. Lola has to wait seven years for Michel. Roland only wins Geneviève because he accepts her child by Guy. Madeleine only gets Guy because she has patiently waited until he was ready. Everyone gasped when Demy announced a year or two ago that he wanted to make a film based on the Perrault fairy-tale *Peau d'Ane*. And yet the fairy-tale element in his films is very strong – not the Grimm/grim kind, to be sure, but the more delicate, sophisticated French sort. Actually, the real counterpart to Demy is not Perrault, but somewhat later writers like the Countess d'Aulnoy and Madame Leprince de Beaumont. In stories like *La Belle et la*

Bête sensibility comes into its own, and everything seems to work out all right in the end. The bad people are pardoned, and in any case, they weren't really so bad, anyway. 'Only in the cinema do people die of love,' says (or rather, sings) Geneviève's mother in *Les Parapluies*. 'Anyhow, time solves most problems.' And Geneviève finally is forced ruefully to admit, 'I would have died for him, but why aren't I dead?'

In spite of this tempering cynicism, Demy's preoccupation with romantic love is distinctly unfashionable. So also are the exterior aspects of his world – décors and costumes. He and Godard may both use white walls, but in Demy's films, they are white in order the better to set off the gracefully twirling iron bed-steads, the art nouveau-ish furniture. Demy's decorative universe would seem to be that in which he grew up – 1900 high style as it slowly filtered down through provincial France. It is not slavishly reproduced, and Demy has achieved a strict selection, thus avoiding the claustrophobic effect so many French interiors still create. For all his admiration of Max Ophüls, there is nothing of the gauzy appeal to the past, nothing fusty or old-fashioned about his sets.

His women, too, seem mostly to belong to another age. Jackie in *La Baie des Anges* with her monkey fur, her boas, and her *guêpières* (Gay 90s corsets) comes from another age. As Jean remarks, 'I didn't think women like you existed any more.' Well, they don't. But nature imitates art, and perhaps they soon will. It is in fact true that several stores in Paris are now offering for sale the highly coloured early Matisse-like wallpaper featured in *Les Parapluies*. (A terrible mistake, says Demy; it would be hell to live with!)

The truth is that Demy is an unashamed sensualist. People are always afraid of bad taste, he says. In *Les Parapluies* he wanted a real riot of colour, and that is exactly what we get. But those who are still haunted by the Bauhaus aesthetic – never more than one colour at a time; straight lines, preferably crossing at right-angles; functional furniture – can't really take Demy's swashing baroque. Or rather, I suspect, they are afraid to let themselves like it. Puritanically, charm is to be resisted. If it doesn't taste bad, it can't be doing you any good.

On the other hand, Demy's film technique is distinctly modern, and he can cut an ellipse with the best of them. (Example: the four shot sequence in *Les Parapluies* after Geneviève and Guy have gone to bed together for the first and only time: from his bedroom, we cut to the entrance to his house, again to the lane, then to Geneviève's street, and finally to her living room with her knitting mother and then – and only then – Geneviève magically runs into frame.) He is also great on movement – the final tracking shot back into the Casino as Jackie and Jean rush out into the light in *La Baie des Anges*; and the scene in *Les Parapluies* when the camera pans along with the just-married Roland's car leaving the church until it sweeps into an exultant close-up of Madeleine: with Geneviève safely married, perhaps she has a chance!

A study of Demy's technique could well be the subject of another article. My point is simply that Demy's sets and costumes are part of his subject matter, and that his predilection for the old-fashioned has been deliberately adopted. To put it crudely, it is not because he doesn't know any better: his directorial technique demonstrates this. Some people have felt, however, that in his two most recent films Demy has been forced by the relative commercial failure of *Lola* to oversimplify, to restrain his natural invention. It is good news, then, that his next film – also a musical, but this time with dancing as well – will mark a return to the construction of *Lola* with its surprises, coincidences, and choreographic complications.

Demy's literary baggage and cultural universe are slight compared with the encyclopaedic erudition of a Godard. And Kierkegaard is certainly more fashionable than Perrault. But Demy's virtue is to have created his own world and to stick to it, slowly elaborating and perfecting his expression of it. One extraordinary example of this is his obsession with Bresson's *Les Dames du Bois de Boulogne*. This was the first film, he tells us, that showed him what the cinema could do. He was 14 years old, and probably saw it at the Katorza cinema at Nantes! He has now completely annexed it into his own folklore – but minus what many people would consider the important part of the film, the character of Hélène, and the story of her revenge.

Instead, Demy concentrates on the three other characters, chiefly on the mother and daughter. In *Lola*, Madame Desnoyers (Elina Labourdette) is actually the Agnès (Elina Labourdette) of *Les Dames*. When she shows Roland (Marc Michel) a picture of herself when she was young, it is a still from *Les Dames*. At the same time, Madame Desnoyers is not only Agnès grown matronly, she is also – and perhaps therefore – the Lucienne Bogaert character, her own mother in *Les Dames*. Like her, Madame Desnoyers has lost everything; like her, she saw her furniture being carried off ('Et moi comme une idiote, attachée à mes meubles, mes bergères, mes consoles qui partent' ['And I, like a fool, attached to my furniture, my bergère chairs, my console tables, as they disappeared']), passing from opulence to poverty in a day. 'My husband was a gambler. He had every vice.'

In *Les Parapluies*, the mother–daughter relationship of *Les Dames* reappears. Anne Vernon, the mother, even looks a lot like Elina Labourdette – and we must not forget that when Cécile Desnoyers ran away from Nantes, she went to Cherbourg. Once again the mother is a widow in a difficult situation; once again she counts on the charming mature man to marry her daughter and get them out of it. Echoes even of the Cocteau dialogue appear and reappear in Demy's films. To describe the growing separation of Geneviève and Guy, he doesn't hesitate to use the uniquely Cocteau-esque phrase: 'Son cœur se détache de lui' ['Her heart detaches itself from him'].

But the real theme of *Les Dames* is not vengeance but the triumph of love over hate, and we are back again with Demy's *Sleeping Beauty*. 'I prefer', he admits, 'blue to black, births to funerals, red wine to Vichy water, the sun to the rain.' The provinces to Paris, one might also add. For with the exception of the prologue to *La Baie des Anges*, Demy's films are all set near the sea — Nantes, Cherbourg, Nice, Monte Carlo. *Les Parapluies* and *Lola* seem to be drawn almost directly from his own life growing up in Nantes. The provincial bookshop of *Lola*, the somehow uniquely provincial dinners which are so important in both films … Demy's father owned a garage like the one in *Les Parapluies* (Demy claims that he himself can to this day *smell* the difference between Shell and BP), and it would seem that for him, too, the Passage Pommeraye in Nantes was the nerve centre of his sentimental life.

How to sum up? If Godard is Picasso, then Demy is Matisse. No, too *Cahiers*. Godard, however, does make a good comparison – for the two men have almost as much in common as not. Let's try again: if Godard is a hare, is Demy then a hedgehog? No, the best animal metaphor for Demy is the snail, the sea-snail, or the periwinkle. Gaston Bachelard tells us that the snail is the only animal who does not build its house in order to have a place to live. Rather, it lives in order to build its house. And it was thought that it builds its house from its own saliva. Like the snail, Demy carries his house with him everywhere; like the snail, his house is created from within; like the snail, his world is intensely self-contained.

The snail is the great example of organic geometry: his shell is circular and spiral, like the circular movements and geometric patterns of Demy's films. Round and round, ever spiralling outwards and yet ever attached to its beginnings, the shell is refuge, protection, and one of the supreme examples of that will to form which alone can make life meaningful. 'The shell', wrote Valéry, 'stands out from the common disorder of most living organisms. Shells are privileged objects, more intelligible at first glance, and yet on reflection more mysterious than any other.' Perhaps it was no accident that Venus Anadyomene was conceived of as bursting upon a startled world from a seashell.

SOURCE: 'RONDO GALANT: THE WORLD OF JACQUES DEMY', *SIGHT & SOUND*, 33.3, SUMMER 1964, 136–9

2.6 THE RED DESERT

NOTE: Michelangelo Antonioni is a key reference point for Roud. Prior to this piece on The Red Desert, *Roud had written an excellent overview of Antonioni's career up to the revelation of* L'avventura *at Cannes in 1960, 'Five films' (*Sight & Sound, 30.1, Winter 1960–1, 8–11*). In 1962 he presented Antonioni and his work on the BBC film pro-gramme* The Cinema Today. *Later, Roud would write an extensive review of* The Passenger, *which is included in this anthology.*

The Triple Split

As part of her attempts to 'reintegrate herself with reality', Giuliana, heroine of *The Red Desert*, has decided to open a small shop. When a friend drops by, he finds her trying out various samples of paint for the walls and ceiling. Giuliana has nearly decided on a light green – it will be less distracting. Distracting, echoes Corrado? Yes, from what I'm selling, the things … There is a pause, and suddenly Giuliana wheels on Corrado: What do you think I should sell?

Antonioni may not have intended this scene as a reference to the vexed problem of form and content, but the image of Giuliana carefully decorating a shop before she knows what – if anything – she is going to sell in it, underlines very early in the film that rift in *The Red Desert* between what it is *about*, and what it *is*. Actually, there is a three-way split between what Antonioni says his film is about, what it is about, and most important of all, what it is as film.

As film, it is a remarkable achievement. All the more reason, then, for a close examina-tion of why – as a statement – it is something less than satisfactory. Antonioni has pro-claimed that this film is a new departure for him, that everything he has done so far no longer interests him. And yet there are enough elements of the past in *The Red Desert* partially to belie this claim, enough of the past to undermine it.

The Undistributed Middle

May 1960: La Napoule. At a press conference the day before the presentation of *L'avventura* at the Cannes Festival, Antonioni read the now famous statement: 'There is today a very serious split between science on the one hand – completely projected towards the future and ready each day to repudiate its past if by so doing it can conquer even the smallest fraction of its future – and, on the other hand, a static, rigid morality, to which Man, fully aware of its obsolescence, nevertheless continues to cling.' Antonioni then proceeds to deplore the contrast between man's conformism to his moral heritage and his willingness, in the scientific domain, to try any likely hypothesis. He offers no solu-tion to the problem, saying only that *L'avventura* is neither sermon nor denunciation: simply a statement of the problem. He concludes, however, with a query. Why is it that, knowing the old Tables of the Law no longer offer us anything more than an all too chewed-over message, we none the less remain faithful to them? Why is the man who is not afraid of the scientific unknown still afraid of the moral unknown?

At the time, there seemed little reason to ponder deeply on this statement, partly because it appeared irrelevant to *L'avventura*, and partly because one discounts general philosophical pronouncements from film directors. But now, in *The Red Desert*, Antonioni seems finally to have attempted a dramatisation of this statement. So perhaps it is time we took it seriously, especially as Antonioni declared, in a recent interview in *Cahiers du Cinéma*, that only by adapting ourselves to the new techniques of life can we find a solution to our moral problems.

Taking Antonioni's La Napoule statement seriously, then, we can see immediately that it betrays a certain degree of confusion. It implies that while science has made enormous progress in the last hundred years, morality has remained where it was in 1860. This, I believe, is untrue – at least in England and America. So manifestly untrue is it that there is little need to offer proof: one has only to read the newspapers and keep one's eyes open. In any case, Antonioni assumes that it is possible to make a valid comparison between science and morality. This seems to me as untenable as his statement that, in *La notte*, he was trying to show that his characters did not live up to the beauty of the modern architecture in which they lived. But architecture, like any art, is an idealisation, a concentration, an incarnation of life: one cannot 'live up' to the Pirelli building any more than the Greeks 'lived up' to the Parthenon or the twelfth century French to Chartres.

One does not want to maintain that 'human nature never changes.' It does. But it changes much more slowly than science and for different reasons. Surely the difference between science and morality is that science is ... scientific: i.e., it deals with matters that can be empirically measured or ascertained. But how could one prove that monogamy is inferior to polygamy?

Travellers on the Red Desert

Giuliana (Monica Vitti): Giuliana is happily married to an engineer; together with their boy they live in Ravenna. Two years ago she tried to commit suicide, but managed, with the help of the doctors, to pass it off as a car accident. In spite of prolonged treatment, she still has great difficulty adjusting to reality. Her husband is very kind to her, but this does not seem to help. His colleague, Corrado, finds her extremely attractive; perhaps he will be able to protect her from all the things of which she is afraid. After a particularly violent crisis, she goes to him for help. They end up in bed together, but the experience is inconclusive. Somehow she manages to achieve a kind of stability thereafter, but for how long, we do not know.

Ugo (Carlo Chionetti): Ugo is an engineer, happy in his work and happily married. After the shock of his wife's automobile accident (which occurred while he was in London: he did not, however, return) he found her rather difficult to live with. On the other hand, he gets much pleasure from teaching his son the rudiments of science. Were it not for Giuliana's neuroses, he would be very happy indeed. The only cloud is the inordinate interest she seems to be showing in his colleague, Corrado Zeller. But Zeller is off to South America soon.

Corrado (Richard Harris): Corrado came to Ravenna to recruit workmen for the factory he is going to run in Patagonia. The task takes him much longer than he expected, but in the meanwhile he becomes very attracted to Giuliana. He is pleased that she seems to like him, too, but disturbed by her rather peculiar behaviour. When she finally tells him that she has tried to commit suicide, he begins to understand her a little better. She demands from him, however, more than he, or perhaps any man, can give. One night she goes to his hotel in a particularly disturbed state; they end up by going to bed together. The experience is not very satisfactory for either of them. Corrado feels that he must complete his arrangements for the expedition; at the same time he experiences a certain lassitude, an unwillingness to keep moving, as he has done for years, from one place to the next.

Objective Correlative?

To judge from the reasonably objective statements I have invented for each of the three leading characters, *The Red Desert* would seem to be a film about a neurotic woman. And Antonioni admits in the *Cahiers* interview that it is not the milieu in which Giuliana lives that provokes her crisis: it only makes it explode. Her husband and her lover do seem to be happy enough, and reasonably well adjusted.[4] If Ugo and Corrado have come to terms with their world, and Giuliana and the other women have not, would not this seem to indicate that the moral of the film is really the same one that moralists have preached for centuries: the Devil finds work for idle hands.[5] This is further borne out by Antonioni's personal statement that if he could not work, could not make films, life would not be worth living.

But this is not at all what Antonioni claims he is saying. Throughout the film, Giuliana's tangled neuroses are contrasted with the clean forms and austere beauty of industrial architecture. Further, her life is compared with the slag heaps, the rusted iron, the refuse: the waste products of industrial civilisation. We see her first in the wasteland surrounding the factory, crouching grotesquely amidst the brush and the waste, against the belching yellow poisonous exhaust from the factory, devouring a half-eaten sandwich which she has just bought for 2,000 lire from an astonished workman.

Antonioni might reply that women are simply more sensitive, and react more strongly than men to the contagion that menaces us all. And it is true that the cry (*il grido*) which heralds the arrival of the plague ship is heard only by Giuliana and Linda: the men hear nothing. And yet, the ship arrives, flying its yellow flag.

The problem is not entirely philosophical, however. Perhaps Antonioni might have succeeded with another actress in rendering significant Giuliana's neuroses. But it must be said, with all respect, that Monica Vitti is inadequate for this purpose. From her first appearance, slouched inside her coat, her fingers jammed in her mouth, staring wildly from right to left, she looks more like a Monica Vitti character who has finally taken complete leave of her senses than the result of the split between science and morality.[6] The problem remains: whether because of the way she is played, or because of the action of the film, Giuliana remains a pathological case. Therefore, when Antonioni assures us that, because Corrado sleeps with her when she comes to him for help, she is consequently the victim of her own outmoded world of sentiments, one can but demur. If she had gone to someone really well adapted like Ugo, Antonioni says, he would have tried to cure her rather than 'profit' by her dismay. But as the character is played by Miss Vitti, any 'treatment' other than the most basic would seem to be of little use.

But this remark of Antonioni's demands investigation, for it displays an unexpected attitude towards sexual relations. If he is against our outmoded morality, why then does he feel it so beastly of Corrado to have slept with Giuliana? And why does 'Nothing Happen' in the so-called orgy scene? One hopes Antonioni is saying that the fact that nothing happens is another proof of how these people are prisoners of their morality. But the arrival of a worker (seen in a heroic low-angle shot from the point of view of the entangled mass of bourgeois limbs on the floor) may signify a condemnation of these wicked, if abortive, upper middle class goings on. The meaning of the scene remains vague, perhaps because of a confusion between Antonioni's old left-wing sympathies (corruption and decadence of the bourgeoisie) and his current view that it is the rising engineer class who – adjusted to science and technology – will inherit the earth. One could say that it is precisely this confusion which is the subject of the film, but it would have been more convincing had Antonioni seemed clearer in his own mind.

There are other examples of basic uncertainty in the film: the husband (admirably played by Carlo Chionetti, a non-professional) is supposed to be the only character approaching Antonioni's ideal, and yet we are astonished to learn that he did not come back from London when Giuliana had her 'accident'. Corrado (and we) cannot help but find this reprehensible. Is this because we are tied to the old morality, too? This seems hard to believe: if it is not true, then perhaps well-adjusted Ugo is *too* well adjusted?

One could go on picking holes in the film's message, but as Antonioni admits, he is not a philosopher, and these considerations have little to do with what he calls the 'invention' of his film. Not being a philosopher (or a scientist) has taken its toll, none the less. Antonioni has been a victim of that deductive reasoning abhorred by scientists: he has imposed an idea or a belief on his materials, rather than inducing one from them. This is a fault of which he was rarely guilty in his previous three films (except, perhaps, for the party scenes in *La notte*). But the specific virtues of *The Red Desert* were largely absent from these films, too.

Figure or Carpet?

These virtues are purely cinematographic, or, to put the fat in the fire, abstract. How can this be, you cry? We all know that films deal with human relationships, not spatial relationships. But do they? I defy anyone to deny that *The Red Desert* is a 'great' film. And yet anyone could – as I have done – pick gaping holes in it as drama, as statement. Ergo: its virtues must be non-intellectual, and, in a measure, non-dramatic. The colour, one anxiously suggests? Yes, it is beautiful. But that's not it. At least, that's not all of it. To go back to the old argument, is it simply that a painting is, before being a battle scene or a nude, first of all an arrangement of lines and colours in a certain order? There is much in *The Red Desert* to justify this view.

This is not an entirely new departure for Antonioni: his early *Cronaca di un amore* and *La signora senza camelie* were distinguished by an autonomous and non-functional use of camera movements, a formal choreography which accompanied the film, providing a non-conceptual figure in the carpet, an experience in pure form. But about the time of *L'avventura*, he seemed to abandon all this; declaring, in fact, that he had tired of what he called experiments in film syntax. None the less, in *La notte* (particularly the great sequence of Lidia's walk) one found him experimenting again. Now, in *The Red Desert*, non-representation is well to the fore. Antonioni says that it was the use of colour which prompted a certain modification of his style. But it goes deeper than that: he has quite consciously foregone realism. For example, he says, he has made much use of a telephoto lens precisely in order to avoid that depth of focus so indispensable to realism. In fact (perhaps because of nearby Ravenna?) many shots have a Byzantine two-dimensionality, a lack of perspective which comes close to creating purely painterly effects.

Then, too, landscape and even people are treated as elements to be arranged and placed in a frame: people are inserted into landscape, inserted into frame; surging up from

Il deserto rosso (1964)

the bottom, sliding in from the side. The arrival of Corrado at Giuliana's shop in the Via Alighieri begins with the irruption from the right of an abstract white form along the bottom of the frame: a second later we see that this is the roof of his car.

Because he has treated the film abstractly, or rather, concretely as film – something which is made up of frames arranged in a certain order – he has also paid more attention to the problem of the cut. But the cut used not for dramatic purposes (to reinforce the action), but almost autonomously for its own sake. For example, the early scenes of Giuliana with the strikers: the camera pans down over her, then cuts to an empty frame into which she slides from the bottom. In the old days, Antonioni used to say that his camera followed his characters 'beyond the moments conventionally considered important for the spectator.' In *The Red Desert*, he pays as much attention to objects and landscape as to the characters. Only a moment after the characters have walked out of frame does he cut to a bit of landscape; seconds later, the characters reappear in frame. Landscape was used extensively in *Il grido*, too, but here its use is not so much expressive as formal. Not completely, of course: there is obviously a relationship, however tenuous, between the emotional mood of the film and the objects, the trees, the fragments of landscape. But it is tenuous. It approaches the pure beauty of, say, the opening sequence of *Marnie*, which also has little to do with the plot or theme of the film, but everything to do with cinema.

If the Hitchcock reference is too shocking, one might further compare *The Red Desert* to *Muriel*. Apart from a few superficial resemblances (the use of a singer in the music score, the relatively choppy montage, the fascination in rendering beautiful the essentially ugly, like the Medicina housing estate), both films are alike in their espousal of a construction which is dictated more by formal considerations than by dramatic relevance or expression.

SOURCE: 'THE RED DESERT', *SIGHT & SOUND*, 34.2, SPRING 1965, 76–80

2.7 OBJECT LESSON

Une Femme mariée (1964)

Une Femme mariée (Cameo-Royal) is sub-titled 'Fragments of a film', and this, in fact, is what it is. Or rather it is a collage made up of four kinds of film materials. There are the ordinary – if anything shot by director Jean-Luc Godard can be called ordinary – scenes of a day in the life of a married woman: afternoon spent with her lover, the evening with her husband, son, and a friend; the following day with her doctor (she discovers that she is pregnant, but doesn't know by whom); and finally the afternoon with her lover again.

Interspersed amid these scenes are seven cinéma-vérité-type interviews. In these seemingly unscripted meditations by the husband, the friend, the girl herself, the child, the maid, the doctor, and the lover, Godard manages to extend our knowledge of the characters and, in some cases, to broaden and deepen the meaning of his film.

The husband's monologue deals with memory – the pretext being a discussion of concentration camps; the wife's with the present, her preference for it, and her refusal to be imprisoned in the past. This of course ties up with her own problem, her preference for her present lover over what her husband represents; in short, her rejection of the past. The friend's monologue deals with the superiority of understanding to action, etc.

The third element of the collage is the tremendous importance given by Godard to the ephemera of modern life, the significance of the world of advertising to the lives of the characters. Charlotte is literally besieged by these intimations of sexuality: ads for bras and girdles, ways of developing the bust, ways of determining if one's bust needs to be developed, gramophone records of music to make love by, of how to strip-tease for your husband, etc.

Finally, there are what one can only call the still-lives, the three sequences of lovemaking, two with the lover, one with the husband. Graphic as these scenes are, they are as un-

Decades Never Start On Time

erotic as they could possibly be, mostly because they are treated as still lives, patterns as abstract as the fragments from the Beethoven string quartets on the sound track of the film. But they are also meant, I suppose, to show the girl being treated as an object — an object which gives pleasure, but an object none the less.

The references to the conflict between past and present culminate in the screening of a fragment from Resnais's *Nuit et brouillard*, the film about the concentration camps. However disparate this yoking together of concentration camps and the problems of Charlotte may seem, the result is no more shocking than a poem of Donne where the same thing happens.[7]

Une Femme mariée (which was originally titled 'La Femme mariée' until the sensitive French censors insisted on the change) is, as I have tried to suggest, a very complex film. It is not perhaps the most completely successful of Godard's films, but it is certainly his most adventurous. In spite of the impression I may have given, it is also extremely funny. There seems little point in the kind of summing up which tells readers whether they should go to see the film or not. Anyone who is likely to like the film will go whatever I may say (and will be right to do so). To the others, I can only say that in this film one of the top four or five directors working today has extended himself, and enriched the cinema. Coming a week after *The Red Desert*, it almost seems like more than we have a right to expect.

SOURCE: 'OBJECT LESSON', *GUARDIAN*, 8 APRIL 1965, 9

2.8 ANGUISH: ALPHAVILLE

LEMMY CAUTION: 'Never forget that Revenger and Reporter begin with the same letter.'

It is seventeen minutes past midnight, Oceanic Time; having driven all night through inter-sidereal space, secret agent Lemmy Caution — disguised as Ivan Johnson, reporter for Figaro-Pravda — arrives in the suburbs of Alphaville. The road is empty, the night grey; Lemmy is alone, with only a revolver in the glove compartment.

Thus begins *Alphaville, or a Strange Adventure of Lemmy Caution*. Another title Godard wanted to use was 'Tarzan versus IBM', and the first time I saw *Alphaville* it was the pop art aspect of the film that struck me most. Of course, Godard, like Marker and Resnais, had been intrigued by comic strips for many years before the term pop art existed. Comic strips seem to represent many things for Godard: first, a source book for the contemporary collective subconscious; secondly, a dramatic framework derived from modern myth — in much the same way as Joyce used the Ulysses myth; thirdly, a reaction against the subtleties of the psychological novel; finally the attraction of comic strip narrative with its sudden shifting of scene, its freedom of narration, its economy.

The plot of *Alphaville* is pure comic strip; Caution (Eddie Constantine) has been sent to Alphaville, city of the future, to bring back or kill Professor von Braun, architect of this capital of computers. Three agents have already failed: Dick Tracy, Flash Gordon, and Henri Dickson. Caution eventually succeeds in his mission, even managing to carry off Natacha von Braun (Anna Karina), to whom he succeeds in teaching the meaning of love. The Robot has been redeemed.

Alphaville (1965)

Just like a Lichtenstein painting ('Oh, Brad, (gulp) it should have been that way'), the dialogue often echoes the balloons: 'Let this serve as a warning to all those who try to …', etc. Characterisation, too, has been reduced to a minimum. The musical score, by Paul Misraki, is extremely effective as used by Godard, but in itself it is (intentionally) the nearest he could get to the Max Steiner of the 1930s. Furthermore, Godard uses all the typographical symbols beloved of pop artists – arrows, buttons, neon lights – all the signposts of modern life.

But *Alphaville* doesn't look like a comic strip, and this is where Godard diverges from the true pop artist, who has been defined [by Robert Rosenblum] as 'a man who offers a coincidence of style and subject, one who represents mass-produced images and objects in a style which is also based upon the visual vocabulary of mass production.' In other words, the pop artist not only likes the fact of his commonplace objects, but more important, exults in their commonplace look. Godard resembles much more pop fringe figures like Larry Rivers and Rauschenberg who, although fascinated by pop imagery, translate it into a non-pop style.

The second time I saw *Alphaville*, it was precisely the great refinement and plastic beauty of its style that impressed me. Like the volume of Eluard poems which the dying Henri Dickson (Akim Tamiroff) presses into Lemmy's hand, Alphaville is the Capital of Pain (*Capitale de la douleur*), and the visual style of the film is painful, menacing, anxiety-ridden. Alphaville is Paris. The swimming pool where the intractable citizens are machine-gunned and finished off by knife-wielding girls in bikinis is actually on the outskirts of Paris. The new Electricity Board building is one of the computer centres; the hotel where Lemmy stays looks to me like the Continental[8] (home of the Gestapo during the Occupation). The problem was to film Paris to make it look like the city of Alpha 60, the city whose inhabitants have become the slaves of electronic probabilities, where tranquillisers come with every hotel room, and logic and the eternal present reign.

On the other hand, there was no real problem, for Paris has always been for Godard the Capital of Pain, and his style has always been anguish-ridden. Without trick shots and special effects, menace is rendered in the usual Godard/Coutard fashion: avoidance of extra lighting creates not an effect of realism, but of a city where the blackness is stronger than the occasional pools of light. Again, because he does not generally use special lighting, he can make play with reflection and shadow in a manner which cannot always be planned in advance, but which always gives the same inevitable effect of mysterious dread. One cannot be sure that individual shots in a Godard film have been planned to create a special dramatic effect, but they always contribute to the mood and general tenor of the film. For example, the glass-enclosed lift in Lemmy's hotel is the excuse for some fabulously disturbing reflection effects. These are beautiful in themselves, but I don't think they have any specific relevance at the moment we see them. On the other hand, the ambiguity of the reflections, the fact that we are often unsure of where the camera could have been placed, are of course an effective mirroring of Lemmy's *dépaysement* and fears.

As befits a study of a totalitarian state, much of the film takes place in long bureaucratic corridors, labyrinths of power, mazes at whose centre lies death. Here again, Coutard's flat underlighting and the graininess of the image render the East Berlin effect in all its greyness and desperation. But the palaces of the government, on the other hand, are all sinister elegance, more like New York. In the same way, the northern suburbs are covered in snow and ice, while the southern suburbs are hot and steamy.

For *Alphaville* is built visually on extreme contrasts, or so I realised more fully the third time I saw it. Basically there is the contrast of the straight line and the circle. For Godard, the circle represents evil: a man must go straight ahead, says the condemned man on the diving-board. So everything in Alphaville that represents the tyranny of the computers is circular. Lemmy's hotel suite is built in circular form; the staircases in the government buildings are spiral; even the city itself is, like Paris, circular, and to get from one place to another one must take a circular route. The corridors may be straight, but one always ends up where one started. And of course the computers move in circles. Time, says Alpha 60, is an endless circle. Lemmy, however, maintains that all one has to do is to go straight ahead towards everything one loves, straight ahead: when one arrives at the goal, one realises that one has nevertheless looped the loop (*boucler la boucle*).

The inhabitants of Alphaville even talk in circles. Whenever anyone says hello, the reply is invariable: 'Very well, thank you, please.' 'You must never say *why;* only *because,*' admonishes Natacha. Death and life are inscribed in the same hopeless circle.

Contrast is also displayed in Godard's treatment of the sound. The main musical theme is, as I have said, syrupy and romantic, but it never gets beyond the introductory cadence. And it is inter-cut with harsh discordant noises: the slamming of doors, the whirling of the computers, and worst of all, the electronic grating voice of Alpha 60, which is as unpleasant as it is indescribable. It would sound like a death-rattle were it not for the absolute evenness and soulless monotony of its delivery. Godard has always liked to flash brutally from a bright scene to a dark one, but this is carried to extreme proportions in *Alphaville*, where the greyness of the streets is continually contrasted with the blinding floodlights of the electronic nerve centres. Like so many lasers, they torture the brain, at the same time exercising a hypnotic fascination in their rhythmical flashing.

In describing a film as extraordinarily individual as *Alphaville*, it seems somehow an anti-climax to talk about the acting; so suffice it to say that Eddie Constantine is the perfect intergalactic private eye, and Anna Karina seems to have gone through a second metamorphosis. Just as the difference between her performances in *Une Femme est une femme* and *Vivre sa vie* was incalculably startling, so she has left behind her earlier incarnation, and now stands before us, no longer the wistful little girl of *Bande à part*, but a woman perfectly capable of rendering both the brainwashed and deadly 'Seducer, second class' (her job in

Alphaville), and also the woman who can just barely remember life before words like red-breast, autumn light, conscience, tears, and tenderness, were eradicated from the Bible/Dictionary owned by every inhabitant of Alphaville, new editions of which are produced daily.

It seems equally anti-climactic to point out that Godard's sense of humour is well to the fore in *Alphaville*. Some of it can't possibly come out in the subtitles, though, so perhaps it should be explained. Caution learns that while the intractable members of society are killed off, the reclaimable ones are sent to HLMs – *Hôpitaux de Longues Maladies*: Hospitals for Long Illnesses. (HLM actually means *Habitations à loyers modérés*: in other words, council houses.) When the fluorescent lights go on in the corridors of Alphaville, someone remarks, 'Ah, dawn is breaking: *Le jour se lève*.' Then there is the efficient method of subduing criminals: a second-class seductress is ordered to tell one of the official repertory of jokes; when the victim doubles up with laughter, he is hit over the head and taken away.

Most anti-climactic of all would be a summing up, in which I would say that for me *Alphaville* is not only Godard's best film, but one of the most important in recent years. But it is.

SOURCE: 'ANGUISH: ALPHAVILLE', *SIGHT & SOUND*, 34.4, AUTUMN 1965, 164–6

2.9 NEW FILMS

To any who may have felt that the ending of *Alphaville* offered a too facile resolution to its problems – Love Conquers All – *Pierrot le fou* now comes as a conclusive rejoinder, and as a reminder that Godard's art and his life-view are essentially tragic. For *Pierrot le fou* (Cameo-Poly) is nothing less than the story of the destruction of a man by love.

Except, of course, that being a Godard film, it does not tell a story. Rather Godard uses a story to express a point of view, a philosophy of life, an anatomy of the emotions. The real Pierrot le Fou was a gangster; our hero Ferdinand, an ex-Spanish teacher, ex-television director, falls hopelessly in love with Marianne, one of those 'students' who haunt the terraces of the Paris cafés. It is she who dubs him, against his will, Pierrot le Fou. Her brother is an arms smuggler, and she is involved in various illegal traffic with most of the world's trouble spots. Murder and violence are familiar companions to her, and in falling desperately in love with her, Ferdinand tacitly accepts a kind of complicity with her world.

After disposing of a corpse they find in her Paris flat, they decide to strike out for the Riviera. On the island of Porquerolles they start to live out an idyll, but Marianne gets bored. Refusing to accept her betrayal, Pierrot follows her in the knowledge that from this moment on there can be no turning back. All too soon, the inevitable occurs: Ferdinand, completely disillusioned, kills Marianne and blows himself to bits.

In many ways, *Pierrot le fou* is Godard's freest, most experimental film to date. Rather than waste time on exposition, he often simply stops the story to allow, as if in a Noh play, one of the characters to advance towards the camera and tell us something. Occasionally, as in the wheat field scene, this procedure can be a little self-indulgent; for the most part it works and it forces one to a reconsideration of the nature of narrative in the cinema. Perhaps the most successful example occurs during the flight from Paris, which is accompanied by a double commentary. Both Pierrot and Marianne speak in turn, but their voices are slightly out of phase with the action giving the effect of a disjointed, antiphonal litany.

Visually, Godard's will to abstraction is given free rein throughout the film, but especially in the already mentioned sequence in which Ferdinand and Marianne drive through the night to the south; the camera is fixed on them behind the windscreen and movement is suggested by an alternating sequence of red and green lights which flash over the faces at rhythmical intervals. Although the motif is obviously derived from reality (cars flashing by, traffic lights, etc.) the effect is a kind of quintessence of flight.

This is Godard's third colour film (and when, pray tell, are we going to be allowed to see *Contempt* and *Une Femme est une femme*?) and from this point of view it is his most inventive. After *Alphaville* one can nevermore be surprised at the greatness of Anna Karina, but the return of Jean-Paul Belmondo to the Godard world shows us that all these years of appearing in trifles has done nothing to impair his talent: as the doomed Pierrot, he is superb.

Morgan: A Suitable Case for Treatment (Carlton) is Karel Reisz's third feature film, and I think it is far and away his best. Morgan, the hero (David Warner), is indeed, even more than most of us, a suitable case for treatment. Born of a bed-rock Communist family (your father's dream was of you waving the red flag in the rubble of Buckingham Palace), he identifies with Trotsky. But also with gorillas, in particular, King Kong: 'gorillas are big, but good.'

When his rich wife, Leonie (Vanessa Redgrave), decides that although he is amusing, a girl can't, in Anita Loos's immortal words, go on laughing all the time, and proceeds to divorce him, the film begins and so does the slow downfall of Morgan Delt. For he does not accept the divorce: for him, his rival, Napier (Charles Stephens), is Stalin to his Trotsky; 'she married me,' he tells Napier, 'to achieve insecurity, and now you're trying to take that away from her.' For all his booby-trapping the bed, his kidnapping of Leonie, his King Kong-like attempt, dressed in a gorilla suit, to break up the wedding party, he fails because although they are all as unbalanced as he is, they at least do not have his integrity; they cover up. And I suppose what Reisz is saying is that the world belongs to those who can adjust, settle for something less than their dreams – but isn't it a pity?

The first half of the film, up until the time when Morgan is finally forced to leave his ex-wife's house, is shot in an extremely nervous, rapid manner. Every frame seems packed to bursting with people or objects, until suddenly another character lunges into frame and the action threatens to spill out over the edges. The cutting is what is inaccurately called 'quick' and most of the cuts are on action: from someone moving to someone else in flight. Occasionally Reisz even speeds up the action, a device generally used only for comic effect, but which here has an edge of hysteria.

The second part of the film during which Morgan begins to drift rapidly towards madness is much slower. There is far less dialogue, a use of slow-motion photography and freeze-frame effects. Farce has given way to a looser, more lyrical mood. I won't spoil the final gag for anyone but it is enough to say that anyone who remembers the final shots of Buñuel's *El* will not be too surprised.

At first one is disappointed at David Warner's lack of charm, but on reflection this is what saves the film: it would have been far too easy to grab for easy and irrelevant sympathy, and Morgan must not be patronised in this way. *Morgan* is not an easy film because 'you don't always quite know where you are,' but it is for that very reason that it is so gripping. Nothing runs along expected narrative or cinematic patterns: here is a film which is fascinating, original, and disquieting.[9] [...]

SOURCE: 'NEW FILMS', *GUARDIAN*, 15 APRIL 1966, 11

2.10 FILM CRITICISM IN BRITAIN

NOTE: This typewritten text from the archive does not appear to have been intended for publication. It would seem to be a text that Roud prepared for a public talk, or more likely for a series of group discussions, presumably among film critics from different countries, gathered at the Cannes Film Festival. From internal evidence we can date the text as May 1967, for example the reference to reviewing various films 'a month ago', including the world premiere of The Honey Pot *(which was at the end of March 1967). For an earlier discussion of film criticism in the UK, see 'Prestige through print',* Guardian, *9 April 1964, 8.*

I almost began by stating that the conditions under which the British critic works are unique. I shan't because I suppose delegates from every country would be able to say the same thing. On the other hand, England is an island, and one given to the eccentric, the anomalous, the peculiar.

Ever since the war, I believe, one very peculiar condition has been the lot of most British critics: we write only one article a week, and almost on the same day – Thursday or Friday. Furthermore, unlike most countries where the critic reviews one film at a time, the English critic is more or less obliged to do all the week's film in one piece – and often that piece must be the same length regardless of whether one, two, three, four, or even no films have come out that week.

This has perhaps one advantage: the reader knows when and where to find a critic's views on all the new films of the week. But, the disadvantages are sometimes great: if several very good films appear the same week, the critic is generally obliged to discuss them in much less detail than he would like. Conversely, if only one or two bad films appear, then the critic is obliged to either discuss them at great and unnecessary length, thus giving them undue prominence, or else devote his piece to general reflections on the state of the cinema, etc., and we all know what those can be like.

A contributing reason for this state of affairs is yet another anomaly: films are shown to the press at special shows which are all arranged through a central clearing house, the so-called Film Publicity Guild, an organisation supported and paid for by the major distributors. This means, in practice, that films are shown to the press on Monday and Tuesday of each week, one performance in the morning, another in the afternoon. The films themselves almost always open to the public on Thursday or Friday. Were the shows not so highly organised, it is doubtful whether the system of one article per week would work. Of course, exceptions can be and sometimes are made: a film of great importance – a world premiere, for example – can be exceptionally reviewed on another day of the week by itself.

Then, too, some newspapers are more flexible than others: the luckier critic can adapt the number of words he is allowed to correspond to the importance of the week's films. But there are always upper and lower limits: these can vary from 750 words to 1500, according to the newspaper.

The weeklies are almost as tightly controlled as regards space as the newspapers; their great advantage is that the critic is freer to decide whether he will cover all the films of the week, or concentrate on the one or two he is most interested in. Then, too, the weekly critic is generally free of the necessity of paying more attention to the English-language films. For the popular press demands generally of its critics that it devote most space to the films which will be most widely shown: and, alas, given the state of affairs in England, this is automatically the English or

American film. The subtitled film – dubbing is practically unknown here – is generally reserved to the art-houses, the specialised cinemas, of which there are fewer than the others.

The monthly magazine critics, and a fortiori those of the quarterlies are generally quite free of these pressures of time and space. For them, films are shown at special 'magazine shows', generally a month before the film is due to come out.

Most film critics in England, I am happy to say, can *almost* live on their earnings as film critics. They all supplement these earnings by working for television, radio, writing books, even, in one case, keeping an antique shop. But by and large, critics are not scandalously under-paid, as I believe they are in countries such as France, and perhaps elsewhere. This, of course, has the great advantage of helping the critic to resist any pressure – were it to be offered – from the major film companies. A relatively secure critic is not easily tempted.

This financial independence is obviously a good thing, for it generally follows that if a paper values a contributor sufficiently to pay him well, then he will be treated with professional respect by his editor. The English film critic is, I think I can say, almost entirely independent, with the exception mentioned above: critics in the more popular papers have to pay maximum attention to English and American films; they can say these films are bad but they must do it at great length. Obviously, I am simplifying, because any newspaper exercises control over its critics if only in the very act of choosing whom they will hire. And some papers, it is well known, try very hard not to hire what they might call 'intellectual' or 'avant-garde' critics. In fact, they often choose the critic who corresponds most closely to the general level of what they conceive to be its readers' interests. This is naturally an element which conditions the critic's reviews.

As regards the critic's relations with the film industry, these are generally good. However, there have been incidents in the past: for example, one Hollywood company, tired of universally unfavourable reviews of Jerry Lewis films, decided simply that they would not show these films to the press. Now a critic can write about whatever he wants, but there is a kind of tacit gentleman's agreement that if a company does not show a film to the press, then the critic is supposed to realise that the company knows it is bad and therefore politely not mention it. This has occasionally led to some grotesque situations when a company has not shown a film, but the critics have decided that they thought it was in fact very good and reviewed it anyhow. One famous example was Ophüls's *Letter from an Unknown Woman* which the press rescued from the oblivion the distributor thought it deserved! This kind of thing points up the fact that although the press, by and large, get on with the industry, the two often judge films from widely opposed standpoints.

More recently, a certain amount of trouble was caused by the bad reviews of Chaplin's *Countess from Hong Kong*. The two evening papers came out with very unfavourable reviews on the very night of the *grande première*, thus apparently reducing the première party into something like a funeral wake. In an attempt to avoid this happening again, another company refused to show *The Night of the Generals* to the press after its première. This caused much ill will among some critics, and steps may be taken by the Critics Circle (a free association of the film critics) to combat this tendency.

Having established the material and general conditions of the film critic, we must now go on to the more complex and interesting problems of the content and standards of British film criticism.

Generalisations are always very risky, but one can say that film critics of Great Britain can be divided into two categories: those writing for the popular press and those for what are known as the 'quality papers'. The popular press, I have already said, labours under the obligation to give most of its attention to the films which will be widely circulated. Their function, by and large, is to tell their readers whether or not they will like a film. The critic will obviously convey his own reactions to the film, he will explain what it is about, but ultimately his chief function is to let the reader know whether he should go to see a film. And the criterion used is generally that of 'entertainment'. This word is difficult to define, and even harder to translate: it does not necessarily refer to comedy: a drama can also be called entertaining. But what is clear is that in determining the entertainment value of a film, aesthetic considerations do not play the major role.

Occasionally social considerations can weigh upon a critic's advice: the reader is told he must see this or that film because it is good for him: in such cases, however, the critic's advice is often unheeded. This actually happened in the case of Wajda's *Kanal* which got very 'good' reviews but ones which made the film sound so grim that the readers ignored the critics' advice.

The critics of the 'quality papers' (*The Times*, *The Guardian*, *The Financial Times*, *The Daily Telegraph*, *The Sunday Times*, *The Observer*) are of course in a different position. The best critics of these papers try not only to tell their readers why they liked certain films, but they also try to convince the reader why he should like them, too. In fact, they proselytise. They make great efforts to bring a broader public to the foreign — that is, non-English speaking — film, they try to discover the smaller films that might otherwise escape the public's notice, and a good Japanese film will get more space than a bad English one.

However, their judgment is almost universally an aesthetic one. English critics by and large do not think of the cinemas as an element of public education, or at the most, only to a minor degree. Social elements do get a certain degree of attention, generally in proportion to the degree of radicalism of the newspaper. Unless, of course, the film they are discussing — like, say, Romm's *Ordinary Fascism* — calls out itself for a special orientated criticism. And a film like Peter Watkins's *The War Game* was almost universally praised not for its aesthetic value — which indeed was small — but for its value as a social document and as a tract for our times.

The very best of these critics try to avoid judging each film as an isolated phenomenon, and rather attempt to discuss it in the context of other works by the same director or of the same national school. Less often are they able or tempted to situate each work in a kind of grander historical/cinematographic context, partly because they suffer from lack of space, and partly from a tendency towards that empirical view, which has often been characterised as essentially British.

Fifteen years ago, *Les Cahiers du Cinéma* published a survey of French film critics which covered much of the same ground as our *Semaine de la Critique*.[10] One of the most interesting questions asked was whether the critic thought that he should judge films from the standpoint of a coherent cinematographic aesthetic approach or whether he thought a kind of impressionist approach was more valid. Most of the French critics who replied decided against the impressionist approach. As I have tried to suggest above, most English critics would be in favour of it. This might be imputable to the difference between French Cartesianism and British empiricism, but it might also be due to the different way in which the cinema itself is considered in the two countries. I think it is fair to say that the cinema is *still* considered in Great Britain as somewhat less important than, say, music, ballet, or the theatre. This is less true than it was ten years ago — much progress has, I think, been made in the last decade — but nonetheless there are many people in positions of power in the newspaper and magazine world who simply refuse to take the cinema very seriously. This is regrettable in itself, and it cannot help but have an adverse influence on the critic. He is not encouraged to take too serious an approach because he always feels that he can be accused of being pretentious. So one often has the ridiculous situation whereby a critic has to praise a difficult or experimental film in terms that will not make it sound too difficult or too experimental. There is nothing basically wrong with trying to reach one's necessarily non-technical public by any means one can, but all too often limitations of space being what they are, the critic does not have enough space left to pursue a really rigorous or systematic discussion of the film with which he is concerned.

If I may be allowed a personal example, a month ago, just before Easter I was obliged to review five films in 1000 words. As if this were not bad enough, one was Orson Welles's *Chimes at Midnight*, another the first British screening of Godard's *Une Femme est une femme*, and a third, the world première of Mankiewicz's *The Honey Pot*. With the best will in the world, no critic can pursue anything but an impressionistic approach when confronted with this task. And I repeat, the reason a critic is so confronted is because of the relatively low esteem in which the cinema is held. One cannot imagine a book reviewer obliged to perform such an impossible task. So here we can see that the criteria and methods of the critic are affected gravely by what looks to be only a physical or material problem but which turns out on further examination to be of a general aesthetic and perhaps a social attitude.

Given this basic limitation, the British critics have, I think, done a great service to the British cinema. In fact, to a certain extent – although not nearly as much as in France – the British cinema has come from the critics. It is perhaps not too well known outside England that Tony Richardson, Lindsay Anderson and Karel Reisz have all been film critics in the past. Not on newspapers, but first of all in that most important quarterly *Sequence*, and then, when its editor Gavin Lambert was hired by the British Film Institute to edit its *Sight & Sound*, for that publication. In fact, just as the *nouvelle vague* can be seen as the creation of the Cinémathèque Française and the *Cahiers du Cinéma*, one *could* say the British Film Institute – for whom Karel Reisz was programme director for several years, and for whom Lindsay Anderson worked – and the magazine *Sight & Sound* (itself a publication of the British Film Institute) were very important in the growth of the new British cinema. Furthermore, the British Film Institute's Experimental Film Fund commissioned the early shorts of Richardson, Reisz and Anderson.

A few of the important daily and weekly critics used to work for the British Film Institute as well, so *that* has only reinforced the influence that the critical climate of *Sequence/Sight & Sound* has had on the young British cinema. This has served well not only native talents, but in particular the films of a man like Joseph Losey. Settled in Britain since 1952, his first really favourable reviews came from *Sight & Sound*. Then, slowly, influenced perhaps by the climate of opinion in France, and also that of the British Film Institute/*Sight & Sound*/National Film Theatre complex, most of the press began to look more closely at Losey's films and to appreciate them more. Critics do have some influence at the box-office, if only for what are generally called films of quality. What I mean is that if they all say that *Cleopatra* is bad, audiences will still flock to see it; but they can at least lead audiences to the more difficult films. An excellent example was the recent Losey film, *Accident*, in which its distributors had little faith. They had planned a brief first-run showing, and that was about all. It received such ecstatic reviews from most of the critics that it was quickly given a full circuit and has, in fact, been something of a success financially, partly as a direct result of the influence of the critics.

1963–9

The question of 'provincialism', raised in the working paper for these discussions, is one which does relate very importantly to the situation in Britain. As I suggested earlier, most critics are very strongly affected by a certain 'provincialism' – that of language. It is natural, of course, that they should give more attention to British films than those of other countries, and in a certain sense, it is appropriate, for it is their duty, I think, to support local endeavour. The real problem is that, as is well known, Americans speak – more or less – the same language as the British. This has meant that ever since the advent of the sound film, the Hollywood movie has had a very preferred status in this country. Given the enormous number of films turned out by Hollywood since 1929, and their often very high quality and popular appeal, the British public has grown up preferring English-language films. In other countries, all foreign films are, *grosso modo*, competing for an audience on equal terms; this is not true in Britain where American films are – to use George Orwell's phrase – more equal than the others.

This may in some way explain the fact mentioned earlier that very few films are ever dubbed. For some reason, it has been more or less proven that English audiences will *not* accept them, as do audiences in other countries. If an Englishman wants to see a foreign film, he insists that it be in a subtitled version. Aesthetically this is doubtless a very satisfactory state of affairs, and one which has been encouraged by the critics who always complain bitterly when a distributor tries to show a dubbed continental film. But it does mean, alas, that foreign films do not get a very wide showing in Britain. Audiences will not accept dubbed versions, but the great wide public does not like reading subtitles either! In London, of course, there are quite a large number of cinemas that *do* show subtitled films, but it is in the provinces – the largest market, after all – that they are not very widely shown. The few exceptions –*Le Salaire de la peur*, the Brigitte Bardot films – only confirm the rule.

In the past few years there have been some encouraging signs of change: the British Film Institute itself has established branches of its National Film Theatre in half a dozen provincial cities, bringing to them an interesting selection of foreign films they would not otherwise have seen. Furthermore, the second chain of BBC Television has instituted an excellent weekly series of foreign films, including such important works as *Alexander Nevsky*, *Senso*, *Une Partie de campagne*. These programmes reach millions who might never have had the opportunity of seeing such films. One can only hope that these efforts of the BBC and the British Film Institute will prosper and grow, thus remedying a very unhealthy situation.

The critics up till now have felt that all they can do is to encourage their readers to be tempted by the French or the Italian film. As a result, very few films of countries other than these privileged ones get released. France and Italy, Scandinavia to a lesser extent, plus America and Britain – make up almost one hundred per cent of Britain's film diet. Recently there has been a certain interest in Eastern European cinema; Polish films had a certain vogue several years ago, and in the past year or two there has been a discovery of the new Czech cinema, but these discoveries have been limited to a half dozen works. The Japanese and the Indian cinema – or rather Kurosawa and Ray – have always had a certain public. But as for the rest of the 'third World' – well, hardly any have been shown, with the exception of a few Brazilian and Argentine films and the more recent Buñuels.

Critics do what they can to encourage a broader view, but their efforts are tempered by the necessity of *breaking through the English-language barrier* and by the fact that they tend to judge films on either an aesthetic or an entertainment basis, and not as '*instruments for the circulation of ideas*'.

It is not for me to conclude; it is rather for you to decide now whether the state of criticism, the position of the film critic, is better or worse than in your own countries. Or perhaps,

Decades Never Start On Time

give and take a little, much the same. I myself would conclude with a not *too* unfavourable view; but self-satisfaction is the critic's worst enemy, and as that great Englishman, Samuel Johnson, *reminded* us: patriotism is merely self-interest *multiplied*.

SOURCE: 'FILM CRITICISM IN BRITAIN', ARCHIVE DOCUMENT, MAY 1967, RICHARD ROUD COLLECTION, HOWARD GOTLIEB ARCHIVAL RESEARCH CENTER, BOSTON, BOX 1, F8, ITEM J.27, 8 PAGES

2.11 MASCULIN FÉMININ

In spite of its modest, unassuming appearance, *Masculin féminin* (Cameo Royal and Cameo Victoria) is, I think, Godard's best film to date. Looked at casually it might almost be a television film; it appears to have been very simply shot, and its interest would seem to be almost entirely sociological.

Godard has gone on record as saying that after Marker's *Le joli mai* and Rouch's *Chronicle of a Summer*, he wanted to do Paris in December. It was, however, a very particular December, that of 1965, the month between the two elections. (After de Gaulle failed to win on the first ballot there was a second run-off between him and Mitterrand.) During the autumn of that year, Godard had been alone in Paris, and found himself mixed up with a group of young people, and he decided to make the film about what was already for him (at 35) the 'younger generation'.

He describes this generation in one of the film's interspersed titles as 'The Children of Marx and Coca-Cola.' Paul, his hero (played by Jean-Pierre Léaud) is a Communist who has just come to Paris after completing his military service; an introduction to a girl gets him a job on the magazine she works for. He falls in love with her and they sleep together; she has no desire, however, to marry him. In spite of all their precautions she becomes pregnant, and the film ends with Paul's death: suicide or accident? Madeleine is left investigating the possibilities of an abortion.

The main point of the film is that while Paul and his friend Robert spend long hours signing petitions, putting up anti-Vietnam posters, etc., the girls they get involved with do not share their preoccupations. They are definitely self-proclaimed members of the Pepsi generation. The only social problem they seem to have in common with the boys is the birth control problem (it's still illegal in France). The girls are not unaware of this disparity, and one of Madeleine's friends tries to convince Paul that they can only make him unhappy. At bottom he knows it, too, but the secret of controlling physical desire cannot be found in *Das Kapital*.

There is not enough space to go into formal considerations here; they are, however, what succeed in giving the film the structure that at first glance it seems to lack, and which makes it, in spite of its modest air, one of Godard's most achieved films. Briefly, although this may only become apparent on a second viewing, it is in the revolutionising of traditional narrative methods and in the finely balanced resolution of the claims of reality and those of abstraction that Godard has succeeded, even more than in *Une Femme mariée* (which this film most resembles), in creating a new kind of cinema.

SOURCE: '*MASCULIN FÉMININ*', *GUARDIAN*, 22 JUNE 1967, 5

2.12 FAR FROM VIETNAM

Some people – perhaps those with guilty consciences? – have tried to dismiss *Far from Vietnam* (Paris Pullman, from 28 December) out of hand. Their line has been that propaganda films preach only to the converted; only those who are already opposed to the American presence in Vietnam will go to see the film, and they – so the argument goes – don't need further convincing.

This is not quite true. There are many people who are vaguely against the war, who think vaguely that something ought to be done, who are sort of unhappy about the whole situation. It is to them that the film is really addressed, as an attempt to help them crystallise their attitudes, to make up their minds once and for all. I know, because I am one of them.

Loin du Vietnam is a propaganda film; it is not, by and large, objective. Its six nominal directors (Jean-Luc Godard, Alain Resnais, William Klein, Joris Ivens, Agnès Varda, and Claude Lelouch), to whom one must add the conceptual organiser of the film Chris Marker, all feel very strongly about the war in Vietnam, and think that they, as artists, should have the right to express their feeling. Each in his own way, of course, and if only to compare Godard's way with, say, that of Resnais, the film is well worth seeing.

Resnais's is the only fictional episode – acted, dramatised, directed. Also, and typically, it is the most generous: his hero is very much like Resnais, a man with great feeling for Americans, gratitude to the liberators of 1944, an admiration for, and fascination in, American pop culture. His attitude is the one which will probably be shared by most British viewers, as will his pain at the role the Americans are playing today.

Godard's episode is the simplest, the most direct: Godard himself, half hidden behind a big camera expressing directly to the real camera his feeling about the war in a sequence that is as moving as Resnais's by its very simplicity and directness.

When the film was shown at the New York film festival, it was violently acclaimed by the audience and bitterly attacked by the press. What right, said the critics, did the French, of all people, have to criticise us? And they all declared that although they were against the war, they still thought the film was Maoist, Communist (cries of 'Moscow gold' were even heard). In any case, and above all, it was anti-American. But this is criminally to oversimplify, for moments like the interview with Mrs Norman Morrison (the widow of the man who burnt himself in front of the Pentagon) made one actually proud to be American.[11]

Far from Vietnam is an important film, a beautiful film, a moving film. Rare indeed have been the occasions when contemporary art has successfully involved itself with politics. In this film, the cinema at last has its *Guernica*.

SOURCE: 'FAR FROM VIETNAM', *GUARDIAN*, 20 DECEMBER 1967, 5

2.13 A LANGLOIS UNTO HIMSELF

In a week during which the cinema in London has so little to offer us, *The Helicopter Spies* (Ritz) and *A New Face in Hell* (Carlton), it seems appropriate to take up again the cause of a man who has done so much for the cinema, not just in France, but throughout the world. Anyone who reads Peter Lennon's *Guardian* pieces from Paris will know that I am referring to Henri Langlois and his dismissal from the post of director of the organisation he singlehandedly created, the Cinémathèque Française.

Even he, with his vast and insatiable appetite for collecting films, would probably not go after prints of this week's two films (though I suppose if they were offered him, he wouldn't say no: he never does). *A New Face in Hell* does in fact have quite a good script by Philip Reisman, junior, and boasts one of those competent performances by George Peppard that he has led us to expect. But the direction by John Guillermin is flat and uninspired. *The Helicopter Spies* is another in *The Man from U.N.C.L.E.* series, sillier and duller than usual if even more apocalyptic: one of those takeover bids which has as its object nothing less than the whole world. This puts it squarely in that tradition which goes back through Hitchcock to Fritz Lang and finally to Feuillade, whose *Les Vampires* seemed to have started the whole thing off.

And conveniently, this takes us right back to Henri Langlois, who is responsible for the fact that we can still see Feuillade's masterpiece. Unlike many archivists, he never pretended that his job was simply to collect 'the best'. Quite straightforwardly he has always declared that he just didn't know what 'the best' was. No one ever did; at the time he got the negative of *Les Vampires* out of Gaumont, it was considered to be rather unimportant trash, and I am not sure whether Langlois himself realised at the time what a great film it was. But he believed that, as part of the history of the cinema, it should be saved.

His point, of course, was that our ideas of what is good or bad change with every generation; we can never be sure – so when in doubt, preserve. In fact, his theory is that a film archive should perform, to the best of its ability and means, the same function as the Bibliothèque Nationale or the British Museum: to collect everything, because someone sometime somewhere will want to see it, and ought to be able to.

The fact that this great man has been deprived of his position by the French Government is no less than a disaster as can be seen by the violence and breadth of the protest movements that have arisen in France. But why, I hear someone saying, should *we* care about it, here in England? It's their problem, not ours.

This is not so. In the years between 1959 and 1967 when I was programme director of the National Film Theatre, hundreds of films from the Cinémathèque were shown in London. Sometimes they arrived late, sometimes the wrong film turned up, but by and large they got here. Without Langlois, London would never have had the chance of seeing Feuillade's *Les Vampires*, Buñuel's *L'Age d'or*, the new longer version of Stroheim's *Queen Kelly*, the complete sound-scored print of Stroheim's *The Wedding March*, many of the films of Jean Renoir, the complete print of Ophüls' *Lola Montès*, the Abel Gance retrospective, including a tinted original print of *Napoleon*, and dozens of others.

In the old days before the war, Langlois used actually to bring films over to present at the BFI's London Film Institute Society (the ancestor of the NFT). As early as 1938, Olwen Vaughan, then secretary of the institute, welcomed endless shows called 'How Do They Stand Now?' and 'Evolution of the French Cinema.'

Furthermore, Langlois has done a lot for the British cinema abroad, going all the way back to his revelation of the British documentary school of film-making in 1937. Immediately after the war was over, Langlois brought over Grierson, Basil Wright, and Paul Rotha to Paris, and showed their works; in 1956 he put on an enormous cycle entitled 'Fifty Years of British Film'; as recently as last year he presented a homage to the GPO films in Paris, and a more complete one than has ever to my knowledge been put on in London. Many of today's best-known British film-makers have received their European premieres at the Cinémathèque –

Tony Richardson, Karel Reisz, Lindsay Anderson. Their gratitude to Langlois (as well as that of directors like Peter Brook and Joseph Losey) has been expressed in their protests to the French Government and more importantly in their statements that they will not allow any of their films to be shown at the Cinémathèque until Langlois is reinstated.

So it is not just a local problem; we all have a stake in it. Furthermore, without getting paranoid about it, the defeat of Langlois would be a victory for the faceless bureaucratic 'Them' – the people who prefer what they call efficiency to actual achievement. And perhaps Langlois has not run the Cinémathèque 'properly' – that is to say he is not orderly, well-organised, or even always rational. But the achievement is there; the results speak for themselves.

Hopefully, the tide may be turning: the telegrams and letters which have poured in from almost every important film-maker in the world (from Dreyer to Welles), from production companies, from people like Picasso, Samuel Beckett, Jean-Paul Sartre, Ionesco, seem to have had some effect on the Government. Obviously the more letters and telegrams received by André Malraux, or by the French Embassy (Knightsbridge), or by *Cahiers du Cinéma* (who are centralising the protest movement under the direction of Godard, Renoir, Truffaut, Resnais, and just about everyone you can think of), the more the Government is going to wonder if it hasn't made a mistake.

SOURCE: 'A LANGLOIS UNTO HIMSELF', *GUARDIAN*, 23 FEBRUARY 1968, 8

2.14 WEEKEND IN PARIS

The first question most people asked when I got back from Paris was about the new Godard. And the answer is that his latest film *Week End* is something of a triumph, and that there is another film almost ready to come out. This last was made, like Rossellini's *Louis XIV*, as a co-production between French television and a cinema producer. Its final title is *Le Gai Savoir*, and it has been announced as being inspired by [Jean-Jacques Rousseau's] *Emile*, the famous novel on education by one of Godard's most celebrated compatriots.

Jean-Pierre Léaud plays a character called Emile Rousseau, and the feminine lead is named Patricia Lumumba. What this mixture of Rousseau and Nietzsche (*Le Gai Savoir* is the French title of his *The Gay Science*) will bring we will have to see.

Meanwhile, *Week End*: the film is based almost entirely on a remark Godard made a year or two ago about contemporary French society. People are prostituting themselves all week long, working at jobs they don't like, selling things they don't believe in, and all for what? To be able to buy a car and spend the weekend at the sea. But all they find are blocked highways and traffic jams.

That, basically, is the plot line of the first two thirds of the film: a young middle-class couple set out in their Dauphine – not without having had one of those typical present-day incidents: The Battle of the Scraped Fender – in order to try and wheedle some money out of his mother who lives deep in Normandy. The usual weekend jam on the highways is evoked in a brilliant single shot lasting no less than seventeen minutes, tracking along stalled cars, bloodied victims of car crashes, accompanied by a symphony of klaxons – as well as by background music specially composed for the film by Stockhausen.[12]

When they finally – after an hour of film-time – get to his mother's house, she refuses to give them any money, so he kills her (in counterpoint to shots of a skinned rabbit). On the way back, our couple's picnic is interrupted by a band of Maoist hippies who have taken over the Seine-et-Oise; from this point on the film goes way out (leaving the *Carabiniers* far behind, a model of elegant civilisation even), and our heroine ends up participating in a cannibalistic repast. She has joined the Maoists, and they sup on the leg of an English tourist who has recently passed that way.

Dramatically speaking, it's his most fast-moving and hard-hitting in some time, which might account for its quite successful run. It also stars that idol of French sex films Mireille Darc, here unrecognisably good.

One French product that is cleaning up in Paris and will no doubt do equally well abroad is Michel Deville's *Benjamin*. The French press was ecstatic: 'Entertaining, roguish charm, alluring elegance.' The names of Watteau and Renoir have been trotted out and all seem agreed that this eighteenth-century piece represents Gallic charm, wit, and true *libertinage*.

Well, in a way it does, but it still adds up to very little. As a seventeen-year-old male virgin, Pierre Clémenti (the boy with the gold teeth from *Belle de Jour*) struggles hard, but doesn't make it. He is miscast. Michel Piccoli as an ageing Don Juan and Catherine Deneuve as a clever young girl do much better, and when the kissing has to stop, when the ooh-la-la gives way to the melancholy of satisfied desire, the film gets much better.

Still, *Benjamin* was produced by Mag Bodard, and the money she makes on this will help to pay for what she lost on *Mouchette* and *Deux ou trois choses que je sais d'elle*. It's not a film anyone need be ashamed of, after all, and if it allows new Bressons and new Godards to be made, then why not?

Apart from the Godard, the best films I saw were Jean-Pierre Melville's *Samourai* and Chris Marker's television film on the Rhodiacéta strike.[13] Perhaps the most amazing thing about the latter was that it was shown at all on the heavily Government-dominated television. Marker's great talent in this kind of exposé is his sense of fairness. No slanted shots, no muck-raking, although he does not hide the fact that his sympathies are with the strikers and against the industrial complex.

Beyond that, he seems to know just how long to keep his camera trained on the people he is interviewing. He hangs on way beyond what one would have thought the essential had been said, waiting for the unimportant gestures, the details – the man spreading mustard on his plate. After a worker goes off to the factory, the camera remains on his wife who smiles, somewhat embarrassedly at the camera, and in that moment becomes a real person, not just a striker's wife in a striker's kitchen. How typical, too, of Marker that his 'hero', the strike leader, should be called by the unprepossessing nickname of 'Yoyo.'

Melville's feature is on the opposite side of the form/content spectrum: a highly formalised gangster film. As the title suggests, some of the techniques of the Japanese cinema have been applied to the story of a modern French samurai, a hired killer (played inscrutably by Alain Delon). The story is classic, but ingeniously worked out, and the main interest of the film is aesthetic. A complete change, in fact, from the somewhat sloppily made *Le Deuxième Souffle* which we saw in London last year, and a (for me) welcome return to the style of some of Melville's earlier films – *Les Enfants terribles*, *Bob le Flambeur*.

I wouldn't like to have to choose between the Chris Marker brand of generous, individual cinéma-vérité and the hieratic ingenuities of Melville, but it is a healthy sign for the French cinema that it can contain two such extraordinary and opposite talents.

SOURCE: 'WEEKEND IN PARIS', *GUARDIAN*, 2 APRIL 1968, 8

2.15 THE END OF THE CANNES PARTY

Although the Cannes Festival closed down officially last Sunday at noon, for all I know it may still be going on even now.[14] I left on Wednesday – and what with the strike in France, it's taken me three days to get back to London. But until the moment I left, the festival, though dead, wouldn't lie down. Of course, one had suspected the festival was going to be overtaken by the events, and one didn't have to be much of a prophet to predict that something dire was going to happen. But the actual way in which the festival shut down – and then partially reopened – was totally unexpected.

It all began with the meeting scheduled by Godard, Truffaut, and Resnais for last Saturday morning: it was supposed to be about new developments in the affair of the Cinémathèque, but by that time history had taken over and pushed Langlois into the shade. Resnais never got beyond Dijon, because of the train strike, and Godard began the meeting with a call to all film-makers to withdraw their films from the festival in sympathy with the students and the workers This was quite eagerly taken up, and in less than an hour the whole group had left the Salle Jean Cocteau and taken over the large Festival Auditorium. Speech followed speech, and there was definitely an air of 1917 over the whole proceedings.

After lunch (which was brought in to the sit-down strikers in the form of sandwiches and Coca-Cola – shades of Godard's 'Children of Marx and Coca-Cola') a compromise was reached between the revolutionary committee – which included Claude Lelouch as well – in which it was decided that only the foreign films would be shown and that access to the festival would be free and open to all. This was announced by the director of the festival, Monsieur Robert Favre le Bret, to a cheering audience, and it seemed that that was that. Alas, it was not to be. By later that night, the more intransigent film-makers and agitators decided the festival would have to shut down altogether. Some said that the CGT, the trades union council, had sent orders from Paris: the more paranoid claimed that the whole thing was being managed from Peking. But it soon became clear that the festival really had to close down, since four members of the jury had resigned, and the rest had declared they would not go it alone.

Furthermore, Favre le Bret decided that if the screenings could not take place in an orderly and normal fashion it was better that they not go on at all. And I think he made the only possible decision, given the really frenzied atmosphere obtaining now in France. In fact, he personally came out of the whole situation very well – dignified, reasonable, and brave, he made a good show. Of course, the locals didn't see it that way: they claim he should have called the police (there was not one in sight), should have cut off the electricity, thrown the strikers out. But that would have led only to the kind of bloodshed that has been going on in Paris, and heaven knows how it would all have come out.

However, such was the force of inertia, or the tenacity of the determined that the festival did not stop entirely. The screenings of the *Marché du Film*, the film market which is held outside the festival in town cinemas kept on going for a couple of days at least. All of a sudden the festival was reduced to a kind of mysterious underground affair. Word flew around that this Swedish producer was going to show his film that night, that Chabrol's *Les Biches* would be screened the next day. Finally, a little order was put into the business, and the festival from Monday on was centred round a small bulletin board in the lobby of the Carlton Hotel. No more press releases, no more efforts of vast public relations machines, just the most primitive means of communication: little slips pinned on to a board.

It was a refreshing change, and surprisingly effective.

Actually, Chabrol's *Les Biches* was a delightful reward for all of us who braved threats of anarchy to stay on. However linear its psychology, it nevertheless marks Chabrol's return to the top of his form where he hasn't been, really, since *Les Bonnes Femmes* all those years ago. It is a triangle love story involving a lesbian photographer (Stéphane Audran), an undecided young girl (Jacqueline Sassard), and a seductive architect (Jean-Louis Trintignant). It's due to turn up at the Berlin Film Festival, so more then. (Actually, the two happiest men in Cannes last week were Dr Bauer, director of the Berlin Festival, and Professor Chiarini of Venice: they were quietly going around like discreet vultures grabbing what they could of the films that were not shown in Cannes. But who could blame them?)

The very best film of the festival just got in under the wire last Friday: Milos Forman's *The Firemen's Ball*. Curiously enough, it was the exact opposite of Nemec's *Party and the Guest*: it, too, was an allegory about the Czech situation, but unlike Nemec, Forman knows how to give his first level of discourse a life of its own. In fact, one enjoys the film first of all for its basic story, and only gradually does one become aware of the other possible significances it could have. The setting is a small town: the firemen are giving a ball for one of their retired colleagues. The Flaubertian nastiness of the observation is countered however, with a kind of affection for all these really terrible peasants. The result is that, in spite of its biting humour, it leaves you with a kind of warming sadness. Some people said it was Chaplinesque; they meant this as a compliment but I think from now on one will have to say that it is Formanesque, for with this, his third feature, Forman has imposed himself as a major director.

If Forman was the king of the festival, Harlow was its queen. He/she is the star of an American documentary shown in the critics' week called *The Queen*: its subject is a contest held annually in New York to choose the most beautiful transvestite of the year. It isn't really much as a film, but the material is fascinating, and somehow the presence of Harlow, the winner of the contest, at Cannes made it seem even better than it was. And after all, for the queen of the festival to have been a man was highly fitting, for never has there been a stranger, more surrealistic Cannes festival than this one. Except perhaps for the very first. MGM had sent a luxury liner, George Raft and Norma Shearer danced in the streets of Cannes in a pre-festival party. The only thing wrong was that the festival never actually began, for its starting date was scheduled for September 1, 1939.

SOURCE: 'THE END OF THE CANNES PARTY', *GUARDIAN*, 25 MAY 1968, 7

2.16 MINIMAL CINEMA: CHRONICLE OF ANNA MAGDALENA BACH

Minimal art is much in the news this year, and the recent Knokke Festival Grand Prix winner, *Wavelength*, was, theoretically, an excellent example. Forty minutes (not however without cuts, as most people would have it, and not without certain … minimal changes of angle) moving slowly down a room to the window wall. Then in London in April, we finally saw one of Warhol's minimal films. Not the 12-hour *Empire*, but *Harlot*, a seventy-minute film which consists only – or as nearly as 16mm film magazines will let it – of one shot. Amusingly, Warhol plays with the idea by including a rather rambunctious cat who is the only uncontrolled element in the shot; his (or her) constant efforts to escape out of frame did indeed provide a certain tension, a certain playful attitude towards the problems of minimal cinema.

But it seems to me that Warhol with his aleatory cat will go down in history as the Marcel Duchamp of the post-war period: an artist who has thrown out a steady stream of ideas, who has changed our way of looking at things without being able – or willing – to realise them fully. It is not an unenviable position. However, the important thing about minimal cinema, it seems to me, is that it must be meaningfully minimal. 'Less is more,' Mies van der Rohe told us, but less implies less of *something*. Stripped-down cinema, as in Bresson, implies both that there was something to be stripped down in the first place and, even more important, that when the stripping has to stop, something – however minimal – is left.

So when I say that Jean-Marie Straub's new film (actually, it was co-directed with his wife Danièle Straub-Huillet), *The Chronicle of Anna Magdalena Bach*, lasts ninety minutes and contains scarcely more than a hundred shots (instead of the usual eight hundred to a thousand); that all movement, whether of camera or within the frame, is held to a minimum; and that what one sees consists almost entirely of period-costumed musicians executing selections from the works of J. S. Bach, I do not mean that these facts in themselves suffice to make the film an important achievement.[15] If such were the case, then I would have to call *Harlot* a masterpiece. For all its ground-breaking, it isn't. But Straub's film, I think, is.

To be sure, readers of *Sight & Sound* will know that I have always had a weakness for the film that extends one's idea of the cinema, of what it can do, and what, in fact, it can get away with. But apart from the excitement of cliff-hanging, if one does not believe that there is any such thing as a definable, 'essential' cinema, that rather it is in a perpetual state of becoming, then it is only natural that one should prize those films which go out on a limb. Like, for example, *Gertrud*. Those who judged it by received standards found it talky and slow; it never moved, and certainly, they added self-confidently, the one sure thing about movies is that they must *move*.

True enough, but there is movement and movement. Whole sequences of *Gertrud* consisted of a single shot of two characters sitting on a divan, talking. But in such scenes Dreyer was able to achieve with a smile, a turning of the head, that same exhilaration of movement which other directors can only get from a whole army crossing the Super Panavision Alps. True, one was constantly holding one's breath: would the scene, like Warhol's cat, suddenly slip away from us into boredom? (And this was not the least exciting element of such sequences: let the psychiatrists explain why.)

But Dreyer at least had a story. Those who saw Straub's first film, *Nicht versöhnt* (*Unreconciled*) will remember his diabolical skill in taking a straightforward, if complex, novel and reducing it – abstracting it – into an unchronological series of extremely brief Brechtian/Bressonian tableaux; of bafflingly elliptical moments. *The Chronicle of Anna Magdalena Bach* works the other way round: Straub starts with the tableaux in the first place. In a sense, the construction of the film is very much like that of Bach's *St Matthew Passion*. The story, as it were, is almost entirely confined to the recitative of the Evangelist. But for the most part it is the arias and choruses, the set-pieces, which really provide the drama. Simply and straightforwardly, we are given the information in order to clear the decks for expression of the emotional significance both of what we have been told, and of what we have not.

The St Matthew role of narrator is taken by Anna Magdalena, so the film only covers Bach's last years, from his second marriage in 1721 to his death in 1748. Throughout, performances of music are linked by Anna Magdalena's calm, non-expressive narration, or occasionally by the words of Bach himself. The film begins, for example, in the Music Room of the Prince of Anhalt-Cöthen: Bars 154 to 227 of the Allegro of the 5th Brandenburg Concerto are performed. Then, we cut to 'A Wall and a Clavichord' and Anna Magdalena begins her tale: 'He was a chapel-master, director of the chamber music at the court of Anhalt-Cöthen. My father was a trumpeter at the court … His wife had died a year before; and from their marriage three sons and a daughter survived … For Friedemann, his father had started a little clavier book …' And then we hear the sixth Prelude from Wilhelm Friedemann Bach's Clavier Book.

In this section, the music has been chosen, at least partly, to illustrate the text. At other times, the music is only very tenuously related to the text. Or rather, the other way round. Because the film is not really about Bach, but about the *music* of Bach. Just as it could be said that *Diary of a Country Priest* was not a film about religion, but a film *of* religion, so this film *is* music. Not musical: music. Except in a very special sense, it does not attempt to express the music; rather it lets it express itself. This may sound pleonastically futile; the same was said about Bresson when he had his actor read out loud what we could all see written on the screen.

In somewhat the same way, Straub lets the music speak for itself, and yet the final result is much greater than the music alone could achieve. For just as his cantata-like form achieves drama without plot − through the music − so he has managed to find a way of filming music without 'copying' it, and of achieving action without movement.

On the one hand, the film is shot in an extremely simple manner − any attempt to compete with Bach's architectonics would be doomed to failure. Instead, Straub intensifies the dynamics of the music by positively limiting the visual effects, and this contrast throws into brilliant perspective the complexity of the music. However, the apparent simplicity of his style should not fool us. Each of his thirty-two scenes is cunningly composed; many of them find a kind of imaginative equivalent to the baroque quality of the music by employing certain of the principles of baroque painting − notably what we might call the oppressive diagonal. Many of the sequences … make effective use of the baroque practice of 'dissolving the logic of the plane and giving to space a troubled directional energy, a compulsive and oblique drive.'[16] Thus the diagonal gives its own impression of movement to an essentially static scene. Furthermore, Straub's compositions are often heavily weighted, alternately to the left and to the right, so that when he cuts from one diagonal to another, he achieves a strangely effective sense of motion. Oftentimes within one of the sequences, the camera at a certain point in the tableau will make a kind of lazy arabesque starting from the right and circling down and then up to the left. On other occasions it tracks in, making a new diagonal in opposition to the original set-up.

At Knokke, much was talked about the triumph of the contemplative cinema, of which *Wavelength* was the prime example. And it was true that after staring at that damned room for forty minutes, some rather startling effects occurred. But these effects were almost purely retinal. Straub's film is also a kind of contemplative cinema, but infinitely more important, and certainly more rewarding in that the contemplation is on a far more profound level and results in that sense of exaltation which is after all the surest sign of the presence of great art. 'Music,' wrote Lévi-Strauss, 'is the middle way between logical thought and aesthetic perception … We know that music is a language, since we under-stand what it is saying, but its absolute originality, what distinguishes it from articulated language, is that it is untranslatable.' This could also be said about *The Chronicle of Anna Magdalena Bach*.

SOURCE: 'MINIMAL CINEMA: CHRONICLE OF ANNA MAGDALENA BACH', *SIGHT & SOUND*, 37.3, SUMMER 1968, 134–5

2.17 THE COSSACKS GO IN AT PESARO

Last night the Pesaro International Festival of New Cinema was violently – and perhaps permanently – interrupted by a display of police brutality the like of which I have only seen in films like *Potemkin*. The 'Siege of Pesaro' as the Italians are calling it may be small pota-toes compared with all that has been happening in Paris and Rome, but I don't think it has been equalled anywhere in Western Europe for the disparity between the lack of provo-cation and the monstrousness of the attack.

From the very beginning of the week, the spectre that has been haunting European Film Festivals made its appearance in Pesaro. A misguided attempt on the part of local students – to stop the opening of the festival – was easily coped with, however. It was made quite clear to them that of all festivals Pesaro is the least dominated by industry, the least socialite, the least glamorous. It was, and is, a working festival and one that has been dom-inated by centre-left tendencies. This year, for example, a whole panorama of Cuban films was announced: three have already been shown. The students, convinced, held out for free entrance to the festival: this was accorded, and all began very well with a brilliant Cuban film *Memoirs of Underdevelopment*.

Trouble began yesterday. In the afternoon there was a screening of *The Time of Furnaces*, an effective, if somewhat flashily executed, Argentinian film against neo-colo-nialism. This was followed by a call for a meeting in the town square to express solidarity with the French in their struggle against de Gaulle; actually, the meeting was more a local affair with the festival only taking a marginal part.

It all began peacefully enough. The police – that is to say the Carabinieri – lined up on one side of the Piazza del Popolo, the manifestos on the other, and then a little squabble broke out – some say provoked by the Fascist sympathisers who were spread out along the sides of the square. Valentino Orsini, a youngish mild-mannered film director was arrested. When this became known about 100 people, the most committed among the fes-tivaliers made a sit-down protest in the corner of the square, chanting 'Che Che Che Guevara' etc. Around them were about 1000 onlookers.

Then the police began to move. They started up their 3 jeeps, shifted into first gear, and then waited while a strange ritual took place: a policeman came forward and blew three notes on a trumpet: another meanwhile announced through a loud hailer that the population was 'invited' to disperse. People started to run – and I soon found out why. Apparently once those 3 notes are sounded the police (and, I repeat, it is the *Carabinieri* I am talking about, who take their orders from Rome, not the pleasant local police who depend on the mayor) feel freed from all restraint, and as it turned out from all vestiges of civilisation.

Then the jeeps charged — there is no other word for it — the sit down strikers. They began to run as the jeeps bore down on them: having thus achieved their aim of clearing them off, you would think the police would stop. But no, they began to circle round and round the Piazza, chasing, hunting down anyone they could get at. Bystanders, tourists, journalists, anyone who was there and could not run fast enough was brutally clubbed, or worse still, crushed by the jeeps against the walls.

Then tear gas bombs were thrown. A young woman was clubbed to the ground and while she was lying there, kicked and beaten, the most terrifying thing — apart from the sheer stomach-aching panic of those jeeps on the prowl — was the gratuitous, unprovoked nature of the attack. If the police had not charged, those 100 people would have sung a few more songs and then gone home quietly. But apparently violence was being actively sought. In Paris there was at least the excuse that the students were throwing paving stones or setting up barricades. Here there were just those 100 people sitting down on the pavement like so many boy scouts round a campfire. To attack them was vicious. To go into the film theatre where no one was doing anything, to throw tear gas bombs, and then to club those who tried to escape was, well — Fascist.

Some say that the whole affair was deliberately worked up by the present Government in Rome to embarrass the left-wing mayor and his festival. It may well be. Something has to explain the horror of what happened. Miraculously, no one was killed: about 70 were hurt. This morning 19 people are in jail. In an extraordinary general meeting, all the festival participants agreed not to leave town until their colleagues are released. Other means of protest are being investigated. What the outcome will be, no one knows. But fresh in everyone's mind, and certainly in mine, is that Cossack-like motorised charge. In our happily meliorist civilised island we tend to forget what the rest of the world is all about. If such things can happen in this sleepy Adriatic resort town, what is in store for Europe, for the world, during what looks to be a long hot summer?

SOURCE: 'THE COSSACKS GO IN AT PESARO', *GUARDIAN*, 6 JUNE 1968, 6

2.18 IF WITH NO BUTS

Almost 13 years ago now, the first Free Cinema programme was presented at the National Film Theatre. The films included Lindsay Anderson's *O Dreamland*, Lorenza Mazzetti's *Together*, and *Momma Don't Allow*, co-directed by Tony Richardson and Karel Reisz. From this beginning sprang much of the best in British cinema. But over those years Lindsay Anderson managed to make only one feature film, and even that, *This Sporting Life*, was not as impressive as one might have hoped. And now, after all these years, he has at last made the masterpiece his early promise led us to expect.

For *If* .... (Paramount) is indeed something of a masterpiece, the best British film of the year, and one of the best from, as they say, 'any source.' What is particularly interesting is the way in which it is both like and unlike what one remembers the Free Cinema ideals to have been. In most people's minds Free Cinema meant realistic documentary, non-professional actors, films of social protest. And yet in the film generally considered at the time to be the least important, *Together* (which was, by the way, edited by Mr Anderson), one sees the path which led ultimately to *If* .... for Miss Mazzetti's film, however tiresome it may

If.... (1968)

have seemed, pointed the way to that kind of mingling of reality and fantasy which one finds in *If ....*

But, on the other hand, *If ....* uses professional actors, although they may not always be recognised as such. On the night of the film's premiere, the leading actor, Malcolm McDowell, was annoyed by an old lady who came up to him in the foyer to ask if he were a 'real' actor! ('After all those years I slogged away in rep,' he said.) Of course, the lady was paying both Mr McDowell and Mr Anderson the highest compliment.

Then, too, *If ....* is not naturalistic; this story, written by David Sherwin, of rebellion in a boy's school, is convincing enough (friends who have suffered through public schools have assured me of that), but it goes way past naturalism to find a kind of free-wheeling fantasy which reminded me of Vigo's *Zéro de conduite*. But fantasy need not mean whimsy; as in Eisenstein's *Strike* fantasy – or surrealism, if you will – is used to heighten an explosive exhortation. The final outburst of violence, in which the band of three boys pit themselves against the school, against the Church, against society, in fact, engenders that kind of palm-sweating fervour one hasn't felt in years.

Decades Never Start On Time

For indeed it is rare for a director to be able both to express himself completely and fully in a film and at the same time convincingly to yoke that self-expression to social protest. Perhaps it is because the metaphor Anderson has chosen – a school – is particularly apt both to the state of Britain today and to his own emotional life.

Last of all, Mr Anderson has achieved a properly distancing effect through his use of the episode form, his mingling of black and white with colour photography (both sensitively and powerfully handled by the Czech Miroslav Ondrícek), and the even more important fusion of fantasy with reality. These formal elements not only give a shape to the film but in some paradoxical way serve to heighten the excitement and tension of the film.

Thirteen years is a long time, but it was worth the wait. If only we don't have to wait that long again! Somehow, I don't think we will, for I feel absolutely convinced this film is going to have the success it deserves. If it doesn't, then there's no hope for the British cinema.

SOURCE: 'IF WITH NO BUTS', *GUARDIAN*, 19 DECEMBER 1968, 6

2.19 LE GAI SAVOIR

After he got back from that trip to Damascus, old Saul-called-Paul must have been something of a drag to his old drinking companions. 'What's gotten into him?' one can hear them say, just like most of Godard's admirers who have been bitterly complaining about *Le Gai Savoir* (which although begun in December 1967, was only completed after the apocalyptic Month of May, 1968). And a possible reaction to this film – indeed, it was mine the first time I saw it – was one of nearly total rejection: it just wasn't like the others; one felt almost cheated. Here we had a young couple sitting in a TV studio for an hour and a half: talking, just talking. To be sure, there was the occasional shot of a street, but by and large the film could be seen as a masochistic exercise in which Godard systematically – almost religiously – stripped himself of all his aesthetic trump cards, all his aces. The screen actually goes black for minutes at a time, which is about as self-effacing as you can get.

Of course, another reaction was possible: to try to find in this film those elements which *are* like the earlier work. To examine it as an aesthetic object, picking out the good bits. And there are quite a few. The first image, for example, of the orange-ribbed transparent umbrella, is as beautiful as anything he has ever done. The photography of Jean-Pierre Léaud and Juliette Berto is good enough for a shampoo commercial, so lustrously does it render their hair, shining with mysterious highlights. The Cuban revolutionary hymn with which he ends most of the episodes; the piano sonata which turns up as punctuation; the extraordinary mask effects, now with Léaud's face hidden behind Mademoiselle Berto's, now the opposite, and, most effectively, with her lips synching his words spoken behind her: the remarkable camera movements going from left to right to pick up Léaud, then Mademoiselle Berto, and in the same shot, Léaud again. The list is, if not inexhaustible, then at least long; her yellow gown with its purple peignoir, seen against the figures of Batman and two other comic strip heroes; the nearly invisible construction of what looks to be a formless film.

But such an appreciation would run totally counter to Godard's intentions. He did not want to make an 'aesthetic object': the 'work of art' is all too easily assimilated by the very society it is attacking. The work of art can be isolated, defused, reabsorbed by society.

He has not totally avoided this danger, but from the disastrous reactions at Berlin, at least, he came pretty close.

The most intelligent way of approaching the film would seem to be to take it *sui generis*: given Godard's career, and *assuming* he has not completely cracked up, what did he think he was up to?

Godard always was a critic as well as a film-maker, so one should be neither surprised nor upset if *Le Gai Savoir* is something of an essay; a pamphlet, even. One could say that he should in fact have *written* a pamphlet. But this would be fatally to misunderstand his new position. Film must be made for that enormous portion of the globe (60%, some say) that is illiterate. He is too clear-headed to think that *this* film is for the Cambodian coolie or the Peruvian peon; and his final disclaimer is neither false modesty nor masochistic self-beratement. When he says, 'This film didn't want, couldn't want, to try to explain the cinema, nor even constitute its object. More modestly it tries to give several effective means of so doing. This is not the film that should be made, but rather it shows that, if one has a film to make, one would necessarily pass by some of the paths trodden here.'

But film is valuable not only for illiterates: it can *show* what is being hidden. It is both practical and theoretical. It's more fun, says Godard, than an equation or a blackboard demonstration. Accepting this, we must now examine what this blackboard demonstration is about, what this equation stands for. Originally the commission from the French television network was for a film about education, and *Le Gai Savoir* was announced as being a modern version of Rousseau's *Emile*. But it turned out otherwise: the film is really about language.

The recently rediscovered writings of the German critic Walter Benjamin shed much light on Godard's development, not as a film-maker, but as a critic who uses film instead of paper. Benjamin's great unfinished work (*Paris, Capital of the 19th Century*) was to have been a study of the complex links between economic evolution and cultural facts. Benjamin, before his untimely death in 1940, began to feel certain that this was in fact the essential task of the critic. Like Godard, he was prey to more and more frequent psychological depressions, and this, combined with the growing Fascist threat, brought Benjamin's work to an ever more exacerbated state. Like the flame between two carbon arcs, he was stretched, almost to breaking point, between Marxist politics and the metaphysics of language. 'The most worn-out Communist platitude,' he wrote, 'means more than the most profound bourgeois thought, because the latter has only one true sense, that of apology.'

Godard has always been as sensitive to cultural climates as the most intellectual barometer, so I doubt whether the comparison with Benjamin is fortuitous; equally important is the whole recent French interest in linguistics, and, most recently, in the American writer Noam Chomsky, whom Godard actually cites in *Le Gai Savoir*.

This does not mean that Godard has pored over the works of Benjamin or Chomsky; he doesn't have to. He is like the bookstore employee he talks about in *Le Gai Savoir*, who over the years had had just two or three seconds between the time he took the books from the customer and the time he wrapped them up to glance at their contents: over the past thirty years he has educated himself, beginning with the alphabet and the multiplication tables. Now, says Godard, he is launching into Faulkner and Chomsky. It would appear that Godard has a magpie talent for picking up a book, mechanically leafing through it, and maddeningly coming up each time with its essence.

From his leafings through Chomsky and the other linguistic philosophers, he has reached the conclusion that language is the key to our problems: it is the enemy. As Juliette Berto says at the beginning of *Le Gai Savoir:* 'I want to learn, to teach myself, everyone, to turn back against the enemy that weapon with which it attacks us: language.'

'Yes,' replies Léaud, 'we have to start again from zero'. 'No,' she answers, 'before starting again, we have to go *back* to zero', and going back means disintegrating man and his language. Thus also Chomsky: 'The renewal of the study of language should lead to a liberation from all our behaviouristic conditioning, and should ultimately lead to a political criticism of our alienation.' All thought has been consciously or unconsciously bound up with the conditioning of bourgeois society of the past hundreds of years; it takes a great effort to look at everything afresh, questioningly, and *Le Gai Savoir* is an attempt at this most arduous of intellectual exercises.

However, it has to be admitted that often the effort proves too great, and Godard spills over the edge of common sense into intellectual dishonesty. To the unsympathetic, much of the dialogue will sound like naive gibberish; on the other hand, it is not easy to divest oneself of the preconceived ideas of a lifetime; and Godard must be allowed something for having made the effort.

He has, in a sense, left the film unfinished. The sequence of Juliette Berto's song he assigns to Bertolucci to do; the analysis of an 'honourable family' is willed to Straub, etc. Although Godard might not like it (he isn't too partial to Bach) one might usefully compare *Le Gai Savoir* to *The Art of Fugue*. Both are didactic, methodical; both unfinished; both have little overt emotional subject matter; both are grandiosely simple in means; finally, both have their boring moments. If this is to be the cinema of the future, God help us. And yet, it seems to me certain to exercise a profound influence on younger film-makers. Just as Bach's audience dwindled to nothing in the early 19th century (*The Art of Fugue* was actually given its first performance only in the 1920s), but continued to have a great influence on the composers of the period, so *Le Gai Savoir* will never be a popular film, but it might well turn out to be an extremely important one.

SOURCE: '*LE GAI SAVOIR*', *SIGHT & SOUND*, 38.4, AUTUMN 1969, 210–11

Notes

1. For some background to the setting up of the NYFF, see Raymond J. Haberski, 'The first New York Film Festival and the heroic age of moviegoing', *It's Only a Movie! Films and Critics in American Movie Culture* (Lexington: University of Kentucky Press, 2001), 144–64. For Roud's assessment of the second NYFF, see 'New York Film Festival', *Guardian*, 5 October 1964, 7.
2. The *Guardian* text is not entirely clear here: the last two words of the sentence appear to be 'the best' but the sense of the phrase is somewhat vague.
3. We have cut a couple of short paragraphs about other films out that week.
4. Roud's note: Antonioni denies this in part: he maintains that Corrado's meeting with Giuliana unhinges him; perhaps because of the inadequacy of Richard Harris in the role, this is never visible.
5. Roud's note: True, there is the worker at Medicina who was in Giuliana's clinic, but he remains a shadowy symbol, rather than a character, expressly put in to show that workers can be neurotic too. In any case, when we see him he is happily back at work, and only his wife displays neurotic tendencies.

6. Roud's note: This is neither his nor her fault: it would seem that the only way he can get a film set up is with the commercial guarantee of the presence of Miss Vitti.
7. Allusion to Samuel Johnson's celebrated description of English seventeenth-century 'metaphysical' poetry (exemplified by John Donne), in which 'the most heterogeneous ideas are yoked by violence together'.
8. The hotel is, in fact, the Hôtel Scribe. The Continental was a military court, not the home of the Gestapo.
9. We have cut the short final paragraph about a Laurel and Hardy compilation film out that week.
10. The 'Critics Week' is a parallel section of the Cannes Film Festival, established in 1962 in order to promote the representation of up-and-coming or less well-known film-makers at the festival. The survey to which Roud refers is 'Notre enquête sur la critique', *Cahiers du Cinéma*, 15, September, 1952, 33–50.
11. On 2 November 1965, Norman Morrison (1939–65) set fire to himself outside Secretary of Defense Robert McNamaras's office, in protest against the USA's military presence in Vietnam.
12. Music by German composer Karlheinz Stockhausen (1928–2007) was used in *La Chinoise* (1967); we are not aware, however, that Stockhausen composed music especially for *Week End*.
13. Chris Marker and Mario Marret's *À bientôt, j'espère* (1967); the strike that took place in the Rhodiacéta textile factory in Besançon, France, February–March 1967.
14. Roud's first *Guardian* report from Cannes on 14 May 1968 had begun with the sentence: 'It looks as if it's going to be a nice festival, interesting, calm, and not terribly exciting.'
15. Roud's note: Cf. Alain Resnais: 'I won't admit that the image counts most; why not the other way around? It all depends on the subject, but a film which consisted entirely of a sound-track with nothing in the frame would still be a film as long as the rhythm of the splices was in harmony with the rhythm of the words or the music.'
16. Roud's note: Wylie Sypher, *Four Stages of Renaissance Style* (New York: Doubleday, 1955).

PART 3 1970–6

3.1 THE VARIETIES OF TYRANNY

Many years ago, Claude Chabrol wrote an article for *Les Cahiers du Cinéma* which demonstrated that 'important' subjects generally made unimportant films and vice versa. The truth of this assertion has once more been confirmed by Costa Gavras's new film *L'Aveu* as well as by Chabrol's own latest work *Le Boucher*. The Gavras film has been a tremendous hit in Paris, and indeed, for the first time within living memory, reviews of the film were given front-page prominence. The Chabrol was also a great success, but not in quite the same breathless way.

L'Aveu, based on the book by Artur London, tells the story of the author's imprisonment for Titoist-Trotskyism or some other form of revisionism in Prague during the fifties, his subsequent trial, confession, and his ultimate release and rehabilitation. It aroused great interest in France because it is a criticism of the Communist world from within: London has not 'gone over to the other side,' or at least he hadn't when the book was written.

The film ends with London's triumphant return to Prague in the summer of 1968, to supervise the official publication of his book by the Czech Writers' Committee. In one of those improbable ironies of history, he arrived the day the Russians invaded.

Here, surely, was an important subject, and as if in tribute to its seriousness, Gavras has abjured the facile melodramatics of *Z*, and tried to make a Bressonian film. The result is even worse than *Z* because it is more ambitious. But the film also fails because Gavras is more than a little opportunistic, and wants to have it both ways; he has hedged his bets by casting Yves Montand as London, and Simone Signoret as London 's wife. It is very difficult to make films about living personages with well-known actors, and by casting Montand alongside his real wife, the spectator is never for a moment allowed to forget the artifice of the situation.

My neighbour murmured appreciatively, half way through one of the torture scenes, 'Montand certainly earned his money on this one,' and this reaction, though trivial, is inescapable. Furthermore, although the subject may sound fascinating, Gavras is incapable of achieving the one thing that would have made it really interesting – he has failed to get inside the character. Instead, he gives us a Jewish Red Riding Hood surrounded by evil wolves – and to make sure we know they're wolves, they wear funny broad-rimmed hats.

Occasionally, there is a telling stroke, like London's meeting years later with his chief tormentor (now also expelled from the Party) who perplexedly asks him if he has ever been able to make out what it was all about. But then Gavras and his scriptwriter Jorge Semprun ruin it by driving the point into the ground.

Le Boucher, on the other hand, has a plot so 'unimportant' that it could be classed as a straight thriller. In a small town in the Périgord, a sadistic murderer has killed several women. The local schoolteacher (Stéphane Audran) begins to suspect that the killer is her friendly neighbourhood butcher (Jean Yanne). Her surmise is correct, but instead of killing her, he kills himself: end of film.

Knowing Chabrol's great esteem for Hitchcock, one might think the film sounds like a Hitchcockian pastiche. But unlike Truffaut, whose attempts at imitating Hitchcock are unsuccessful because he neither retains his own qualities, nor attains those of the master, Chabrol is here successful because he is able to bring to a Hitchcockian subject that humanity one generally associates with Truffaut.

For the first time in his career, almost, Chabrol has managed to present rounded characters with whom one is in full sympathy, and that goes for the sadistic butcher, too. Even in Hitchcock one rarely cares much about the characters; they are simply convenient ciphers with whom an audience can identify. Here in *The Butcher* Chabrol has painted a picture of the town and of his two leading characters that is almost Balzacian in its attention to detail and its effectiveness. It is significant that he has not used his usual regular scriptwriter, Paul Gégauff; as a result, the more nerve-wrackingly cute conceits are absent from the film. And perhaps because Chabrol himself wrote the script and dialogue, he has been able to get still better performances from both Mademoiselle Audran and Yanne than in their previous films with him: Yanne, in a sympathetic role, has really surpassed himself, and moved up into the pre-war Gabin class.

Chabrol has moved up, too. I know there are some enthusiasts who have always claimed him as a truly great director. Maybe they were right, and I was just slow. I would prefer to think that they mistook the potential for the actual. In any case, with *Le Boucher*, he seems to me to have entered on the major phase of his career. His brutalised ex-army butcher tells us more about the nature of tyranny than all the discussions of *L'Aveu* because, however limited its subject, *Le Boucher* is precise where the other is vague, because all the beautifully managed accumulation of significant detail builds up effortlessly to the concrete solidity of a sculpturally realised whole.

SOURCE: 'THE VARIETIES OF TYRANNY', *GUARDIAN*, 4 JULY 1970, 8

3.2 FILMS TO CHANGE THE WORLD?

Whether we like it or not (and many don't), it seems that the political film is here to stay. Looking over the films I have seen this year, I find this conclusion inescapable. But even more important than the numbers of political films is the fact that we are now obliged to look at films differently in the light of politics. Back to the thirties, some would say.

But there is a difference – there always is. Just the other day, Jean Renoir was heard complaining – somewhat petulantly – of the uselessness of committed film. 'I made *La Grande Illusion*,' he said, 'in 1938. Now there was a film almost universally recognised as one of the most powerful anti-war films ever made. And what happened? A year later war broke out.'

W. H. Auden has been complaining of the same thing. 'I got a reputation,' he has said, 'as a poet in the thirties, but none of the changes I was aiming at came true. In the end, my poems didn't save one Jew from the gas chambers. Ever since I've been very suspicious of politically committed writing. By all means, let a poet, if he wants to, write engaged poems, protesting against this or that political evil or social injustice. But let him remember this. The only person who will benefit from them is himself; they will enhance his literary reputation among those who feel as he does. The evil or injustice, however, will remain exactly what it would have been if he had kept his mouth shut.'

Let us grant for the sake of argument that these two distinguished artists are right. But does it matter? Both Auden's and Renoir's responses seem to imply that they had some choice in the matter. Surely, Renoir must have made *La Grande Illusion* because that was how he felt about war; surely Auden must have written his poems of the thirties because they arose out of his personal, and therefore unavoidable reactions to what was going on in Spain and Germany. To complain that they did no good is foolish; surely the artist writes (or films) what he wants to, what he *has* to. If his work has no practical results, too bad.

The writers and film-makers of today have achieved a more sophisticated attitude towards the problem. An artist is not, cannot be, on the one hand a man who creates poems, pictures or films, and on the other, a taxpayer, voter and political animal. That way schizophrenia lies.

It is true that the relationship between art and politics has always been complex. Both Léger and Matisse, for example, were members of the French Communist party. While one can see something of this in Léger's later paintings, it is hard to distinguish any overt political comment in those of Matisse. And yet one could say that although Matisse's political views were not directly expressed in his works, there could be a relationship, however covert, between the life-affirming joyousness of his paintings and his social creed. 'Each true work of art,' wrote von Hofmannsthal, 'is the blueprint for the only temple on earth.'

But in the cinema, a more direct confrontation of art and politics cannot easily be avoided. For even if a film has nothing whatsoever to do with contemporary problems, that too is a kind of political statement. As Sartre explained twenty-five years ago, doing nothing is also doing something. Some film-makers feel the need of distance. In his *Othon*, Jean-Marie Straub has gone all the way back to ancient Rome – or at least to Corneille's seventeenth-century version of it – to say something pertinent about the power struggle in the antechambers of government. In his *The Inheritors*, the Brazilian director Carlos Diegues has gone back 40 years to give us a panorama of Brazilian life which perhaps tells us more about contemporary Brazil than a more directly political film could. The Italian director, Bernardo Bertolucci, has, in both the films I wrote about from Rome this winter (*The Spider's Stratagem*), and the one from Berlin (*The Conformist*) returned to the Fascist Italy of the thirties: for many artists, contemporary reality just, in Henry James's useful phrase, 'won't compose.'

On the other hand, there are many film-makers who prefer to tackle contemporary problems head on. I have written about some of them during the year – Godard's *Wind from the East* and Marin Karmitz's *Comrades*, and here in New York I saw another remarkable one, *Street Scenes 1970*.[1] A group effort, it was made by the New York University Cinetracts Collective, and is first of all an attempt to tell us what the media forgot to about the demonstrations on Wall Street and in Washington this spring. In form, it is our old friend, cinéma vérité, but its distinction is that although its makers very clearly are committed to a point of view, they are neither blinkered nor unfair: even those whose opinions are least sympathetic to them come out as recognisable human beings.

By tackling social and political problems head on, they may – or may not – have made a more successful, a more useful film than those artists who have taken a more oblique approach. But the point, I think, is that all these directors have made the kind of films they felt they had to make. And whether the film has any direct social effect is almost irrelevant – irrelevant because this would imply that they could have done something else, that the work had no internal necessity.

Maybe their films will not change the world; maybe they will. The point is that in the cinema, at least, one is likely to get better films from whole men than from splintered ones.

SOURCE: 'FILMS TO CHANGE THE WORLD?', *GUARDIAN*, 26 OCTOBER 1970, 8

3.3 FATHERS AND SONS

It appears to be characteristic of the relationship between father and son that the father should excite in the son both feelings of admiration, love and loyalty, and also impulses of anger, jealousy and self-assertion. The more the son learns to 'idolise' his father, developing … the 'conscience of the sentiment', so that any muttering of jealousy or hostile criticism is suppressed as disloyal, the more acute will become the tension of the inner attitude. It is such an attitude that can find relief in imaginative activity wherein both the love and the repressed hostility have play. (Maud Bodkin, *Archetypal Patterns in Poetry*, London, Oxford University Press, 1934)

Bernardo Bertolucci has described *The Spider's Strategy*, one of the two films he completed in 1970, as 'a sort of psychoanalytical therapy, a journey through the realm of pre-conscious memory.' But even without this hint, and without the knowledge of Bertolucci's recent interest in and exploration of psychoanalysis, it would be evident that both *The Spider's Strategy* and *The Conformist* are linked by more than their 1930s settings and their concern with the problem of Fascism.[2] […]

Bertolucci was born in 1941, so that both *The Spider's Strategy* and *The Conformist* are concerned with a period he never knew. One's most intimate acquaintance with the past comes precisely from one's family, in his case from his father. It would be much too pat – and not very interesting – if Bertolucci's own father had been a Fascist. In fact, he was very much not. But Bertolucci's relationship with his father, as expressed in these two films, is interesting in so far as it is not a case of a simple or obvious rejection. In fact, he and his father were and are very close, so that it becomes more a question of an essential affirmation of identity: the specific problem of being the son of an intellectual. 'The more the son learns to idolise his father … the more acute will become the tension of the inner attitude …'

In *The Spider's Strategy*, the father ultimately triumphs: not only does he impose his will on his son, he also reduces that son to being just that – not a man, simply the son of his father. The relationships of the central character in *The Conformist* with his father, and with the various father-figures that dot the film, are still more complex; but they contribute to a better understanding of this subterranean theme which flows so importantly through both pictures, and which was already more obscurely present in Bertolucci's earlier films.

The Conformist, however, is a much more complex work, for in it Bertolucci has settled for nothing less than a re-creation of the world of the Fascist 1930s: all Rome is his stage, and it is peopled by a large and diverse cast. Until now, his films have been intimate in scale and scope; here he gives us an almost Balzacian portrait of a dying civilisation.

Il conformista (1970)

While Trintignant's interpretation of the conformist is brilliant – only a slightly twisted smile and a tight-hipped scamper betray his plausibly charming exterior – this is not a one-character film. The petit-bourgeois world is exemplified in his fiancée's apartment, an interpretation, not a copy of a 1930s décor: its venetian blinds casting jazzy patterns on the wall and its gramophone scratching out nostalgic tangos are the expression of the life that is lived within these art-deco walls. And when, ten years later, we find the conformist Marcello and his wife installed therein, the difference in the state of the flat tells us what has happened in the intervening period: the war, and the toppling not only of the regime, but of a world.

Bertolucci has always attempted to relate psychological problems to a social context, but this film is more successful than either *Before the Revolution* or *Partner* in achieving this integration of Freud and Marx, partly because the relationship between Bertolucci and his hero is less direct, partly because his canvas is broader, more dramatic. The earlier films had their set-pieces, but the Communist picnic or the opera premiere in *Before the Revolution* had little *dramatic* relevance: their importance was thematic. In this film, every sequence, every lyrical flourish – the blind people's ball and the Parisian dance-hall; the sleeping-car honeymoon and the murderous car chase; the radio station and the Chinese restaurant – is both spectacular and significant. Story line and psychological undercurrents at last come electrifyingly together.

Like *The Spider's Strategy*, *The Conformist* is an adaptation of a pre-existing literary work. But Bertolucci has cut a good many elements from Moravia's novel, and added more; and once again, it is in these suppressions and additions that one looks for the most reliable evidence of the film's deeper significance. Both novel and film tell somewhat the same story: a young boy is the object of a homosexual assault, which he escapes only by shooting his assailant. The result of this adolescent incident is to imbue the boy with an overpowering thirst for normality. When Marcello (Jean-Louis Trintignant) grows up, he joins the Fascist party, and is so desirous of total identification with the establishment that he even volunteers for counter-intelligence work. His first assignment is to go to Paris to make contact with Quadri, his old university tutor, now an anti-Fascist leader in exile. Meanwhile, he has coolly decided to marry a nice middle-class girl (Stefania Sandrelli) who is 'good in bed, good in the kitchen'. Their honeymoon will serve as cover for his mission to Paris. By the time they get there, however, his orders have been changed: Quadri is to be killed.

After the mission is accomplished, Marcello and Giulia return to Rome. The last section of both film and novel takes place on the day Mussolini is deposed, the day when Marcello discovers that Lino, the man he thought he had killed all those years ago, is actually still alive. Suddenly his guilt over the murder (if not of having somehow 'provoked' the homosexual assault) seems to vanish, leaving a great void in his life. In the novel, he and his wife and child are killed by enemy aircraft on the following day as they take refuge in the country. The end of the film is quite different, but this is only one of the key changes Bertolucci has made.

First of all, the book tells the story chronologically; whereas Bertolucci has chosen to frame most of it in the sequence of the murder of Quadri and his wife. Significantly these flashbacks leave out almost all of Marcello's early life. Moravia had provided a somewhat old-fashioned 'psychological case-history' to establish basic aggressions and fears; we first meet young Marcello killing lizards. We see much more of his relationship to his father and we are even treated to a Freudian chestnut: Marcello stumbles upon the 'primal scene' – he sees his parents having sexual intercourse.

Moravia fully paints Marcello's schooldays as one long torture: the other boys find him effeminate, and even try to beat him up and tie a petticoat on him. Further, Moravia establishes the father's incipient madness, preparing us for Marcello's visit to his father in an insane asylum just before his own wedding.

In contrast, Bertolucci shows only the attempted seduction of Marcello by the chauffeur Lino; and this comes some twenty minutes into the film as part of Marcello's pre-marital confession and absolution. A few other elements are omitted from the film (a second homosexual pick-up attempt in Paris); but as in *The Spider's Strategy*, Bertolucci's additions are generally more significant. Most important, he has invented a new character, Italo, who serves as a confidant for Marcello but also plays the more telling role of one among three father-figures. It is he, we are led to believe, who has introduced Marcello to the doctrines of Fascism, and secured his entree into the upper echelons of the government. Significantly, Italo is blind – like the real father who is mad, and the ex-tutor who is stunted and short-sighted.

Another minor but not insignificant change is in the treatment of Marcello's mother's lover, the chauffeur Alberi. In the book, Marcello is content simply to express his jealous dislike of the man; in the film, he has him thrown out of the house, and probably expelled from the country. Another change: in the novel Marcello's father is incapable of any communication; in the film, Marcello has a very unpleasant scene with him in the asylum. The father, presumably an ex-soldier, is taunted by Marcello about the 'punitive expeditions' in which he had been involved: 'Did you use clubs on them, or just castor oil; did you torture them?'

Finally, 'Did you actually kill?' The father refuses to answer, and growing more and more upset grabs hold of a straitjacket and folds his arms into it himself – asking, as it were, to be restrained. The gesture is moving, but it also reminds one of the way in which Marcello always holds himself: legs close together, even while walking or running, always restraining himself. Marcello's sadistic torturing of his impotent father is perhaps self-torture: he himself has engaged on a career which will lead to torture and murder. It is also an indication of how Marcello may eventually end up, and a telling exposition of the unbearable load of conflicting desires.

The two major changes, apart from the introduction of Italo, come towards the end of the story. In the novel, Marcello's mission is only to identify Quadri to an underling; he himself is to have no part in the killing. In the film, although he is accompanied (indeed chauffeured) by his assistant Manganiello, he is supposed to perform the act himself. When the time comes, however, he is seen to be incapable of action – paralysed, impotent. And just as he got Manganiello to dispose of his mother's lover, so it is Manganiello who actually kills Quadri and his wife. It is as if Marcello's shooting of Lino has rendered him forever incapable of action.

The novel ends, as I have said, with death in an air attack. In the film, Marcello discovers the still living Lino in a Coliseum crowded with squatters and refugees, one of whom Lino is trying to seduce. Marcello's rage when he accuses Lino of Quadri's murder frightens the chauffeur away, and Marcello is left with the handsome young Roman Lino had been trying so hard to seduce. The boy starts to strip down for the night; Marcello, fascinated, stands watching. In the last shot of the film, his glance fixed on the boy's naked body, he blinks. The implication is that the discovery that he had not killed Lino after all, coupled with the shock of the end of Fascism, of his career, have so shaken him that he is at last able to face what has probably always been his true nature. And this ending, along with the other changes, gives a meaning to the film which is quite different from that of the novel.

In a sense, Bertolucci's *Conformist* can be taken as his attempt to overthrow authority in all its forms. There is Marcello's true father reduced to an insane asylum; which, significantly, resembles in its architecture and accessories, and the way they are filmed, both the Fascist Ministry we have seen earlier and the Fascist headquarters in the brothel we are shortly to see. And just as his 'replacement', the mother's chauffeur, is ignominiously sent packing, so Marcello's aggressive taunting of his father is equivalent to a total rejection.

Secondly, there is the father-figure, Italo. In the climactic last scene on the day of defeat, Marcello runs into him in the streets of Rome. And the blind Italo has never, as it were, been blinder. As they walk across the Sant' Angelo bridge, all the trappings of dictatorship – the enormous busts of Mussolini, the larger-than-life imperial eagles – that we saw in the Ministry scenes are being unceremoniously dumped into the Tiber. They walk on through the streets to the Coliseum, where the encounter with Lino will take place, preceded by throngs of marching people singing the Red Flag, the Internationale, *Fratelli d'Italia*. When Marcello discovers that Lino is not dead, he turns on him; but he also tries to transfer his burden of guilt to Italo. He denounces him to the crowd not only as a Fascist, but as an assassin, as a homosexual. It was Italo who had first expounded the doctrine of normality to Marcello, and the irony inherent in a blind man praising normality was pointed in a scene in which Italo claimed never to be mistaken in detecting normality or its opposite. As he says these words, the camera slyly moves down to show us that the man who never makes a mistake has on shoes of different colours.

Logically enough, we find that the impotent fathers are doubled in *The Conformist* by the aggressive chauffeurs. The homosexual Lino is a chauffeur by trade, and his picking up the young Marcello and taking him for a ride sets a certain pattern. Manganiello, Marcello's supposed subordinate, also acts twice as chauffeur, 'picking him up' as he makes for his mother's home, and more importantly, driving him to the scene of the assassination. Bertolucci links the two episodes by cross-cutting Marcello's attempts to be let out of the car (cf. *Spider's Strategy*, when both father and son want to be let out), both in the frame story of the ride to the assassination and in the ride with Lino which will end with Marcello shooting the chauffeur. The passivity of the back seat role (cf. also *Partner* where there is a similar situation), the sense of being 'driven' by someone older, is not unrelated to Marcello's sense that he is not his own master. And even while he is physically guiding the blind Italo in the early scenes, he is actually being *led*, psychologically and philosophically, by Italo − the blind leading the blind, as it were.

The theme of blindness also occurs in the episodes devoted to the short-sighted Quadri, with his shuttered flat in which he reminds Marcello of Plato's myth of the cave. While Marcello is being driven to his fatal rendezvous, he tells his chauffeur of a strange dream he has had. He has gone blind, and he goes to Switzerland for an operation; it is Quadri who conducts the operation, and the result is successful: he can see again. So we have the true father insane, Italo blind, but the myopic Quadri as the man who could restore Marcello's sight. The reference to Switzerland is somewhat curious, especially when one bears in mind that the address given for Quadri in Paris, as well as his telephone number, are the actual address and number of none other than Jean-Luc Godard. Hardly a coincidence, of course, especially when one remembers that Quadri's wife was originally to have been played by Anne Wiazemsky.

What is the significance of this detail? Is it simply a private joke, a pun? I think not, although obviously whatever significance it has is bound to be lost on 99 per cent of the film's audience. Nevertheless let us consider: Godard and Bertolucci have been very close friends and Bertolucci has certainly been influenced by Godard. Since the events of 1968, however, their friendship has diminished as Bertolucci's political evolution ceased to parallel Godard's. We also know that since Bertolucci signed to make *The Conformist* for 'the enemy' (actually for Paramount), he has had no further communication with Godard. It is also true that both this film and *The Spider's Strategy* mark an almost total liberation from the Godard influence. By equating Quadri with Godard, Bertolucci is perhaps establishing once and for all their separation − one that was forced upon him by Godard's rejection, but which is none the less real and perhaps definitive.

Bertolucci's sense of spectacle as well as of decoration has always been more instinctive than that of Godard, but in *Partner* one got the feeling that he was not giving it its head, that he was purposely depriving himself of what he did best − as, indeed, he had to, given the subject of that film. Here in *The Conformist* he lets rip; one sequence after another is breathtaking in its spectacular virtuosity. I have already mentioned the scenes in the Ministry, the insane asylum, and the brothel; the other great set-piece is the *guinguette* at Joinville, beginning with the suggestive tango of the two girls (Sandrelli and Dominique Sanda), and culminating with a snake-like farandole around, through, inside and out with the crowd of dancers exploding with the sheer joy of movement.

But even simple scenes are brilliantly conceived, like that early one in the radio station with the Andrews-sister team followed by Italo's propaganda speech. Bertolucci shoots this in such a way that we see neither the speaking Italo nor the watching Marcello; rather both of them are reflected on the glass wall which separates them. The resulting spatial

Decades Never Start On Time

ambiguity is not only handsome in itself but, like Quadri's recounting of Plato's cave myth, tells us something about both men and the regime they serve. The already famous still of Marcello, flowers in hand, walking past the great marble monument inscribed with thousands of names, is even more impressive in the film, since it consists actually of three shots, each taken from a widely different angle, but all contrasting this tiny, almost ludicrous figure with the enormous slab which symbolises the cause he supports. The discrepancy between the two, the massive weight soon to crush Marcello, is yet another example of Bertolucci's ability to sum up in one telling image.

There may be something masochistic about Bertolucci's identification – in this particular instance – of himself with Marcello and of Godard with Quadri; but the important thing is not the very limited similarity of the two, but the act itself. If one can forget for a moment the *character* of Marcello, one can see in his story a metaphor of Bertolucci's liberation from the past; and one can even see in Marcello's final self-revelation a symbol of Bertolucci's separation from his father and from all the father-substitutes. In this context, it is not without significance that his next film is to be a love story between a man and woman who are roughly contemporaries. This may not sound very striking: 75 per cent of all films are about exactly that. But not Bertolucci's. Leaving out the first film, with its story by Pasolini (another father-figure, by the way), and which in any case has no protagonist, the Bertolucci heroes have been involved with women much older than themselves (*Before the Revolution*, *The Spider's Strategy*), or narcissistically with their own double (*Partner*). Even in *The Conformist* Marcello's relations with his wife could hardly be called passionate. So this mass disposal of father-figures is a very important step in Bertolucci's career.

Another interpretation is of course possible: one could say that the new direction Bertolucci has taken corresponds to Fabrizio's betrayal of the revolution – that, objectively, Bertolucci like him is simply rejoining the ranks of the bourgeoisie. You could say that if you were an old-line Marxist aesthetician; but results are what count, and these last two films are so much more successful in their own terms than *Partner* that one is allowed to doubt the correctness of such a hidebound judgment. Just as Straub has declared his inability to make 'instant history', to make films about current events, so Bertolucci has tacitly acknowledged where his abilities lie. Having now swept away the past, having in effect filmed his Declaration of Independence, he has before him a clean slate; and one can hardly wait to see what he is going to write on it.

SOURCE: 'FATHERS AND SONS', *SIGHT & SOUND*, 40.2, SPRING 1971, 60–4

3.4 LOOK BACK IN SHAME

Like the Louis Malle film [*Le Souffle au coeur*] I wrote about a few days ago, *Le Chagrin et la pitié* (*The Sorrow and the Pity*) is also an historical film, but it is set back in the dark days of the Occupation. This is a very touchy subject in France – so dangerous in fact that there has not been a film in the past 25 years that dared to suggest that all France had not been behind de Gaulle from the very beginning. Further proof that the French are not ready for a dispassionate account of those terrible years is the fact that *The Sorrow and the Pity* – a film made for television, and which indeed has been seen on German and

Swiss stations – cannot be shown on French television. And that decision came straight from the Prime Minister. In fact, it was only because the new Minister of Culture wanted to inaugurate his regime with a gesture of liberality that this film, made two years ago, can now be seen at all.

Significantly, the only theatre that agreed to show it is a Latin Quarter cinema with 200 seats. But those seats are full – all the time, and the queues begin at 10 o'clock in the morning. The reason for the morning shows is that the film, directed by Marcel (son of Max) Ophüls runs for nearly four and a half hours: two television shows of a little more than two hours each.

Four hours is a long time – especially for a smoker – but I was still there at the end. For *The Sorrow and the Pity* is not 'just' a documentary – it is also a film beautifully structured and powerfully edited. It has, of course, a point of view, but it never ridicules or anathematises those who held different views. The great miracle of the film is that Ophüls and his associates, André Harris and Alain de Sedouy, managed to get everyone to talk. Everyone from Anthony Eden to Pierre Mendès-France, from General Spears to Laval's son-in-law, from Georges Bidault to the German General Warlimont.

In order to give as complete and as accurate a picture as possible of those years, Ophüls and his associates interviewed dozens of people, shot hours of film; and then from this mass of material he built up his film. Much of it is hard to believe.

The professional cyclist who says he never noticed any Germans in Clermont-Ferrand during the Occupation – followed by a few photos of the town square crawling with German soldiers. The English secret agent who tells us that, being homosexual, he unfortunately fell in love with a German officer in Paris during these years; that he lived with him for seven months, without betraying either his country or his lover; only then did the strain begin to get too much for him and he asked to be recalled to London. The French films of the thirties which were shown in revival but with the names of all Jewish actors or technicians blacked out in the credits. The French girls who steered clear of German soldiers during the day, but who worked willingly by night in soldiers' brothels.

I suppose the most extraordinary single thing in the film is the series of interviews with Christian de la Mazière, one of the 300 survivors of the 12,000 Frenchmen who enlisted in the French division of the Waffen SS – his explanation of the climate of the period, the feeling of many of his contemporaries that the defeat of France was a judgment rendered by God, and that in order for the country to rise again, they had to go through the humiliation of Occupation. And that the fastest way to get through it was to service one's penance by fighting for the Germans. This kind of thinking seems incredible today, but it does help to understand a lot of the things that happened in France from 1940 to 1944.

Curiously enough, it makes one respect the incredible nerve of de Gaulle who, representing practically nobody, nevertheless managed to get himself accepted as the legitimate spokesman for France. For in the early years of the Occupation, there were very few resistants: life went on, Maurice Chevalier sang songs to the glory of Marshal Pétain; a troupe of French actors are seen going off to Germany to meet their colleagues from beyond the Rhine.

A German soldier stationed in Clermont-Ferrand (the directors chose this town to centre the film around because it was both close to Vichy and an important centre of resistance) is interviewed today somewhere in Bavaria. He explains to us that he never learned much French, just enough to go courting. And when be repeats for the camera's benefit his tiny stock of blandishments: 'Bonsoir, mademoiselle, voulez-vous vous promener avec moi,' a shiver goes down one's back, for of course, one is certain that a fair number of girls *did* 'Go for a walk' with him.

But we must beware of sitting smugly in judgment: when the interviewer asks Anthony Eden whether he didn't think the French behaved shamefully during the Occupation, Eden simply refuses to answer the question. We were lucky enough not to be occupied, he says, and therefore we cannot know what it was like; it is not for us to condemn.

None the less it is terrifying to hear how the French police behaved – worse apparently, than the police of any other occupied country. When the Germans ordered all the Jews in Paris over 16 to be rounded up, the French police decided to be over-zealous, and they rounded up children as well. This done, the Germans decided that the kids might as well be sent to extermination camps as well, and they were.

The madness of war is without limits: today an ex-German officer feasting the marriage of one of his children is heard to expostulate about the disgraceful behaviour of the French Resistance. One day his men were marching down a country road: by the side were a dozen peasants digging potatoes. Suddenly they dropped their spades, picked up rifles, and shot down the German squad. That's not guerrilla war, says the German; that's plain murder. Partisans, he explains indignantly, should wear either armbands or a badge or cap of some sort to identify themselves.

For, of course, there were resistants, and some of the Auvergnat peasants in the film do much to cheer one. Alexis and Louis Graves, two brothers from the country round Clermont are in fact perfect examples of the kind of image we have of all Frenchmen during the Occupation: tough, gentle, good. When Louis came back from Büchenwald whence a letter of denunciation had sent him, he didn't rest until he found out who had written the letter. But then he didn't do anything about it – what would have been the point then? And for the past 25 years, he has seen, doubtless every week, the man who had written that letter to the Gestapo.

But before we get too enraged about French television not showing this film, we might well ask why it hasn't been shown on our own television. It has been seen in Germany and Switzerland; it's been bought by television companies in Holland, Belgium, Sweden, and Hungary. Isn't it time now perhaps for it to be seen here? Of course it might be considered too 'political'. One point that is made by the English secret agents and the aviators who were shot down is that they were always helped by working-class people, especially railwaymen. The middle classes? They were rather 'neutral' says one, tactfully. But then he adds, it is only those who have 'nothing' to lose that can afford to act on their convictions. Perhaps that's considered subversive?

The only fault I could find with the film was one curious omission from this attempt to show all sides or the period. And that was the year between the debacle in June 1940, and September 1941, when, because of the Hitler–Stalin treaty, the French Communist Party, so soon to take a major part in the Resistance, lay rather low. It would have been another contribution to this portrait of the insanity that war brings to have interviewed a man who was a young Communist at the time: what did it feel like to have overnight to switch gears, as it were? One day, it was an imperialist war; the next, a people's war. No stranger, I suppose, than a lot of the other things that happened during the war, but it would have rounded out the picture.

As it would, to conclude, have been to see the two versions of Pagnol's film *The Well-Digger's Daughter*. The version shown during the Occupation ended edifyingly with the wayward girl and her father reconciled listening to an uplifting discourse by Marshal

Pétain. When the film was revived after the war, the last scene was changed to show father and daughter no less uplifted, but this time, listening to the broadcast of General de Gaulle from London.

SOURCE: 'LOOK BACK IN SHAME', *GUARDIAN*, 4 MAY 1971, 8

3.5 GOING BETWEEN

The best recipe for a successful marriage of minds – as for any other kind – is naturally that the partners should have much in common. It is equally important, however, that they should be dissimilar in as many ways as they are alike. These two qualifications are abundantly fulfilled in the collaboration of Joseph Losey and Harold Pinter. They are alike in that both are outsiders. Neither was born into the kind of English aristocratic or upper middle-class world their films describe. Losey is, of course, American, and therefore out of the running. Pinter, though English, was neither born nor educated in the kind of world which fascinates both him and Losey – at least when they are working together. For it is curious that when Pinter is on his own, he deals with a seedy world of derelicts, outsiders, tramps. And when Losey is on his own, the milieu of his films is seldom the same as in the films he does with Pinter.

Together, if not separately, both men seem fascinated by the possibilities offered by a depiction of a privileged world, from the smart Chelsea house of *The Servant* to the spires of Oxford and now, in *The Go-Between*, the splendours of upper-class life at the turn of the century. Such a world offers the film-maker and scriptwriter many advantages. For one thing, it provides the best kind of setting for that portrayal of the differences between appearance and reality that interest both men. In *The Go-Between* everything in the garden, in the house is lovely; it is only underneath the white muslin dresses that beat the savage hearts, and Losey and Pinter burrow beneath the veneer of a civilisation of manners to lay bare what lies there.

Mrs Maudsley (Margaret Leighton) seems at first the perfect hostess, well-bred, cultivated, delightful. It is only as the film progresses that we see beneath that surface to her sexual jealousy of her daughter, her determination that Marian should make a suitable match, and that scandal must at all costs be avoided. And it is precisely because people like Mrs Maudsley impose restraints on themselves – in the name of 'good form' – that they are so tempting for Losey and Pinter; for in this contrast between behaviour and desires lies the essence of drama. Throughout the film there runs a secondary thread, this battle of wills between mother and daughter which is all the more gripping because it is expressed only in guarded looks, conversational gambits, and raised eyebrows.

Another advantage of this kind of milieu is that it allows for concentration: no one has to go to work, and the action of the film can be compressed. This links up with Losey's and Pinter's experience in the theatre. Pinter, of course, is both playwright and actor; but Losey, too, began his career on the stage, and it was only after eighteen years in the theatre that he began work in films. Therefore (or is it vice versa?) both men are fascinated by closed universes. The Pinter rooms, to be sure; but most of Losey's films, too, are studies of small worlds – the two characters of *Figures in a Landscape*, the house in *Secret Ceremony*, the prison in *The Criminal*, the island in *Boom*. Because of this need to concentrate, to crystallise, we have yet another reason why the Losey–Pinter films prefer upper-class settings. And because they have imposed spatial limits on themselves, they are naturally tempted to play tricks with time; to compensate, as it were, for the smallness of their stage.

It has often been remarked that Losey and Pinter share, above all, a certain tendency to misogyny. This, I think, is true of the two men individually. One has only to think back to the treatment of the woman in *The Homecoming* or to Losey's portrayal of Susan Gilvray in *The Prowler*, or the character Jeanne Moreau plays in *Eve*. However, in the films the two have made together another element seems more important. The female characters *are* often predatory. Anna, in *Accident*, chalks up a death (William) and two very unhappy men (Stephen and Charlie). In *The Go-Between*, Marian Maudsley betters this record with a suicide (Ted Burgess) and two ruined lives (Leo and Trimingham). But the fact that the Sarah Miles character in *The Servant* is only an accessory to the downfall of Tony indicates that what concerns Losey and Pinter is less the destructive female than the self-destructive male. They are simply saying that when men give themselves up entirely to their sexual obsessions, they are in fact committing a kind of suicide. The Servant destroys the master by pandering to his lusts and weaknesses. Anna is not really *responsible* for the havoc wreaked around her: that must in all honesty be put down to the self-indulgence of the men. Marian, in *The Go-Between*, is selfish and reasonably heartless, but the men all *want* to be walked over.

Leo is too young to be aware of the nature of Marian's relationship with Farmer Ted; nonetheless he is aware that he is somehow betraying the Maudsleys' hospitality by carrying the secret messages between the Hall and the Farm. But he is so pleased by the self-importance given him by his function as messenger that even when he begins to suspect that Marian is only using him, that she does not really care for him, he blinds himself to this knowledge. Lord Trimingham, Marian's fiancé, suspects, as does everyone except Leo, that Marian is having an affair with Ted; yet he closes his eyes, goes through with the marriage, and accepts Ted's child as his own with never a word of reproach. Ted knows that Marian is using him sexually, just as she is using Leo as messenger; he knows she will never marry him. And when the scandal breaks, Ted commits suicide, presumably to save Marian from further embarrassment. Leo, far from harbouring any vindictive thoughts towards Marian for having embroiled him in a situation which is to leave him an emotional vegetable, remains true to her to the end. And Trimingham? 'Hugh was as true as steel. He wouldn't hear a word against me. But everybody wanted to know us, of course. I was Lady Trimingham, you see, I still am. There is no other.'

Losey and Pinter, then, are united more by their understanding of man's self-destructive instincts, his masochistic vulnerability, his over-dependence on sex, than by any form of misogyny. Their men 'fly too near the sun', and they get scorched. Which is perhaps just another way of saying that both Losey and Pinter share what is generally called a tragic view of life.

But if their background, psychology, and preoccupations are often similar, their differences as artists are equally important. Losey is generally thought of as baroque, and his visual style is indeed often complex and convoluted. Pinter, on the other hand, specialises in monosyllables, in deceptive simplicity. Where Losey has occasionally been led by his exuberant temperament to overdo effects, Pinter is more of a miniaturist, using tiny brush strokes to make up his canvas. If the tempo of Pinter's plays could be described as *moderato assai*, Losey often prefers an invigorating *allegro furioso*. Finally, if Losey has in the past tended towards explicit social comment, Pinter in his plays has fought shy of statement of any sort. Day and night, one could say; but day and night do of course meet in a twilight zone, and it is in that late afternoon of the 19th century that *The Go-Between* is set, one of those beautiful Edwardian summers like the one we are told preceded the outbreak of the war in 1914.

And indeed in the beginning of the film, hostilities are about to break out at Brandham Hall. 'The past is a foreign country: they do things differently there …' Marian is engaged to Lord Trimingham; at the same time she is carrying on a passionate affair with Ted Burgess, a farmer on the estate. Everyone knows, or suspects it; no one says a word about it. Into this charged atmosphere, fate brings young Leo Colston, a boy from a shabby-genteel home invited by a richer schoolmate for the summer hols. Leo, like Losey and Pinter, like us, in fact, cannot help but be seduced by life as it is lived at the Hall. The charm of the Maudsley family is irresistible. During the course of the film, however, we gradually discover that beneath the surface blandishments, beneath the formal pleasures of tennis and tea, and above all, cricket, there lies something far less pleasant. And the tragic irony lies in the fact that while we see it all, poor Leo, blinded by his vanity and pleasure at being taken up, sees nothing.

In order for this contrast between appearance and reality to work, the surface has to be as alluring as possible. And it is. Gerry Fisher, whose photography of Oxford made of it some impossible dream of romantic spires, here makes Brandham Hall and the surrounding Norfolk countryside achingly, nostalgically beautiful, the essence of an English summer as old colonials must have dreamed of it. Carmen Dillon, whose art direction for *Accident* was so accurate, here works miracles, so that we feel, as does Leo, that the people who inhabit such beautiful rooms, wear such beautiful clothes, must also have beautiful souls.

But above all, the acting is centrally necessary to keep up this illusion, and Margaret Leighton and Michael Gough as Marian's parents, and Edward Fox as Trimingham, succeed strikingly in creating the illusion of being truly well-bred that so much impresses little Leo. Alan Bates, good as he is as Ted, is no match for them; nor is Julie Christie. Only Dominic Guard, as Leo, amazingly holds his own against such competition. And when, towards the end, the masks come off, Margaret Leighton breaks up terrifyingly: the charm and beauty gone, she becomes a Fury. Even Leo suddenly becomes dimly aware of the abyss into which he − and they − have fallen.

One of the reasons why I prefer *The Go-Between* to the earlier Losey–Pinter films is its greater scope, its broader canvas. Like all their films, it is an adaptation, but whereas *The Servant* and even *Accident* were fairly short novels, L. P. Hartley's *The Go-Between* is a full-length work, if anything psychologically over-elaborated. And, therefore, it makes a much better subject for what I think of as the Losey–Pinter dialectic, their two-fold process of analysis and synthesis. First, the original material is scraped down, all excrescences chiselled away, so that the original screenplay is not just a condensed version of the novel, but something more like a quintessence. (One can imagine L. P. Hartley, like the cow in the old Oxo ad, looking at the tiny cube and saying, 'Goodness, *me*?') And once Pinter (or Pinter and Losey − it is not important who did just what: we know they work closely together) has reduced the novel to its essence, then the work of the director is, in a sense, to blow it up again, to restore the novelistic density, the texture, the life by cinematic means.

For example, the novel of *The Go-Between* begins with a prologue in which Leo Colston, now grown old, comes across a youthful diary. The main part of the novel is concerned with the evocation of the fatal summer at Brandham Hall. The book ends with an epilogue in which we discover what the effect of that traumatic summer was, what kind of man Leo has become, and it closes with Leo's return to the Norfolk village. The film gets rid of both prologue and epilogue; instead, there is a double articulation of time: as the story of the summer runs along, it is interrupted from time to time – at first only by occasional flashes, later by longer scenes, of Colston arriving in Norwich *now*, making his way to the village, meeting Marian's grandson, and finally being asked by Marian to do one more errand, for the last time to act as go-between.

The effect of this playing with time is more intense, even, than in *Accident*. For at first, we feel terribly uneasy; what are those strange flashes? Who is that grey old man? What are these modern cars doing here? Only slowly do we realise that this man (Michael Redgrave) *must* be young Leo grown old; and in a strange way, this gradual discovery counterpoints our gradual discovery of the realities of the Maudsley household. While we are penetrating the reality which lies beneath the charming exterior, we are also finding out what the effect of Leo's ultimate discovery has been – through Colston's sloping shoulders and deadened features.

But Losey and Pinter have done more than simply translate the novel into film terms; they have added much themselves. Pinter, for example, has not written much new dialogue; he has contented himself with 'adapting' it. But what he has done, often only by cutting a word or a line here and there, is to create his own very special brand of what the Greeks called stichomythia, that achieving of rhythm and speed through alternation:

TED: She cried when she couldn't see me.
LEO: How do you know?
TED: Because she cried when she did see me.

And this sense of movement which contrasts with the sultry summer heat is achieved by Losey in other ways. He has commissioned from Michel Legrand an extraordinary score – a formal set of variations for piano and orchestra in what could be described as a Bach–Stravinsky style, and he uses it in a formal way, too. No question of the music underlying certain scenes or trying to express emotions: no, it is used almost autonomously to punctuate the film, and, more important, to give it shape and impetus. And the music's driving *ostinato* parallels the tremendously exciting forward movement of the camerawork and the editing. Which may have been suggested by Leo's activities as messenger: Trimingham compares him to Mercury, the messenger of the gods, and the film's frenzied movement could also be described as mercurial.

Take the opening shots: we begin with a fast tracking shot laterally following the carriage bringing the two boys to Brandham Hall. We then cut to a long shot of the carriage moving across the screen from left to right, and at the same time, as one of the boys rises to grab at some leaves from a branch, the camera moves (or zooms) in towards them. This compounding of movement gives a breathless start to the film, plunging us into this new world in much the same way as Leo must have been plunged into a world he had never known and which was to destroy him. His first vision of Marian and her family comes from high up on the balcony of the house as he looks down on to the grass. In Norwich Cathedral, we see him dwarfed from the vaulted ceiling, and the plunging verticals give us some sense of the vertiginous nature of what is to befall him throughout the film. All through *The Go-Between*, the double staircase plays an essential role, and we are always looking down with Leo, or looking down on him. Even outside the house, when Leo is frantically running off on his errands, we see him, a tiny figure against the Norfolk countryside. Very flat, Norfolk, and it makes him look flatter, too. But Leo is no passive figure: like some tragic hero, he rushes headlong to embrace his fate.

These are only a few examples of how Losey and Pinter have not only transposed the novel into film terms, but also, in a sense, transformed it. More even than in his previous films, Losey here achieves an almost palpable sense of reality, which gives the moral force of the film a greater intensity because of the heightened contradiction between apparent surface and true subject. You can feel the clothes, you can smell the heat; and because all these sensual details are so physically realised, you end up hearing the unsaid, seeing the unseen. If only they could tackle Proust now.

SOURCE: 'GOING BETWEEN', *SIGHT & SOUND*, 40.3, SUMMER 1971, 158–9

3.6 THE INTERNATIONAL GRAVY TRAIN

Over the past 10 years or so, I have spent about three months a year attending film festivals.[3] That's a statement, not a complaint; in spite of the boredom and the eye-strain, the foolishness and the folly, I don't regret it. But both the friends who commiserate and those who are envious are right. Festivals are hell, and they are also fun. But they are very different from the average layman's conception of them.

What you don't understand till you've been to Cannes or Venice is that film festivals are not public affairs. Trying to buy a ticket to a film festival screening is well nigh impossible; they are only given away. But to whom? You may well ask. Festivals are much more like trade fairs or conventions than one would think possible. The man in the street or even the film lover doesn't have a chance unless he can somehow snag an invitation. And short of being a producer or distributor, the only way is to be a journalist.

If the industry men are the actors in the play then the journalists are the indispensable audience, without whom there would be no show. For it's not enough for festivals to show films, give prizes, serve as the setting for deals. All these things have not only to be done; they have, like justice, to be seen to be done: they have to get into the papers. For the more that gets written about festivals, the more people think they're important. And, circling viciously, the more important they're thought to be, the more gets written – and published – about them. Editors are not exempt from festival fever, either. Witness this article.

But how did this self-perpetuating gravy train ever get on the tracks in the first place, I hear someone asking. The answer has nothing to do with the cinema; the very first film festival – Venice in the early 1930s – was someone's bright idea of how to compensate for the dearth of tourists at the end of the summer season. Times were hard in 1932, and the film festival helped fill the Lido hotels. To be sure, the hotel-keepers had to offer reduced rates to the festival organisation, but a full house is always better than an empty one; furthermore, the great discovery was that in the long run the film companies spent more money in Venice than the festival had to fork out in 'hospitality.' And it was all good publicity for the city.

Things have moved on since then, but the basic impetus behind the creation of film festivals remains tourism and the chief instigators remain the Chamber of Commerce stalwarts. (The Italians with their realism recognise this: they have a Cabinet post called Minister of Tourism and Spectacles, thus cynically linking the two.)

Occasionally, however, politics has played a part. In fact, when Cannes was established in the late '30s, the motivation for this second international festival was the fact that the prizes at Venice were too much influenced by Mussolini. So, as an alternative to a Fascist festival, the French announced the creation of a 'free' one. Biarritz and Cannes fought it out for a whole winter, not so much for the honour as for the tourists; finally Cannes won. The opening was to be grandiose. MGM even sent over a shipload of stars. The pre-opening festivities featured Norma Shearer and George Raft dancing in the streets of Cannes, and the whole town worked itself up into a frenzy for opening day. Alas, that day was 1 September 1939 – and the first Cannes Festival shut down before it started: the ship set sail, the tents were folded, and that was that until 1946.

Politics, too, played a part in the Berlin Film Festival – it was one more event to persuade the beleaguered Berliners that the rest of the world hadn't forgotten them. Whether it will now survive the relaxing of tension between East and West is doubtful. But film festivals die hard: the Soviet invasion of Czechoslovakia in 1968 made many think that the Karlovy Vary (ex-Karlsbad) festival would wither away, but in spite of troubles of one sort or another, it hasn't and it still alternates with Moscow as the prime Eastern block festival.

The miraculous thing about the good film festivals is that in spite of their ambiguous origins, they really perform a service. Many directors well known today owe their initial recognition to film festivals. The discovery of the Japanese cinema came about directly as a result of the presentation of *Rashomon* at Venice in 1951. Up until then, no Western distributor would even look at a Japanese film, let alone pick it up for distribution. But the enormous success and brouhaha over *Rashomon* succeeded in changing people's minds.

Up until 1960, the name of Michelangelo Antonioni was known to about 200 people in the whole world. But the premiere of *L'avventura* – and its scandalous reception – soon made him almost a household name. The film was roundly booed and hissed: but that didn't matter – the important thing was that it got talked about – and of course, there were some people who liked it. Coming closer to home, it wasn't until the Cannes screening of *Easy Rider* that its producers realised what they had. Up until then, they hardly dreamed they had a $30 million winner – but the enthusiastic Cannes reception made a lot of people revise their ideas pretty quickly. Fortunately, the film business has always been pretty good at that.

Besides bringing otherwise unknown directors to the limelight, festivals also serve the useful function of bringing together in one place a mass of films, a slap-dash panorama of world production. Some are selected, some just come. Anyone with a little money in his pocket can hire one of the fringe theatres, put up a few signs, and be certain of getting some kind of audience for his film. Naturally, one sees a lot of lemons this way, but occasionally, you make a real discovery, too, like, in 1960, Godard's *Breathless*.

Along with all these positive elements, film festivals have many ludicrous aspects, and not a few sordid ones. I mentioned earlier the important role of the journalists: they're also part of the rat race. Festivals like Cannes or Venice are indeed lavish in their invitations: some journalists get a week, others two weeks of free room and/or board, plus fringe benefits in the form of invitations to cocktail parties, receptions, lunches on the beach. So important are these fringe invitations, in fact, that festivaliers (well, that's what *Variety* calls them) spend almost as much time gossiping about who got invited to what than discussing the films themselves. There are, for example, those receptions to which everyone is invited – but to which it's smarter not to go. Then there are the more select parties which are so considered because you actually get lunch, dinner or something approaching a full meal.

Naturally, fewer invitations are sent out for these affairs and it is often hard to discover how the lists are drawn up. I remember the Russians giving a big party at Venice to which

I was invited but to which the most important French Communist film critic (and historian of Russian film) was not. Any attempt to figure out how these lists are made up reduce the inquirer to Kafkaesque paranoia. The neophyte, of course, takes any invitation he may get – and as his festival invitation often covers only his hotel room, he can be seen gobbling up canapés and tiny sandwiches. Some of the less cool have even been observed slipping tidbits into handkerchiefs and pockets, like so many thrifty squirrels.

But how do you snag a festival invitation in the first place? Well, to start with, the festival administration wants to know the circulation of your magazine or newspaper. If it meets their requirements, you're half-way there. That is to say, you get your invitation for the first year. But the catch comes the next time. They don't care what you have written – all that counts are the column-inches. If you haven't written enough, you're out. And whether you're invited for one week or two the second year depends solely on your word-count.

Some clever guys manage to live for nearly a year on the festival circuit. It takes some imagination, a lot of guts, and a thick skin, but it can be done – as long as you don't mind the occasional night sleeping under the board-walk. Starting with Cannes, you move on, with hardly a hiatus, to Pesaro (films by young directors), to Annecy (cartoons), to Berlin, to San Sebastian, to Moscow or Karlovy Vary, to Locarno, to Bergamo, to Venice and so forth. These people may be known as festival bums, but their nerve is much admired. You see them in the lobby of the Carlton, the Kempinski, or the Excelsior, waiting around to get invited to lunch, or at least a drink (during which they greedily devour the peanuts and olives); towards the end of the festival, they reappear with their bags packed, ready to bum a lift from anyone about to depart.

But even among the more legitimate festival invites, there is a serious pecking order which hinges on what hotel you are put up at. There are various schools of thought on the subject: in Berlin, many feel that the Kempinski is a little more prestigious than the Hilton (I agree): at Karlovy Vary there is no problem: either you are in the Moskva Pupp, or you're in outer darkness (literally: the other hotels have 40-watt bulbs). Venice and Cannes are more complicated, because larger. The Excelsior would seem to be the best place on the Lido, but there are some who prefer the relative calm of the Grand Hotel des Bains. True, it's farther away, but doesn't that very fact make it more select? And now that Visconti has used it for *Death in Venice*, I'm willing to bet that it's going to be chic-er than ever.

The most complex is Cannes. Most Americans wouldn't dream of going anywhere but the Carlton. But the Majestic is riding it a close second, partly because it has a swimming pool, and partly because the Carlton lobby during the festival looks more like a bazaar or a machine-tools convention than a luxury hotel. Then, too, the staff of the Carlton is famous for reminding the festival guests in various subtle ways that they are there only through the hospitality of the festival: that they could never afford it otherwise. This is not always appreciated by more sensitive guests.

The French, Italians, and the Japanese prefer the Martinez. The largest hotel in Cannes, it is somewhat barnlike, but it has three great advantages. It is outside the Blue Zone so can park your car easily: the personnel is charming: and, most important, it is so big and rambling that there is no problem in sneaking bed-partners into it. In fact, such people have lived there for a week without the hotel being any wiser. Or perhaps they do know, and just pretend not to, on the notion that a happy journalist will write more glowingly than a frustrated one.

And although the festival administration may be appointed, as in Venice, by a government Ministry, or at Cannes, by a strange consortium of national and local officials, ultimately the money comes mostly from the town itself, that is to say, the hotel-keepers and the restaurateurs, the gift-shops, and the hairdressers. So all of them have a vested interest in trying to keep the journalist happy, or at least not letting him realise how much he is being milked (prices in shops rise by 20 per cent the day a festival begins).

All this may be silly, but not terribly serious. Graver charges have been levelled at the way festivals are run, notably the whole question of prizes, which many people think are 'fixed'. They're not, at least not in the way you might imagine. I doubt very much if a jury ever gets bribed – at least not with money. For one thing, it's too expensive; for another, it's too dangerous. But they are 'fixed' in more subtle ways. Hardly any jury ever escapes the geographical squeeze. Every major film-producing country has to get something – if they don't, their sensibilities are so tender that they may refuse to participate the following year, and what would a festival be without a Russian film, or an American one, or an Italian one?

This fact of life is explained to the jurors, and they quickly accept it as something they have to live with. Of course, the most sensitive are us (the Americans) and the Russians. One year the Russian delegates were so distressed when they heard advance news that they were to get nothing, that they pleaded with the director of the festival – telling him they'd lose their jobs, or worse, unless they got 'something.' Now in a case like this, the jury can be persuaded – not indeed to give them a major prize – but at least something.

What the Russians got that year was 'The Prize for the Best Evocation of a Revolutionary Epic.' The fact that the Russian film was the only revolutionary epic in the festival didn't faze anybody. There were a few giggles on the night they gave out the awards, but by and large, everybody played the game.

The same device has been used for the Americans, not once but several times. When it looked like we were not going to pick up anything, someone suddenly had the brilliant idea of creating a new prize, and cynically (or sentimentally – it often comes to the same thing) seized on the fact that Gary Cooper had died that year and that's how the 'Prix Gary Cooper' was born. Oh, it was tarted up with a few lines to explain that this prize was to recompense films whose 'humanitarian qualities' were exceptional and which promoted better understanding between nations, but this didn't fool anybody, and it thereupon became a useful prize whenever the American selections weren't up to scratch.

Cannes, in particular, specialises in such solutions. This spring they used the fact that this was their 25th anniversary to break the deadlock between Losey's *The Go-Between* and Visconti's *Death in Venice*. Actually, it was not much of a deadlock; at Cannes most people preferred the Losey film, but it was felt that Visconti had to get something, so while Losey got the Golden Palm. Visconti had the Prize for the 25th Festival of Cannes palmed off on him.

Some festivals don't give any prizes at all. When the New York Film Festival was founded in 1963, I didn't have very much trouble in persuading Lincoln Center to follow the non-competitive model of the London Film Festival: the idea being that (1) every film got a prize, that of just being in the festival and (2) how do you compare apples with oranges – Hitchcock with Antonioni, John Ford with Godard? And in recent years, more and more festivals have given up the whole prize business. Especially since 1968 when the first victim of the 'events' in France was the Cannes Festival, shut down by a group of militants. (Some of them have since somewhat sheepishly returned to Cannes, but that's another story.) The Pesaro Festival was also interrupted, and gradually the idea got around that prize-giving was undemocratic.

But the ferment of 1968 changed many aspects of European film festivals. For one thing, a festival is a pushover for even a small band of militants, perhaps because of the ambiguous nature of its financing and origins. And also because there has been a general failure of nerve among the big film producing companies all over the world.

The plain truth is that the producers don't know what they're doing any more – they don't know which of their films will succeed, and when they do, they often don't know why. So they were in no position to resist the pressure from the festival direction – which in turn was not able to answer the objections of the contesters – to change the festival formats. Cannes, for example, didn't give up prizes, but it did allow the creation of a counter-festival. A group called the Society of French Directors has presented for the past three years an enormous group of films in opposition to the official selections. The same thing happened in Berlin this year, as a direct result of the jury scandal of 1970 when it was charged that the chairman of the jury, George Stevens, had said that he would oppose a German film about Vietnam on the grounds that it was anti-American. By and large, these counter-festivals are a Good Thing, even though their selections are often no better than the official ones – anti-festivals have their own pressures and prejudices, too.

In any case, these new developments on the festival scene may finally kill the legend that festivals are just a barrel of fun, free-loading, and folly. Maybe it used to be that way in the palmy pre-1960 days, when the great event of the day was a Robert Mitchum posing with a nude starlet on the beach. Festivals have changed because the film industry has changed. There aren't any starlets on the beach any more because there is no place for starlets any more. A long hard stint on TV is likely now to be a better introduction to a film contract than a night with the producer.

If any proof were needed of this, it can be found in the dramatic increase of prostitutes, of both sexes, that now litter the Croisette once night has fallen. (In the streets behind the Carlton and the Martinez, they don't even wait for the evening: from three o'clock in the afternoon, they're there on the back street corners, hard by the English church and Avis.) In the good old days there was too much non-professional competition: now, the 'Amazones' cruise back and forth in their shiny Mercedes, ready to console the distributors, the producers, the money-men.

And they need consolation: doing a festival seriously (which is the only way anyone can afford to do it these days) takes a hell of a lot out of you. There are something like 40 screenings scheduled each day: no one can see them all, of course, but, like busy worker ants, one scurries from one to the other trying to make sure that one doesn't miss the film that's going to turn out to have been the revelation of the festival – invariably the one that was shown on the rainy Thursday at 11.45pm.

Cannes retains its function as market-place: deals are consummated – Rumanians sell their films to Uruguayans – but the old euphoria is gone. Every year you hear them swear they'll never come back to Cannes, that they need another vacation after those hectic two weeks, that the weather isn't as good as it used to be. But, come March, as winter is crawling to its slushy end, you see them in London, Rome, and New York asking each other, 'You going back?' And, the answer comes, hesitantly, reluctantly, but invariably, yes. It sounds better this year, they say: or, I hear the Riviera's in for a good spring. They may even believe it. And who knows, maybe this year it will be true.

SOURCE: 'THE INTERNATIONAL GRAVY TRAIN', *GUARDIAN*, 11 DECEMBER 1971, 8

3.7 VISCONTI MISSES THE GONDOLA

Nicole Stéphane, the producer, has announced in Paris that her film of Proust's *Remembrance of Things Past* will now be directed, not by Visconti, but by Joseph Losey. And that the script of the film will be by Harold Pinter.[4]

The original announcement of the Visconti version caused much turmoil, even reaching the leader pages of this newspaper which seldom devotes so much space to film. Having gone on record myself that it would be a wonderful idea if Pinter and Losey could tackle Proust after *The Go-Between*, I feel somewhat as if the mantle of prophecy had descended upon me, a not very cosy feeling.

The reasons why Visconti is no longer going to do the film are complex and as the matter is *sub judice* at the moment, it would not be wise to go into it too closely. One can, however, speculate – did he get cold feet? In any case, it is a matter of fact that he has preferred to start another film in the meanwhile – his version of the story of mad King Ludwig of Bavaria starring Helmut Berger and Romy Schneider. The Proust film was scheduled to have begun in January 1972. Whatever the reasons for the delay – Mademoiselle Stéphane seems to have decided that she had better think again.

It is not as if she were the impatient type. On a recent visit to London she told me that she first acquired the rights to Proust back in 1965. At the time, she thought about Visconti for the film, but it then seemed impossible. *The Stranger* had just come out, and it was something less than a success. Then, too, the xenophobic French had complained about this trans-Alpine laying his hands on Camus – what would they have said about his daring to touch Proust? She then considered René Clément who at that time still was thought to be a distinguished man of the cinema.

That never panned out, and after the success of *The Damned*, it was at last possible to set up the project with Visconti. Joining forces with another French producer, Robert Dorfman, Mademoiselle Stéphane began in 1969 seriously to plan out the project. Much work was done – a script, by Visconti and Suso Cecchi d'Amico was elaborated, and it was announced that the film would mainly cover the latter part of the work – from the end of *The Guermantes Way* to the outbreak of the First World War. Casting was announced: the role of the narrator was to be played either by Alain Delon or Dustin Hoffman; Olivier would do Charlus, Garbo the Queen of Naples, etc. Locations were sought out, expeditions were made, and everything seemed to be getting satisfactorily under way.

But when Visconti announced that he would do the Ludwig II film first (perhaps to give Helmut Berger the big starring role he had earned), the producers were forced to think again. Then came this year's Cannes Festival with the confrontation of Visconti's *Death in Venice* and Losey's *The Go-Between* – and it appears that I was not the only one to begin to wonder if Visconti was after all the ideal choice for Proust. Although critics and audiences in this country were favourably impressed by the Visconti film, this was very far from being the case on the Continent (or in America, in fact). Everyone admired the way Visconti handled the hats and the hotel, but they felt (as I did) that he had essentially missed the gondola.

Furthermore, as for the physical recreation – or better, reinterpretation – of the past, Losey managed all that just as well, if not better, in *The Go-Between*, then, too, the treatment of time in the film seemed to indicate that Pinter and Losey would be very much at home with Proustian chronology.

And this is, in fact, so. Both in their *Accident* and *The Go-Between*, Losey and Pinter have shown themselves fascinated by the way in which the cinema, to use the phrase of the *Guardian* leader writer, 'can be used to illuminate or deliberately confuse the nature of past and present, and of the permanence or impermanence of memory in our minds.'

It is too early to be able to say much about the form the film will take: the script is not yet written. But from what Mademoiselle Stéphane reported, one thing seems clear. The film will centre on the Swann story. In a sense, the film will go back to Proust's original conception for the work: *Remembrance of Things Past* was supposed to be a three volume work – something roughly corresponding to the present *Swann's Way*, *The Guermantes Way* and *The Past Recaptured* – and the extension of the work to include the Albertine books (*Cities of the Plain*, *The Captive*, and *The Sweet Cheat Gone*) only came later, probably as a result of Proust's relationship with Agostinelli.[5]

This decision brings the project down to workable dimensions. Perhaps the finished film will be something like the 'Overture' to *Swann's Way* – those first fifty pages or so where so many of the characters make their first dream-like appearance – even Charlus is already there as the supposed lover of Odette. All this, right down to the madeleine, should be very much Losey's and Pinter's – you should excuse the expression – cup of tea.

So much for speculation; but there are some hard facts. For one thing, the film will be shot in English – there may, however, be a second version, filmed simultaneously, in French. In any case, only Proust's own dialogue will be used in either version, although as with the L. P. Hartley book, Pinter may fiddle with it a bit.

It will be a French–English co-production, shot largely in France. If there is any studio work, that will probably be done here, but the producers (Mademoiselle Stéphane and Monsieur Dorfman on the French side, and Martin Rosen for this country) are fairly confident that most of the film can be shot on location. Naturally, one wonders about the casting of the film, but it is still early days. From the fact that Mademoiselle Stéphane was very eager to see Alan Bates's performance in *Butley* during her stay here, I would deduce that he has been suggested by either Losey or Pinter, or both, as a possibility for an important role in the film – maybe Swann? But then one thinks of the other actors Losey has used in the past – like Bogarde and Burton – and one wonders what roles they might play.

If there are going to be two versions, one could also consider those marvellous French actresses who are known to be bilingual, like Simone Signoret, Delphine Seyrig, Jeanne Moreau, Danielle Darrieux and Catherine Deneuve. Actually, the very first person to think of filming Proust was the late Raoul Lévy – and his idea was to do just *Swann in Love* with Jeanne Moreau as Odette. My own choice for Odette now would probably be Catherine Deneuve, and I would love to see Danielle Darrieux as Madame Verdurin, and Delphine Seyrig as Oriane de Guermantes. Of course, there would be a problem with accents, as each of these ladies speaks English differently, and they would have to fit in with the English actors as well. Then, too, one hopes that the idea of using Greta Garbo as the Queen of Naples will still be possible; and what a Morel Alain Delon would make!

One could go on for hours conjecturing; but we will just have to wait and see. If the wait seems long to us, think what it must be like for Mademoiselle Stéphane – who has waited since 1965. But then, she is not your usual producer. She is perhaps best known in this country as an actress: she was the unforgettable Elisabeth in the Melville–Cocteau film of *Les Enfants terribles*. But her acting career was cut short by an automobile accident which laid her up for several years. After that, she decided to investigate other aspects of film-making. After working as Franju's assistant, she then directed several documentaries herself, the most notable being a classic work on hydrocephalic children.

After that, she turned to production, first working with the director Frédéric Rossif, whose *Mourir à Madrid* and *Les Animaux* she produced. Her most successful film at the box office was *La Vie de château*, and her most experimental were Allio's *L'une et l'autre* and Marguerite Duras's *Destroy, she says*. Most recently she produced the Nelo Risi film about Verlaine (Jean-Claude Brialy) and Rimbaud (Terence Stamp) called *A Season in Hell*, which will be coming out in January.

A varied career, to say the least, and one which could be said to have prepared her for anything, even Proust. And the fact that she was born into a well-known aristocratic French-Jewish family also uniquely qualifies her for this venture.

But it could also be said that Losey and Pinter are ideal choices to do Proust precisely because neither of them is French. For one thing, Proust's greatest early success was in English-speaking countries. For another, just as Proust himself was always something of an outsider in the world he was describing, so Losey and Pinter will be, too; even more so, of course. But that is all to the good. The great danger with Visconti was that we would have had a kind of copy of Proust – and that never works. With Losey and Pinter, we will have a critical reinterpretation. And if one is to translate Proust from one medium to another, this seems to me to be essential if the film of *Remembrance of Things Past* is to be an autonomous work of the cinema. It must revolutionise the cinema just as Proust did the novel. That is what one expects from Losey and Pinter, and that, I reckon, is what we are going to get.

SOURCE: 'VISCONTI MISSES THE GONDOLA', *GUARDIAN*, 22 DECEMBER 1971, 8

3.8 JEAN-MARIE STRAUB

NOTE: Published in 1971, Roud's study remains an excellent introduction to the work of Jean-Marie Straub and Danièle Huillet. Roud continued to write about the couple's work after this book, notably 'Verse against Vespas' about Othon *(Guardian, 11 February 1970, 8) and 'Golden bull' about* Moses and Aaron *(Guardian, 26 February 1975, 10).*

A book about Jean-Marie Straub may seem premature. After all, it could be objected, he is only thirty-eight years old. Moreover, he has made only three features and two shorts; not a very considerable body of work, it might be said, and not enough matter for a monograph. And it is true that this book must, by its nature, be more a progress report than a definitive statement about a director who has many films still to come. Nevertheless, Straub's *oeuvre*, limited though it may be, is of an importance great enough to outweigh all objections. The fact that his work is not very well known seems to me a positive rather than a negative factor. Many people find his films difficult, frustrating, and unrewarding. Because I feel so strongly that they are among the most significant of the decade, it seemed that any attempt to widen the circle of their admirers was well worth making. And Straub's films do present certain problems: to be sure, there are those who have been drawn to them instinctively, but there are others who are still unfamiliar with his world, and it is to them that this book is addressed in the hope that with familiarity will come understanding, followed by appreciation and pleasure.

Roud's study of Jean-Marie Straub, 1971

Straub is in many ways a unique figure. Although French by birth, his early years in German-occupied Lorraine and his decade spent in Munich have not been without their effect. Although he shares many of Bresson's preoccupations, and although he is a great admirer of Grémillon, Renoir, and Godard, there is at the same time in his work a pronounced reaction against much of what is thought of as typically French and an accompanying bias towards what is thought of as typically German. The fact that neither of these stereotypes is accurate is unimportant: clichés contain a modicum of truth. If his philosophy is more Hegelian than Cartesian, then his sense of ellipsis, of understatement, and of plastic values, belongs well west of the Rhine.

Straub is also unique in that he is that rarest of animals: a formalist with left-wing views, the first perhaps since Eisenstein and Dovzhenko. It has long been a subject of concern to many people (*Partisan Review* used to have long, tormented symposia about it during the war) that the greatest writers of the twentieth century – Yeats, Pound, Eliot, Valéry, Mann, Proust – were all in varying degrees socially and politically reactionary, whereas those writers with exemplary political views were less satisfactory as artists.

Now we have in the cinema a great formalist who is also concerned with social problems; and naturally he has been rejected by the stupider left-wing critics, especially in France, because his artistic honesty has kept him from caricature and from over-simplifications. And in spite of his anti-militarist, anti-authoritarian viewpoint, he, or at least his films, are not without certain mystical tendencies: the end of *The Bridegroom, The Comedienne, and the Pimp* is on as exalted a plane as any scene from Bresson.

The catalogue of contradictions is endless. Straub believes very strongly in the necessity of the documentary approach – he uses only non-professional actors and direct sound – and yet this almost *cinéma vérité* approach is applied to a seventeenth-century verse drama, to the life of Johann Sebastian Bach, to a novel or a short story by Heinrich Böll. For Straub, documentary statement does not preclude an interest in literature and other pre-existing works of art: his next project is the Schoenberg opera *Moses und Aaron*, which will also be filmed from a 'documentary', materialist angle. When Straub takes a literary work, he neither alters nor adapts it – it, too, is treated as documentary raw material. Yet like Bresson, while apparently negating the cinema by subordinating it to literature, he actually renews and enriches it.

Although he will not tamper with sound by post-synching, he subjects sound to a treatment which reduces it to the level of an object. Even though the sound is captured live, he has already altered it by his direction of the actors, obliging them to speak in a deliberately inexpressive manner – or even, as in his last film, in a manner which is often unintelligible. For him, the soundtrack of a film is at least as important as the visuals, if not more so. But it, too, must be subordinated to the *total* effect of the film as a whole – which he once defined as simply the application of space to time.

Decades Never Start On Time

The total effect is also one of complementary values: content is important to Straub, but he has achieved an extraordinary fusion of form and content, and it is difficult to dissociate the two. He has achieved this, I propose, through the complex structuring of his films. Apart from anything else, they are extremely rich patterns of sound and light, articulated in the cutting-room by Straub's rhythmic sense. These structures can in fact be expressed in mathematical terms, yet I would not suggest that they were so engendered. But music and mathematics share a great many elements both with each other and with the cinema, the most important being proportion, number, and rhythm.

The foregoing may make Straub sound forbiddingly formidable, and yet, I suggest, this is not so. For he is the most unaristocratic of film-makers: he makes the viewer a party to the process of creation. When he takes his creative leap into the dark, we are right there behind him. If the spectator is not merely passive, he can find the experience of a film like *Not Reconciled* a highly stimulating form of controlled participation, always provided he is willing to suspend any attempt at total understanding until the film is over. Surely this is not too much to ask: the reward is the excitement of seeing all the pieces, whether of plot or design, slowly begin to fit together.

Of course, as with a lot of contemporary art, Straub's films are as much 'about' themselves as 'about' anything else. Apart from their subject-matter, they are also 'film-films'; that is to say, they are concerned with the processes and materials of film itself. This, in fact, is probably the biggest hurdle to general appreciation, as it was in the past with writers like Joyce. Many people have an underlying and ineradicable feeling that art can only be justified by life. This somewhat puritanical view has naturally brought an opposing reaction: that it is only art that can possibly justify life. Without pronouncing on what is so obviously a futile problem, one can at least say that with Straub the choice does not have to be made: his films resolve the contradiction.

As they do all the other contradictions. Straub is not interesting because of the conflicts in his work, but because these conflicts are somehow resolved. He is militant, yet mystical; materialistic, yet musical; minimal in means, and yet in the end maximal in effect. A film like *Not Reconciled* can deal directly with the problems of Nazism and yet at the same time achieve a state of exaltation equalled in the cinema only by a Dreyer or a Bresson. He may construct his films from the most realistic materials, and yet the result is a musical structure which transcends realism – but without rejecting it. His rooms may be bare and white, but his diagonal views of them make those empty walls vibrate with life. He may not move the camera very much, but when he does the effect is stimulating in inversely geometrical proportions.

And although these films are self-contained works of art, they do call on our participation: they must be completed by us. A review of the Bach film by Penelope Gilliatt (which began unfavourably) concluded that: 'The terrible restraint is probably justified. It deliberately creates a vacuum which you have to fill yourself, in your own sloppy way. Sometimes I watched the moments when the pretend Bach changed manuals on the harpsichord, and sometimes I fell into things that never get into reviews, like thoughts of dinner, and what to do with your life …' And this is true, not only 'what's for dinner', but 'what to do with your life'. I suggest that the greatness of Straub lies in the fact that, although he doesn't *tell* you what to do with your life, one does have a better idea of what the possibilities are, what one could do, after seeing his films. The idea that Art should somehow ennoble and purify is impossibly old-fashioned, not to say Platonic; and yet, Straub's films share with the greatest music and the greatest painting an effect of elevation which is all the more powerful for the obscurity of its origin.

It may therefore seem contradictory to want to shed a little light on this obscurity. But to illuminate is not to dissolve; and a fuller understanding of Straub will only heighten our sense of that insoluble mystery at the heart of every true work of art.

'I was born under the sign of Capricorn, like Johanna, the old lady in *Not Reconciled*. As Max Jacob said, all Capricorns are born old. More precisely, I was born on the Sunday after Epiphany in Metz, capital of Lorraine, the city where Paul Verlaine was born, Verlaine who wrote: "And if I had a hundred sons, they should have a hundred horses/all the more quickly to flee the Sergeant, the Army."'

'The name that was given me was that of one of the first conscientious objectors – Jean-Marie Vianney, the Curé d'Ars. And the year was precisely the one in which Hitler came to power. Until 1940 I only heard French spoken; that was the language I learned at home and at school. And then I was suddenly obliged to speak only German: any French word at school was absolutely forbidden. We were taught by the "direct method", and I remember my older sister who came home from her first day at school having learned two sentences in German: "The bad wolf ate the seven lambs," and "God created the whole world." Unfortunately, when she was asked what the *first* sentence meant in French, she replied: "Le Bon Dieu a créé le monde entier."'

But Straub's biography begins much earlier than 1933. Actually, we should start a thousand years ago when, on the death of Louis Le Débonnaire – son of Charlemagne – the whole Empire was divided into three parts: Charles was given the Western Kingdom, Louis the Eastern, and everything in between (Flanders, Alsace, Lorraine, Burgundy, and all the rest down to Rome) was given to Lothar, the third son. As every schoolboy knows, poor Lothar was the weakest of the three, and the history of Western Europe has suffered ever since as a result. During the past century, for example, Straub's birth-place has been part of Germany for more than fifty years. So when the Germans invaded France in 1940, they treated both Alsace and Lorraine, not as Occupied Territory, but simply as parts of Germany. They even went so far as to oblige shopkeepers to repaint their signs in Gothic script.

History is seldom irrelevant, and Straub can be described as a man of the Middle Kingdom: one who is imbued with both French and German culture. While this has caused him great personal hardship, it has also greatly enriched his life. One cannot call Straub a German director; on the other hand, he does not belong entirely to the French school either.

After the Liberation, Straub went to St Clement's, a Jesuit school, where he learned, he says, that insubordination had virtues other than poetic; he then entered a state *lycée*. During his second year he took part in a demonstration against the unenterprising programmes of the Metz cinemas, and on that occasion had his first brush with the French police. The second, even more brutal contact, came a little later during a protest against police harassment of the Algerians in Metz.

At that time, Straub wanted to become a writer, and he did half his *License-ès-Lettres*. But he tells us he was not a good student: 'I was so lazy I missed out on both maths and music. My parents brought me up very badly; if children were taught music at the time they are taught Latin and Greek, they'd be much better off.'

He first became interested in the cinema just after the war.[6] [...]

After the overwhelming experience of *Les Dames du Bois de Boulogne*, Straub decided that he wanted to write about the cinema. At the same time, he swore that he would never make a film himself. He preferred, he said, to explain them. Four years later, he left Metz

Decades Never Start On Time

for Paris ... with the intention of making a film about Bach. After his arrival in Paris in 1954, he was assistant/apprentice to Abel Gance (*La Tour de Nesle*), Renoir (*French Cancan* and *Eléna et les hommes*), Rivette (*Le Coup du berger*), Astruc (*Une Vie*) and, of course, Bresson (*Un Condamné à mort s'est échappé*). The two most important events of his Paris years were his meeting with Danièle Huillet and the Algerian revolution.

Danièle was already interested in the cinema before meeting Straub; and she was in fact preparing to enter the French Film School, IDHEC. But, she said: 'I never passed the entrance exam. They showed us Yves Allégret's *Manèges* and asked us to analyse it. I left my exam book blank, except for three lines in which I said it was scandalous they should show us such a terrible film. Perhaps if I saw the film now, I'd find it entertaining – Simone Signoret was really good in it. But then I was indignant that they should consider this film worthy of extended analysis.'

The outbreak of hostilities in Algeria and the increasing number of men called up to do their military service there presented Straub and the other young Frenchmen who were violently opposed to colonial war with something of a moral dilemma. So, in 1958, Straub left for Germany. During his first year there, he went all through East and West Germany, hitch-hiking most of the way, to look for locations for the Bach film. Part of the time he was accompanied by Danièle (she went back and forth to Paris to raise money). Straub discovered that it was going to be impossible to make the film on the original sites; so much had been altered during the nineteenth century that substitutions would have to be made. Meanwhile, he microfilmed the documents that were to appear in the film.

By the end of 1958, he had finished the script. He then looked for someone to help him modernize the eighteenth-century texts enough to make them understandable without distorting the language. In Paris he had a friend who knew a German called Böll who might be able to help. Straub went to see him, but Böll convinced him that he had hardly to change more than a word or two, arguing that the eighteenth-century language was an essential part of the film.

The meeting with Böll turned out to be of great importance: it prompted Straub to read his works. By 1959, when the Bach project had to be dropped for lack of money, Straub had read Böll's *Billiards at Half Past Nine* (the basis for *Not Reconciled*) and *Bonn Diary* (which he was to film as *Machorka-Muff*). At the end of 1959, Straub and Danièle Huillet married and settled in Munich, where they were to remain for ten years. (In fact, Straub has now lived almost as long outside France as within.)

The next two years were spent in trying to find a producer for *Billiards at Half Past Nine*. Round and round Germany they went, but the project was always turned down. One of the chief reasons was Straub's insistence on direct sound. Germany, like Italy, has a long tradition of dubbed film, and everyone thought Straub was mad. But his belief in direct sound was confirmed by a number of films he saw in those years which made a profound impression on him. They were as different as *Man of Aran*, *Toni*, *L'amore*, and *La Chienne*, but all of them relied on sound, original sound. 'The most beautiful films in existence are Renoir's first sound films. Not only because the actors speak so beautifully, especially those with *Midi* accents, but because it is original sound. The Bach project only made sense if the sound was recorded while the film was being shot, directly. And all my other projects grew out of the Bach film.'

After *Billiards at Half-Past Nine* was turned down by everyone, Straub began to try to put together a third, less ambitious, project. And this third project, the short *Machorka-Muff*, was the first to be realized. After Homeric struggles, two-thirds of the money was put up by Atlas Film, and the other third Straub got together from friends and acquaintances. But he was also obliged to write, edit, and direct, without remuneration. The film was sent to the Oberhausen Short Film Festival, where it was first rejected, then finally shown, early in 1963. Straub was then thirty years old.

SOURCE: *JEAN-MARIE STRAUB* (LONDON: SECKER & WARBURG; NEW YORK: VIKING PRESS, 1971), 'INTRODUCTION' AND 'BACKGROUND', 6–27

3.9 DADDY OF 'EM ALL

Whatever else can be said about Francis Ford Coppola's *The Godfather*, it is, to use Paramount's publicity phrase 'now a phenomenon.' It is, in fact, an event – the likes of which one hasn't seen here since *Gone with the Wind*. It has been playing now in New York for a fortnight in five cinemas, and according to *Variety* it has already grossed almost a million dollars. I went to see it on a weekday afternoon and had to stand in line for half an hour. In the evenings and on the weekends, the wait averages an hour and a half.

But numbers and dollars don't tell the whole story. Unlike *Love Story* which everyone went to see but didn't much talk about, everyone – at every level – is talking about *The Godfather*. What's more, everyone, almost without exception, thinks it's great.

And, in its way, it is. It's your big commercial film which, without advancing the art of the cinema a millimetre, without a real directorial presence behind it, is nonetheless an extremely satisfying three hours. Old-fashioned? Of course. From the beginning with the wedding of the godfather's daughter serving as set-piece backdrop for a myriad of short expository scenes which effectively get us into the story, to its slam-bang penultimate sequence with the baptism of the new godson intercut with a flashy montage of the slaughter of the family's enemies (we cut from 'I renounce Satan' right into the most brutal of slayings) the film is sheer economical story telling.

What is unusual is that unlike blockbusters of the past it boasts only one real star: Marlon Brando who plays the ageing Don Corleone. It took me about ten minutes to get adjusted to his performance, because at first it looked as if he were imitating Orson Welles. His mouth is stuffed with cotton wool, the jaws sag all too convincingly, and the diction is pretty far out.

But then the magic begins to work, and one forgets the obvious 'acting' and to notice the real acting that's going on underneath. Brando is best of all in his scenes with his favourite son Michael, charismatically played by Al Pacino, who some will remember from *Panic in Needle Park*. Pacino has got the makings of a star, and it was particularly heartwarming to see him in his sequences with Brando. Neither tries to hog, to steal scenes. In fact, each is at his best when playing with the other. And as Pacino uncannily and almost imperceptibly begins to resemble his father, the effect is all the more telling.

As Vincent Canby of the *New York Times* neatly summed it up, this is 'the year's first really satisfying, big commercial film. One of the most brutal and moving chronicles of American life ever designed within the limits of popular entertainment …'

The success of the film does not entirely lie in its cinematic qualities. Mario Puzo's novel is supposed to have sold here as well as the Bible, and this has contributed much to the film's popularity. But the subject matter has had a lot to do with its success. Although you'd never know it from the film, it's about the Mafia. But nowhere are the words 'Mafia' or 'Cosa Nostra' mentioned.

The Italian-American League had no objections to ethnic slurs like 'wop', 'Dago' or 'guinea' which pop up quite frequently – but Mafia – never. Without coming to grips with the problem, the film occasionally, and obliquely, attempts to 'explain' it in terms of an immigrant morality. When the Italian undertaker comes to the Godfather for the vengeance the courts refused to grant him, Corleone doesn't miss the chance of rubbing in the fact that the undertaker was mistaken in thinking that American justice and institutions were strong enough to take care of him. The point he is making is that just as the Mafia arose as an attempt to deal with problems that the various invaders of Sicily either couldn't or wouldn't handle, justice in America is also neither universal nor impartial, and the Mafia is there to 'supplement' it.

The Godfather (1972)

Later in the film Michael's WASP girlfriend expresses horror at his decision to go into his father's 'Business,' he makes the point that there is little difference between his father and traditional American power figures. The point is never argued: she calls him naive, and he retorts that it is she who is being naive – but while audiences may not agree, they will at least accept the argument as valid. We have come a long way from the Frank Capra populist days: almost every day one reads of scandals like the Beard/ITT affair, or the more recent earthshaking indictment of such a bourgeois bulwark as Dun and Bradstreet for fraud.[7]

On the other hand, there is an undeniable fascination with the romantic side of the Mafia. In a time when court cases drag on inconclusively and people are beginning to have less and less faith in American institutions, an organisation like the Mafia has the appeal of directness – an eye for an eye, and all the rest of it. Then, too, the code is simple, dramatically simple and in an age where justice seems lost in interpretative waffle, and the Supreme Court is upsetting cherished prejudices, there is a dangerous nostalgia for law and order, even in the particularly brutal form dear to the Mafia.

Some people have questioned the morality of the film; I think it simply reflects current unease and fears of anarchy, but I don't think it panders to them. On the other hand, this is also why Canby was right in circumscribing the film within 'the limits of popular entertainment,' for surely that is one of the differences between art and entertainment: the latter reflects; the former provokes.

SOURCE: 'DADDY OF 'EM ALL', *GUARDIAN*, 6 APRIL 1972, 10

3.10 THE DRAGON ...

The Wheel of Fortune turns pretty fast these days. Maybe not like a film projector, at 24 images a second, but fast enough. It is only four years now since Henri Langlois was thrown out of the Cinémathèque Française by the French Government. Four years, too, since the film world in France discovered that Governments can successfully be fought, and got him reinstated within months.

Now with the blessings of the Government, he has just opened a new film museum in the Palais de Chaillot with an exhibition that will run on for the rest of the year. It is not the first show he has mounted, but it is the largest, with a choice selection of the material he has amassed over the years – Cocteau called him 'the dragon who jealously guards our treasures.'

There are some who might question the whole notion of a film-museum – why bother collecting costumes, sets, stills, posters: what counts are the films themselves, they say; the rest is sheer fetishism. Maybe so, but such people can never have seen a Langlois exhibition. For it is in itself a kind of *mise en scène*, a three-dimensional film. No one realises more than he the dangers of simply putting on display a lot of faded costumes, so what he has done is to create a kind of environment where, as you wander from space to space, the whole history of the cinema unfolds before your astonished eyes.

Tidy, it's not. Through the wings of the set of *The Cabinet of Dr. Caligari*, one suddenly sees a blow-up of a still from Lubitsch's contemporary *Madame DuBarry* ... it doesn't belong there, but seeing it tells you more about the coexistence of various styles than chapters of film history.

It is true that Vivien Leigh's ball-gown from *Gone With the Wind* has gone yellow with age, and yet seeing it casually draped near Esther Williams's pearl bathing suit and not too far from Chanel's costumes for *Marienbad* prompts the most fruitful musings about the relationship between history and the cinema, and between cinema and fashion.

Each period is treated differently: the Italian neo-realist epoch is brilliantly done in one room with huge blow-ups of shots from *Bicycle Thieves*, *Open City*, and *La strada*. Of course, film itself is not totally absent: through the show, strategically placed cartridge machines repeat important sequences from film history.

Perhaps what I found most extraordinary is the great charm of so many of the artefacts of film history. The Méliès painted backdrops – his models are nearly works of art in themselves. The robot from *Metropolis*, the tiny houses which form the set for René Clair's *Under the Roofs of Paris* turn out to be enchanting in their own right.

Nor is Art with a capital A absent: there are a number of drawings by Léger as well as the original wood sculpture he made for his film *Ballet mécanique*, right alongside such lesser objects as the shoes of Little Tich (obligingly lent, says Langlois, by a lady from Brighton). There are Tom Mix's cowboy suits; the shrunken head of Tony Perkins's 'mother' from *Psycho*, the crown from Kurosawa's *Throne of Blood*. Each in itself might be trivial; but somehow, and this is where the art of *mise en scène* comes into play, together they form a staggering show, an atmosphere unmatched anywhere in the world.

The exhibition ends, fittingly enough, in a small theatre, a cinémathèque within the cinémathèque, where films will be shown nonstop. This, combined with the regular theatre downstairs which already shows three – and sometimes four – films a day, plus the Left Bank branch on the Rue d'Ulm which shows three films a day, will mean that there is now no place in the world where you can see more films in a given period of time: ideal for a crash course.

After the Film Library (for that is what cinémathèque literally means), the Film Museum: Langlois and his two associate dragons – Mary Meerson and Lotte Eisner – have completed the consecration of the cinema. If film has its museum, who can doubt that it is an art? But the exhibition also proves that a museum itself can be a work of art. Strange to think that the most enduring results of the ferment of 1968 is a museum. And that Malraux, inventor of the Imaginary Museum, the Museum without Walls, is out, and Langlois, creator of a very concrete museum, is back in place.[8] But these are just a couple of the ironies which history so often lavishes on us.

SOURCE: 'THE DRAGON AND DESPAIR', *GUARDIAN*, 1 AUGUST 1972, 10

3.11 IT TAKES TWO TO TANGO

Having already broken my self-imposed rule about not writing about the New York Film Festival (of which I am director) in discussing the new Buñuel, I might as well break it again to report on our world premiere of the new Bertolucci film: *Last Tango in Paris*.

It was something of an event. Pauline Kael, a lady who does not often lose her cool, wrote in the *New Yorker*: '*Last Tango in Paris* was presented for the first time on the closing night of the New York Film Festival … that should become a landmark in movie history comparable to 29 May 1913 – the night *Le Sacre du printemps* was first performed – in music history.

'There was no riot, and no one threw anything at the screen,' conceded Miss Kael, 'but I think it's fair to say that the audience was in a state of shock, because the film has the same kind of hypnotic excitement as the *Sacre*, the same primitive force, and the same thrusting, jabbing eroticism. The movie breakthrough has finally come.'

By which she means that at last a director has come along and used the 'new permissiveness' to make a film about sexuality which is both intelligent and moving. Part of the shock came from the fact that much of the film is in English: Marlon Brando can, and does, speak French, but the key scenes were in our own language, and they were spoken by nothing less than a household name. Furthermore, it was generally conceded that he was giving his best performance in 20 years. This was no mere 'character part' as in *The Godfather*, but the real thing.

More than that, he spoke, for the first time in film history, the way people do about sex when they're having it. And during much of the film, that is just what he and Maria Schneider are doing. The variety and explicitness (too explicit to recount in a family newspaper) of their sexual encounters also drew gasps. I have used the phrase 'having sex' because that is what they are doing – they are not making love, at least not at first. Brando plays an American in Paris whose wife has just committed suicide. He meets a young girl while they are both flat-hunting, and he launches a purely sexual relationship with her.

No names, no addresses, no past – those are his ground rules. The couple are to meet only in the flat, and they are never to talk about their outside life. The girl (brilliantly played by newcomer Maria Schneider) at first fights the idea, but gradually gives in. The twist, of course, is that as time passes, it is *he* who grows dissatisfied with the arrangement: her reaction is as unpredictable as it is quickly seen to be inevitable.

The film is based on an original script by Bertolucci and Kim Arcalli (who has also been Bertolucci's editor on his last three films), but Bertolucci modified the original script to fit the actors in much the same way Renoir did in *Rules of the Game*. Bertolucci's original choices for the two main roles were Jean-Louis Trintignant and Dominique Sanda. But the film as it stands now could never have been played by those two. In the same way, Renoir, after casting his film, began to modify it by bringing the documentary method into fiction film-making. Long before the term was invented, Renoir was creating his own kind of cinema vérité in which the film is almost as much a documentary on the actors as it is a story.

And this is also a film about Marlon Brando and the American tough-guy ideal he has so completely incarnated over the years. When Paul begins to talk about his childhood, Bertolucci abandoned his script and trained his camera on Brando who begins to improvise, and in fact tells us about his own childhood.

But apart from the film's many qualities (and I have been able to sketch in only a few of them) there was a special air of excitement that night because there was some doubt if anyone who wasn't there would ever see the film in its original form. Although shot entirely in Paris, it is an Italo-French co-production, and as such, if it is to benefit from all that the Italian system offers in the way of subsidies, etc., it cannot be exported before it is passed by the Italian censorship board.

An exception was made for the New York Film Festival, but the print was whisked in and out of the country too fast for there to be more than the one solitary screening – there was not even a press show. At the same time, the producer Alberto Grimaldi, flew in a half dozen Italian journalists: the idea is that the Italian censorship board is very responsive to foreign opinion: it is generally agreed that Pasolini's *Canterbury Tales* would never have got past them if it had not first won the Grand Prize in Berlin.

There are no prizes in New York, but the closing-night spot is much sought after, and those journalists had plenty to write home about. Whether it will work, we shall know in the next few months. Both producer and director are adamant that they will allow no cuts to be made.

What they always can do if the Italian censors don't pass the film is to surrender the film's nationality: it may cost them a little, but they would surely make it up on the film's American release. But where else can it be shown? Germany, Scandinavia – yes. But France or England: I wonder. It is certainly the best possible test for a censor: everyone here agreed the film is not pornographic. On the other hand, it is graphic and explicit. In fact, it poses something of a quandary. But I dare say it will be solved eventually: *Last Tango* is manifestly too important a film to be put on the shelf. Meanwhile, the fur is going to fly.

SOURCE: 'IT TAKES TWO TO TANGO', *GUARDIAN*, 20 NOVEMBER 1972, 8

3.12 HOW CAN WE KNOW THE DANCER FROM THE DANCE?

NOTE: Roud wrote several excellent texts for the programmes of the Film Society's gala tributes – for example, those devoted to Alfred Hitchcock in 1974 and Martin Scorsese in 1977 (see Bibliography for details of these pieces).

It is universally recognised that musical comedy is one of the greatest of American contributions to world cinema. But it is perhaps less well understood that the true originality of musical comedy lay not in the music or the comedy, but in the dancing.

Operetta and light opera were nothing new – they had reached their peak as an art form in the Vienna of Johann Strauss, Jr, and the Paris of Offenbach. What Hollywood brought – first in the massively manic symmetry of the Busby Berkeley musicals, and then in the pure dance of the Astaire films – was the fusion of music and comedy, of romance and dance: that sheer exhilaration of movement which only the cinema can offer, the conjugation of camera movement with the movement of the dancers. And for this no one deserves more credit than Fred Astaire.

Like the greatest stars however – and here Garbo and Keaton also spring to mind – Astaire was much more than a star. He was not just a dancer, not just a choreographer: he was in a very important sense also a director. From the very beginning of his

The Sky's the Limit (1943)

career in motion pictures he was determined to have control over the filming and cutting of his numbers. And already by 1933, Arlene Croce, in her definitive study of Astaire, tells us the RKO bosses had begun to let him edit his own numbers.[9]

Except for the writing of the songs, she tells us, Astaire controlled every development of every number, and there are instances when he affected even the actual composing. Composers trusted him: Irving Berlin said that he would rather have Astaire introduce his songs than any other performer, and Jerome Kern, 'a notably fussy man who concerned himself with every aspect of production, used to say "Astaire can't do anything bad."'

He was technically the greatest revolutionary in the history of the movie musical. He forced camerawork, cutting synchronisation and scoring to the highest standards of sensitivity and precision. He fought on every front, Miss Croce tells us, and in the cutting room, he was a stickler. It may have *looked* to some at the time that he was doing nothing but having the camera reproduce his stage dancing, but that was far from the case: it was he who created film dance.

But his justly enormous popularity derived from other causes: it was not his technical skill, but the converse – that illusion of spontaneity which only he could supply. Like Tarzan, he made it all seem so easy. Nor did he look like a movie star, either. (There is the famous if apocryphal story about the comment by some movie mogul on his first screen test: 'Can't act. Can't sing. Balding. Can dance a little.') In fact, he makes his routines look so smooth and so simple that people could, with a slight suspension of disbelief, imagine themselves dancing like that, too.

For his was the art that conceals art: Miss Croce points out how revolutionary his technique really was. Unlike the earlier 'Mickey-Mousing', where steps were mechanically matched to music, he often worked *against* the beat, the steps in counterpoint to the music. Often he choreographed to the accompaniment as well as to the melody. Never mimicking the music, he preferred to run the dancing alongside the music or against it in a countercurrent.

More than any of his successors, Astaire created the dance film, one of the true glories of the cinema, and one that was not destined to last more than a few decades. In fact, it is a genre that no longer exists. But as long as film exists, Fred Astaire will be remembered.

'O body swayed to music/O brightening glance/How can we know the dancer from the dance?' wrote William Butler Yeats. In the case of Fred Astaire, the answer is clear: he was both director and dramatist, choreographer and cameraman; the singer and the song, the dancer and the dance.

SOURCE: 'HOW CAN WE KNOW THE DANCER FROM THE DANCE?', PROGRAMME, FILM SOCIETY OF LINCOLN CENTER'S TRIBUTE TO FRED ASTAIRE, 30 APRIL 1973

3.13 HOLLYWOOD EMBERS

Renaissance is a dangerous word to use: I prematurely employed the word a few years back in writing about the New German Cinema, and thereupon, with three exceptions, it folded up and died. This has been one of the best years the American cinema has seen for a long time, with half a dozen new films by young directors that could – at the very least – be termed promising, so let's take the plunge and call it a renaissance.

They are all 'Hollywood' films, too, if that term still has any meaning. The three I want to write about were made independently but *Mean Streets* was snapped up by Warner Brothers, *American Graffiti* by Universal, and *Electra Glide in Blue* by United Artists. Strictly speaking, this is nothing new. Over the past five years, an 'independent' company like BBS has produced for Columbia an extraordinary series of films – *Easy Rider*, *Five Easy Pieces*, *The Last Picture Show*, *King of Marvin Gardens*. But BBS has family ties with Columbia, and anyway there has never been a single year with quite so many encouraging films at once.

Whether this 'experiment,' if that is what it is, will continue will be determined by the success of these films at the box-office, this kind of dollars-and-sense speculation is unavoidable. As Richard Corliss points out,[10] in his forthcoming book on American screenwriters: 'The American cinema is a most peculiar child, conceived by the shotgun marriage of art and industry, raised in a circus, brought to maturity under a whole world's watchful eyes – and then abandoned in its prime. It costs money to make movies, especially for the dwindling audience of the 1970s; and unless self-enlightenment and self-interest can continue to co-exist, the talking picture could die out.'

So far, and it is probably too early to tell, at least two of the three movies mentioned above look as if they will do all right at the box-office. The exception is *Electra Glide in Blue*. As I wrote from Cannes, it is not a perfect film: there is something fuzzy about its conception, and it has more than a few awkward moments. Unfortunately, the *New York Times* review of the film (which is all-important, to a point that may be hard for Londoners to understand) was a terrible pan, concentrating only on the film's defects and not even mentioning its considerable virtues.

This, I am afraid, was partly caused by the truly unfortunate publicity campaign for the film, which was built entirely around the not-terribly-engaging personality of the director, Guercio, with full-page ads of him all got up in black boots looking balefully out at his audience like some sulky star of the 1960s. And so the *Times* review began: 'For a long time

Decades Never Start On Time

now, the ads have been everywhere. Ads for a movie, yet they feature not the movie, but a man: An American Movie by a New Director. A lot of money has been spent to make Guercio very, very public.'

So, many people were prejudiced against the film from the start – and the *Times* ended up by calling it 'the most strangely inflated movie of the season.' True, in an attempt to counter its own blast, there did appear an article the following Sunday in favour of the film, but the damage was done.

And yet, another film, *American Graffiti*, which also has its flaws, has been praised to the skies by everyone. The one thing both films have in common is their very strong sense of place – their vision of small town American life. *American Graffiti* is very much a California film; its theme may be universal, but it is firmly rooted in the automobile culture, the drive-in civilisation of California, sometimes described as more a state of mind than a State of Union. And the Arizona landscapes of *Electra Glide*, and its director's feeling for them, give his film its truly indigenous qualities.

American Graffiti is, however, more of a piece than *Electra Glide*. It is George Lucas's second film as director (the first was the underrated sci-fi film *THX 1138*) and in spite of its fragmentary plot it makes its effects more purposefully than *Electra Glide*. The whole action takes place on one night in the early sixties: it's the weekend of a high school graduation in Modesto, California, and we follow four friends on a Saturday night out. One of them is off to an Eastern university; another is hesitating; a third is involved more with his automobile than anything else; and the fourth is desperately trying to get laid. Three of the characters are projections of the author/director: 'I spent my teen years cruising the main street in Modesto. I was Terry the Toad, fumbling with girls. Then I became a drag racer, like John. I was interested in cars until a bad accident almost killed me. And finally I became Curt: I got serious and went to college.'

As long as the film doesn't 'get serious' all is well, but in a misjudged attempt at higher significance Lucas has tacked on an epilogue which suddenly and unsuccessfully tries to give the film more weight of meaning than it will bear, tries to make it the story of a generation, rather than of four guys. Curiously enough, the most believable of the four was the one not modelled on Lucas's youth – 'I was never a big wheel at high school like Steve,' he has declared; 'he was totally fictitious, and the most difficult character to create.' Maybe so, but he is also the most credible, and there must be a lesson there somewhere.

Mean Streets could also be described as a 'nostalgia' film, except that the director, Martin Scorsese, couldn't afford to set it in the three-week period before Kennedy's assassination in 1963 as he wanted to. So it is sort of timeless, but with very strong suggestions of the early sixties. Unlike the other two films mentioned, it has an urban setting, Manhattan's Little Italy. It is a world Scorsese knows well, and his portrait of the Mulberry Street Mafia is both sympathetic and critical. (Remember Graham Greene's remark – 'the camera can note with more exactitude and vividness than the prose of most living playwrights the atmosphere of mean streets and cheap lodgings.')

This is not a first film: Scorsese has fought long and hard. He began at the New York University Film School, made an extraordinary short (*The Big Shave*), some semi-underground features, and then a Roger Corman special, *Boxcar Bertha*, which passed almost unnoticed in America but which was well received in London.

It seems fair to predict that *Mean Streets*, after its world premiere at the New York Film Festival, will do very well. Vincent Canby of the *New York Times* called it an 'unequivocally first class film' and Pauline Kael in the *New Yorker* gave it the *Last Tango* treatment –

four pages of unqualified praise – 'a triumph of personal film-making,' 'dizzyingly sensual,' 'a thicker-textured rot and violence than we have ever had in an American movie, and a riper sense of evil.'

She may have overstated the case, but there is no denying it is a remarkable achievement, a film which looks and sounds like nothing else. And certainly not like *The Godfather*, although the material and milieu are similar. That was first-rate commercial entertainment: *Mean Streets* is less perfect, but more genuine, more unsettling, truer to the violent reality of urban America.

SOURCE: 'HOLLYWOOD EMBERS', *GUARDIAN*, 29 OCTOBER 1973, 10

3.14 APPLE PIE BEDLAM

Recently I wrote about three new movies which seemed to me to herald some sort of American renaissance. One of them, *Mean Streets*, premiered at the recently concluded New York Film Festival: but there were two other American films shown there too. *Kid Blue* and *Badlands*. Originally called *Dime Box* (a much more appropriate title), *Kid Blue* is set in 1900 and has been described as the first comic Marxist western. That is something of an exaggeration, but Brecht probably would have enjoyed this tale of a failed young bad-man (Dennis Hopper) who comes to Dime Box, Texas to go straight, only to find that incipient capitalism (The Great American Novelty Company) runs the town like a penal colony. But the film is not only concerned with Kid Blue's desperate (and ultimately unsuccessful) efforts to go straight – there is also an odd triangle drama between Kid Blue and a couple who befriend him. The man (beautifully played by Warren Oates) is something of a latent homosexual: when his attempt to make all three of them one happy family ends with his wife seducing Kid Blue, he feels betrayed on both sides.

One hopes fervently that Fox will release the film in England, even though they got badly burned here. This is director James Frawley's first film, and it is both enjoyable and pertinent.

Badlands was received unanimously as one of the most exciting American debut films in a long time. What was controversial, however, was what the film was saying. Its director, Terry Malick, is only 29 years old, a philosophy teacher (and Rhodes scholar) until a few years ago he suddenly threw it all up, enrolled in the American Film Institute's film programme and wrote the script (filmed by someone else) of *Pocket Money*. Those who saw it called it a gently nihilistic comedy about two American cowboys getting taken for everything they own in contemporary Mexico.

So there is no body of work to which to refer in working out the film. There is however an historical jumping-off place: the true story of Charlie Starkweather who, in 1958, went on a killing spree totalling a dozen victims, including the mother, step-father, and half-sister of his girlfriend. He was executed, but the girl is still in prison, and is now in fact up for parole. This, Malick admits, was his starting point, but for many reasons, including legal ones, he was obliged to change the story – and in particular that of Starkweather's accomplice: in the film, her complicity is never established, and she ends up marrying her lover's lawyer.

What was it that interested Malick in this story of a mass-murderer?

He has no obvious sociological axes to grind: we are told nothing about Kit's life before he met Holly. He is presumably from the lower middle class, but there are no suggestions

Decades Never Start On Time

Badlands (1973)

that his murders are motivated by economic resentments. Nor are there any psychological explanations – he seems like a nice kid, and as we are carefully told nothing about his background, we cannot assume that there was anything there that drove him to his actions.

When asked at a press conference about Kit's motivation, Malick said he didn't really know: he thought of Kit as a force of nature, like a great wind, one of those tornados that periodically chew up the Middle West. I think there is more to it than that: it's easy enough to say that this is an 'existential' thriller, with no explanations, no psychology. But there are some things to go on.

The very first conversation in the film is between Kit and a friend: 'I'll give you a dollar if you eat that collie,' says one of them. The answer comes back quickly enough: 'I wouldn't do it for a dollar, and besides, he's not a collie.' From the very beginning, then, murder is accepted as something natural enough to be joked about.

As Kit and Holly get to see each other more, her father begins to get angry – mostly, he says, because of the difference in ages: Holly is 15, Kit 25 – so he shoots her pet dog as punishment for disobeying his order not to see Kit. It seems that Malick is making some kind of point about the world of his characters – that world where violence is, as H. Rap Brown said, as American as apple pie.[11] The violence of the film, though never lingered over, is all the more appalling because of the contrast between it and the pastoral beauty of the small towns and countryside in which it occurs. The leisurely rhythm of mid-west life in the mid-1950s further reinforces this contrast, as does the music, a strange but telling mixture of Erik Satie, Carl Orff, Nat King Cole as well as a hauntingly original theme.

The suspicion that for all of Malick's denials the film is something of a microcosm, is reinforced by the scene in which Kit, after killing Holly's father, sets her house on fire, and we see, cut into the burning of the house, the destruction of her doll's house, a house within the house.

And then they go off on a woodland forest idyll, living in tree houses: 'Better spend a week,' says Holly, nourished by her constant reading of film magazines and romantic novels, 'with someone you love, than years of loneliness.'

The film comes into its own in the final third, when Kit and Holly cross the great plains, endless miles of open range, of lunar landscape. They are eventually caught. First, Holly gives herself up, and is assumed into heaven like the Virgin Mary, assisted by a helicopter and religious sounding music. Their separation is somewhat matter-of-fact – he says, 'I'll meet you at Grand Coulee Dam on New Year's Day in 1964.' All right, she says, but we know that she won't keep that appointment, that he'll be dead by then.

And the final quarter hour of the film sees Kit finally caught by the police, and taken off, by plane, through billowing clouds reminiscent of Hitler's arrivals and departures in *Triumph of the Will*. But he is still unconcerned by his killings. When he is captured, he quickly makes a small cairn of rocks, so that future generations will be able to find the exact spot. As he is driven off to the airfield, he straightens his hair in the rear-view mirror; at the same time, one of the policemen takes a pot shot into the prairie – at nothing. When he finally is led into the plane, he shakes everyone's hands, congratulates them on their good job, and wonders if he can get himself a hat like those the State Troopers wear. Far from resenting his captors, he seems very impressed with them, as if they had a great deal in common with him. And I suppose Malick is saying that they do.

I'm still not sure, after two viewings now, that I really understand what Malick is getting at. This piece is an attempt to come to grips with the experience of the film – and it's an extraordinary cinematic experience. The performances, the photography, Malick's extraordinary way of manipulating the camera: things are seen at angles which appear odd at a second, then suddenly right. The camera movements are spasmodic, yet serene – if that makes any sense. But the whole film doesn't 'make sense' in any conventional way. It has been compared to *Bonnie and Clyde* – because of the subject matter. In treatment it is much more like *Night of the Hunter*, the Charles Laughton/James Agee work – a film Malick much admires.

It is also, like that film, very American. I don't know quite how to explain this: it's something everyone here felt instinctively. Perhaps because of the feeling it gives of people who have no roots, no responsibilities other than to themselves – an obscene parody of the high principles with which the country was founded. Kit is engaged in the pursuit of happiness, and if that happiness depends on killing a few people, why then, they will just have to be killed. Not in anger, just to get them out of the way. The same way, I suppose, that the Indians who once peopled these prairies were killed; just to get them out of the way.

I don't think I am reading too much into the film: there must be some explanation of the powerful effect of this story, of two people for whom, as Holly writes in her diary, 'the world is a faraway planet to which I could never return.' She, of course, does return, but he doesn't. If there is no God, then everything is permitted, said one of the Karamazov brothers.[12] And one could see *Badlands* as a reduction to absurdity of America's protestant ethic which says that God will help those who help themselves and which exhorts us all to enrich ourselves as best we can.

Malick is a great admirer of Pasolini's work, and while there are no direct signs of this, there is a certain coolness about the film, a certain disposition to present us with a metaphysical situation that is not unlike, say, *Theorem*. *Badlands*, too, may be a kind of theorem, and one that is particularly appropriate to this country in the year 1973.

SOURCE: 'APPLE PIE BEDLAM', *GUARDIAN*, 27 NOVEMBER 1973, 14

3.15 THE RULES OF THE GAME

It may sound snobbish to choose *The Rules of the Game* as one's favorite film, for it is generally considered one of the world's greatest films; to say that it is one's favorite seems like showing-off – only the best is good enough for *me*.

Choosing a film as one's favorite implies that one has personal reasons for liking it; that is, in fact, the case. For some, like Leo Braudy, the main subject of *The Rules of the Game* is 'the retreat into theater.' For Bazin, it was probably the most total expression of depth of field used to present the ambiguities of reality. For me, it was something much simpler and, to me, more important: it was the discovery that life, and particularly love, was not as simple as I had been brought up to believe.

I first saw the film in January 1951 in Paris. I was twenty-one years old; I had been in France on a Fulbright for several months; and I was troubled.

Of course, Europe had been a very enriching experience; like Henry James's Chad Newsome (in *The Ambassadors*, which I was only to read the following year) I had had a vision of another world, a richer reality. But also a disturbing one – not because, like Chad, I suddenly discovered that these charming, witty Europeans were all evil. I was too sophisticated for that; lots had happened since James's hero had sailed forth out of New England.

No, it was the discovery, which the film crystallised, that there was in fact a Game which everyone was playing, and that it had its Rules, and that I didn't know them.

I think what shocked me most in the film was one character saying about another that he was 'too sincere.' I had never heard anyone talk that way in an American film – to make it worse, the character who said it was no Benedict Arnold, but a reasonably sympathetic person.

How could you be *too* sincere? I puzzled. Hadn't we all been brought up on the notion that sincerity was the highest virtue? I even remember people saying during the war, 'Well, I think Hitler is *sincere*,' as though that were somehow an attenuating factor.

Now, of course, looking back, I see that although American society pretended to believe this, it did not practice it. But I was too young to realise that; I had left home too soon. Something else became clear at that moment: although I had majored in English, minored in French, and read a large number of the classics, my notions about love and personal relations corresponded much more to Hollywood movies than it did to Dostoyevsky, Flaubert, or George Eliot. What was the point of reading Proust if one expected one's love affairs to follow the lines laid down by Lenore Coffee or any of the hundred Hollywood scriptwriters who, I suddenly realised, had given me my notions as to how people behaved when they were having an affair?

But if I was shocked by 'too sincere,' I recognised myself all too well in another state-ment made in the film: Dalio, at the end, saying 'I am suffering, and I hate that.' I still naively thought that if one person loved another, then it was bound, somehow, to come out all right. Tragedy was something awe-inspiring and noble; the notion that tragedy could pop up into everyday life without any flashes of lightning or clashes of cymbals was a new idea – one which I have since, like everyone else, learned to live with.

Then too, André Jurieux, the aviator, was there for me to identify with. Hadn't he, after all, come from America, as I had? He was simple and sincere, and here he was mixed up with all these people who managed somehow to be in love with several people at once. His bewilderment was mine, but not quite, for I had been there long enough to realise that although he and I were obviously in the right, there were an awful lot of other people – nice people – who felt differently about the matter.

Or perhaps I was already corrupt: I still know dozens of people who firmly maintain that marriage means fidelity, that it is *impossible* that a man can love his wife and also be car-rying on an affair. Either he *really* loves his wife or he doesn't, and if he does, then he can't have an affair with anyone else. And what *The Rules of the Game* confirmed (for nothing can teach you something you don't already know, however obscurely) is that it all depends on what is meant by *really*, and that anyhow people's needs are much more complex than we had been led to believe. The Marquis de la Chesnaye *does* love his wife Christine; he also loves Geneviève. Christine *does* love her husband, but she also loves André; and it is also possible for her to contemplate an affair with Octave. Pretty strong stuff for someone who had been brought up on *Now, Voyager!*

But there is another reason why I was struck by the film: the way it brought absurdity, which I was beginning to realise was inherent in human life, into art. The previous year saw the first productions of the plays of Ionesco, and a year after that we had *Waiting for Godot*. But obviously the 'theater of the absurd' was in the air, and in January 1951 I was very aware of it in *The Rules of the Game*. It was the first film I had ever seen that was neither comedy nor tragedy, melodrama nor social realism, but rather an insane combination of them all.

And what had me on the edge of my seat was the central Walpurgis Night sequence: the after-dinner 'entertainment' in which everything comes to a head, and which is treated like a Marx Brothers film scripted, not by S. J. Perelman, but by Feydeau (whose bedroom farces had just begun to be revived in France at that time). But more exciting than the far-cical treatment of serious things was the feeling that, underneath, the farce was more truly tragic than any I had heretofore experienced. The phrase 'tragic farce' is well established nowadays, but at the time it was new and daring. (Of course, when the film originally came out in 1939, it was totally unacceptable, as witness the disastrous first-run career of the film. By 1951, however, we were ready for it.)

And this mixing up of the genres seemed to correspond to the content of the film. Just as love and life were not so simple as one had thought, so a film that was to express this new vision had to be different from those made before. And the mixture of farce and tragedy corresponded, in my mind, to the ambiguities of the characters.

What I was not aware of at the time was that Renoir's *mise en scène* brought this out all the more. I probably noticed that the camera moved around a lot, but I was certainly not aware that his emphasis on long-ish sequence shots created an effect of simultanity which only reinforced the themes of the film. But I dare say this had its effect on me; I didn't notice, for example, that the whole Walpurgis Night sequence – from the beginning of the show to that fantastic moment when Dalio says to his maitre d'hôtel, '*Faites cesser cette comédie!* ('Stop this farce!'), and the answer comes: 'Which one?' – was done in an incredibly small number of shots – about fifty in all. But it had its effect, nonetheless.

All this is ancient history now. But seeing the film over and over again through the years, it is still as fresh as ever. Naturally, one is impressed with different things now, its encyclopedic quality, for example. The French have always gone in for the big novel – or rather sequence of novels – which portray a whole society. They were the first nation to produce an encyclopedia, and their novelists have gone on producing them – Balzac with his *Human Comedy*, Zola with the *Rougon-Macquart* series, Proust, Roger Martin du Gard with his pre-1914 saga *The Thibaults*, even Jules Romains's endless *Men of Good Will*.

If France were destroyed tomorrow, and nothing remained behind except *The Rules of the Game*, the whole country and its civilisation could be reconstructed from it. We have nothing like it here in America – not *Citizen Kane*, not *Birth of a Nation*, not anything. The only Great American Novel which even tried to bring it off was Dos Passos's *USA*, and although I persist unfashionably in thinking it a remarkable achievement, it seems, next to *The Rules of the Game*, overly fabricated.

Everything is in *The Rules of the Game*, every strata of society – with the possible exception of industrial workers and peasants, but even here there are glancing references to Monsieur and Madame de la Bruyére's factory in Tourcoing, and a glimpse of the peasant class in the character of the poacher Marceau.

But it is not just twentieth-century France that is present in the film: we know that Renoir was inspired by Musset's *Les Caprices de Marianne*, and that he carefully reread Marivaux before writing the script. It is France itself which the film explores, and this gives the film an incredible richness and takes it beyond a simple tableau or portrait of 1930s France.

Nevertheless, it is also very much of its own time, as a double bill consisting of this film and *The Sorrow and the Pity* would clearly reveal: one could almost predict how each of the characters would react in Vichy France (Schumacher joining the French SS, and Marceau joining the Resistance, for example).

But no matter how important a film's themes may be, and how revolutionary its technique, it stands or falls in the long run on its material qualities, and in the case of this film that means, above all, the performances, the direction of the actors – who are after all what we *see* and *hear* in the film: the raw material. And one is amazed at just what Renoir has done. It is an open secret, for example, that he chose Nora Gregor for the part of Christine because he had fallen in love with her, and only as he began to make the film did he realise her inadequacies – her physical awkwardness, her difficulties with the French language. What he did was to modify not only her role, but the whole film: Mila Parély's role (as Geneviève, La Chesnaye's mistress) was built up so as to compensate for whatever Madame Gregor could not bring to the film. His use of Dalio to play the Marquis raised a lot of eyebrows, for he was not exactly the most aristocratic of types; it works because Renoir convincingly changed him from a patron of the arts into a half-Jewish collector of musical toys.

What he did was to bring the documentary method into fiction film-making. Long before the term was invented, Renoir was creating his own kind of *cinéma verité*, in which the film is almost as much a documentary on the actors as it is a story. Improvisation plays a large part in Renoir's technique, and it helped to enrich his treatment of the characters. Because he had got the marvellous trio of Carette, Gaston Modot, and Paulette Dubost, for example, he decided to develop the 'servant' part of the story while downplaying the Nora Gregor role.

La Règle du jeu (1939)

And then there is the role played in the film by Renoir himself. It is as though he included himself through a kind of scrupulous honesty: he could not except himself from his portrait of society; he did not wish to stand outside. Renoir's character, Octave, is more than a little ridiculous, and I feel sure that Renoir knew this and did not shrink from it. (A friend has suggested that the *real* reason I like the film so much is that I identify with Renoir/Octave, and I must admit there is a certain resemblance in face and physique, and in his bumbling gesticulations; Octave is always clumsily throwing himself around.) The film would not be the same without Renoir/Octave; he serves as the standard against which reality and fiction can be measured. And as in a Pirandello play, the two become ultimately confused; that would seem to be Renoir's point, even if he did not grasp it fully at the time.

It seems that Renoir did not 'know' what he was doing – when the film had its catastrophic premiere, he was amazed by people's reactions. He may not have been intellectually aware of his audacity, but the film is no accident. Everything in his career leads up to it, just as everything since is a development of elements that are already present – however unconsciously or inarticulately – in this watershed film.

There is yet another reason why this is my favorite film: I have emphasised its riches, but the spectator has to dig for them. He has to contribute, and in so doing, he becomes a part of the film, in much the same way as the director became a part of it by playing Octave.

And this may be why, ultimately, I prefer it to another of my favorite films – Bresson's *Les Dames du Bois de Boulogne* – an almost perfect film, but one which hardly needs the viewer to complete it. It is a much more conscious work of art; everything has been planned, nothing left to chance. Rather than *use* the actors as Renoir has, Bresson has obliterated them. They become Bresson's puppets, whereas the opposite is the case with

Decades Never Start On Time

Renoir. And here again one sees the significance of his acting in the film. Bresson's films are Bresson. Renoir is saying, this is me, these are the others; put them all together and, to misuse Carson McCullers's phrase, you get the we of me.

The Rules of the Game is an open work, from which no one is excluded, either in the making of the film or in the experiencing of it now. I love Vigo's *L'Atalante:* it is perhaps the most purely 'poetic' film ever made, but it is not my favorite film because – because Vigo didn't *want* it to be. It is his film, his vision, and we are kept a little outside of it.

In *Citizen Kane*, another favorite, Welles does indeed play a role in his film, as Renoir did, but the difference is monumental: Welles plays Kane in such a way as to keep Welles *out* of the film, to keep us at our distance from him. It is, of course, a much finer performance than Renoir gives; but it is also a much less personal one. Welles hides behind Kane, whereas Renoir, almost indecently, exposes himself as Octave.

Oddly enough, a film that much resembles *The Rules of the Game* is Resnais's *Muriel*, another favorite of mine. Like the Renoir, it is a panorama of French life, this time post-war. And Delphine Seyrig, although a much greater actress than Nora Gregor, also gives a performance which is against the grain for her; Renoir made a 'mistake' in casting Gregor for the part, and that is paradoxically why she is so moving. Resnais chose Seyrig purposely to play a part for which she must have seemed – and is – oddly suited. And paradoxically she is great in the role just because the Seyrig of *Marienbad* was all wrong for the Hélène of *Muriel*. And while Resnais did not go so far as to appear in his own film, the actor he chose for Alphonse is in fact playing a version of Resnais himself – an unsympathetic, unflattering version, showing himself at his vacillating, temporising worst, just as Renoir showed himself at his worst as Octave. Masochism, objectivity, or humility? A mixture of all three.

One admires some people and some things because they are different from oneself. And one admires others because they are the same. I like Bresson's, Godard's and Straub's sensibilities because they are totally unlike mine. I go all gooey at Demy's *Lola* and Ophüls's *La signora di tutti* because their sensibilities are all too much like my own. But I think what I like most is a mixture of my own temperament with something a little different; or, shall we say, my view of myself on one of my better days. That is why I like Bertolucci, and that is why *The Rules of the Game* remains my favorite film.

SOURCE: '*THE RULES OF THE GAME*', IN PHILIP NOBILE (ED.), *FAVORITE MOVIES: CRITICS' CHOICE* (NEW YORK: MACMILLAN, 1973), 97–104

3.16 HOLD THE FRONT PAGE

It's not very often that a film review gets the honours of the front page of *Le Monde*, but Louis Malle's new film *Lacombe, Lucien*, has made it: indeed, it was acclaimed a masterpiece. I'm not sure that it's exactly that, but it is certainly Malle's masterpiece, the film in which he finally has got together both sides of his cinematic psyche, the social documentary, and the psychological study of character.

Malle has always been an uneven director, stringing back and forth not only between good films and bad, but also one who couldn't seem to settle down, as it were. After his first feature, that taut thriller *Lift to the Scaffold*, he gave us the Brahmsian langours of *Les*

Amants. The next film *Zazie dans le Métro*, was again a total switch. With the exception of the *Le Feu follet*, his later films (*Vie privée*, *Viva Maria*, *Le Voleur*) were entertaining disappointments. One felt, like one's teachers at school, that he could do better if he tried.

There then followed a gap, with nothing except for some documentaries, until 1970 and *Murmur of the Heart* which re-established him as an important director. 'Some documentaries': one always, forgets that before his official first feature, Malle co-directed *The World of Silence*, with Jacques-Yves Cousteau, and throughout his career he has continued to make documentary films: there was the one about the Tour de France bicycle race in 1962, *Calcutta*, and *Phantom India* in 1967, and last year, one about an assembly-line factory, *Human, Too Human*, which has still to be seen.

His new film *Lacombe, Lucien*, is set in the past, like *Murmur of the Heart*; perhaps he needs distance from his subject matter. This time, however, it's not an amorally joyous evocation of middle-class youth, but a tough-minded view of a likeable, if surly, peasant boy whom we first meet in June 1944, somewhere in South West France. The war is still on, and France remains occupied. At 17, Lucien works in a hospital, disgustedly cleaning out bedpans, pausing only to bring down a bird with the cruelly sure aim of his slingshot.

Given a few days leave, he goes home to the country, only to find his mother installed with another man. His father is in a German prison camp, but 'just wait till he gets back,' he threatens. After this cool reception at home, and fed up with the hospital, Lucien makes a feeble stab at joining the *maquis*, but is turned down, none too tactfully, by his old school teacher who heads the local resistance movement.

So he goes back to town, but a flat tyre on his bike brings him in after curfew, and he is taken in by the local Quislings for interrogation.[13] They soon conclude there is nothing suspicious about him, but they get him drunk, hoping he will reveal something of interest. Flattered by all this attention, stupid Lucien begins to brag about knowing the leaders of the *maquis*.

From this moment on, he is trapped. He can no longer leave the pro-Germans. Dumb as he seems, he knows that he will be held responsible for the arrest and torture of the schoolteacher. But also, he now finds the excitement he was looking for in the *maquis* in working for the Germans. He is adopted as a kind of mascot, and the gun they supply him with gives him his first feelings of self-importance. He is all-powerful: if anyone protests, he has only to mutter 'Police Allemande', and opposition miraculously melts away. At last, he is somebody.

Never before, I think, have the attractions of Fascism for the peasant (or the lumpenproletarian) been so powerfully evoked. Lucien sees his chance at last to get back at all those bourgeois who have despised him for his accent, his cheap clothes, his lack of education. What some French people have found shocking is the way in which Malle seems to be saying that the appeal of the Resistance and that of the other side had much in common, but psychologically it seems to me a completely defensible position.

The only aspect of the film that is slightly miscalculated is the love–hate relationship between Lucien and the Jewish tailor from Paris who has holed up in this little town with the hope of making it across the nearby Spanish border. He lives with his mother and his beautiful daughter, and it doesn't take long before Lucien falls for the girl. The course of their growing passion is sensitively rendered, but unfortunately the tailor is played by the only big-time professional in the cast, that old Bergman favourite Holger Löwenadler. He's good, but much too actor-ish for the kind of film Malle has made.

Occasionally, too the dialogue about the Jews gets a little heavy with irony, as when the young French Fascist says he has to admit that when you put a Jewish girl up against French women, the French women look like horses.

But this aside, Malle handles his story with total sureness; it has to end tragically, and it does, but off-screen. When the Allies start moving into France, Lucien and the girl take off for the countryside, and the film ends with an idyllic sequence of the two of them making love in the green fields. There is only the final rolling title to tell us that in October 1944, Lucien Lacombe was captured, tried, and executed. We never find out what happened to the girl or her father.

The story, although partially invented, was apparently based on a true incident. But even without that knowledge, one is forced to believe in the truth of the situation. Malle doesn't gloss over any of the ambiguities. We are never sure just how much the girl is attracted by Lucien and how much her interest in him is conditioned by her desire to survive. As Malle admitted in an interview: 'it is perhaps not a love story.' What is certain, I think, is that their relationship is highly charged both with sensuality and brutality, and Malle makes us see how close the two can be.

The absence of a 'positive' hero is supposed to be box-office poison, and Lucien is not someone with whom one would care to identify. This, plus the well-known French resentment at any blot on their national honour, might mean the film will not do well commercially. I hope not, because although it is less perfect than *Murmur of the Heart*, it is also less superficial. It is Malle's finest film: it is also the proof that he can do still better.

SOURCE: 'HOLD THE FRONT PAGE', *GUARDIAN*, 19 FEBRUARY 1974, 10

3.17 THE PASSENGER

Writing about Michelangelo Antonioni's early films fifteen years ago, I said that 'the desolate autumnal wastes of the Po Valley through which Aldo aimlessly circles in *Il grido*, the oppressive presence of the horizon, the perspectives which open on to infinity, are the exact reflection of Aldo's state of soul.' I see now that I got it the wrong way round. The *subject* of those sequences was in fact the desolate autumnal wastes, the oppressive horizon. These were the things that inspired Antonioni, and the plot of the film — including Aldo's state of soul — was an expression, so to speak, of the landscape, not the other way around.

In Antonioni's latest film *The Passenger* (or *Professione: reporter*) there is a sequence which takes place on the roof of Gaudi's Hotel Milà in Barcelona. One of Gaudi's most complex constructions, this multi-levelled roof is dotted with groups of chimney-stacks, ventilators and stair-wells. Maria Schneider is on one side, Jack Nicholson on the other, and when they try to come together they find that, although it looks as if they could walk straight across to each other, they actually have to follow a sinuous and complicated route: up, down and around. This sequence may have been in Mark Peploe's original story, or in the script (credited to Peploe, Peter Wollen and Antonioni), but I doubt it. I don't think that this sequence arose from anyone's desire to find an analogy for the difficulty which the two characters have in communicating; rather, I feel sure that the roof itself suggested the scene, and in doing so enriched Antonioni's — and our — perception of the characters.

Even if the scene was there in the original story, it would only show how perceptively Peploe grasped the fact that Antonioni is inspired by figures in a landscape. For that, it now seems to me, is what his best films are essentially about. Not alienation, not the problems of love in an industrial society, not revolution; although these elements may all be part

Professione: reporter (1975)

of the landscape. But what seems most to excite Antonioni is that problem confronted by all Italian painters, from the great Venetians onwards: how to place figures in a meaning-ful relation to a landscape. It can be an active urban setting, as in *The Eclipse* or *La notte*, or a remote and rocky one, as in *L'avventura*. And often the most memorable scenes in his films are the closing ones: the hotel terrace at the end of *L'avventura*, the *terrain vague* where the streetcars end in *The Eclipse*, and now the plaza in *The Passenger*. It seems as though these final tableaux are what generated the whole film, that the vision of such a scene retroactively created everything which leads up to it.

This is certainly the case in *The Passenger*. One can see the whole film, in a sense, as so much exposition, setting us up in order to allow him to shoot that ultimate sequence.[14] [...]

Locke [Nicholson] is lying on the bed in his ground-floor room; the camera is pointed past him at the window. On the window are wrought-iron bars; beyond the window is a huge square. It is almost empty; there is only an old man sitting against the wall that closes off the perspective. Slowly the camera begins to move. It moves past Nicholson, towards the window. We see a driving school car circling clumsily and aimlessly round the square; someone is prac-tising. Schneider crosses the frame from lower right to upper left. Music begins: a *pasodoble*. A little boy in red passes by and throws something (a stone?) at the old man. A car arrives,

Decades Never Start On Time

with a black man and a white one. (Are they the agents of the African state?) A girl in red walks to the right; a dog crosses the frame to the left. Schneider reappears in frame. A man talks to her; the men move towards lower right, then laterally left, then towards upper right.

The camera has almost reached the bars on the window. Another car drives up; we move closer. Schneider talks to the old man. Sirens begin to wail. And then, with an effect of exaltation and surprise only comparable to that of the resurrection scene in *Ordet*, we pass through the narrow bars of the window. And it's not just the trickery that is exciting: we feel we are setting off on a fantastic voyage with no knowledge of where and when and how it will end – except that we feel it must end with death. At the same time there is a sense of liberation; we don't know what lies in wait for us out there, but we know that we are leaving something behind for ever. So, in a sense, the comparison with the resurrection scene in *Ordet* – which simply popped into my mind – is relevant; only this time it will be more an ascension than a resurrection.

The police are there; a crowd of kids appears. Then the camera begins to inscribe a movement in the shape of the (Greek) letter omega. That is to say, it tracks out and then to the left following Schneider, and when it reaches the back of the square it circles right, again following her. Meanwhile more police cars arrive, this time with Rachel [Locke's wife] and her producer friend. We continue right, and then slowly curve back towards the entrance of the Hotel de la Gloria. When we reach the façade, the camera moves laterally along it as Rachel and Schneider go inside. As we move along the façade towards Locke's window, they (invisibly) go down the corridor to his room. And the camera comes to a stop only when it has reached the wrought-iron bars of his window. Inside Locke is still lying on the bed, but he is now dead. Presumably he has been shot by the men trailing Robertson [whose identity Locke has adopted]. Rachel bends over him and says, 'I never knew him.' Schneider says, *'I do.'*

Cut to the façade of the hotel from the square. Night is falling, the sign is illuminated, the old man walks away, and the credits begin to roll up. The film is over.

The long detour is over: Antonioni has come home. All my reservations about his last three films – which were also his first colour films – had melted away in that extraordinary seven minute shot. And any reservations that I might have had about *The Passenger* itself suddenly seemed less important. I still find its political meanderings not very effective, since it is impossible to put across generalised political messages: unnamed and therefore unreal countries in which guerrillas (good) and government (bad) are fighting can hardly evoke more than stock responses. There are some reservations about the schematic nature of the plotting: Rachel and Martin's dashing about Spain is rather seriously under-motivated, and these sequences are in any case none too convincingly acted by Jenny Runacre and Ian Hendry. Reservations, too, about some of the contrivances: the all too recently white-painted (funeral?) coach in Munich, the waiting for Godot aspect of the quest for Daisy (who is she?), who naturally never appears. (Unless 'She' is she; and if so who cares?)

These things might be enough to swamp a lesser film, but Antonioni emerges triumphant. Why? Literally, because of his *mise en scène*, the way he places people on his stage, in landscapes, against buildings, in their physical context. Jack Nicholson succeeds (no easy task) in giving us Antonioni's first positive male protagonist. At first I suspected that he might be too realistically humanising an actor for Antonioni, but actually it is precisely the contrast inherent in his naturalistic way of playing a non-naturalistic role that makes the shadowy figure of Locke so effective. Nicholson does not play him as a cipher, nor does he over-personalise him, but strikes just the necessary balance between reality and abstraction. Maria Schneider, in an equally difficult role, succeeds as well: it is as if Antonioni were determined to show that she could be used in a way diametrically opposite to the way Bertolucci used her in *Last Tango*, and so she is all understatement, wan, pale, but with that residual toughness just visible.

The theme of the film is not related to these figures in the landscape in the same direct way as in Antonioni's Italian pictures (although Mediterranean architecture and landscapes do seem to suit him better than more exotic ones). There is in *The Passenger* a much less direct, less 'expressive' relationship. In fact, the theme of the film – the search for identity, for commitment – is expressed only glancingly, by ironic contrast. The more closely Antonioni relates his characters to their physical environment, the more dissociated from it they seem to be. The Hotel de la Gloria is a modest, simple hotel, much less flamboyant than the Gaudi buildings in Barcelona or the church in Munich. And the plaza is much less monumental than the Bloomsbury precincts in which nothing (except that first fleeting glimpse of Schneider) occurs. And indeed perhaps even the fuzziness of the political message, the vagueness of the aims of the gun-runner and the guerrillas, may be an ironic contrast to the almost religious importance which Antonioni gives to the Journey. One death in a tropical hotel room, another death in another tropical hotel room: these are the termini of the odyssey. And what has been accomplished between these two deaths? 'There was a birth, certainly/We had evidence and no doubt. I had seen birth and death,/But had thought they were different . . . I should be glad of another death' (Eliot again, in *Journey of the Magi*).

Conventionally, the Schneider character, the one who speaks up for life and youth, is the one we are supposed to take as 'right'; but the way the film is made leads me to believe that although Antonioni may intellectually side with her, poor Locke's rebirth as Robertson in one hotel room could only end in 'Robertson's' death in another. In, however, the Hotel de la Gloria.

Writing about Antonioni's use of the camera fifteen years ago, I mentioned 'his autonomous and non-functional use of camera movement to create spatial patterns which are satisfying in their own right ... He proposes to us a formal choreography of movement which accompanies the film, providing a non-conceptual figure in the carpet, an experience in pure form.' And that I'll stick by, even though many insist that there can be no such thing as pure form. But there has to be, or else Antonioni's films wouldn't work. However intelligent he may be, he is not an 'intellectual' director. However much ideas may interest him, they do not inspire him. However interested in people he may be, psychology is less important in his films than we have thought. However committed politically he may be, he is not a director of political films. ('The cinema is not in essence moral; it is emotional,' he said recently.)

The plaza sequence at the end of *The Passenger* does not bear directly on the ideas of the film, or on its theme. The theme is its point of departure, and its end-point. Everything that happens between the time the camera begins to move and the time that it stops is about ... itself. The great painters were concerned with light and shade, colour, texture and composition; and so is Antonioni. The great architects and town-planners of the Renaissance and the Baroque were interested in scale and the relationships of bodies, buildings and space; so is Antonioni. But unlike them, he can also define space through movement and sound, and all the more tellingly now that he has settled down to colour, since it has stopped monopolising his concern to the extent it did in *Red Desert*, *Blow-Up* and *Zabriskie Point*. Antonioni no longer paints the scenery; and the essential architecture emerges more clearly.

Decades Never Start On Time

There are three slightly different versions of *The Passenger* (for commercial reasons). The one I saw lasted 125 minutes, and those 125 minutes, those 7,500 seconds each with its 24 frames, those 180,000 images and compositions, are conjugated with movement, dialogue and sound into a unique perceptual experience. This may sound like a minor achievement or a sterile exercise − but to me it was a more meaningful, more exhilarating experience of the world we live in than the colour-dominated (colour-destroyed) and trendy last three films, and more cinematic than the more 'psychological' first five. Architecture has been described as frozen music. Antonioni's moving camera unfreezes it, and this non-linear, non-narrative thaw pours forth a cascade of sound and images, spatial music.

SOURCE: '*THE PASSENGER*, *SIGHT & SOUND*, 44.3, SUMMER 1975, 134−7

3.18 FILM OF THE CENTURY

Contrary to any reports you might have heard, Bernardo Bertolucci's *1900*, far from being uneditable, is completed. I know because I have seen it, all five and a half hours. Far from being un-releasable, it is due to come out this spring. True, it was three years in the making, but the time was well spent: it is a masterpiece, and all the more startling in that it has all the makings of a very popular film. Because of its great length, it will have to be shown in two parts. The idea is to run each part simultaneously at two theatres side by side; those who want to see it straight through can do so; those who want to take a break can do that; and those who want to see the two a few days apart will have that possibility.

I saw it all in one day, with an hour for lunch. It may seem like a dauntingly Wagnerian experience, or like reading *War and Peace* straight through but once into the film nothing short of an earthquake could have got me out. The story Bertolucci has to tell is supremely engrossing, and he lets nothing come between the audience and that story. Gone are the grandiloquent set-pieces, gone the elaborate camera movements. Or rather, he uses his camera in such a skilful way that one is not aware of it as such.

And one is held by the actors. This may sound like a return to square one, for the most simple-minded spectators all over the world will invariably reply when asked why they liked a film that it was because of the story and the actors. But it is just such a return to square one that Bertolucci wanted to make.

Ever since the 60s, the gulf between the popular film and the art film has been growing. Ninety per cent of the films I have raved about in these pages were never seen by very many people. Films which have been universally panned by the critics have made millions. This has not always been the case; the films of Griffith and Feuillade, Stroheim and Lang, Chaplin and Keaton were almost always box-office successes. *Citizen Kane* was not an art film.

But Bresson, Straub, Godard, even Resnais have usually been confined to the art-house ghetto. When Bertolucci said three years ago that, not content with the tremendous success of *Last Tango in Paris*, he wanted his next film to reach an even wider audience, I concluded that he was suffering from galloping megalomania. Either that, or he was contemplating a sell-out of some sort. No, no, he protested: we were wrong in the 60s, it's the director who must 'do the work' before the film comes out so that the audience won't have to 'work' at experiencing it. After all, he said, it's been done before, it can be done again.

History is irreversible; I wasn't convinced. And I still think so. Nonetheless, Bertolucci has succeeded. He has found a way of submerging his psychological and visual preoccupations into a social and historical epic that takes as its subject nothing less than the 20th century. That's what the Italian title means, by the way: not 1900, but the 1900s, or the 20th century. But because of the Hawks film called *Twentieth Century* the English title will probably misleadingly remain *1900*.

The basic plot-line is by now pretty well-known. On the first day of the 20th century, two boys are born on the same estate in the province of Emilia. Alfredo (Robert De Niro) is the son of the lord of the manor, Olmo (Gerard Depardieu) is born to a peasant woman of an unknown father. And in the story of those two boys and their families, the social and political history of Italy from 1900 to the end of the Second World War is embodied.

So richly textured and intricate is the film that it is almost impossible to write about, at least after one viewing. Even with limitless space at my command, it would be difficult because Bertolucci has put it all together so tightly that it is not easy to separate the various strands for analysis or description.

Let's take just one character, Ada, as she is played by Dominique Sanda: she almost steals the film, her performance is so extraordinary. And surprisingly so, since her recent appearances (*The Mackintosh Man* or *Steppenwolf*) have been so zombie-esque. Bertolucci has given her a great role – the New Woman of the 20s. Alfredo meets her at his uncle's, whose mistress he assumes her to be; she is different from any woman he has ever met. She smokes, she drives her own Bugatti, and she writes futurist Odes to Speed. Little wonder that our provincial squire is overwhelmed. He finally succeeds in seducing her only to discover that she was a virgin. Why didn't you tell me, he asks. You'd never have believed me, she replies, and he can only concur.

She, too, falls in love with him, but makes him swear he'll never become like his friends, a fat vulgar land-owner. Small chance, he assures her, and off they go, with the uncle (who turns out to be homosexual) on a wild trip to Naples where they experiment with everything, including cocaine. Then comes the news that Alfredo's father has died. And what Ada has always feared comes true. With the death of his father, not only must Alfredo take over the estate but he inevitably becomes a land-owner. Not fat, perhaps, and not vulgar, but a member of his class. Not a Fascist, he makes use of them for his own purposes, and in so doing, becomes as one of them.

The couple drift further and further apart. Ada takes to drinking, and eventually, unable to stand Alfredo's degeneration and that of the society in which they live, she leaves. The transition from bright young thing to solitary tavern-drinker is conveyed by Dominique Sanda with accuracy and pathos.

But the story of each of the main characters is equally engrossing, all the actors equally effective: Depardieu as the solid Communist peasant, Stefania Sandrelli as his school teacher companion whose faith in the future of socialism is so great that she is willing to teach 70-year-old men how to read. There is Attila, the Fascist overseer played almost unrecognisably by Donald Sutherland, who gradually acquires a position of great power by being so useful to Alfredo and also by marrying into the family.

It is impossible to summarise the plot; there are too many major characters, and their inter-relationships are too complex and varied. At the same time, as befits an epic, each is representative of different types of behaviour, of different classes, of different reactions to the events of the half-century. They are always seen in context, and by the end of the film, the context, as it were, takes over.

When liberation comes to Italy in 1945, most of the main characters have left the stage free to be turned over to the peasants, the people. After the settling of accounts, they proceed to divide the land among those who work it, and they all celebrate what they take to be the beginning of a new era. The boss is dead; the boss no longer exists. However, they don't kill Alfredo; he is to remain alive as living proof that the bosses are dead. The execution is indefinitely postponed. But Alfredo knows better, and so do we. The moment the peasants give up their arms to the 'National Liberation Committee,' the revolution is over, and as Alfredo gloats, 'the *padrone* is alive.'

I realise that I haven't begun to scratch the surface of Bertolucci's achievement. I haven't even mentioned the performances of Laura Betti, Sterling Hayden, Alda Valli, and Romolo Valli. Nor have I said anything about the complex relationship between Alfredo and Olmo with all its careless ambiguities, nor the breath-stopping epilogue to the film with the two men, like Beckett tramps, pushing each other along the road to eternity. I have said nothing of how Bertolucci uses landscape, the picnics among the lines of poplars, the 1908 strike scenes, the wedding of Ada and Alfredo, the great red flag of 1945, the funeral procession in the piazza.

Just as well, perhaps, to leave the reader to make these discoveries himself. One thing I do regret: I'll never be able to see the film again with its original soundtrack. Given the enormous cost of the work, it simply had to be an international production, and the version I saw was as it was made: in Italian, English, and French. Sometimes the actors would speak one language, sometimes another. They mostly try for English – to help the lip-synch of the English version, but whenever a scene got really intense, the actor usually lapsed into his mother tongue.

The 'master' version release will naturally be the Italian one – which means that De Niro and Depardieu will be dubbed by other actors. Dominique Sanda will be spared that indignity, because she is described as being half French and she can do herself, with accent.

This version will be the one shown first all over the world, at least in the major cities. But there will also be an English version, in which Sandrelli and Depardieu will have to be dubbed. I can't help regretting this; but it seems to be economically inevitable. The Italian public won't even notice the difference, so used are they to the whole dubbing process. The rest of us will just have to put up with it. It seems a small price to pay for such a great film, which surpasses the psychological intensity of *Last Tango*. By going back to his roots – to the landscapes of *Before the Revolution* – Bernardo Bertolucci has found the classical simplicity of 'invisible' *mise en scène*.

SOURCE: 'FILM OF THE CENTURY', *GUARDIAN*, 7 JANUARY 1976, 8

3.19 MEMORANDUM ON PROCESSES OF PROSPECTION AND SELECTION

NOTE: This typewritten document appears to be Roud's contribution to a debate within the Lincoln Center regarding the mechanisms and procedures employed for the choice of films to be shown at the New York Film Festival. Although it provides some evidence of the kind of personal tensions and budgetary pressures that surely must exist in all such cultural institutions, we have rather included it here for the light that it throws on the run-

ning of a film festival from Roud's resolutely cinephile point of view. It also provides an extraordinary insight into the tribe of film festival people – critics, archivists, programmers, producers, directors – who formed Roud's personal network of contacts across the globe.

The process of programming the New York Film Festival divides naturally into two separate parts: prospection and selection. The second function, selection, is done by half a dozen people – the program committee. The first is done by me and dozens of unpaid advisors and informants.

Over the sixteen years since I have been running a film festival (London began in 1960, New York in 1963) I have slowly built up a large and useful network of people on six continents on whom I count to alert me to developments in their respective countries or fields of interest.

Much of this prospection takes place at the Cannes festival which has traditionally been the place that new film-makers from all over the world come to show their films to the rest of the world. And it has always been true that a significant portion of the films we show come from Cannes – especially since 1969 when the Cannes festival expanded to take in the competition: i.e., the counter-festival that began as a result of the political 'events' of 1968. The result is that now over 200 films are shown at Cannes in one category or another.

But Cannes is important for another reason, too. For it is there that my 'network' comes together, there that I get reports on the latest and best from various countries all over the world. For the Cannes Film Festival invites each year 1,500 film journalists and critics, and it serves as a meeting-place, a mart where ideas are exchanged.

For example, it is there that I learn from Aito Mäkinen what is going on in Finland; from Mrs Kashiko Kawakita and Hiroko Govaers the latest news from Japan; from Adriano Aprà, Gianni Amico, John Francis Lane, and Morando Morandini about the new Italian films; from Freddy Buache about the news from the Swiss film industry; from Louis Marcorelles and Jean Rouch about African cinema; from Michel Demopoulos about the Greek cinema and the films shown at the Salonika Film Festival; from Françoise Jaubert and Jean Lefevre about new Canadian films; from Sylvie Le Clezio about Australian product; from Fabiano Canosa and Claudio Bojunga about new Brazilian films; from Claude-Antoine about South American films in general; from István Dósai and Claire Kristoff on new developments in Hungary, from Jan Aghed and Anna-Lena Wibom about new Swedish films. (These are but a few examples: there are many others.)

The second avenue of prospection takes place the whole year round, starting, in fact, almost the minute the previous New York Festival ends. Now that we have become established as one of the two most important festivals in the world, it is the film-makers and producers who seek us out, who write to us from places as far off as Patagonia to propose to us their latest films. This happens both in New York and in Europe: the letters pour in throughout the year. Each lead is carefully followed up because you can never tell. *Harlan County, USA* was a film that came to us through the letter-box, as it were, but it was preceded by a phone call from D. A. Pennebaker, a distinguished documentary film-maker whose own films played in the first New York Film Festival back in 1963. *Badlands* was physically brought to us by an unprepossessing young man who turned out to be, not just a messenger as we thought, but the director himself. But it, too, was preceded by two letters: one from Arthur Penn telling me that he had seen bits of it and recommending the film to us, and one from Bert Schneider, the producer (but not the producer of *Badlands*) telling me to look out for a first film by one Terence Malick.

Not all of these tips turn out to be so interesting, of course: but the point is that with this large body of unofficial and unpaid advisors, I think it is fair to say that there is little or nothing that does not come to our attention.

The third means of prospection are the other non-competitive festivals like Paris, London, and Rotterdam: each shows about 80 films that have been gathered from all over the world by the organisers of these events. One does not have to agree with their taste, but it is a chance to see an enormous amount of films cheaply and conveniently. And since there is no rivalry between us, I often get together with the organisers of these events to hear about the films that they *didn't* manage to get, for one reason or another, and which we might be able to procure for New York. And these festivals also see a meeting of a large number of professional colleagues who are only too eager to have their brains picked and their opinions asked. So we benefit from the travels and explorations of Huub Bals and Monika Tegelaar, from Rotterdam, Ken Wlaschin, […][15] and John Gillett from London, Pierre-Henri Deleau from Paris, not to mention Ulrich and Erika Gregor from Berlin, Lino Micciché from Pesaro, Moritz de Hadeln from Locarno and Nyon, etc., etc.

Fourthly, there is simply doing one's homework, i.e., keeping up with the trade papers (not only *Variety*, but also *Le Film Français*, *Il giornale dello spettacolo*, and *Movie Marketing* (for the Far East)). There are also the organs of the National Industries: *Hungarofilm Bulletin*, *Film a Doba* from Czechoslovakia, as well as the large number of film magazines from all over the world.

Fifth, Paris has now become the most important center in the world for film *exhibition*. Throughout the year, there are Film Weeks put on there by various countries and groups: I have just attended here a Soviet Film Week. Next on the list is a week of films from Bulgaria, etc. There are now 300 movie theatres in Paris; most of them are small, and this allows them to program more adventurously, and it allows countries to rent one or two of them cheaply in order to present panoramas of their current production. Now I have set-tled in Paris, it will be even easier to keep up with these various manifestations − which, because of the political climate here, include a large number of films from the 'third world' (African, Asia, South America).

Inevitably, however, the bulk of the films shown in the New York Film Festival are by already well-known directors. This is not because we do not know about the younger film-makers, but is a function of the selection process.

Which brings us to the second part of the programming procedure: selection. This is an area which might perhaps be improved (or altered). It seems to me that our programming selection has become less adventurous over the past few years than it used to be. And this for the simple reason that no matter how often I try to impress upon members of the program committee that they should give their opinions on a film without considering whether the film in question is going to be a 'success' or not with our audience and/or the critics, they cannot help but feel the pressure (which we all feel) to fill those seats, to make the deficit as small as possible. As board-members, you too may feel that we are right to concern ourselves with this problem. And yet I fear that this can be a very inhibiting fac-tor. For one thing, it is almost impossible to second-guess either critics or audiences. Secondly, if the festival does not take chances in its programming, it will die. Many of the established directors who now automatically sell out were not always in such a position. The chance had to be taken in the first instance, and one had to persevere in what one believed in. The most stunning example of this phenomenon can be found among the West German directors. The first Fassbinder film we showed (in 1971) was not well attended nor was it particularly well received. But each year, the situation changed, until now he is an automatic sell-out. The same is true of Herzog.

I suppose I would do a better job of convincing the program committee members that they should not concern themselves over much with their estimate of how a film will sell, of how much *others* will like a film, if only I could be a bit more convinced myself of support from the Board. But when one knows that success is judged by the percentage of seats sold, this is difficult to achieve.

Another problem in selection: efficiency and perfect democracy do not always go together. (If they did, our country would still be run by Town Meetings.) There are some cases, generally the result of deplorable, but understandable, vanity – both personal and national – where it is impossible for me to get a film to New York for the committee to view and vote on. This is one of the reasons we have had so few Soviet films in recent years. The Russians simply will not 'submit' (as they see it) to the indignity of submitting their films. If one happens to see a Soviet film and then asks for it definitely, then there is a fairly good chance of getting it for the festival. But they consider it humiliating to be asked for a film on spec. The same applies to certain directors and producers: it is a grave mistake to think that the film world runs on purely economic motives; the so-called business men in this so-called business are often, through vanity, quite prepared to cut off their noses to spite their faces.

And this is why, each year, I have had to take several films off my own bat or with the opinion of only one other member of the committee. This is something that some of the committee members do not very much like (and understandably), but most of them see the necessity for it. The only other solution would be the prohibitively expensive one of having the committee travel as a group for four months.

The question to which this memorandum was supposed to address itself was 'How can we effectively broaden our procedure for finding films?' At the risk of sounding complacent, I cannot think of any way in which the procedures could be improved. We could, of course, follow the example of Chicago: they don't even have a program committee, but they do feature strongly in their program book the names of the 'International Advisors'. We could include in our program the names of our foreign correspondents so that the procedure would be seen to be as broad as it actually is. But there seems little point to me in hiring strangers in far-off places when we already have a host of unpaid stringers; and little point in hiring someone to circle the globe when the films themselves already make the rounds more cheaply. Things may have been different before the jet era: now there is not a film-maker from Phnom Penh to Peru who doesn't know how to get his film to Cannes, Rotterdam, London, or Paris.

If, however, we could decide as a matter of policy to take more chances, to experiment with more 'difficult' films, with films that do not *sound* as if they would automatically appeal to our audiences, then I think we could improve the *selection* process enormously. Of course, this not a decision to be taken lightly. Our financial problems are serious, and unless there is a *clear mandate* from the board, no-one will want to run the risk of pushing for a film he or she thinks is important only to find him or herself saddled with the (implicit) blame for having landed us with a flop. But there are films that were shown in the early days of the festival to half-filled houses (admittedly, it was Philharmonic Hall, then) and whose directors have subsequently established themselves as being fully as important as the directors of those films which did sell out the house. *If we don't keep just that little bit ahead of our audience, we will soon find that we have fallen way behind them.*

Decades Never Start On Time

One final plea: ever since Special Events had to go by the board for financial reasons in 1971, many have particularly regretted the absence of full-dress retrospectives like the Renoir show in 1969 or the Gance in 1968 or Westerns in 1970. If some way could be found to finance a new series of full-length retrospectives, the festival would be immeasurably enriched.

SOURCE: 'MEMORANDUM ON PROCESSES OF PROSPECTION AND SELECTION', ARCHIVE DOCUMENT, 16 DECEMBER 1976, RICHARD ROUD COLLECTION, HOWARD GOTLIEB ARCHIVAL RESEARCH CENTER, BOSTON, BOX 1, F17, ITEM B; ALSO: BOX 3, F10, 1971–6

3.20 MOVIES VERSUS MOTION PICTURES

NOTE: *This discussion of the* That's Entertainment *compilation films is a typewritten text that was clearly written for publication, although we have not yet found a published version of it. Along with his beautiful tribute to Fred Astaire ('How can we know the dancer from the dance?'), this piece demonstrates Roud's abiding love for classical Hollywood cinema.*

In the 30s and 40s film fans and critics could usually tell which studio a film came from by just looking at it. Each studio had its own stars, tightly bound by contract. The mere presence of an actor or actress – or especially the crew of secondary players each studio had on its payroll – was a sure sign of the film's origin.

There were other reasons, too. Each studio specialised in a different *kind* of film: Warner Brothers in night-city thrillers; Paramount, because of the Lubitsch heritage, was known for its 'continental' comedies, as well as for its DeMille epics.

And MGM? MGM meant the big musicals and it meant the worthy costume dramas. It meant high-gloss production values, it meant 'more stars than there are in heaven', and it meant Garbo.

At the same time, for the 'advanced' and 'liberal' film critics, the studio system was the villain of the piece. Directors and actors inveighed against its power, its regimentation. The studios were supposed to be stifling the creative powers of those who worked for them, and independence from the system was thought to be the only way for film to become art.

But, as W. H. Auden noted, 'All works of art are commissioned in the sense that no artist can create one by a simple act of will, but must wait until what he believes to be a good idea for a work "comes" to him. Among those works which are failures because their initial conceptions were false or inadequate, the number of self-commissioned works may well be greater than the number commissioned by patrons.'

Now that the major studios have lost much of their power and individuality, we can now see their role in a different light. For when a certain number of directors in the 60s finally did achieve the freedom to make the films they had always wanted to, these films turned out to be inferior to the ones they had been forced by the system to make. For all but the greatest directors, the collective system of creation that the studios had developed worked out better. All too often, freedom was counter-productive.

Looking back at the prodigious series of films from which the extracts of *That's Entertainment* have been chosen, one can but marvel at the richness of MGM's film production of the 30s and 40s. First of all, the musicals: they could only have been produced

Singin' in the Rain (1952)

by a major studio, for they depended on great numbers of talented musicians, dancers, and singers who were under yearly contract and always available. They depended on the Anglo-Saxon market which in those days was sufficient for a film to get back its costs. For it is a curious fact that except for America, England, and a few other English-speaking countries, musicals are just not popular. Which explains why a film like *Singin' in the Rain* was shown only in art houses in countries like France. Now that the American market is not as important as it used to be, musicals are not being made very often. Even when a musical show like *Irma la Douce* was made into a film, the songs were dropped.

The reason for the superiority of the MGM musical was the presence of a truly creative producer: Arthur Freed. There are differences between 'Freed' musicals directed by Minnelli and those by Donen, but they had a lot in common: it was Freed, seconded by Roger Edens, who nurtured the talents of Donen and Kelly, Minnelli and Charles Walters, and who was midwife – and more – to the most glorious string of musicals in the history of the cinema.

But musicals and costume pictures were not all that MGM had to offer, as *That's Entertainment, part 2* makes clear. There were sophisticated comedies, like *Ninotchka* and *The Philadelphia Story* and there were also the Marx Brothers comedies from *A Night at the Opera* on.

The curious thing is that if one looks back at the critics' Ten-Best lists of the past, one finds that they have constantly underrated the musicals and comedies. (The same, by the way, is true of Westerns and thrillers.) And yet if there is a lesson to be learned from *That's Entertainment, part 2* and from its predecessor, it is that what was thought of as 'mere' entertainment turns out to have more artistic validity now than the films that were considered to be serious attempts at being works of art.

The adaptations of novels by Nobel prize winners not only look stilted and boring now, but they can also be seen as inferior as film art. Is the moral that movies hold up better than Motion Pictures? That Fred Astaire and Gene Kelly, Judy Garland and Frank Sinatra, the Marx Brothers and Laurel and Hardy are finally greater film artists than the Oscar-honored stars who are now largely forgotten, and whose performances, when seen on television re-runs, now seem either dull or grotesque. That there was finally more art in the entertainment movie than in the Art Film? After seeing *That's Entertainment, part 2*, I think there can be only one answer. What Auden said about books applies equally to films: 'Some are undeservedly forgotten; none are undeservedly remembered.'

SOURCE: 'MOVIES VERSUS MOTION PICTURES [MGM]', ARCHIVE DOCUMENT, 1976, RICHARD ROUD COLLECTION, HOWARD GOTLIEB ARCHIVAL RESEARCH CENTER, BOSTON, BOX 1, F8, ITEM J.28, 3 PAGES

Notes

1. This film is now generally credited to Martin Scorsese, a member of the New York University Cinetracts Collective.
2. We have cut the discussion of *The Spider's Strategy* in order to focus on the analysis of *The Conformist*.
3. Some five years earlier, Roud wrote for the *Sunday Times* an amusing piece on a similar theme, 'Playing the festival game', *Sunday Times* magazine, 3 July 1966, 30–2.
4. This version was, of course, never made. Roud would follow the saga of the Proust adaptation right through to the appearance of *Swann in Love* (Volker Schlöndorff, 1984). See 'At last! Proust the movie', *Tatler*, 279.3, March 1984, 76, 84.
5. Alfred Agostinelli, Proust's real-life secretary, with whom the novelist was in love, is said to have inspired the female character Albertine in the later novels of *À la recherche du temps perdu*.
6. Here we have cut a passage in which Roud discusses the influence exerted on Straub by the films of Jean Grémillon and Robert Bresson, especially regarding the importance of Grémillon's use of sound and the 'stripped-down' aesthetic of Bresson.
7. In 1972 it was revealed that the American conglomerate ITT had funded the Republican National Convention in return for favourable treatment from the Justice Department. Dun and Bradstreet is a financial information services company whose origins go back to the nineteenth century; Roud is referring to an indictment for fraud in relation to a mortgage scandal in the early 1970s.
8. André Malraux, French novelist and art historian, was de Gaulle's Minister of Culture from 1959 to 1969. As such he had played a key role in the so-called 'Langlois affair' in 1968 when Langlois was temporarily removed from the head of the Cinémathèque Française (see 'A Langlois unto himself', 23 February 1968). Malraux wrote an influential book about museum culture called *Museum without Walls* (1947), in French *Le Musée imaginaire* or 'The Imaginary Museum'.
9. Arlene Croce, *The Fred Astaire and Ginger Rogers Book* (London: W. H. Allen; New York: Dutton, 1972).
10. Roud is referring to Richard Corliss's *Talking Pictures: Screenwriters in American Cinema* (New York: Overlook Press, 1974).
11. The actual phrase by H. Rap Brown, Afro-American political activist of the 1960s is: 'I say violence is necessary. It's as American as cherry-pie.'
12. This phrase is attributed to the character Ivan in Fyodor Dostoyevsky's novel *The Brothers Karamazov* (1880).
13. A 'Quisling' is a term coined during the Second World War to denote local Fascist or otherwise collaborationist organisations in countries occupied by the Germans.
14. Here we have cut a descriptive account of the film's narrative; we then return to Roud's analysis of the famous final sequence of *The Passenger*.
15. Here there is an illegible hand-written name.

PART 4 1977–83

4.1 HENRI LANGLOIS

> He disappeared in the dead of winter
> What instruments we have agree …
> The day of his death was a dark cold day.[1]

I was in Rome when I heard that Henri Langlois had died on 12 January. There was no snow on the statues, but there had been an incredible hail storm that day, the day 'the provinces of his body revolted'. It was sudden, in one sense: he had been saying of late that he knew he was not going to live much longer, but we all thought him indestructible.

I first met Henri Langlois nearly twenty years ago, when *Sight & Sound*, having commissioned a pamphlet on Max Ophüls for its short-lived second Index Series, bundled me off to Paris where the Cinémathèque was going to show me Ophüls's French films of the '30s. All this had been arranged with Mary Meerson, Langlois's companion (as the French always put it) since the war, and the *éminence grise* of the Cinémathèque. But the meeting with Langlois was, typically, explosive. The very fact that I had been sent by the BFI seemed to him (or at least so he pretended) to prove that I must be mixed up with some now long-forgotten dispute between the two organisations about a print of *L'Age d'or* that had somehow found its way to Tel Aviv. My protests of innocence, indeed of total ignorance, went unheeded; he ranted on, until Mary Meerson came in to tell him to stop it. Then the two of them began to fight with each other. I didn't know what to do, so I just stood my ground and waited for them to finish. Suddenly, he stopped, turned round, looked at me, and grinned. He had apparently decided that I had passed the test – whatever that may have been. From that day on, all (well, almost all) was sunny, and we became friends – although he always called me Roud. Always, that is, until the last time I saw him, a week before his death, when he suddenly started calling me Richard. Looking back, it seems significant; maybe not.

> You were silly like us; your gift survived it all …

Langlois was a difficult man sometimes, but he was a good man and a great one. And with any luck, his gift, his creation – the Cinémathèque Française – will survive. At the first meeting after his death of the Steering Committee of the General Assembly, Mary Meerson was confirmed as General Administrator, and we can trust her to carry on in Langlois's spirit. Indeed, even during his lifetime, she was responsible for many uncredited (*her* choice) achievements – like the Chaillot theatre.

The collection has survived too, in spite of all the tales of rusty cans. They *were* rusty, but in all the years that I borrowed films from the Cinémathèque for the National Film

Theatre and later for the New York Film Festival, I always found that beautiful prints came out of those admittedly rusty cans.

He became his admirers ...

But even if the collection had turned to dust – as his enemies have always predicted – his memorial would be a living one, the school of French directors which used to be known as the New Wave and who always proclaimed that the Cinémathèque was where they had learned most about the art of film-making. Of course, the conditions of screening were not impeccable; the films were often not subtitled, or if so, in Serbo-Croat. And often the film announced was not the film shown. Sometimes a reel was missing: when someone complained about this to Mary Meerson, her ready response was, 'Darling, when you go to the Louvre, you don't complain because the Venus de Milo has no arms.'

Now he is scattered among a hundred cities
And wholly given over to unfamiliar affections

Even before his death, Langlois's activities circled the globe. The French are often accused of being chauvinistic (and Chauvin himself was a Frenchman), but if ever there was an internationalist, it was Langlois. He sometimes attributed this to his birth in Smyrna (where his father was a stationmaster for the French-run Turkish railways). And there was that American grandmother he used to brag about. But the fact was that he had a world-view of the cinema, and therefore he was interested in the world (or was it the other way round?). He was particularly fond of London, and nourished great affection for what he called the Old Guard of the BFI. Some of them are now dead, like Olwen Vaughan and Norah Traylen; some long gone from the BFI, like Denis Forman and James Quinn; one is still around: the editor of *Sight & Sound* [Penelope Houston].

Follow, poet, follow right
To the bottom of the night
With your unconstraining voice
Still persuade us to rejoice

And these words of W. H. Auden about Yeats, like the others I have quoted, apply to Langlois: he loved the cinema and wanted others to rejoice in its glories. And that love was all-embracing. Unlike some archivists, he didn't tickle his ego by picking and choosing the films he was going to preserve. Not for him the selection committee. He had his own ideas, but he was wise enough to know that his taste was conditioned by his date of birth, his upbringing and all manner of things, and that the true archivist has to allow for this. He was very fond of the late Iris Barry of the Museum of Modern Art in New York, but he disapproved strongly of her decision many years ago that as there were only four 'great' films of Buster Keaton, those four were all she took, although the Museum had been offered them all. He just didn't understand how she, or anyone, could be *sure*. So often films which were considered unimportant by their contemporaries (Feuillade is the great example) turned out to be greatly appreciated by later generations.

Earth receive an honoured guest ...

Henri Langlois is laid to rest; his achievements, his personality, his wit and intelligence will not, I think, be forgotten – at least not by me, or by any of those who knew and, therefore, loved him.

SOURCE: 'HENRI LANGLOIS', *SIGHT & SOUND*, 46.2, SPRING 1977, 119

4.2 THE LEFT BANK REVISITED

Fifteen years ago, faced with the luxuriant flowering of new talents in French cinema, I tried to draw a distinction between the *Cahiers du Cinéma* group (Chabrol, Truffaut, Godard) and what I called the Left Bank group: Resnais, Marker and Varda. As I said at the time, this classification was only a kind of analogy; it proved nothing, and was only valuable if it could tell us more about what was being classified. At that time, Chris Marker's work was totally unknown in Britain and America; we had seen Varda's *Cléo* and some of her shorts. But we had seen *Hiroshima, mon amour* and *Marienbad*. And we knew that Resnais had edited Varda's first feature, *La Pointe Courte*, that Marker and Resnais had co-directed a subsequently banned film, *Les Statues meurent aussi*. What else did the three have in common? Agnès Varda suggested it was their shared love of cats, but admitted that there might be something more.

So the article printed in *Sight & Sound* was called 'The Left Bank'. That was where they all lived, but Left Bank implies a state of mind and what is now – loathsomely, but usefully – called a life-style. A fondness, then, for the Bohemian life, a rejection of Right Bank conformity, a high degree of involvement in literature and the plastic arts, and a consequent interest in experimental film-making. It also implies a political viewpoint well to the left of centre.

Since those days, many things have changed: 'Right Bank' Godard became perhaps the most left-wing of all, and the differences between Chabrol and Truffaut became greater than the similarities. But the Left Bank group, although they no longer work with each other, still maintains a kind of identity. What kind?

Before answering that question, one must trace what has happened to each of them over the past fifteen years. Resnais went on to make *Muriel* in 1963; to many, his finest film, it was a commercial failure and a lean decade for Resnais was the result. Only three films, *La Guerre est finie*, *Je t'aime, je t'aime* and – most successfully, in my view – *Stavisky*. Varda had her biggest commercial hit with *Le Bonheur* and her biggest flop with *Les Créatures*. Then came *Lions Love* in 1969, and after that nothing. Unless one counts a film for French television (*Nausicaa*) which they refused to show for political reasons, and a film for German television (*Daguerréotypes*) that fell somewhat short of the standards she had previously set for herself. Marker's *Le joli mai* appeared in 1963; then there followed *Le Mystère Koumiko* and *Si j'avais quatre dromadaires*, his last 'personal' film. He went on film-making but only as a member of various co-operatives. He 'co-operated' on *Far from Vietnam* (as did Resnais and Varda), *Classes de lutte*, *The Sixth Side of the Pentagon*, and a number of politically militant films. But the Chris Marker we had known died, he insisted, in 1967. Well, yes and no. He did sign one film in the 70s, a documentary on Yves Montand called *The Loneliness of the Long Distance Singer*.

Then came 1977. Why this year should have become the *annus mirabilis* for the Left Bank group, I really don't know. A series of circumstances, the swing of events, the turning wheel of fortune? Whatever the reasons, 1977 saw the return – *en force* – of all three directors. The first to arrive was Resnais with *Providence*. Gilbert Adair reviewed the film in the Spring issue of *Sight & Sound*: if I read him correctly, he thinks, as I do, that this was Resnais's best work since *Muriel*. But there is one point I would like to make about the film – and it is a point relevant also to Marguerite Duras's new film *Le Camion*. I think too much has been made of the narrative device of *Providence* – the notion that we are seeing reality through the eyes of an author trying to write a novel. To me, this is simply a device, and the interest of *Providence* does not lie in any light it might shed on the creative processes. The interchanging of characters that goes on in Clive Langham's mind is not only an expression of the way a novelist's mind is supposed to work. It is much more the expression of an important truth about human relationships. We do take on other roles, and these roles are usually derived from our family history.

Before Freud, Tin Pan Alley discovered that men choose and act towards their wives as their fathers did towards their mothers: 'I want a girl/Just like the girl/That married dear old dad.' And women towards their husbands as their mothers towards their fathers. More bizarrely, but just as frequently, the analysts tell us, one can find oneself acting towards one's spouse as one acted towards one's mother or father; and one can even manipulate the spouse into acting towards oneself as one's parent did. So, when Claude Langham (Dirk Bogarde) begins to talk like Clive Langham (John Gielgud), when his mistress is played by the Elaine Stritch who also 'plays' his dead mother, when he kills his brother as if he were killing his father, these are not just fascinating examples of the way a writer's mind works; the film is about how *all* our minds work.

Providence was soon followed by Agnès Varda's *L'une chante, l'autre pas* (*One Sings, the Other Doesn't*). Although it is more accessible and much warmer than her earlier films, it is clearly the work of the author of *La Pointe Courte*. The title itself is an expression of Varda's persistent interest in 'doubling'. *La Pointe Courte* doubled a political film with the story of a marriage on the rocks. *Lions Love* also doubled several stories and (scandalously, to some) even related the story of a hippy *ménage à trois* to the assassination of Robert Kennedy. And there was an ambitious project called *La Mélangite* which was to have been about a woman who got everything mixed up. ('La Mélangite', a personal neologism of Varda's, can translate as 'Mixitis'.) And, like everyone of her generation, she was fascinated by Faulkner's device in *The Wild Palms* of two stories printed in alternating chapters which did not have any obvious connection with each other.

In her new film, she begins with two fused stories, one of a young woman with two children who lives with an unsuccessful photographer, and the other about a younger former neighbour who tries to help her friend get an abortion. Then the lines abruptly diverge: the photographer hangs himself and Suzanne (Thérèse Liotard) is forced to go back to her peasant family. The lines converge ten years later at an abortion rally: each of the women has come, in a different way, to a consciousness of the condition of womanhood. The meeting is warm, but circumstances force the two apart, and the distance that separates them (Iran to Hyères) is bridged by postcards. Pauline (alias Pomme, and played by a great new discovery, Valérie Mairesse) pursues her singing career, meets an Iranian economist, marries him, and bears him a child – only to discover that with the birth of a son his profeminist façade drops to reveal the traditional *pater familias*.

Suzanne, on the other hand, raises her three bastards, starts a family planning clinic, and marries a paediatrician. Only in an epilogue do they all get together again to wind up the film like the last chapter of a 19th-century novel. Wind it up as far as the plot goes; but the film asks many more questions than it answers. Although it is clear that Varda has views, she does not impose them on her audience. And in any case, the differences between the two women themselves give us alternative approaches. So without being didactic (except in a few of the songs), the film has a great deal to say. Varda's dialogue is as wittily literary as always, but there is a new simplification of *mise en scène* which neatly sets off the occasional verbal preciosity.

Of all three directors, however, the master of the word is Chris Marker. The title of his new film is even too clever to be translatable. *Le Fond de l'air est rouge*: well, the *'fond de l'air'* does not exist as a concept in English, but it does in French folklore, as when people say on a day in May that the 'fond de l'air' is still cold – meaning that although it is warm in the sun, the atmosphere has not yet warmed up. So, if the 'fond de l'air' is red, this means – putting it crudely – that although the real revolution (I almost said the real right revolution, but that Jamesian expression could be gravely misinterpreted) has not yet occurred, it is, shall we say, 'in the air'. And Marker's film traces the vanguard revolutionary movements from 1967 on.

The film has not yet opened. At the time of writing, however, editing has been completed, and that was the major task since the film (all four hours of it) is to be made up of pieces of other people's films. Not extracts (this is no *That's Revolution*), but the parts that never got into finished films. Sections that were cut by censors, sequences which the directors censored themselves, scenes dropped for other reasons. Marker is also using pieces of television film – films which were shown, but only once, and which were thereafter buried forever. 1967, Marker says, was the decisive year. The Chinese Cultural Revolution was 'taken in hand', and the failure of the revolutionary left in Venezuela was, he thinks, even more significant, if less spectacular, than the murder of Che Guevara in Bolivia. From 1967 on, the powers that be began to infiltrate and control the 'subversive groups', and traditional politicians (from *all* parties, right *and* left) began to secrete the necessary antibodies to check the advance of the leftist infection. But, says Marker, 'we' didn't know that then; and, using a typical and inimitably Markerian comparison, the leftist movements continued like Boris Karloff's bowling ball in *Scarface* to knock down the tenpins after the hand that bowled the ball was already dead. Continued to the apex of their influence in the stunning if futile parades of 1968: the Prague spring, May in Paris, Mexico …

But was it all futile? That remains to be seen. Yes, Czechoslovakia was occupied, Allende was crushed, and the Chinese myth, so long protected by our Euro-centrism, was shattered. And yet, even these failures do not affect the fact that nothing can ever be as it was before 1968. Certain acts were committed, certain things were said, certain forces came into being. And in the film he will retrace the path traversed by the revolutionary left – not to find the guilty, but the innocent. Even (and especially) when the innocence of 1967 has become the crime of 1977 and vice versa.

But there will be some Marker footage in the film too. In 1952 he had shot the Olympic Games in Helsinki. And running over the film recently, he discovered that a jump-team medallist that year was a Chilean who later became one of the four generals of the Junta. It was indeed ex-horseman Mendoza who thought up the idea of using the Santiago *stadium* as the place to round up political prisoners (see *Providence*). So what was it that Marker had really filmed in 1952: the rider or the future general? The film will be a kind of dialogue. It would be too easy to indulge in facetious contradictions: instead each step of this imaginary dialogue will attempt to create a third voice which will be produced by the meeting of the first two and yet distinct from either of them. Marker doesn't boast that he has succeeded in making a dialectical film. But he has tried (having in his time, he says, abused the exercise of power by the commentator-director) for once to give back to the viewer, through montage, his own commentary; which is to say, his own power.

This sounds to me like a film worth waiting for, and a worthy third panel of the 1977 Left Bank triptych. But there is a fourth film that belongs here too: Marguerite Duras's *Le Camion* (for a wonder, an official French selection at Cannes). Duras can be considered a member of the Left Bank group for many reasons. Her first film work was the script for Resnais's *Hiroshima, mon amour*, and her second a script for Resnais's editor Henri Colpi (*Une Aussi Longue Absence*). And of course she is also a Left Banker in her choice of residence, of lifestyle, in her interest (to say the least) in literature, and in her left-wing non-Communist party politics.

The ostensible subject of *Le Camion* is a film-maker (played by Madame Duras herself) going over the script of a film she wants to make with the other leading player (Gérard Depardieu). Someone joked that this must be the cheapest film ever to compete at Cannes, because all the dialogue scenes were shot in a room in Madame Duras's house, there are only two actors, and the only other footage (but what footage!) is of the truck itself rolling through the desolate wastes of the Yvelines, an exurban department west of Paris where the blank landscape is punctuated only by hideous housing developments and garish hypermarkets.

However, as I suggested with regard to *Providence*, the device of discussing an unmade film is *only* a device; it is not the real subject of the film. True enough, for much of the time we do get Duras reading lines to Depardieu, and the actor asking questions about the characters each would be playing (this is a film in the conditional tense). Who would she be, asks Depardieu of the woman he, as truck-driver, would give a lift to. *Déclassée*, says Duras; that's all one can say about her. But of course there is much more to be said, because this woman is a number of women. To begin with, she is the heroine of *Hiroshima, mon amour* grown old: 'Ah, que j'étais jeune un jour,' says Duras, quoting *Hiroshima*. 'She wanted to die for love … but she lived on.' Depardieu is made to suggest that the woman has perhaps escaped from a local lunatic asylum. Duras neither confirms nor denies the accusation. Perhaps she is on the way to the christening of her nephew Abraham, whose family lives in an impossible spot to which there is only one bus a day. She talks once or twice about her childhood – far, far away from France. 'There was a river.' The Mekong, perhaps? We are never told, but the woman could be the young heroine of *Barrage contre le Pacifique*, she could also be Anne-Marie Stretter, Lol V. Stein. She is almost certainly the Asian beggar woman from *India Song*. But she is probably also Jewish.

In short, she is Marguerite Duras in all her fictional and non-fictional roles – all the women she was, all the women she imagined herself to be. And, like Duras, this woman is someone who has lost faith in politics, lost faith in the proletariat. Blasphemy! So she thought, for a long time, but when she saw the complicity between the bosses and the workers to prevent the occurrence of a real free revolution, when she saw that the invasion of Prague was the direct result of collusion between capitalism and socialism, she knew that she was right: Karl Marx is finished. Towards the end of the film, she would get out of the lorry – in the middle of nowhere. Perhaps, *en route*, they would have stopped at a roadside café, and he would have learned from a waitress that the lady he picked up did the same thing every day: hitch a lift in order to tell the driver her life story.

All the dialogue is shot with the two seated at a table. But much of the action of the film is on the road; for the lorry itself, a magnificent five-axle, blue Fruehauf, is the third character of the film. Its movements through the countryside and the roundabouts are as rhythmical as what Penelope Gilliatt once called Duras's back-stitching dialogue. I must confess that I don't really know what back-stitching is, but it sounds right for Duras's style. And the truck goes in for some back-stitching too; its movements are all the more pre-monitory because we never see its driver, nor do we hear the sound of the engine. Silently, it wanders through the fields, up and down hills, its movements never quite matching the dialogue. When the woman says she would get out in the middle of a heath, we see the lorry slow down and we expect it to stop. But no, it moves slowly on to a more travelled road, merges with the other lorries in the stream of traffic on a crowded highway. And probably the other lorry-drivers don't know what they are carrying either. When the woman asks our driver, he says that he doesn't know – they are all containers and who knows what's in them, or what their final destination is.

'So that's how it ends?' asks Depardieu. Yes, it's over. That is all we ever find out about the two people. The camera then moves forward towards the table where they are sitting and moves past them to a bright source of light: a white-curtained window with what seems to be some mystical light glowing from behind. Then the camera angle changes, and we see past the two actors and their table to an open window: her lips are moving, but the dialogue track has gone dead. All we hear (as we have heard at various moments throughout the film) is one of Beethoven's 'Diabelli Variations'. And then we see through an open window on to a terrace with a tall oak waving in the wind – and, next to it, a single klieg light. So that is what provided the 'mystical' brightness behind the curtain, one could say. Or, the light is there to show us that while pretending to talk about making a film, a film has actually been made: the one we have just seen. One could say both these things, and say them dismissively. But *Le Camion* is *not* an *exercise de style*; it is not just about a woman talking about making a film. Its real subject is Marguerite Duras in 1977, just as the real subject of *Providence*, David Mercer or not, is Alain Resnais in 1977.

Much as I liked *India Song*, I prefer *Le Camion*. *India Song* had many obvious attractions: its gorgeous interiors, its exoticism, its seductive tango music, its even more seductive Delphine Seyrig. *Le Camion* has nothing: nothing but Marguerite Duras and Gérard Depardieu; that room and that truck, that landscape and Beethoven. And with these meagre materials, Duras has made her most achieved film. It is also her shortest: one hour and eighteen minutes. But a film of this intensity, of this spareness, couldn't be borne for much longer. And also of this degree of pessimism: 'Let the world go to wrack and ruin,' says Duras/the Woman. And yet, however pessimistic her intentions, the sheer nerve of a film like this, plus its physical beauty (Bruno Nuytten on the camera), gave me a sense of exal-tation that was anything but a 'downer'.

SOURCE: 'THE LEFT BANK REVISITED', *SIGHT & SOUND*, 46.3, SUMMER 1977, 143–5

4.3 THE BAGGY-TROUSERED PHILANTHROPIST

'Life,' wrote Charles Spencer Chaplin, 'is a tragedy when seen in close-up, but a comedy in long-shot.' The first intimations of this aesthetic philosophy which was to dominate his work came at the beginning of his career in *Carmen*, his last Essanay short. Intended as

Decades Never Start On Time

a parody of both the Geraldine Farrar and the Theda Bara straight versions, it is indeed extremely funny all the way through. Until, that is, Charlie (playing Darn Hosiery) finally stabs Edna Purviance/Carmen.

And suddenly, in an electrifying moment, he plays it straight, and the whole tragic force of the story wells up. Seconds later, he goes back to clowning it up, but that brief moment was unforgettable − and unforgotten.

From then on all of Chaplin's films, no matter how funny, no matter how slapstick, had their moments of pathos, of tragic vision. *The Kid*, the first of his feature films, was also the first in which he no longer hid his intention of showing us, as Sergei Eisenstein wrote, 'the most terrible, most pitiful, most tragic things through the eyes of a laughing child.' There have been some who regret this evolution, who prefer the early two-reelers with their intoxicatingly pure comic pantomime. This may be true: it is also irrelevant. Whether or not one likes Chaplin is also irrelevant: the fact remains that he is a self-made myth, one of the few great mythic figures of the twentieth century. Chaplin was plugged into the collective unconsciousness, and this is why, from the very beginning, he captured the imaginations and the hearts of audiences all over the world.

Lévi-Strauss tells us that myth is an expression of unconscious wishes which are somehow inconsistent with conscious experience. In other words, myth serves to resolve unwelcome contradictions, and this is an important clue to the nature of Chaplin's greatness.

In a medium as realistic as film most early directors tried to get round the unrealistic fact that their characters could not speak. Chaplin, however, built his whole cinema on the very fact that his characters couldn't speak. There was nothing for them to say. Everything was translated into action, into visuals.

Indeed, his great appeal to the younger generation today lies precisely in this fact. But more important still, the figure Chaplin created was the archetypal underdog. He has no parents or relatives; nor has he a wife or children. He doesn't, until the later films, even have a girlfriend. He is the loner: rootless, twentieth-century urban man. His films may have been shot in and around Los Angeles, but they always seem to be taking place in some unspecified, and curiously rather middle-European, city.

And yet this under-dog, this little man, does have his victories − temporary, to be sure. He is never wholly defeated − there is always, until the end of *Monsieur Verdoux*, some hope for the future. As Gilbert Seldes put it, 'the little man … was an attorney − appealing in the highest courts of justice on our behalf … with often a comic accident accomplishing what a cosmic resentment desired.' This, I think, explains why Chaplin attained such universal popularity, for he speaks for men and women everywhere. They may know from their conscious experience that underdogs can't win, that nice guys finish last, but they find sustenance in the fact that Charlie embodies their unconscious, unavowed hope that some day, they, too, might triumph.

Or if not, then they can at least hope to walk undaunted down that straight road that Charlie used to travel at the end of his films. 'It is better to travel hopefully,' runs the old proverb, 'than to arrive.' Most of us haven't much choice in the matter, and this is perhaps the message Charlie has been signalling to us − between pratfalls − over the past sixty years.

SOURCE: 'THE BAGGY-TROUSERED PHILANTHROPIST', *GUARDIAN*, 28 DECEMBER 1977, 8

4.4 ROBERT BRESSON

NOTE: Throughout his critical career Roud wrote passionately about the films of Robert Bresson, who was undoubtedly one of his key film-makers. In this text, which reprises material going back to the 1950s (e.g., 'The early work of Robert Bresson', Film Culture, 20, 1959, 44–52), Roud concludes his account with Lancelot du Lac *(1974). Roud also wrote about* Le Diable probablement *(1977) in articles for the* Guardian *('Talk of the Devil',* Guardian, *17 January 1978, 9) and* Film Comment *('The redemption of despair',* Film Comment, *13.5, September–October 1977, 23–4). On* L'Argent *(1983), Bresson's final film, see 'Cheerful pessimist with the Spartan touch',* Guardian, *23 June 1983, 11.*

Because he has made so few films – only eleven in the thirty-two years from 1943 to 1975 – and because he has never been obliged to make films other than those he wanted to, most writers speak of Robert Bresson's *oeuvre* as if it were a canon. As indeed, in many ways, it is. Because of this feeling, most critics also feel impelled to divide this canon into periods, epochs. Jean Sémolué, for example, sees two groups: the first seven films up to and including *Au hasard, Balthazar* (*Balthazar*, 1966), and then the next three (he wrote before *Lancelot du Lac*, 1974, had been made). Michel Estève sees it differently. For him there are four main cycles. The first includes *Les Anges du péché* (1943) and *Les Dames du Bois de Boulogne* (1945); the second, *Le Journal d'un curé de campagne* (*Diary of a Country Priest*, 1951) and *Un Condamné à mort s'est échappé* (*A Man Escaped*, 1956); the third, *Pickpocket* (1959), *Procès de Jeanne d'Arc* (*Trial of Joan of Arc*, 1962) and *Au hasard, Balthazar*; the fourth, from *Mouchette* (1967) to *Lancelot*.

It is indeed tempting to break up the eleven films, since they do seem to fall into groups. There are the literary adaptations – of Giraudoux, Diderot/Cocteau, Bernanos (two), Dostoyevsky (two – plus *Pickpocket* and *Balthazar*, both of which have their point of departure in Dostoyevsky) – and there are the 'originals'. There are the films with a male protagonist and those with a female one. There are the realistic films and there are the fables. But finally, it seems to me that the most interesting approach is the unfashionable one – a normative view. Taking such a view, it seems to me quite clear that the films fall into two groups. The first ends with what I take to be Bresson's masterpiece, *Pickpocket*. The second ends with *Quatre nuits d'un rêveur* (*Four Nights of a Dreamer*, 1971). This leaves *Lancelot du Lac*, neither with the first group nor with the second.

What I am saying is that the first group, Bresson's first five films, are his best; contrary to the *politique des auteurs*, and also contrary to what I thought at the time, the next five are on a lower level of achievement. Why I think so will become clear, but, briefly, there are three important reasons. The first five films are similar in that they are films about redemption, films which because of this produce in the viewer a sense of exaltation. Redemption is not necessarily a more worthwhile subject than despair or suicide; but it is the exaltation born of the redemption theme which counters Bresson's tendency to greyness, to a glumness which is all too evident in the films from *Joan* to *Quatre nuits*. It is the dialectical struggle between glumness and glory that makes the first five films so enduringly effective.

There is another factor which may be related: in his first five films Bresson seems to be dealing with matters of which he has a profound understanding. It is natural that he should want to extend his range to take in the juvenile delinquents of *Au hasard, Balthazar*, the young peasant girl Mouchette, the married couple in *Une Femme douce* (*A Gentle*

Creature, 1969), but it would seem that this subject matter is somehow alien to him. In his book *Notes sur le cinématographe*, he maintains that the film-maker should avoid subjects which are too foreign to him, that he should stick to what he can draw from his own experience. Without suggesting that Bresson was ever a pickpocket, I still think that the subject matter of the first five films must be closer to his experience and to his understanding. And yet, 'the most important ideas in a film are the most hidden,' he wrote. In the first five films there is a buried erotic stratum which surfaces only in the later films (*Joan* being the obvious exception). And this subterranean sexual significance gives to the earlier films a richness lacking in the more explicit later ones.

Having thus laid down my hand, I can now proceed to a more orderly examination of Bresson's unusual career. He was born in 1907 in central France, and educated in the suburbs of Paris. His first ambition was to be a painter; he did not come to the cinema until 1939, when he was thirty-two years old, when he made a featurette, all prints of which appear to have been lost.[2] It was called *Les Affaires publiques*, and the only description of it comes from Bresson himself: 'It was, how shall I put it, not a burlesque … but a crazy comedy about three days in the life of an imaginary dictator – who was played by a well-known clown of the period called Béby. There were two other actors in it, Dalio and Gilles Margaritis.'

The film appears to have made no impact; in any case, the war came, and Bresson was taken prisoner by the Germans – a fact of great significance in his cinema, when one remembers how many of his films deal with prison: *Les Anges du péché*, *Un Condamné à mort*, *Pickpocket* and *Trial of Joan of Arc*. He spent eighteen months in a German prison camp; on his return to Paris, he met Father Raymond Bruckberger, a 'literary' priest, who was unofficially known as the almoner of Saint-Germain-des-Prés – not of the church but of the cafés and the *caves*. And it was he who suggested to Bresson that he make a film about Bethany, an order of Dominican nuns devoted to the care and rehabilitation of women ex-prisoners. Together they worked out a scenario and succeeded in getting Jean Giraudoux to write the dialogue. It took them a year to find a producer – the subject was not obviously commercial – but when the film was released in 1943, it was a great success. Overnight, Bresson became an important figure in French cinema.

The impact of the film came partly from its unconventional theme. Films had been made before about religious orders, but never one of such spiritual intensity and rigour as *Les Anges du péché*. The plot was a fairly complex one, but there were basically only two characters – Thérèse, the ex-prisoner (Jany Holt), and Anne-Marie, a young novice (Renée Faure). During her first prison visit, Anne-Marie meets Thérèse, the bitterest and most intractable of the prisoners, and there and then, Anne-Marie decides that it is her divinely appointed mission to 'save' Thérèse.

When Thérèse is released from jail a few days later, she does accept Anne-Marie's invitation to live at the convent – but not before having killed her lover (for whose crime she had been wrongfully convicted). Anne-Marie, overjoyed at Thérèse's arrival and at what she naïvely takes to be her own personal success, does all she can to alleviate Thérèse's bitterness – but naturally, Thérèse resents being overwhelmed with all this unsought love.

Anne-Marie's wiser superiors notice this, and also accuse her of neglecting her other duties in order to dedicate herself entirely to Thérèse; finally, in the face of Anne-Marie's stubbornness, the Prioress is obliged to ask her to leave the convent. Anne-Marie goes away, but when she is found in a dead faint one morning in the convent garden, the nuns realise that she has been returning secretly every night since her expulsion. Half-dead, she is brought in, and it is Thérèse who is assigned the task of nursing her. To no avail; on the point of death, Anne-Marie is allowed to take her final vows, but she is too weak to pronounce the words. And it is then that Thérèse, finally touched by Anne-Marie's devotion, understands and accepts; in a kind of spiritual transference, it is Thérèse who pronounces the words. Anne-Marie dies, but she has won: Thérèse gives herself up to the police. She has accepted responsibility for her crime, and has thus opened the way to expiation and redemption. And in the last shot – which prefigures a famous shot in *Pickpocket* – Thérèse extends her hands to the waiting handcuffs. She must be made prisoner before she can be set free.

The great originality of the film lies in the fact that for once a director is really concerned with religion, and has succeeded in giving it dramatic life – even for non-believers. He has stripped from this complicated plot all the inessentials; like Dreyer, he uses the close-up to reveal the souls of his characters. In spite of what Bresson said later, his actresses were superb. The film was almost entirely shot in studio, and the sets of the convent, with their dazzling whiteness, take on an obvious symbolic value, especially contrasted with the darkness of the prison scenes. Like *Les Dames du Bois de Boulogne*, *Les Anges du péché* was much more 'literary' than any of Bresson's later films; Giraudoux's dialogue, brilliant though it is, never swamps the film as it might so easily have done.

I have spoken earlier of that undercurrent of sexuality which I think nourished Bresson's first five films, and it is certainly present in this, his first work. The intensity of the relationship between Thérèse and Anne-Marie may not be sexual in origin, but as portrayed it takes on the aspect of a particularly tormented kind of masochistic courtship: one feels that it is precisely Thérèse's hatred of Anne-Marie and what she stands for that awakens in Anne-Marie her passion for Thérèse.

Bresson's next film, *Les Dames du Bois de Boulogne*, concerns itself directly with redemption through love. Begun early in 1944, it was not released until after the Liberation. Unlike *Les Anges du péché*, *Les Dames* was an almost total failure with both critics and audiences. Almost the only prominent person to defend the film was Jacques Becker. Since then, it has slowly gained a wider audience, and it is often revived – in France, at least.[3] […]

If *Les Anges du péché* is a film about religion, Bresson's next film [after *Les Dames du Bois de Boulogne*], *Le Journal d'un curé de campagne*, is a drama of religion. Analogically, like the first two, it is a drama of salvation and grace, the triumph of love over hate, of grace over sin. But it is much starker than the first two, less conventionally beautiful. Instead of the elegance of Philippe Agostini's camerawork (he shot Bresson's first two films), we now have the simpler, starker photography of L. H. Burel, a veteran who began his career with Abel Gance. And this starkness was essential to express the profoundly harrowing mood of the film.

It was an adaptation, by Bresson, of the novel by Georges Bernanos, and he once again reduced his material to its essentials. The masterstroke was to have kept to the *form* of the novel – first-person narration, for everything is seen from the point of view of the country priest. For the first time Bresson used non-professional actors, and they are totally subordinated to the interior drama – the Passion of the priest of Ambricourt. In the earlier films, there was a stylisation of the actors – here they are positively hieratic.

The most startling stylistic innovation of the film was its apparent use of pleonasms – the narrator telling us something while we are actually watching it happen. The effect is of a kind of distanciation; as we watch the Curé writing his diary, the film itself becomes a diary. But even more important, these apparent pleonasms are actually a conjugation of

Decades Never Start On Time

text and image, of novel and film. René Briot has suggested that just as *Les Dames* was based on the relationship (contradiction?) between realism and abstraction, so *Le Journal* is based on the relationship between reality and literature.

Certainly Bresson's use of off-screen noises (which will be more important in *Un Condamné*, but realistically justified) tends to confirm this. From the beginning of the film, the sound of the squeaking of a wagon wheel becomes an important leitmotif which contrasts with the literary subject and dialogue. A more striking example is the great central scene, the 'conversion' of the Countess, when in the pauses in the conversation we distinctly hear the sound of a rake scraping the earth from the grounds of the château. Far from lowering the tension of the scene, this seems to increase it by heightening the contrast between the everyday world and the extraordinary spiritual struggle for the redemption of the Countess's soul. And the Countess is redeemed — and dies shortly thereafter; and the priest does triumph over Chantal's pride. By the end of the film, even the non-believer is forced to acknowledge that the little country priest is a saint — whatever that word may mean. His final liberation comes not only from his acceptance of his approaching and painful death, but from the knowledge that his conflicts have not really been with the Countess, or Chantal, or Seraphita, but with himself. And these conflicts are resolved: *Tout est grâce*.

Although Bresson was not the first to make a film with this kind of fidelity to both the form and subject of a novel — the credit for this must go to Jean-Pierre Melville in *Le Silence de la mer* — this film is greater than Melville's both because the Bernanos novel is superior to the Vercors story, and because Bresson has made of Bernanos's novel a Bresson film. He was, in fact, never again to achieve the same effect; *Mouchette* is not as effective a transposition of Bernanos's novel, nor is it so extraordinary a film. The death of the Curé is more *interesting* than the death of Mouchette because his life has been more complex than hers. She is only a victim; the Curé is much more. And the atmosphere of sordid small country town sexuality is all the more powerful in *Le Journal* because it is almost unexpressed. But in the smouldering look of Chantal's face, in Dufrety's mistress, the intrigues of Seraphita, and even in the eyes of the Countess, we feel the presence of a current of sexuality which is only the stronger for being almost totally repressed.

During the five years between *Le Journal* and his next film (1956) Bresson was not idle; he had wanted to adapt *La Princesse de Clèves*, and had gone as far as rehearsing the main characters when the plan was abandoned because of another project to film the same novel. During this time, too, Bresson began work on *Lancelot du Lac*, which was not to be realised for twenty years.

Bresson's next film, *Un Condamné à mort s'est échappé*, is his most popular work to date — and not without reason. This time, basing his film on a true story, he found the sort of anecdote which both would serve his own ends and could also be accepted on a purely realistic basis. Condemned to death by the Gestapo in 1943, André Devigny succeeded in escaping from the Montluc prison fortress only a few hours before his scheduled execution. Excited by the idea of turning Devigny's newspaper story into a film, Bresson was determined to respect the historical truth, but at the same time he wanted, he said, to 'superimpose a truth which would be authentically filmic'. So while he carefully reconstructed Devigny's cell in the studio, and while the exteriors were shot in Lyon, he also made a certain number of significant changes in the original tale. All references to how and why Devigny had been captured were suppressed; he changed the order of some of the incidents in the prison; the character of Orsini is a combination of two characters in the original. But most important of all, although the original insisted on the skill and daring of Devigny as being entirely responsible for his success, Bresson introduced another element, that of chance, or grace: the subtitle of the film, it must not be forgotten, is *The Wind Bloweth Where It Listeth*.

Although the film's success derived largely from the fact that it was acceptable as a realistic story of escape, it is much more than that – it is an exemplary tale, a fable of the relationships between man and man, and between man and God. I have said that redemption is the key concept of Bresson's first five films – here it abounds on all sides. Not only does Fontaine (the name given Devigny) achieve his own escape from despair, but his cell-mate Jost is also redeemed, and so is old Blanchet, whose pessimism and despair have seemed almost invincible. But when Orsini is killed in an attempt at escape, there ensues an exchange of words between Fontaine and Blanchet. Blanchet: 'Orsini had to fail in order for you to succeed.' Fontaine: 'That's extraordinary.' Blanchet: 'You knew that.' Fontaine: 'What's extraordinary is that it's you, Monsieur Blanchet, who is saying it.' For human solidarity is almost as important in this film as grace; and again, this made it acceptable to those put off by Bresson's religious or spiritual attitude.

Most important, however, Bresson's austere style is acceptable in this film because it is set in a prison cell: it is realistically justified. And the use of off-screen sounds is also justified on a realistic level. Shut up alone in a cell, Fontaine pays careful attention to any signs of life from outside: the screeching of tramcars, the hoots of trains, the squeaking of bicycles. This realistic 'justification' does not in any way diminish the film: it remains one of Bresson's greatest achievements, and marked an important advance in his style. For one thing, he at last abandoned the use of a musical score composed for the film; instead he relies only on a few scraps of a Mozart mass. Yet these bits of Mozart are not generally used to underline the great climactic scenes; instead, they suddenly appear in the scenes where the prisoners wash up and empty their slop pails.

Until well over half-way through the film, Bresson succeeds in fascinating us with only one real character – and with very little interaction between that character and the others we occasionally see. But it is just then that the whole film is turned upside down – just as Fontaine's plans are turned upside down – by the sudden appearance of another character: Jost, the adolescent suddenly thrust into his cell, into his life. Is he a spy? Must Fontaine kill him in order to secure his own escape? Finally, he decides to trust him, to tell him his plans and to enlist his aid, to force Jost to accompany him. And he promises that once out, he will help him to make something of his freedom, to transform this reluctant collaborator (Jost was a member of the German–French militia). It is only when they reach one of the walls they have to scale that Fontaine realizes he *couldn't* have made it without Jost. And when they finally reach the street, Fontaine's first reaction is to take Jost into his arms; and Jost, in one of the cinema's greatest lines, says only, 'If my mother could see me!', and the two men disappear into the smoke of a train passing under a bridge.

Le Journal begins with a series of short scenes, which gradually lengthen into sequences. In this film, there are 600 shots, but no sequences: the whole film is one long sequence. These short, sharp shots are articulated by the rhythm of editing and by that of Fontaine's commentary, both holding the film together, urging it onward unceasingly, welding it into a seamless whole.

Bresson tells us nothing about Fontaine – who he is, what he does for a living; he is a blank piece of paper, and yet he is also a very real character. One feels by the end of the film that one *knows* Fontaine without knowing any facts about him except that he presumably is not married, since the only letter we see him write is to his mother, and that he

Decades Never Start On Time

Pickpocket (1959)

has sisters, since he describes the making of a rope as being like the way his mother used to plait their hair. Oddly enough, in the original, Devigny had a wife and three children.

Comparing the film with the original story, Jean Sémolué tells us that Jost is more sympathetic in the film than in the story, and that their relationship is much more strained in the film than in the book. In the original, one of Devigny's major arguments in persuading Jost to escape is that he will take him to a brothel! Naturally, there is nothing like that in Bresson's film – not only because of Bresson's delicacy, but because of the slightly ambiguous nature of Fontaine and Jost's relationship.

This lack of 'information', this openness of the story to many interpretations, will be carried to its furthest extent in *Pickpocket*. Bresson has always been against 'psychology', but in his recent book he explains more clearly what he means: he is against that psychology 'which only discovers what it can explain'. Once a character is 'explained', he loses all interest – he becomes a 'case'. This, Bresson feels, must at all costs be avoided. Hence he leaves all psychological options open. Just as we never see the *whole* of Fontaine's cell, even though almost three-quarters of the film takes place there, so the presentation of Fontaine is, as Bazin noted at the time, 'beyond psychology'.

Pickpocket went so much further in this direction that it was almost universally disliked.[4] [...] Was it the failure of *Pickpocket*, or the feeling that Bresson had gone as far as he could, that made his next film, *Trial of Joan of Arc*, a simpler, less ambitious and less interesting work? Lasting only sixty-five minutes, it is a film of the official transcript of Joan's trial. Bresson's Joan is self-possessed, resilient but vulnerable, sustained by a sense of grace. Alternating between court and cell, much of the film consists simply of dialogues between Joan and her accusers: one scarcely sees the onlookers, and there are no dramatic outbursts. The film begins with a shot of bare feet pattering over the cobbles, then imperceptibly pausing before the stake, and it ends with a series of shots of objects: chains, the faggots, a little dog, the smoke, the cross, some doves, and then finally and terrifyingly the stake itself, charred, still smoking, and *bare*. For the first time in film history, one feels that Joan was really *burnt*.

There is no denying the mastery with which Bresson has reduced the drama to a series of one-shots with a practically immobile camera and a strict minimum of set-ups, and only a minute of music in the whole film. And yet the film is less meaningful than its predecessors because the cards are stacked. We *know* that Joan is a saint, and therefore there is no conflict: she is an entirely pure being – a kind of intellectual Antigone with the symbolic values that go with it. Susan Sontag felt that the problem was Florence Carrez, 'the least luminous of all the presences Bresson has used in his later films. The thinness … is partly a failure of communicated intensity on the part of the actress.' Partly, yes: but the thinness comes from the lack of dialectical struggle. Without sin, what interest has redemption?

Perhaps Bresson made the film because so many other projects fell through: a life of Loyola, *Lancelot of the Lake*, and a film about a donkey. The donkey film, *Au hasard, Balthazar*, was finally made three years later. And it was different from anything Bresson had done before. For one thing, it was a totally original script (I persist in seeing echoes of *Crime and Punishment* in *Pickpocket*), and it was the first film in which he tried to tell several stories at once, to treat several subjects at once. The danger here was a lack of unity, a risk which was consciously taken by Bresson – and he admitted later in an interview with Godard and Michel Delahaye that 'perhaps *Balthazar* did have less unity than the other films'.

Basically, there are two stories: the first is the story of an ass, Balthazar; the second is of two young people, Jacques and Marie, to whom the donkey is given as a companion. As time passes, Balthazar learns first to draw a carriage, then to plough. Eventually, he is sold by Marie's father to a baker who uses him to deliver bread. After Marie is seduced by Gérard, the leader of a motor-cycle gang, Balthazar falls ill, and is almost put away. But Arnold, a tramp, takes him, nurses him back to health, and uses him to give rides to children. Suddenly, however, he turns against Balthazar and sells him to a circus, where the donkey is a great success doing tricks until Arnold appears one night in the audience and Balthazar is incapable of performing. He leaves the circus with Arnold – but after Arnold's sudden and mysterious death, Balthazar is sold at auction to a miller who uses him to turn a grindstone – the same miller with whom Marie now lives, offering her body in exchange for food and shelter. When her parents come to 'rescue' her, they take Balthazar too. On the death of Marie's father, Gérard and the other members of his gang use Balthazar in their smuggling expeditions (the film is set near the Swiss border). On one of their sorties, Balthazar is shot by a customs officer. Wounded, he makes his way down the mountain, and there comes to a halt; surrounded by a flock of white sheep, he sinks to his knees. Two dogs arrive, the sheep slowly withdraw and Balthazar dies.

This is one way of telling the story; another would be to start with the adolescent passion of Jacques and Marie, which ends when Marie prefers the vicious Gérard; or to start with the story of Marie's father and his difficulties with his farm and with the man to whom the land belongs – Jacques's father.

What seems wrong with the film now is the overly complicated plot – too much to digest, too much to 'compose'. Bresson has said it was his 'freest' film, and that's part of the trouble, too. In *Notes sur le cinématographe*, there is the injunction: 'Avoid subjects which are too vast or too remote.' In *Balthazar* one feels that he has avoided neither: the subject(s) are too vast and the subject-matter, especially the motor-cycle gang, is too remote from Bresson's experience. The donkey, of course, is meant by Bresson to act as the unifying factor, but I don't think that this works. Bresson thought of the donkey as both a Christian and a sexual symbol; traditionally the donkey is also considered both the stupidest and the wisest of animals. At the time, it seemed to me that the film could be justified by the notion that Bresson had meant it to be a series of unresolved contradictions, constantly forcing us to question the events of the story. Perhaps this is so, but when one actually begins to question the events of the story, one's doubts as to the success of the film begin. For a director whose style is as rigorous as Bresson's, there are too many fuzzy edges, too many vague, unrealized notions. The first time one sees the film, one is fascinated by its technique: a series of brush-strokes, short, elliptical scenes which give only the barest essence of any action, leaving the viewer to fill in what happened before and after each very short scene, as well as obliging him to establish the various relationships himself – a mosaic, in fact, of perpetually interacting forms, narrative elements and symbols. Unfortunately, the mosaic does not finally emerge. Although Bresson has, as always, pared down each scene to its essentials, he hasn't done the same thing with the film as a whole – that is to say, he never succeeded in distilling what he wanted to express. Perhaps its very freedom militated against this: the fact that he could now allow himself to include explicitly sexual material took something from him. The sexual charge of his earlier films – smouldering underground, as it were – was much stronger than in this film, where sexual relationships are one of the chief themes. There is a lack of tension in *Balthazar*, and this slackness is accompanied by a concomitant lack of exaltation – with the single exception of Balthazar's death scene.

Bresson's heroine, Marie, is too passive to be interesting. Doubtless she corresponds to something in Bresson, but like Joan, like Mouchette, like *la femme douce*, things just happen to her. One can feel sorry for her, but that is not an emotion which goes very far. Bresson succeeds much more, it seems to me now, when he is dealing with positive characters – because of the very positive nature of his *mise en scène*. Michel's aggressiveness in *Pickpocket*, Fontaine's determination in *Un Condamné*, the Curé's stubbornness, Agnès's fortitude – these are the qualities that inspire Bresson, and which he can render best.

Mouchette was based on the Bernanos novel about a fourteen-year-old peasant girl, one of the despised and rejected of this earth. The film deals with the last twenty-four hours of her life, and it is significant that its two most extraordinary sequences are the early moment of joy in a fairground scene and the final scene of her suicide (buttressed by the use of the Monteverdi *Magnificat*). But her passive nature and the single-toned narrative do not allow Bresson any of the occasions for those controlled yet lyrical outbursts of *Pickpocket*. Indeed, there is something almost sadistic in the way in which the girl is treated, not only by the other characters in the film but by Bresson as well. She is a victim, and he is unable to make anything more of her than that. This being said, the film is extraordinarily well shot: not only the suicide, but little things, like the way that Mouchette often comes into frame from the upper left, moves towards the middle, and then, as if unable to cross the frame – with the obvious symbolic meaning – she retreats again to the left.

Bresson's last two films before *Lancelot* were both Dostoyevsky adaptations: *Une Femme douce* (his first film in colour) and *Quatre nuits d'un rêveur*. The first is based on *A Gentle Creature*, and tells the story of a man whose wife has suddenly committed suicide. While he sits by her corpse, he goes back over the past to try to understand why she did it. He never really finds out, and neither do we except in a very open-ended way. Beyond the plot level, the film, like the novel, is concerned with the failure of love, the difficulty in breaking down the walls that separate people.

For the first time since *Les Dames*, Bresson has given us a life-sized woman, neither victim nor abstraction – and all the more real because played by Dominique Sanda, in her first screen appearance. Her presence almost succeeds in making the character real to us. The husband is less satisfactory, and as it is he who gives us the most information, this is a pity. As Eric Rhode pointed out, there is another problem with the portrayal of the 'Gentle Creature': 'I keep feeling that Bresson's treatment of the girl is a little like the relationship of some fathers to their teenage daughters. He wants to share her interests, and even loves her, but, irritably, he cannot quite bridge the gap between them.' This was also, I feel, the case with Marie in *Balthazar*, and it surely has something to do with Bresson's troubled sexuality – the girl in his film is a much more explicitly erotic creature than in the Dostoyevsky original, and Bresson seems to have had some difficulty in handling this.

He had no difficulty with colour, however, and he has created a masterful composition almost entirely in tones of blue and green. This is not done in any obvious way; it's just that after a while you begin to notice that the man always wears a blue suit and the girl a green coat. Even highways take on the colour scheme, with the borders green and the roadway bluish.

Quatre nuits d'un rêveur is based on *White Nights*, and like *Une Femme douce*, it evoked resistance even from Bresson's admirers. Visually, it is among his most accomplished works. Shooting on location in Paris, mostly round the Pont Neuf and the Pont des Arts, he does some fantastic things with urban landscape. What he makes of an illuminated tourist boat gliding mysteriously under those bridges partakes of both science-fiction and entomology. Like some weird spaceship or some tropical insect, these *bateaux-mouches* pass silently under the bridges where our young hero meets the girl of his dreams, who alas is waiting for the return of the man of *her* dreams.

The film is set in the present, and Bresson seems as little at ease with the strolling bands of hippies as he did with the motorcycle boys of *Balthazar*. And the Brazilian folk songs suit him less than Mozart, or Monteverdi. Nor do his non-professional actors have the same spiritual authority as those in previous works. This being said, the film is none the less the work of a master of cinema. In Penelope Houston's words: 'A man pushes a lift button, and a light flashes; a gesture of no special significance to the character, or to the film's meaning. And yet no interruption, short of the ceiling falling about one's ears, could distract attention from that little illuminated panel. How? Apart from Bresson's supreme paring-away, his awareness of essence, one can only posit some sort of telepathic communication, transmitting the intensity of the director's concentration. The object is not a symbol, a clue, a "significant" detail, but simply a conductor for the director's will.'

Three years later, however, when his long-planned *Lancelot du Lac* was finally completed, one could measure the difference between the 'masterstrokes' of *Quatre nuits d'un rêveur* and the triumph of a work which is a masterpiece on every level, including that of its conception and ambitions. Ostensibly the subject of the film is the self-thwarting love of Lancelot and Guinevere, but it is also – or even more – a film about the end of the Middle Ages. The impossible quest for the Grail has ended in failure, and the impossible dream of an ideal society has also proved unworkable. It is no accident that Bresson ends the film with the slaughter of the knights by foot soldiers with crossbows. This may not be historically accurate, but this is not a realistic film. Nevertheless, it presents us with a view

Decades Never Start On Time

of feudal society that is marred by none of the complacency or sentimentality of films like *Les Visiteurs du soir.*

From the very beginning, even before the credits, we are presented with images of horror − skeletons in armour, burned bodies, the feeling of the surrounding forest always ready to reconquer the clearings made by civilization. But before this civilisation crumbles, there is one last great moment, the tournament in which Lancelot proves that he has lost none of his skill or strength. Shot saddle-high, it has Lancelot dispatching his opponents one by one, in a sequence that, like Uccello's battle-paintings, is both unreal and very material. Some critics complained that there was too much clanking of armour in the film, too many scenes of mounting and dismounting. But even though Bresson always avoids direct symbolism, one can see in this insistence on the armour in which his heroes are always encased a symbol of the code by which they live. When Lancelot appears before Guinevere without his armour, it is as if he were stark naked.

The film runs barely ninety minutes, but there have never been so many arresting images in a Bresson film: enormous close-ups of the eye of a terrified horse, the bird that appears at Guinevere's window during the love scenes, the riderless horses at the end of the film, symbolic of uncontrolled instincts. Every shot is a surprise, and every surprise turns out to be justified. Throughout the film, for example, we see Arthur and his knights from below, their contact with the earth always evident. One might wonder at this insistence, but when at the end of the film we have the archers in the trees and the slaughter of the Knights of the Round Table is seen from above, with the mass of armoured soldiers piled up like some monstrous heap of old iron, one suddenly realizes that it was this tragic contrast Bresson had been working towards. Psychologically, the film is his richest − for it is not a simple triangle story. There is also Gawain (Gauvain), who is presented as Lancelot's best friend and also in love with Guinevere − and yet loyal to both Arthur and Lancelot. Between these four characters there is a tension which is all the stronger because it is never clearly defined. Although the film ends in total destruction, there is a kind of transcendent radiance in the relations between the main characters because of the way in which Bresson portrays this birth of desire and a more exalted form of passion. And it is from this struggle that *Lancelot* derives its strength and luminosity and that sense of physical and spiritual exaltation that had been absent in Bresson's *oeuvre* since *Pickpocket.*

SOURCE: 'ROBERT BRESSON', IN RICHARD ROUD (ED.), *CINEMA: A CRITICAL DICTIONARY: THE MAJOR FILM-MAKERS* (NEW YORK: VIKING PRESS; LONDON: MARTIN SECKER & WARBURG, 1980), 141−53

4.5 LOUIS FEUILLADE AND THE SERIAL

NOTE: For an earlier appreciation of the work of Louis Feuillade, see 'Les Vampires', Sight & Sound, *33.2, Spring 1964, 96−7.*

Given the mechanically reproducible nature of film as a medium, the enormous popularity of Louis Feuillade's films in their time, and what now seems their indisputable greatness, it hardly seems possible that a director of the stature of Feuillade could so totally have disappeared from the history of the cinema for so many years. In France he was remembered as the director of *Judex* (1917) and a few other serials, but until the first Cinémathèque revival of *Fantômas* (1913) in 1944, he was never considered one of the great figures of the French cinema.

In Great Britain, Feuillade was completely unknown; his name does not appear in Roger Manvell's Penguin *Film* nor in Paul Rotha's *The Film till Now*. And it was not until the National Film Theatre revival of *Fantômas* and especially *Les Vampires* (1915) in 1963 that British critics had seen any of his films. The same is true in America; Louis Feuillade's name does not appear in the *New York Times Index to Film Reviews* until 1965, when *Les Vampires* was screened at the New York Film Festival.

There are many reasons for this eclipse. First of all, Feuillade was a victim of his very popularity: the enormous success of his films militated against his being taken seriously as an artist. Secondly, his career did suffer a decline after 1919, and in the six remaining years of his life he was never able to equal either the success or the genius of *Les Vampires*, *Tih Minh* (1918) and *Barrabas* (1919). Furthermore, the cinema was undergoing great changes at this period: by the early 20s the French had discovered Griffith, and his mobile camerawork and dynamic montage – both of which are totally absent from the films of Feuillade – became the touchstones for a new generation of film critics.

It is no accident, I think, that the Feuillade revival of the mid-40s coincided both with the rediscovery of location shooting in the Italian neo-realist cinema and also with the new interest – sparked off by the European release of Orson Welles's first two films – in composition in depth, and the concomitant critical downgrading of montage.

The first French avant-garde movement looked upon Feuillade as precisely the sort of commercial film-maker they were fighting against. Louis Delluc's judgement was uncon-ditional: '*Judex* and *The New Mission of Judex* are more serious crimes than those con-demned by courts-martial.' And the distinguished critic André Antoine decreed that Feuillade 'was certainly the man who has contributed the most to make those people with a spark of good sense and of reason disgusted with the cinema'.

The opinion of these critics and film-makers prevailed for many years. The only voices raised in defence of Feuillade during the 20s were those of a few surrealist writers – and the young Buñuel. Georges Sadoul remembered (*Etudes Cinématographiques*, 38–9) Buñuel telling him how much he loathed the films of the 'avant-garde movement' and all the techniques that were fashionable in the 20s – rapid cutting, super-impositions and photographic effects. His models, he told Sadoul, were *Fantômas* and *Les Vampires*, direct translations without any *chichi*, of '*une réalité insolite*' ['an unusual reality']. But the irony, Sadoul tells us, was that 'like all of us, he didn't even know the name of the director of those films'. There was to have been a gala, organized by the surrealists, to render homage to René Cresté (Judex) and to Musidora (Irma Vep of *Les Vampires*) but not to Feuillade who was an anonymous figure. In any case, the gala never took place, but a play, *The Treasure of the Jesuits*, was written by Louis Aragon and André Breton in which the following lines appear: 'Since you're interested in the cinematograph, I am going to intro-duce you to the apotheosis of a forgotten *genre*. Soon it will be generally understood that there is nothing more realistic and at the same time more poetic than those serials which the intellectuals used to make fun of. It is in *The Perils of Pauline*, it is in *Les Vampires* that one must look for the great reality of this century – beyond fashion, beyond taste.'

As Henri Langlois put it, the surrealists *had* to admire Feuillade, since surrealism already existed in the cinema before the actual surrealist movement began: 'One only has to take *Les Vampires* to see that the cinema, because it was an expression of the twentieth

Decades Never Start On Time

century and of its universal subconscious, bore the essence of surrealism within it.'

In fact, the surrealists were able to appreciate the very elements in Feuillade's work that others reproached him with: his use of the serial format and his taste for melodrama. Indeed, Feuillade cannot be defended without at the same time making out a case for melodrama. But before tackling that problem, we should first see how Feuillade came to the cinema.

He was born in 1873 in southern France, and grew up in a very religious family who insisted on his attending church-supported schools. Once he got his *baccalauréat*, he enlisted in a cavalry regiment without waiting to be called up for military service, and spent four years in the army. On leaving, he married and followed his father and brothers into the wine trade. In his spare time, however, he enjoyed amateur theatricals and was an *aficionado* of bullfights. After the deaths of his parents, he decided to leave for Paris, where a friend found him a job in a newspaper office. His journalistic career ended in 1905; a friend had introduced him to the artistic director of Pathé, and he began to write scenarios. The Pathé connection didn't work out, however, so Feuillade went directly to Gaumont, where he was received by the legendary Alice Guy-Blaché. Initially Léon Gaumont's secretary, she had become the first woman director in the history of the cinema, and was the artistic director of Gaumont.

She liked Feuillade's scripts, and one of them, *Le Coup de vent*,[5] was filmed by Etienne Arnaud in 1905. Two years later, she left Paris to follow her husband, who had just taken over the Berlin office of Gaumont, and she persuaded Gaumont to let Feuillade replace her. From 1907 he was in charge of hiring directors, buying scripts, choosing stars and at the same time directing his own films. Francis Lacassin tells us that at the end of his life, Feuillade reckoned he had written at least 800 scripts, of which he had directed 700. One must remember that his earlier films were very short: one- or two-reelers. Still, the total is impressive. Gaumont still preserves the negatives of about 500 of these films. No one alive, I dare say, has seen them all. The early years, from 1905 to 1908, saw Feuillade turning out comedies. The historical series began in 1909, and the *Film Esthétique* in 1910, but he continued to make comedies, in particular the series devoted to Bébé, a child actor. Some of them are still quite funny, but Feuillade first became famous through his series of films under the high-sounding general title *La Vie telle qu'elle est* (*Life As It Is*).

This laudable effort at neo-realism, we are told, came about largely through the need for economy: Pathé, as always, was Gaumont's great competitor, and Feuillade always wanted to turn out better films more cheaply than they could. And when Gaumont told him that a Danish company (Nordisk) was making films for no more than 6.50 francs a metre negative costs, he declared that he could do it for only 6 francs a metre.

And he did, and some of them are very good, although they have more to do with melodrama than with realism – at least in so far as their plots are concerned. One of the earliest and most beautiful is *La Tare* (1911). The story is pure corn: a kind doctor gives a young woman in Paris attached to a wastrel a chance of redeeming herself through hard work in an orphanage. Alas, her Parisian friend tracks her down, and when it is revealed to the trustees of the institution that her earlier life had not been blameless, she is thrown out. She cannot find work, and is close to suicide. In an extraordinary shot, Feuillade shows her in her attic room, with a bright shaft of light cutting the room in two; she goes to the window, climbs onto the sill and is poised there ready to jump when her despairing face is illuminated by the bright sunshine. She hesitates, and then falls back into the semi-dark room. The film leaves her there, her head bowed in misery. Although the plot is melodramatic, the treatment is restrained, and one can already see in this early work that extraordinary combination of realistic treatment and melodramatic subject that was to be the hallmark of Feuillade's *oeuvre*.

There is one tiny, tentative camera movement in the film (which only runs for 900 metres) – a lateral pan from the waiting room of an employment agency to the office. One can almost see Feuillade, having done it once, thinking, well, let's do it again; and so having moved from left to right, haltingly we go back from right to left. But Feuillade's compositions were and remained almost exclusively in depth. One could call it a theatrical point of view, if it were not for the fact that there has seldom been a director who could so escape theatrical perspective through the use of light and the movements of his characters.

The comic series continued, however, throughout the period of *Life As It Is* – the only differences being that the films got longer and that Bébé (René Dary) was replaced by Bout de Zan, who stayed with Feuillade for the rest of the director's career, appearing in both *Les Vampires* and *Judex*.

In the same year as *La Tare*, 1911, two authors, Marcel Allain and Pierre Souvestre, wrote the first instalments of the story of the master-criminal *Fantômas*. 'In 32 volumes,' as Lacassin put it, 'and in 32 months, they thrilled a whole generation.' And in 1913 Feuillade captured the imagination of the world with the first three parts of his five-part film of *Fantômas*.

'It is to be hoped,' wrote T. S. Eliot, 'that some scholarly and philosophic critic of the present generation may be inspired to write a book on the history and aesthetic of melodrama ... Those who have lived before such terms as "high-brow fiction", "thrillers" and "detective fiction" were invented realize that melodrama is perennial, and the craving for it is perennial and must be satisfied ... the frontier of drama and melodrama is vague; the difference is largely a matter of emphasis; perhaps no drama has ever been greatly and permanently successful without a large melodramatic element. What is the difference between *The Frozen Deep* and *Oedipus the King*? It is the difference between coincidence, set without shame or pretence, and fate – which merges into character.'

Eliot wrote this in 1927, in an essay called 'Wilkie Collins and Dickens'. But the surrealists already saw the matter in a different light – as, I think, do most of us today. The main objection to melodramatic novels was that they depended too much on chance and coincidence. On the other hand, both the surrealists and we who have been exposed to the Theatre of the Absurd feel that it is precisely the aleatory nature of the plots – the chance occurrences – which make melodrama more 'true to life' than the classical canons of character and verisimilitude ever did. The surrealists spoke of the encounter of a sewing-machine and an operating table as being the essence of art, and some of Feuillade's (and Allain and Souvestre's) juxtapositions were equally hair-raising, equally absurd, equally meaningful.

The roots of *Fantômas* were double: both literary and political. The nineteenth century was, in Western Europe, at least, the century of universal literacy. But when the illiterate learned to read, they did not want to read Racine or Corneille. And a whole new genre of literature appeared. At its grandest, it was Victor Hugo's *Les Misérables* and *Notre Dame de Paris*. But underneath the lyricism the principles of melodrama were present. An even greater success was Eugène Sue's *Les Mystères de Paris* (and the connection between the three-volume shocker and the cinema was clearly made when *The Exploits of Elaine* was retitled by the French as *Les Mystères de New York*). These were the world's first great best-sellers. (When it is said that great literature was popular in its time, it should always be remembered that this only means that it was popular with the ten per cent of the population who knew how to read. These authors – Hugo, Sue and Dickens, of course – were really read by the masses.)

The *Fantômas* novels clearly belong to this tradition, but they were different in content. The earlier works were what was called 'improving' – by and large, the wicked were punished and the good triumphed – even if only on their death-beds (or even after). Fantômas was the first anti-hero, the first evil hero. To be sure, he had an opponent – Juve – who stood for 'good', but there was no doubt in any reader's mind as to which was the more interesting, the more fascinating character. Both the novel and the film of *Fantômas* are glorifications of evil, and one can only speculate as to the reasons why such a hero should appear in 1911 and why he should have been so popular. There is a connection, I think, with the exploits of the various anarchist gangs that were terrorizing – and fascinating – France at the time.

In a chapter (significantly entitled 'Further than *Fantômas*') from his book on the anarchist movement *La Terreur noire*, André Salmon describes the French reaction to the Bonnot gang: 'Newspaper readers were thrilled. Certainly, they trembled a little; the more sensitive were horror-struck. But a great many people nevertheless found themselves won over by a kind of admiration. The cinema was not yet fully developed; the *série noire* was still to be invented. But they already had a real-life cinema. Were these men scourges of God, tragic bandits? Something like that …'

The 'Bande à Bonnot' was the most famous, but there were others, and this eruption into the bourgeois life of its victims, this rising up of underground forces, this attack on the *status quo*, is closely connected with the popularity of *Fantômas* and, later, of *Les Vampires*. The cover of the first volume of the book-of-the-film of *Les Vampires* significantly shows a group of black figures – masked – crawling up a staircase. Towards what?

The middle classes were terrified of these men, who indeed constituted a threat to authority and even more to property; at the same time, there was a kind of *Schadenfreude*: a thrill at the thought of the retribution which they perhaps felt they deserved. The reaction of the working classes must have been different; they had less to lose and therefore they could simply enjoy the sight of the rich being terrorized. Whatever the reasons, both the books and the films captured the imagination of all France at a time when the anarchist gangs were at their most active.

But today the books seem almost unreadable; whereas the film remains eminently viewable, for the obvious reason that Feuillade was a master of images and Allain and Souvestre were not great prose-writers. However, I don't think that one can separate Feuillade's visual style from his material, and say that the one was great and the other lamentable. If you like the one, you have to take the other. This was not true, as we have seen, with early films like *La Tare*. But it is the sudden introduction of evil into Feuillade's work that provided the stimulus for his talent. All his best films – *Fantômas*, *Les Vampires*, *Tih Minh* and *Barrabas* – are involved with it. Whenever he tried to be moralistic, the films lost much of their force. The reason for this lies in the tensions set up in Feuillade between his consciously held views (we know that he was both a Catholic and a monarchist) and the fascination he found in women like Irma Vep and men like Fantômas.

This is not the only example in the cinema of a film succeeding because of a tension between the author's material and his personality. *Kiss Me Deadly*, which remains a greater film than anything Robert Aldrich did before or after, owes its peculiar grandeur to the fact that the director strongly disapproved of the characters and subject matter with which he was forced to deal, and the resulting tension made for an electrifying film.

Obviously Feuillade could not consciously either approve of or identify with a master-thief like Fantômas, and yet the film can only be seen as a glorification of this evil figure – this omnipotent, ubiquitous master of disguise. Surely it is significant that whenever Fantômas appears to us in action, he is covered from head to foot, with black tights and with a Ku-Klux-Klan slitted hood over his face. This is his disguise; it is also Feuillade's own disguise. And in the film's most famous shot, when Fantômas is seen as he blows up a house, it is with both arms raised in triumph and silhouetted against the smoke from the apocalyptic explosion.

What makes the film so believable is the all-important fact that it is shot in real exteriors. Or, as Annette Michelson aptly remarked about *Les Vampires*, this film, which is all about dislocation, is all shot on location: 'Haussmann's pre-1914 Paris, the city of massive stone structures, of quiet avenues and squares, is suddenly revealed as everywhere dangerous, the scene and subject of secret designs. The trap-door, secret compartment, false tunnel, false bottom, false ceiling, form an architectural complex with the architectural structure of a middle-class culture. The perpetually recurring ritual of identification and self-justification is the presentation of the visiting card; it is, as well, the signal, the formal prelude to the fateful encounter, the swindle, hold-up, abduction or murder.'

This constant interplay between reassuring everyday appearance and the frightening realities which lie just below is the key to the fascination of all Feuillade's best work. He had a genius for location: the great sequence in *Fantômas* of the shoot-out on the Quai de Bercy with Juve and Fantômas darting between the huge wine-barrels is not merely picturesque. Somehow those barrels take on as much importance as the protagonists; indeed, from the way in which they are shot, they become as mysteriously threatening as

some of Magritte's renderings of ordinary objects. And Feuillade's compositions in depth help because on their many levels he can best orchestrate the many levels of significance, disguise and treachery.

What makes *Les Vampires* a greater work than *Fantômas* is the fact that it was written by Feuillade himself, and thus conceived entirely in cinematic terms. But there is still another reason, and that is the presence of the female character – Irma Vep (Musidora). Once again the subject of the film is a gang of jewel-thieves; the nominal hero is not a policeman as in *Fantômas*, but a more ambiguous representative of law and order, a journalist who is determined to capture the gang. But in the first sequence of the film, a painting of a sphinx is pushed back from the wall of an apartment to reveal in the hole cut behind it the black-tighted Irma Vep – and suddenly we realize that the battle is going to be not only political or social, but sexual as well.

Les Vampires (1915)

Decades Never Start On Time

It soon becomes clear that this gang of jewel-thieves is being pursued by Philippe Guérande with somewhat mixed motives. It is important that they are jewel-thieves, that they prey only on the rich. But their method is not haphazard: they have organized a plot against constituted society; they are a potential revolutionary force, an underworld which is rising up to take over the 'real' world. Whether Feuillade totally understood all this is unlikely, but his audiences did: a great wave of protest arose against what was termed his glamorization of crime. The fact that the gang was ultimately vanquished by the police did not deceive anyone. Audiences knew this was only a gesture or a kind of auto-censorship on the part of Feuillade. And it is significant, for example, that the high priestess of the Vampires is killed neither by the police nor by Guérande. It is the reporter's *wife* who guns her down, and in a giveaway shot the hero lingers longingly over her dead body in a vivid expression of the sexual attraction exercised by this dominating woman. It could also be an unconscious recognition of a society in love with its own destruction. When a large party of rich people are gassed by the Vampires, it is significant that the gas is sweet-smelling and that the guests at first think it must be some new kind of incense or perfume. And in the penultimate scenes of the film, when the Vampires think they have triumphed, Feuillade films their celebration, their witches' sabbath, with an enthusiasm and a conviction that more than border on the ambiguous.

Seeing *Les Vampires* today is quite a different experience from what it would have been when it first appeared. Now it is shown in one go – six one-hour episodes strung together, rather than six episodes seen at varying intervals. Furthermore, and I think this is important, the inter-titles for the film have long ago vanished, so that we are obliged to figure out the action without any help. With no help, that is, except for Feuillade's narrative genius which, as the current state of the film proves, is more than adequate for an understanding of the film – without our reading the letters that are constantly being handed to characters and to which they react with surprise, horror and amazement. But the fact that the titles are missing makes the film go much faster, and this is all to the good since present-day audiences are more sophisticated as to film narrative than audiences in 1915. We really don't need a title to say 'The Next Day' – we can figure that out for ourselves.

And there is another difference between our appreciation of the film and that of Feuillade's audience. For us, the film recaptures the mystery and charm of a Paris long since gone: all the urban poetry of deserted streets, *terrains vagues*, half-finished buildings. This of course would not have had the same appeal to the earlier audience. But they got something else from the film – the thrill of seeing all these extraordinary and terrifying things happening in the streets they knew, that they walked down every day. For them (and in some measure for us, too) there was a conjugation of a naturalistic rendering of Paris with the evocation of strange and frightening happenings. This was Feuillade's great discovery: nothing can be more frightening than extraordinary events against a normal, everyday background. (Hitchcock has of course used this principle in many of his films, e.g., the gunning at the crossroads by the 'crop-duster' in *North by Northwest*.) Fantasy is grounded in everyday reality, thus making it both more credible and more frightening. In a perfectly ordinary room, a bishop presses a button, and a cannon comes out of the fireplace, all set to destroy a night-club next door. Before the cannon is fired, however, the window curtains are carefully pulled and the window is opened. After the cannon goes off, the window is closed, and the curtains are methodically drawn.

As Alain Resnais puts it, 'People say there is a Méliès tradition in the cinema, and a Lumière tradition: I believe there is also a Feuillade current, one which marvellously links the fantastic side of Méliès with the realism of Lumière, a current which creates mystery and evokes dreams by the use of the most banal elements of daily life.' The surrealistic method, in fact – the method of a painter like Magritte.

If *Les Vampires* was the greatest of Feuillade's films, there were two others, almost as good, to follow. But not immediately. The fact that one of the episodes of *Les Vampires* had been (temporarily) banned by the chief of police was enough to frighten Feuillade – and Gaumont. So the successor to *Les Vampires* was very carefully worked on to avoid offence. *Judex* was the result, and it turned out to be Feuillade's greatest success – perhaps because of its enlightening moral tone, but also because of its star, René Cresté. As Bardèche and Brasillach so neatly put it: 'Cresté's cape: that was *Judex* … that majestic cape which he threw back over his shoulder in such a noble gesture. The rest was of little importance: the kidnapped girls, the highwaymen … there was nothing in *Judex* that was not already in *The Exploits of Elaine*, *The Perils of Pauline*, and even more in *Fantômas*. But there was that cape. Because of that cape, because of that fatal beauty, that smile, every young man in France dreamed of Judex.' Seen today, *Judex* almost founders in its self-imposed sentimental morality. And *La Nouvelle Mission de Judex* (1917) is unwatchable; Louis Delluc's strictures on Feuillade are justified by this film.

But Feuillade had not completely gone over to respectability; for the two Judex films were almost immediately followed by two serial films which almost equal (and some believe, even surpass) *Les Vampires*: *Tih Minh* and *Barrabas*. *Tih Minh*, as Francis Lacassin puts it, 'leaves the grey streets of Paris for the Riviera, where the bright Mediterranean sun seems to efface the differences between good and evil. The Vampire gang are now bent on world conquest: the film is about their revenge for the death of Irma Vep, and their victim is Tih Minh, a beautiful Oriental maiden. Scenes like the fight on the roof of the Hotel Negresco possess that dreamlike evil magnificence which no one was ever able to achieve so completely as Louis Feuillade.'

And in this context it is illuminating to compare *Tih Minh* with Léonce Perret's masterpiece *L'Enfant de Paris*. Both are largely set on the Riviera, and both make magnificent use of their locations. But while Perret – and properly so, for his purposes – simply makes the Riviera look beautiful, Feuillade makes it sinister – or rather the sinister proceeds from the combination of the landscape and the 'evil magnificence' of the subject. And there are strokes of pure genius – like the 'rest home', the Villa Circe (Irma Vep is dead, but the name of the villa may be a reference to her powers) with its gardens haunted by ghostly forms in white, wandering phantoms, the 'living dead': victims of the gang.

True, the film has an 'improving' end: crime is punished; virtue has its reward. But the criminals are not all killed: Dolores de Santa Fé is taken alive, and the good doctor Clauzel takes her back to Paris to undertake the difficult mission of converting this adventuress and delivering her from the evil spirits. But she outsmarts him – somehow she had managed to procure poison from the wicked Asiatic doctor Kistna, and she escapes conversion through death.

Between *Tih Minh* and *Barrabas* came *Vendémiaire* (1918) – but discussion of that film must be postponed, since it belongs to the beginning of Feuillade's decline, whereas *Barrabas* is the last of the great films. In many ways it is the best, except for its rather slow beginning. The plot of the film is so complex that it necessitated a great deal of exposition, in fact almost two hours of it. There are so many things we have to learn, to register, so that when Feuillade springs his trap, bottomless chasms can open metaphorically beneath the feet of his characters. But once the trap opens – and it is actually the fall of the blade of a guillotine which sets the infernal machine working – the pace never slackens. *Barrabas*, too, was largely shot on the Riviera, in the hills overlooking Nice. It achieves an even greater plastic beauty than *Tih Minh*; and it is also more powerful. The aim of the criminals in *Tih Minh* was 'God strike England'; in *Barrabas*, it is the whole world they are after, and the very title of the film, with its Biblical resonance, seems to suggest the eternal existence of an underworld, of the forces of evil.

Unfortunately, little as *Les Vampires* and *Fantômas* have been seen in recent years, *Tih Minh* and *Barrabas* are even less known. The negatives still exist at Gaumont, and there are prints in both the Cinémathèque Française and the Cinémathèque Royale de Belgique. But their length militates against their being shown; furthermore, legends die hard. Feuillade was for so long unknown that opinion-makers (writers of film histories and teachers of film) are reluctant to revise their notions. Feuillade has been swept away by Griffith and a different school of film-making.

Had his career ended with *Barrabas*, he might have had a greater chance of survival; unfortunately his later films did little to enhance his reputation. *Vendémiaire* is about the only one that looks good today. Photographically, indeed, it is extremely beautiful, particularly the opening scenes of refugees from the north going down the river Rhône by ship. But the patriotic plot (German soldiers disguised as Belgians) is not terribly interesting, and already the signs of the series of tear-jerkers that Feuillade was to make from 1919 until his death in 1925 are there.

But, this being said, and although Feuillade sank into obscurity, he nevertheless did have an influence on the history of the cinema – even if it was a very delayed one. With the exception of Buñuel who, as we have seen, admired his work, and in *L'Age d'or* and some of his other films continued the Feuillade vision of the extraordinary subject filmed as if it were the most ordinary thing imaginable, one must wait until the Feuillade revival of the 1940s to see a direct influence of his work. It is most obvious in the work of Georges Franju and that of Alain Resnais. 'Of course,' Resnais has said, 'I haven't sought systematically to imitate Feuillade. If you try to do it that way, it doesn't work.' (And I, for one, think that this is the reason why Franju's *Judex* is much less authentically Feuilladesque than his *Les Yeux sans visage*.)

But there are other ways in which Feuillade's influence was felt. One doesn't know, of course, and there is no way of finding out, whether Fritz Lang ever saw any of Feuillade's films. But his serial film *The Spiders* (1919–20) looks to me very much as if he had seen and admired Feuillade. And from *The Spiders* there is an apocalyptic thread which leads through the *Dr Mabuse* films straight to Alfred Hitchcock. This cannot of course be proved. It is entirely possible that Lang had been influenced by other, similar films. For Feuillade was not the *creator* of the serial, nor its only exponent. The first serial is generally considered to have been Victorin Jasset's *Nick Carter*, which came out in 1908 and was followed by *The New Exploits of Nick Carter* and a whole series of films about Zigomar. In 1913 there was *Protéa*: the antecedent of Irma Vep, Protéa was a hotel thief dressed in black tights.

The first American serial was *The Adventures of a Girl Spy*, which ran from 1910 to 1913. But this and its successors were all eclipsed by Pearl White and her French director, Louis Gasnier, who were responsible for *The Exploits of Elaine* and *The Perils of Pauline*. And we should remember that it was precisely the forthcoming release of *Les Mystères de New York* (the French title of *The Exploits of Elaine*) that urged Feuillade on to finish the first episode of *Les Vampires*. (Confusingly enough, the French title of *The Perils of Pauline* was *Les Exploits d'Elaine*!) And successful as was *Les Vampires*, it never became a universal craze like the Pearl White films. Their episodes were shorter, they came out regularly and most important, they were backed up by newspaper serializations.

These films were nowhere near such accomplished works of art as the Feuillade films, but they did participate in the same climate of catastrophe, the same melodramatic poetry – however uninteresting they were plastically – and therefore one cannot be sure if the idea of a line going from Feuillade to Lang to Hitchcock is tenable. In any case, that line exists, whether or not it actually started with Feuillade; and it continues on to the films of Jacques Rivette, particularly *Out One: Spectre* where the shots of the Place d'Italie surely must have been inspired by visions of Feuillade – and we know Rivette has seen his work. And some of the Montmartre locations in *Céline and Julie* are reminiscent of Feuillade's use of Montmartre in *Les Vampires*.

The serial as a form continued long after the death of Feuillade, only coming to an official end in the late 40s. The most accomplished American practitioner was William Whitney, and his *G-Men versus Black Dragon*, grotesque though it is, might have amused Feuillade as it does us. The serial was killed by the end of regular weekly cinema attendance – as well as by a greater degree of sophistication on the part of audiences. But of course it never really died, for it continues on television to this day, particularly in those American afternoon dramas, and in such parodies as *Mary Hartman, Mary Hartman,* just as it persevered all through the great years of radio in the 'soap operas'.

We might indeed have had a great television serial if Rivette's original idea for *Out One* had ever been carried out: this film was designed as a series of thirteen one-hour films – which takes us straight back to Feuillade. But the past, as Resnais noted, can never be recaptured directly, and although I have not seen the thirteen-hour version of *Out One*, those who have say that fascinating though it is, it is inferior to *Out One: Spectre*, in which Rivette took his Feuilladesque notion of a thirteen-episode film and transformed it into something else. 'No voice is wholly lost,' and Feuillade the commercial craftsman, Feuillade the fabricator of films, still lives. 'Please believe me,' wrote Feuillade, 'when I tell you that it's not the experimenters who will finally obtain for film its rightful recognition, but rather the makers of melodrama – and I count myself among the most devoted of their number … I believe I come closer to the truth than they do.' And, looking back, there can only be one answer to the question as to whose films come closer to the truth (whatever that may be), Delluc's or Feuillade's.

SOURCE: 'LOUIS FEUILLADE AND THE SERIAL', IN RICHARD ROUD (ED.), *CINEMA: A CRITICAL DICTIONARY: THE MAJOR FILM-MAKERS* (NEW YORK: VIKING PRESS; LONDON: MARTIN SECKER & WARBURG, 1980), 348–59

4.6 JEAN RENOIR: TO 1939

Every man has his own Renoir; indeed, if Renoir is, as I believe, the greatest of all film-makers, one reason is that his *oeuvre* is so varied, rich and complex. There are two articles in this Dictionary: mine, which covers the period to *La Règle du jeu* (*The Rules of the Game*, 1939), and the following one, which takes his career from 1939 on. But there could have been further sub-divisions. For a critic like Noël Burch the essential Renoir is the silent period, or more precisely *Nana* (1926). For me, it is the films from *La Chienne* (1931) to *La Règle du jeu*. There are others who, although admiring the pre-war films, prefer the American period and the later French films of the 50s.

André Bazin and the *Cahiers du Cinéma* group tried hard – and with some success – to prove that there were no dividing lines, that Renoir's *oeuvre* was an integral whole. Others have found different dividing lines: 1936, 1938, 1939, 1950, etc., just as critics have divided Godard's work into different periods. By considering Renoir's pre-1940 films in isolation, I am not saying they are the only good ones, or even that they are very different in nature or quality from the others: I am simply saying that they are the ones that interest me most; therefore, *for me*, the best.

Born in 1894, Renoir was the son of the Impressionist painter Auguste Renoir. His interest in the cinema began at an early age (ten), but it was not until the First World War and the double revelation of Chaplin and *The Perils of Pauline* that he began to think about making films himself. After the war he nevertheless took up ceramics, only abandoning it in favour of the cinema in 1923. He began by producing and writing *Catherine, ou une Vie sans joie* (1924), a vehicle for his wife, Catherine Hessling, whom he had married in 1919 (she had formerly been a model for his father). The film was directed by Albert Dieudonné. In 1924 Renoir directed his first film, *La Fille de l'eau* (*The Whirlpool of Fate*, 1925): it is not a successful work, but it showed that he was already capable of capturing on the screen the atmosphere and beauty of landscape, and of suggesting that almost pagan reverence for nature which was to run through much of his work. On the other hand, there was already present in that first film the darker side of Renoir's persona: what we can call the Stroheim or Zola side. The sequence of the fire in *La Fille de l'eau*, as Bazin remarked, already announces the Renoir of *Nana*, with 'that extraordinary demoniacal shot of Pierre Renoir's head in his pitchfork', and there are other touches of violence and cruelty in the film.

Nana, his next film, was directly influenced by Stroheim's *Foolish Wives*, which Renoir tells us he saw 'at least ten times'. Generally acclaimed his best silent film, its conjugation of Zola with Stroheim created a work which was unlike any other in the French cinema, although its affinity with certain German films was intensified by the presence of Werner Krauss in a leading role. Catherine Hessling played the lead again, and it would seem that one's reaction to the film is somewhat conditioned by one's feelings about Miss Hessling as an actress. I have always found her both touching and abominable, and her Nana something of a caricature of Zola's heroine. But the film is an extremely important one for many reasons.

For the first time, Renoir began to mix his genres, and the same mixture of comedy and tragedy, of the lyrical and the grotesque, that was to culminate in *La Règle du jeu* thirteen years later is already present here. As Noël Burch points out, Renoir also began here his experiments with the opposition of off-screen space to screen space. 'More than half the shots ... begin with someone entering the frame or end with someone exiting from it, or both, leaving several empty frames before or after each shot.' For a formalist critic like Burch, *Nana* is important because it marks the first *structural* use of off-screen space. Bazin, however, finds the film unsatisfying because the shots succeed each other with neither dramatic nor logical rigour.

La Chienne is an expression of the Stroheim–Zola side of Renoir: this is a city drama, and the softening effect of landscape is not allowed to intrude. Paradoxically, it is a very enjoyable film, even though there is nothing very pleasant about its subject – the downfall of a middle-aged man in love with a cold-hearted bitch. An amoral film in intention (Renoir announces this in a puppet prologue to the film), it has also been called a 'cold' film.

Perhaps its 'coldness' is what has preserved it from the ravages of time. What has certainly contributed to keeping it alive is Renoir's sense of realism – not only visual but aural. This was the first sound film in France to be shot and recorded directly, in real locations – the noisy streets of Montmartre with its taxicabs and streetsingers.

Indeed, the use of sound was what was most commented on when the film appeared, particularly in the scenes which lead to the discovery of the murdered Lulu. Renoir fixes his camera on a streetsinger and the crowd gathers round him outside Lulu's house. When her lover goes upstairs, the camera simply rises vertically to the window of her flat, and then slowly descends. This simple movement is repeated later when the concierge leaves the crowd to go up and deliver the day's post. The song, which has gone on uninterruptedly, is only broken off when the concierge thrusts her head out of the window to report the murder. The narrative economy of the sequence (we know from this moment on that Dédé will be falsely accused of Lulu's murder), and the more abstract pleasure of the dialectical use of time and space, make this a great sequence. Dramatically it renders both the warmth of Renoir's response to the Montmartre setting and his objective view of his characters. But objectivity does not imply indifference: as one of his characters says in *La Règle du jeu*: 'The terrible thing about this world is that everybody has his reasons.' And Renoir understands, and makes his spectators understand and even empathize with Lulu and Dédé as well as with his hero. He neither sentimentalizes them nor sees them as types (the Pimp, the Tart, the Client): he does not, in fact, take sides. All are equally justified; all are equally guilty.

The following year, 1932, Renoir made two films: *La Nuit du carrefour* and *Boudu sauvé des eaux* (*Boudu Saved from Drowning*). The first was an adaptation of a Georges Simenon thriller, and if the legend is true, the reason for the almost total incomprehensibility of its plot is that the editor of the film lost three cans of film at the end of the shooting and the film had to be edited without them. The film is none the less fascinating, not least for the performance of the director's brother, Pierre Renoir, as Maigret. The whole film takes place at a semi-deserted crossroads, and the soundtrack is replete with strange sounds of rifles going off, cars back-firing. The film has a *louche* atmosphere which comes as much from the locals from the village as from the drug-smugglers. Not in the main line of Renoir's development, it has none the less been called (by Godard) the only great French thriller, the greatest French adventure film.

One is tempted to say that with *Boudu* Renoir turned the clock back to the rustling landscapes of *La Fille de l'eau*. But that would not be strictly true, for the film is more of a synthesis of his impressionist tendencies and the naturalistic picture of Paris life he gave us in *La Chienne*. Part of the pleasure one gets now from *Boudu* comes from the simple joy of the reality of Paris in the summer, the parks, the *quais* of the Seine. These are pleasant in themselves but they also situate the story of the tramp Boudu in a definite time and place. The plot is schematic: Boudu the tramp is saved from drowning by a bookseller who tries to rehabilitate him. In return, Boudu carries on a brief but stunning affair with the bookseller's wife, and then becomes engaged to his mistress, who is also the maid. During the wedding ceremony, however, he gets fed up with it all, and disappears beneath the waters of the Marne. While everyone mourns his second drowning, Boudu picks himself out of the water a little further downstream, and a beautiful 360-degree pan expresses his joy at his regained freedom. His horizons once again unbounded, off he goes. The sense of place is further heightened by Renoir's use of depth of focus: there are many scenes shot from a point in one room in the bookseller's flat which stretch all the way across an air-shaft to another room in the flat: for once, one feels that this is a real apartment, and that it is inhabited by real people. Which is perhaps why Renoir's faithful evocation of a filmed time and place has dated less than, say, Carné's artistic stylisation of Le Havre in the 1938 *Le Quai des brumes*.

There may seem to be a contradiction in this insistence on reality and Renoir's impressionist treatment of landscape. Superficially one could say that in *Boudu*, as in *Une Partie de campagne* (1936; released only in 1946 in a newly edited version) and *La Fille de l'eau*, there are scenes which remind one of his father's paintings. But the influence of Auguste Renoir goes far beyond a similar taste for atmospheric Ile de France landscapes. We are all too apt to forget that in intention the Impressionists were *realists*. That is, Impressionism was an attempt to render reality more accurately. Renoir painted shadows blue because even though they *appear* black, they really *are* blue. And when Monet painted the Rouen Cathedral at different times of day, it was because he felt that a rendering of reality had to take into account that, because of the action of light, things change. The cathedral did not exist as an essence; it had no immutable form. It had to be shown as it was at a given moment: only thus could an existential impression of reality be achieved. And to do this, the painters were forced to leave their ateliers, just as Renoir left the studios. One of Auguste Renoir's most urgent artistic goals was to integrate figure with landscape: '*Je me bats avec mes figures jusqu'à ce qu'elles ne fassent plus qu'un avec le paysage qui leur sert de fond*' ['I fight with my figures until they merge with the landscape']. In his painting the figures are *in* their landscape, and in Jean Renoir's films of this period his figures are in their milieu. This was important for him not only visually, but dramatically and even politically. Characters cannot be seen as entities apart from their environment; they must be seen *in* that environment.

This intention was already clear in *Boudu*; it was to become more strongly defined in *Toni* (1934). Before going on to *Toni*, however, one must not forget *Madame Bovary* (1934). Long considered one of Renoir's failures, and unseeable now except in a cut version, it has much to recommend it. There is the use of the Normandy landscape, and the contrast between that beauty and Emma's despair; and there is the acting of Valentine Tessier. A remarkable actress, she was none the less an odd choice for Emma; yet, as we will see with Nora Gregor, Renoir often managed to achieve extraordinary effects by casting against the grain.

Thanks to the understanding of Pagnol, Renoir undertook the filming of *Toni* in 1935. Following Pagnol's example in *Angèle*, Renoir abandoned the studios and filmed exclusively on the locations where his story of a *crime passionnel* among emigrant farm-workers took place. Some of the characters were interpreted by actors, others by the local inhabitants of Martigues in the Rhône delta. But even the professionals, with one or two exceptions, belonged to the social classes and nationalities of their roles. Renoir's ambition was that the audience should imagine that an invisible camera had filmed various phases of a conflict without the human beings involved ever noticing!

As in *La Chienne*, this triangle drama is never melodramatic because the girl Josepha is not the sluttish señorita, nor is Toni the good faithful working-man; even Albert is not played as the menace. *Toni* is superior to *Angèle* because its exterior realism is complemented by Renoir's psychological, social and dramatic realism. Then, too, the fluidity of his camerawork, his brilliant compositions in depth, his feeling for figures in a landscape, are much more impressive than anything Pagnol's occasionally clumsy style could achieve. Furthermore, perhaps because his father was a painter, Renoir was never tempted by the merely pictorial. His compositions never seem contrived or consciously beautiful. Because he had an instinctive understanding of painting, he was never tempted by the 'artistic' two-dimensional composition. 'To me,' said Renoir, 'the cinema is photography, and what is interesting is to photograph reality.' Reality was something you start from: there were no shortcuts to beauty.

Toni, together with *Le Crime de Monsieur Lange*, made the following year (1936), was a turning-point in Renoir's career. From here on, until *La Règle du jeu*, his work was to be marked by an interest in social and political problems. This is not unconnected with the climate of the time: the Popular Front was emerging, and artists all over Europe, confronted with the flourishing of Nazism in Germany, were growing more political; in 1935, the Saar had voted for reunion with Germany, Hitler had re-established conscription, and Mussolini was actively intervening in Ethiopia. 1935 was also the year of the First International Congress of Writers for the Defence of Culture.

Le Crime de Monsieur Lange is something of a freak in Renoir's *oeuvre*, for it owes much to its scriptwriter, Jacques Prévert, and it is the only film of Renoir's of which this can be said. All Prévert's qualities are present in the script and dialogue: his verbal invention, his bite, and his sense of humour. But whereas in the Carné–Prévert collaborations Prévert's faults were intensified by that side of Carné which is also pretentious, literary and over-romantic, in *Le Crime de Monsieur Lange* Renoir's sense of reality compensates for Prevert's artificiality. And it is the explosion of the two opposed talents that makes the film so fascinatingly unique. In some ways, it can also be seen as a sketch for *La Règle du jeu*, for it is both a study of personal relationships within a broad social context, and a spontaneous comedy which slowly begins to reveal an incipiently tragic sense of life. In its number and variety of camera movements, combined with Renoir's continued experiments in depth-of-field camerawork, it is something of a dry run for *La Règle du jeu*. Here the movements of the camera are occasionally clumsy, but the famous shot in which Lange kills Batala is worthy of the Walpurgis Night sequence in the later film. Extensively analysed by Bazin, this shot and its effectiveness can be summed up as a combination of two factors. First, the fact that after Lange runs out of the building to pursue Batala, the camera suddenly leaves him and then describes a reverse 360-degree pan round the courtyard which works both dramatically and plastically. Dramatically it reminds us in the few seconds while we pan round the courtyard of the reason Lange has to kill Batala by evoking everything that has happened previously in this very courtyard (the film was originally to be titled *Sur la cour*). Secondly, this shot is also a development of Renoir's experiments, going back to *Nana*, in the use of off-screen space. This conjugation of concentric *mise en scène* and depth of focus, as Bazin pointed out, would lead four years later to the brilliant effects of *La Règle du jeu*.

One must not overlook the political aspects of the film, naïve as they may seem today, for they were an important element, not only of this film but of those that were to follow. Here the sentiments are simply liberal, with the co-operative as the solution to the class struggle. But Renoir's choice of Jules Berry as the wicked capitalist was somewhat self-defeating: to be sure, Batala is an ignoble individual, but Renoir was unable or unwilling to make Berry totally subdue his odious yet telling charm. As we shall see later, Renoir was often led by his actors, his raw material, into changing his original notions of what a film was to be about.

His next film, however, was commissioned by the Communist party itself. *La Vie est à nous* (1936) was re-issued in the mid-70s, and it proved to be interesting in its less political aspects – the love story about the two poor students and the auction in the country. Otherwise mere agit-prop, it was less truly political than the other film he was to make that year, *Une Partie de campagne*. This may sound like provocation; *Une Partie de campagne* is generally thought of as Renoir's most lyrical, most idyllic work – and it is: the final scenes with Sylvia Bataille and Georges Darnoux are unforgettably poignant. But actually the reasons for the tragedy are political and economic. Henriette and Henri are not separated by metaphysical considerations; nor is she a Capulet and he a Montague. They are separated only by class barriers – a marriage between the two is unthinkable, and one of the most effective notes is that it is as unthinkable for *her* as it is for him. Their personal tragedy is that he is a particularly sensitive and gentle member of his class, and that she is a particularly beautiful and sensitive member of hers. But the class divisions exist, and this fact in no way diminishes the emotional power of the film.

Never completed, the film was released only after the war, when Joseph Kosma added a haunting score: although it runs for only forty minutes, it is one of Renoir's most beautiful works, not only for the rendering of the Ile de France landscapes, but also for the performances. Renoir's next film is also distinguished by its acting, but his adaptation of Gorky's *Lower Depths* (*Les Bas-fonds*, 1936) is, I think, a minor work. Louis Jouvet, Jean Gabin and Jany Holt all give remarkable performances, but the combination of Gorky and Renoir was not particularly fruitful. Perhaps if Renoir had gone whole hog and transposed the setting from Russia to France the film would have gained in verisimilitude.

In 1937 Renoir made *La Grande Illusion* (*Grand Illusion*), his most popular film. Of late, critical opinion has tended to underrate the film in order to boost *La Règle du jeu*. But the fact that the latter is superior does not seem an adequate reason for downgrading an extraordinary achievement. In many ways, it is Renoir's most effective film – and also his most accessible. Its plot line is carefully worked out, and its theme is appealing. Once more we have an example of how the choice of the actors determined the final form of the film. Originally, the script was about three soldiers – the officer (Pierre Fresnay) and two ordinary Frenchmen, one of whom was to be played by Jean Gabin. But when his producers suggested he use von Stroheim, whom he had admired for years, in the small part of the German commander, Renoir was reluctant to have him in such a minor capacity. So he

decided to build up the role, and this lucky stroke strengthened his film by adding a new element. No longer was it simply about three different classes of Frenchmen in a German prisoner-of-war camp: it was also to be a commentary on those class loyalties which cut across national frontiers. Furthermore, the original script did not include the Jew Rosenthal (Dalio); the third man was just another Frenchman. But by adding the idea of creed to the ideas of class and of nationality, Renoir significantly enriched the film.

La Grande Illusion (1937)

In spite of the elevated nature of the subject matter, Renoir none the less indulged his penchant for the grotesque and for the breathtaking mixture of genres – taking us suddenly from the ridiculous to the sublime. The scene in which the 'Marseillaise' is sung during a prison camp show to celebrate a French victory was made much more effective by Renoir's insane inspiration of having an *English* soldier, in drag, as the one who leads the singing. All the exteriors were shot on location (in Alsace, the closest he could get to Germany at the time), and even some of the interiors were done there. As usual, this attention to realistic detail paid off.

La Grande Illusion was welcomed by the Left at the time as a committed film, and indeed the sacrifice by the aristocrat De Boëldieu (Fresnay) to save Maréchal (Gabin) was clearly not only an act of comradeship, but also an admission that the aristocracy as a class was condemned. Renoir's next film, *La Marseillaise* (1938), was commissioned by the CGT – the congress of trade unions. It was begun as a co-operative venture, and shares were sold for two francs apiece to anyone who wanted to support 'the film of the union of the French nation against a minority of exploiters, the film of the rights of man and of the citizen'. It didn't quite work out that way. The film takes a series of moments beginning with the storming of the Bastille and ending with the flight of the royal family, and the thread that is supposed to bind the whole thing together is the story of a few Marseillais who march to Paris – singing all the way. In the late 60s the film was re-released in a more complete version than had previously been available, and many acclaimed it as one of Renoir's masterpieces. I wish I could agree. To me, it is often clumsy; the attempts at rendering the soldiers from Marseilles don't ring true; and the best scenes are those with the aristocrats – which doesn't help the general thrust of the film at all. Pierre Renoir as Louis XVI is truly touching; this wouldn't matter if the 'people' were equally so, but they are not. Once again everyone, for Renoir, has his reasons, but this attitude is not particularly suited to a film which is supposed to be about the triumph of the people over their aristocratic oppressors. Some find this basic ambivalence a reason for liking the film – it *is* characteristic of its author, but it doesn't really work here. And I can't help feeling that Renoir was not cut out for the historical fresco: unlike Gance, he is too sensible; nor does he have a sufficiently developed sense of rhetoric to be able to ride roughshod over history in the magnificently loony way of Gance's *Napoléon*. His historical sense and his political convictions were simply not sufficiently rigorous to bring off 'The Film of the Revolution'.

He was much more at ease in his next project, a modernization of Zola's novel *La Bête humaine* (1938). It should not be thought that Renoir was not interested in his subject matter, although it is true that he declared at the time that he couldn't have cared less about Zola, and that all he wanted was to play with trains. But what he meant, I think, was only that he was not very interested in Zola's notions of heredity. *La Bête humaine* is part of the Rougon-Macquart series of novels, and its hero Jacques Lantier (Gabin) is supposed to pay for his alcoholic forbears who have tainted his blood. Such a deterministic idea could not possibly interest Renoir, and the weakest scenes in the film are those when Gabin has to explain his fears of his heredity to the pale and uninteresting Flore (Blanchette Brunoy). Curiously, the 'pure' girl is as unconvincing here as she was in Carné's *Le Jour se lève*.

In Renoir's version the story would have been the same had Gabin had an irreproachable heredity. What interested him was the triangular relationship between the engine-driver Lantier, the station-master (Fernand Ledoux) and his young, minxish wife Séverine (Simone Simon). And it is really a three-way triangle, for a kind of masculine solidarity prevents

Lantier from killing Séverine's husband as he had planned; ultimately, it is the wife who disposes of him. The documentary-like scenes on the Paris–Havre run have been (deservedly) much praised, but the film also contains one of Renoir's most unforgettable sequences: the railwaymen's ball. Renoir has always had a fondness for popular songs, and he knows how to use them to great dramatic effect – as in *La Chienne*, for example, where a song accompanies the murder of Lulu, and in *Le Crime de Monsieur Lange*, where Florelle's singing 'Au jour, le jour' is an important element of the film. But here, in the skimpily decorated room (cf. Olmi's improvised dance-halls), the old song 'Pauvre petit coeur de Ninon' serves as an ironic yet pathetic counterpoint to the murder of Séverine's husband.

At the time of its British release, Graham Greene noted that the film's 'documentary' material, although well done, had been done before, if not so well. 'What is most deft is the way in which Renoir works the depot and a man's job into every scene – conversations on platforms, in washrooms and canteens. Views from the station-master's window over the steaming metal waste: the short, sharp lust worked out in a wooden plate-layer's shed among shunted trucks under the steaming rain.' And the film, despite its unevenness, triumphs because of the way in which the characters and their milieu are integrated. [...][6]

SOURCE: 'JEAN RENOIR: TO 1939', IN RICHARD ROUD (ED.), *CINEMA: A CRITICAL DICTIONARY: THE MAJOR FILM-MAKERS* (NEW YORK: VIKING PRESS; LONDON: MARTIN SECKER & WARBURG, 1980), 835–45

4.7 LONDON AND NEW YORK

From the start, the London Film Festival was lucky.[7] It began just before there was the great outburst of new films, film schools, film groups all over the world – not just in France with the New Wave, but generally. The first festival took place in 1957, and by '59 the whole thing was building up. There was a real revival after the general dullness of the 50s, and certainly in its first ten years the festival benefited greatly from that upsurge in film-making and in interest in cinema.

At the beginning the London festival was a very pragmatic business: in so far as there was a brief for the organisers, it was simply that it should be a 'Festival of Festivals', with the idea of bringing to London films from other festivals which people would not otherwise get a chance to see. I had nothing to do with the first festival, which was organised by Derek Prouse. I think they showed about sixteen films. Then David Robinson put together the second one, which was already a bit bigger. In 1959 there was no single organiser: it was rather a combined effort. I remember that my own first task for the festival, that year, was to look after Truffaut, who was in London for the first time with *Les Quatre Cents Coups*. I was put in charge of the 1960 festival, and that was something of a communal effort. Films were suggested by all sorts of people. James Quinn, who was then director of the BFI, brought *Rocco and his Brothers* from Venice. I remember going over to Paris to see *Shoot the Pianist*. Most of the films that year came from Cannes. *Moderato cantabile* came from Cannes; *L'avventura*, *The Young One*, *Los golfos*, *Virgin Spring* and *The Lady with the Dog*. Not a bad festival. And Chabrol's *Les Bonnes Femmes*, two Hungarian films, and a film by de Broca, who didn't turn out to be much, but still. The first complete screening of *La Règle du jeu*, the reconstructed version. No, it wasn't bad ...

Things were far easier in those days. In New York now we show fewer films than London, only about twenty, and we feel that we are just about getting enough. But in the old days you could afford to be very choosy: this film or that wasn't *quite* good enough. There was never any question of representation by countries, no United Nations business. If towards the end there was a choice to be made between two particular films, then perhaps the edge might go to one from a country not already represented, but that was all. Also, it wasn't true that we showed mainly French films; the trouble was that the French films were the most popular ones, the most widely talked about, so some people got that notion. It's as false as the idea that you could never get into the NFT or the London Film Festival. You couldn't get in for certain films, admittedly, but there were always some seats, even though houses were probably fuller in the early days, when there was only one cinema.

In those days we used to add extra screenings as the films sold out. Then there could be trouble because a distributor would allow you only one screening, for fear that too many people would see the film before he put it on commercially. That was why, when I got to New York and a much larger cinema, I made sure that every film was shown only once. If they were all treated the same way, that was that. There was no question of adding or subtracting screenings, which gave too much leeway for bargaining and hanky-panky. But in the early days in London we sometimes had as many as five screenings of a popular film. Of course part of the point of the festival was to show films that wouldn't otherwise be opening in London, and to attract distributor interest. We felt it was taking far too long for many important European films to reach Britain – something which hasn't improved all that much over the years. Some potential distributors would wait for the festival: it gave them a chance to see the film they were interested in with a British audience, albeit a select one, and to find out what the reviewers were going to say. Also, there are always certain films which are taken by a distributor only *after* it is known that they will be in the festival. This has been true both of London and New York.

What is a festival for, anyhow? Is it run for the benefit of the audience, or for the film-makers and the industry, or to help distributors, or for the prestige of the organisation that sponsors it? As far as I am concerned, it is for the audience and for the people who make the films. It's not enough if 500 people or 1,500 people see a film. I think one only feels really justified when the film goes on to achieve wider distribution.

At the outset, the films were what I chose or what people recommended to me – Tom Milne, John Gillett, or of course, James Quinn. I didn't see all the films beforehand; I was too new at the game. If a distributor came by and told me he had the new Visconti film, say, one couldn't very well insist on seeing it first. I wasn't in that position, and also it didn't seem necessary. There was no programme committee. In fact, for quite a while the programme planning staff was me, Pamela Balfry, who is now a partner in the Artificial Eye company, and a shorthand typist. The whole BFI was so small then that everyone more or less took a hand. Remember those famous festival booking weekends, when just about anyone from the Institute used to come in and help with the forms? The Institute may have wanted the festival as something rather spectacular, to celebrate the launching of the new NFT in 1957, but it never had the money to do anything in a big way.

One limitation on London is that it was, and remains, so largely a festival for BFI members. Another is the size of the theatres – they're really quite small. And also their location, rather inconveniently tucked away under Waterloo Bridge, which seems to me to have become more rather than less of a drawback. But the main thing then was always to get

Decades Never Start On Time

the thing on, to get it sold out, and to make sure that people were reasonably happy with what they saw. I don't think we worried too much about creating a festival atmosphere – though we did try. In any case, the difference between London and other festivals, like Cannes and Venice, is that they are professional junkets, congresses, trade fairs, conventions. Very few non-professionals get to those festivals, they are concentrated occasions for the industry and the film press.

New York is public, and it has more visibility. Because the festival takes place at Lincoln Center, it was from the first day an important event in the city's life. In the days when there were many more New York papers, every paper reviewed the festival daily. Some reviewed every single film, which is something that never happened in London. The fact that the festival took place in a larger cinema, that it had the prestige of Lincoln Center, that it wasn't part of an all the year round operation, that it wasn't under a bridge but in the centre of town, has meant that from the outset it has had more influence on what films get bought and seen than the London festival. This has made it more exciting – and more difficult. All eyes are upon you, whereas in London there was never that kind of public exposure or pressure. The difference is that *anything* that happens at Lincoln Center is considered a media event, whereas for years you had to explain to a taxi driver where the National Film Theatre was. Not any more, but for years you had to. Cities are different, and perhaps the way things are is also the only way the festival could work in London. They *could* have made it more public, found a less eccentric location for it, but that's not the Institute's way of doing things. There were even moves to have an English Cannes at somewhere like Brighton, but that never got anywhere.

In fact, the New York festival came into existence as a direct result of the LFF.[8] In 1962, an American composer called Dr William Schuman had taken over at Lincoln Center. A friend of mine, the *New York Times* critic Eugene Archer, asked why there was no provision at the Center for film, as one of the performing arts. Dr Schuman said that he was interested but didn't know where to start, and Eugene Archer suggested that he might do worse than try to imitate the LFF. So, after some letters to and fro, Dr Schuman appeared in London in the autumn of 1962 and went to see James Quinn. It was on a Saturday, and I remember that we met at Wheeler's, in Old Compton Street. Schuman was keen not to do something *like* the London festival but to do the London festival. One thing I discovered during lunch is that New Yorkers resent English people programming their festivals. 'Where do you come from?' Schuman asked. I told him. 'You're American, ohh!' It was decided there and then – almost. And James Quinn went to New York, and it was agreed that the festivals should be twinned.

This lasted until 1967, when Stanley Reed, who had succeeded James Quinn as BFI director, had reservations about the way things were working out. In the first five years, London and New York showed more or less the same films. I was the 'co-ordinator'. The fascinating thing was to see how audiences differed. Ozu's *Autumn Afternoon*, for instance, was very badly received in New York: Japanese soap opera, people called it. In London, they had already seen Ozu films, they could see beyond the soap opera plot. *Muriel* did just as badly in New York as in London. *Hallelujah the Hills* went down much better in New York. The Munk film *Passenger* did better in London; the New York audience couldn't see the point of showing an unfinished film.

The main difference was in public attitudes, and particularly press attitudes. In London in the early days one didn't feel there was any press opposition to the festival; they just tended to ignore it. Lincoln Center was too big to ignore, so you had to take a stand for or against it. For quite a while *Variety* was almost our only supporter, though they changed their minds later. I remember Judith Crist saying that New York needed the festival like it needed more traffic. The critics didn't want to have to see all those movies: twenty films in two weeks, God, all that work. They didn't see the need for a festival, because they felt that if a film was any good it would always find a distributor. Which of course is not true. Altogether, it was extremely controversial.

It wasn't until I got to New York, in fact, that I realised how much attention *could* be paid to a festival. It was exciting in London when a film you particularly liked was put on, got a good audience response and was bought by a distributor. One was very pleased, but it didn't matter too much if it didn't happen. New York could be more exciting. In 1964, for instance, we showed Bertolucci's *Before the Revolution*. In London, nothing much happened. In New York, the film had a good review in the *Times*, it was bought almost instantly, and suddenly, overnight, Bertolucci was made. The only film I can remember creating that excitement in the early days in London was *L'avventura*, and that already had its reputation from Cannes. Other films from those days? *Il posto* came virtually out of the blue. I had to fight with the producers, who said it was a specifically Milanese film, and that no one else could understand it. I had to argue at length that anyone who had worked in an office, anywhere, could understand it. I think that Pasolini's reputation with English-speaking audiences was made via festival screenings; and the reputation of Milos Forman's early films, *Peter and Pavla* and so on.

Critical reaction has always been more important in New York. Perhaps one reason the New York critics are more influential is because there are fewer of them – and fewer now than in the early days, since we've lost five papers in New York since the early 60s. But one of the points about keeping a festival small, and one reason why New York is still small, is to allow the reviewers to see everything. In London now, it's literally impossible to see, much less review, ninety films in two weeks. In the old days, you *could* see almost everything. Reviews are certainly important to the film-makers as well as to audiences, and producers and distributors would be less likely to give us the films if they didn't think they were going to be reviewed.

Perhaps I ought to mention that there are other, less publicised advantages for them in a festival screening. It costs a great deal of money to launch a film in New York and a festival showing can reduce some of that cost. For instance, a *New York Times* advertisement actually cost less if a film had been in the festival because when it opened later it was considered second run. A strange anomaly; they may have stopped it by now. For another thing, a festival press show means that you don't have to hire screening rooms. In New York, they have individual screenings for individual critics. It's just not done, for instance, to have Pauline Kael and Vincent Canby at the same screening. It's mad, but they do cater to them madly.

In the early days, of course, there were great problems about getting American films for the London festival. You couldn't expect the major Hollywood pictures, only smaller movies like *Studs Lonigan* or *Too Late Blues* which the distributors thought were 'difficult'. In New York the problem has not been so bad. Most of the major companies have in fact been co-operative, though not necessarily all at the same time. For a couple of years Columbia was very interested in the festival; then Paramount gave us support. It keeps changing. Universal was the one company that would never give a film to the festival until last year, when we got *Melvin and Howard* because the producer, Verna Field, believed in the festival.

Some people have never seen much point in the New York festival using screening time

Decades Never Start On Time

on Hollywood movies, since audiences will have no problems about seeing them in the normal course of events. But there are advantages, apart from the fact that it makes people happy to feel that the American cinema is represented at an American festival. One practical benefit is that when you ask for a film for the festival some high-powered foreign producers almost immediately ask what American films you have. They think that if there are Hollywood films they are in good company. Another advantage, particularly important in New York, is that you get decent projection in the proper ratio. We showed *Mean Streets*, the world premiere, and it was nice to show Scorsese's first feature after programming his shorts. We were very pleased to show *Badlands*. I don't know what Warners would have done with it. As things turned out, it didn't do well commercially anywhere, but perhaps without a festival screening it might not have come out so soon. Our showing certainly got *Melvin and Howard* a quicker opening: the exhibitors had not been very interested, and Universal were prepared to keep it on the shelf. When we showed *Kid Blue*, James Frawley said that audiences had reacted just as he had intended, and that whatever happened to the film afterwards that kind of experience made it worthwhile. Are screenings like that an advantage to the festival or to the film-makers? Perhaps that's a false distinction.

In recent years, London has gone one way and New York the other. The London festival has expanded to a point where it's hardly possible for any one person to get an idea of the festival as a whole. It's strange, in fact, that so many festivals have gone in for showing more and more films at a time when the overall number of good films is certainly not increasing. They think they can make up in quantity what they lose in quality, which is debatable. Or they think it is elitist to talk about 'good films' at all. You think you know what the good films are, but do you? Perhaps the good films are the other ones. Our New York programme committee thinks it knows what the good films are, but then it's elitist. So what is London: permissive … omnivorous … non-normative, perhaps? Cannes went the same proliferating way in an effort first to placate and then to swallow up the opposition, but in London no one ever suggested starting an alternative festival in Battersea … Oh yes, in 1968 there was an alternative screening of *One Plus One* outside the NFT. It was run by a group who put the film on in a sort of tent; their generator didn't work so they had to plug it in to the NFT supply. That could only have happened in London.

The London festival has so many different categories now. In fact, there might be more justification for this diversification in New York, where apart from the Museum of Modern Art, whose screenings are mostly during the daytime, there is nothing to compare with the NFT seasons running through the year, often showing the same kind of films that are presented in the festival. But there is a real difference between the two situations. London is not a great movie town, and the United Kingdom is not a great film market. North America, after all, represents half the world market, while Britain is only four per cent. New York is influential because most of the distributors are there, because a festival showing can lead to a film being bought, and because there is still an American market outside New York itself. Not everywhere, but in key cities. Sadly, that is no longer true of Britain.

Through the 60s, the New York festival was expanding. Unlike London in the early days, when there was no money at all, there seemed to be almost unlimited cash. There were all sorts of adjuncts, extras, free things. Then in 1970 the money ran out and the festival very nearly went under. It had been taken over by the Film Society of Lincoln Center in 1968, instead of being run by Lincoln Center itself, and from 1971 the programme was cut back to below its present size. The budget is now about $200,000, but it would be difficult to make valid comparisons with costs in London. For instance, something like a quarter of the budget goes on rent for the hall. There are stage hands to be paid. Every time anyone uses a microphone on stage, it's two four-hour calls, one man to bring the microphone out and one to turn on the switch. And there are the advertising costs, like a full page in the *New York Times* (in the old days it was a double page), which now costs over $40,000.

We could get the costs back from higher ticket prices, but we want people to be able to afford the festival – the festival as a whole, not just one or two films. Seats used to be cheaper than the regular New York cinemas; now the price is about the same, which is still cheaper than London West End cinemas. So we raise about $100,000 from ticket sales, and for the rest we depend on fundraising and grants.

There doesn't seem to have been much change in the type of people who make up the audience, except perhaps in one respect. No one would bother to go to the festival now for the sake of seeing uncensored films, or sexy films, as they certainly did in the 60s. It's a much more mixed audience than the London one, from the fur-coat ladies to the jeans crowd, and it reacts rather differently. When a film goes well, it's more exciting. When it goes badly, it's a disaster. People feel they've been cheated and stomp out in fury, whereas the NFT crowd … they know what they've come to see, they know what they're in for. Saturday night in New York always has to be an easy film, for an audience who want to have fun. The more experimental films go on during the week, and you try to signal them in the blurbs. There was a rather good piece by Morris Dickstein in the *Bennington Review*, in which he makes fun of the blurbs' basic honesty: 'the film may seem slow, but …' or 'in other hands than Kurosawa's this would be sentimental.' But there is no sense in getting the wrong audience for a film, and I feel you have to let them know, guardedly, what to expect. For Duras and the Straubs the blurb may end up saying 'its rewards are commensurate with its demands.' The warning is in there somewhere, and I think that over the years people have come to read them carefully.

Attitudes do change. Before the 1980 festival, Vincent Canby wrote a piece in which he mentioned past festival films which he had thought were endlessly long and boring, like Jancsó's *Red Psalm* (which is actually only 85 minutes) and Marguerite Duras's *Nathalie Granger*. He added that in view of the junk he had to see all that year, he would really be very grateful to see something like that now, whatever he might have thought of the films at the time. All the same, you have to get the notion across to the film-makers that you can only help films which are helpable. Some film-makers have the idea that if a film is in the festival it will be a success – like the other ones. But putting a film in a festival isn't going to make people love it.

So where do we go now? New York could always, I suppose, founder for lack of money, as it nearly did ten years ago. London is more solidly based on the National Film Theatre. But we have to reckon that soon everything is going to be on cassette or disc, and it is no longer going to be simply a matter of showing films, but of showing the best print in the best possible way. It is going to be like hardback and paperback. Paperbacks will be the cassettes. But there will always be people who will want to see the film properly: the festivals will be for them, and their policies will be more selective as a result.

SOURCE: 'LONDON AND NEW YORK', *SIGHT & SOUND*, 50.4, AUTUMN 1981, 233–6

Decades Never Start On Time

4.8 GROSS CAN BE BEAUTIFUL

When I saw the world premiere of Steven Spielberg's *E.T. – Extra Terrestrial* at Cannes this year, I thoroughly enjoyed it – more, in fact, than any Spielberg movie I've seen. But I could never have predicted that it would be not only the most popular film of this summer's season in America, but that it may soon turn out to be one of the top-grossing films of 'all time,' to use the industry's lunatic but consecrated phrase. Of course, top-grossing is a tricky concept; it means that a film has made a lot of money, but it also means that a film that costs $5 admission (today's price) is competing in the 'all-time' stakes with films (like *Gone With The Wind*) that only cost $1. (This is why house records are constantly being broken: raise your ticket price and you break your record.)

But a contact at Universal, the happy studio that produced the film (after Columbia reportedly turned it down), says that by August they may be able to announce that at has actually been seen by more people than any film ever made. And this, with the European returns still to come, since *E.T.* will not open outside North America until autumn.

Meanwhile, the lines – and I use the plural, because the three theatres showing the film in Manhattan have two queues, one to buy a ticket, and one for ticketholders, to get into the cinema – are long. The film has grossed $87 million in three weeks in a smaller group of cinemas than is usual for a block-buster.

Why has it attracted so many people? I think it is not only because the film is fast-paced and well made, but because it is also extremely moving. It is not unusual to see grown men coming out with tear-stained cheeks. Ostensibly, a science-fiction film about a creature who by mistake is left behind on earth and befriended by a boy, it is really a love story. Never mind that one member of the couple is only ten years old and that the other is a fairly repulsive 'thing' with a long neck and a head that looks like a foetus: love is love, whatever the objects.

E.T. the Extra-Terrestrial (1982)

It is also very much every child's wish fulfilment dream: a real friend, intensified in this case because the boy's father has just left the wife and kids to go off with another woman. The boy has a nice older brother and an adorable younger sister (Drew Barrymore, grand-daughter of the famous actor John Barrymore), and a good mother, but in E.T. (the extra-terrestrial being) he has found a friend outside the family: they are, to use the Penguin translation of Goethe's novel, *Kindred by Choice*.

As Spielberg put it in an interview in *Rolling Stone*, 'it was like when you were a kid and had grown out of dolls or teddy bears or Winnie the Pooh, you just wanted a little voice in your mind to talk to. Then I thought, what if I were ten years old again – where I've sort of been for 34 years, anyway – and what if he needed me as much as I needed him. Wouldn't that be a great love story? So I put together this story of boy meets creature, boy loses creature, creature saves boy, boy saves creature – with the hope that they will somehow always be together, that their friendship isn't limited by nautical miles.'

But as well as being a homoerotic adolescent fantasy, it is also a kind of child's ver-sion of Walter Mitty: doing something really impressive like saving a creature from another planet. But, Spielberg says, he might not have made the film had it not been for the encouragement of François Truffaut (who acted in Spielberg's *Close Encounters of the Third Kind*). During the course of the making of that film, Truffaut apparently said to him: 'I like you with *keeds*; you are wonderful with *keeds*, you must do a movie just with *keeds*.'

I think that another reason why people enjoyed the film so much is that it is extremely simple. There is practically only one set, and while emotionally it may be Spielberg's most complicated film, technically it's his simplest. And then, too, for those who don't usually like science fiction, it has the advantage of having only two premises to accept: one, that there are intelligent beings in other planets, and two, that one of them might have been left behind on earth when a spaceship was forced to take off in a hurry. But that's it. Everything that follows is logic and simplicity itself.

The same, alas, cannot be said of another Spielberg film that is also doing very well (fourth place with $37½ million) this summer. *Poltergeist* was actually directed by Tobe Hooper (director of that loathsome cult film, *Texas Chain-Saw Massacre*) but it was pro-duced and written by Spielberg. In *Poltergeist* one has to swallow one unlikely incident after another, and in the end they add up to very little. Of course, had the film been better made, one wouldn't be sitting there thinking about its plot inconsistencies. Nonetheless, critics and others have been gossiping that the film was really directed by Spielberg, while Hooper has been claiming that it was he and he alone who directed the film.

I wouldn't be eager to claim credit for anything to do with this rather silly film. But they have, and as a result, the Directors Guild of America has set up an investigation to ascer-tain whether it was Spielberg's fault that this film about a housing estate built over a grave-yard has been credited to him. Spielberg (or his lawyers) have taken the matter seriously enough to pay for a full page in *Variety* to reprint a 'Dear Tobe' letter from Spielberg, in which he regrets that some of the press has misunderstood the 'rather unique creative relationship which you and I shared through the making of *Poltergeist*.'

However, in an earlier interview in *Film Comment*, Spielberg had admitted that he designed the film … from the story-boards to postproduction. 'I'm saying,' he goes on, 'that I was the David Selznick of the film. I won't go any further on a limb. I'll just say that I func-tioned in a very strong way.' When asked why he didn't direct it himself, he replied that he was doing *E.T.* and, 'you know, it's sort of illegal to direct two movies at the same time.

Even my involvement on *Poltergeist* as a writer-producer somewhat was flirting with a moot infringement.'

Spielberg has also said that he wanted *Poltergeist* to be one of the scariest movies of all time; I don't think he and/or Hooper succeeded in making it that. In fact, it is often quite amusing, and the funniest thing about it is a joke that has little to do with the plot, but rather with the relationship between movies and television. It is through the television screen that contact is made by the ghosts, and the last sequence of the film shows the family, out of their haunted house at last and safely ensconced in a Holiday Inn motel. The door closes behind them, and that, one thinks, is the end of the film. But suddenly the door opens, and Daddy firmly and violently thrusts the motel's TV set out of the room onto the balcony.

Would that it were so easy for the film industry to get rid of TV competition. But the only real way to get people from their televisions and out into the movie houses is to make a film like *E.T.* and now that Spielberg seems to have gained enough confidence to make films about people rather than automobiles and spaceships, it is encouraging to learn that this next project will be a film about adults, albeit with a fantasy touch: a remake of Victor Fleming's 1943 film called *A Guy Named Joe*.

SOURCE: 'GROSS CAN BE BEAUTIFUL', *GUARDIAN*, 15 JULY 1982, 9

4.9 BITER BIT

When the newscaster on Radio Three announced the death of a well-known German film director on 10 June, I said to myself, oh yes, it must be Douglas Sirk. So when it turned out to be Rainer Werner Fassbinder, it came as a shock. I was surprised, but after a few seconds thought I realised – to use a distinction much favoured by Henri Langlois, one of Fassbinder's greatest admirers – although surprised, I was not astonished. It could have been foreseen: Fassbinder had long been on a collision course, and suicide (if it was that) or an accidental overdose was only to be expected.

I heard the news from a car radio and all during that day's drive from Crianlarich to Carlisle I went over the fourteen years since I first became aware of Fassbinder's exis-tence. It began in Munich in 1968, when Jean-Marie Straub and Danièle Huillet showed me their film *The Bridegroom, the Comedienne and the Pimp*. Fassbinder starred in it, playing the *louche* pimp, Freder, who in the play-within-the-film supplies a dilettante count-ess with the Veronal with which she eventually commits suicide; he also plays a pimp in the framing story. The play-within-the-play was a Straubian 'digest' of Bruckner's *Sickness of Youth*, the rights to which had been bought by Fassbinder's Anti-Theatre group for pos-sible future production. Straub had actually directed Fassbinder in the stage version and had then filmed it.

It was perhaps unfortunate that I had seen the Straub film, because when Susan Sontag and I saw Fassbinder's first film, *Love Is Colder than Death*, at the 1969 Berlin Film Festival, I remember complaining in writing that this young director had attempted an impossible amalgam of Straub and Godard and it hadn't worked. I was so annoyed by his 'copy' of Straub's long tracking shot along the Landsbergerstrasse (a notorious prostitutes' hang-out in Munich) that I was unable to appreciate what was new and different in Fassbinder. Susan Sontag, on the other hand, although she didn't like the film that much, predicted that here was someone we had to keep an eye on. But when I saw his *Whity* at a 'market' screening in Berlin the following year, I found its portrayal of a Southern American milieu unconvincing and more than a little silly. It was only with my third Fassbinder film – *Pioneers in Ingolstadt*, shown in the Directors' Fortnight at Cannes in 1971 – that I realised he was a major figure, not only on the German scene but in world cinema. So reluctant was I to accept the evidence of my eyes and ears that I remember going back to see it a second time; only then was I sure. I invited the film to the 1971 New York Film Festival, the first time any Fassbinder film had been shown in the States.

The theatre was not full, and the reviews were not very good, but a number of people came out impressed with the film, and particularly with an unknown actress called Hanna Schygulla. The film featured other players who were to become part of the Fassbinder stock company (Irm Hermann, Harry Baer, Klaus Löwitsch); the photography was by Dietrich Lohmann and the music by Peer Raben. I still think it was one of his best films. Unfortunately it has not been much seen, because the author of the play on which it was based, Marieluise Fleisser, was so upset by the changes Fassbinder had made that she refused to let the film be shown commercially anywhere.

Perhaps if I had seen the other eight of the ten films which separated *Love Is Colder than Death* from *Pioneers* (in the space of three years), I might have appreciated Fassbinder sooner. On the other hand, what I had seen of him personally had rather turned me off: when the festival audience in the Zoopalast (where *Love Is Colder than Death* was shown in competition) booed his appearance on stage, Fassbinder had carried on like a victorious prize-fighter, arrogantly strutting back and forth, hands linked above his head, pretending that he was being cheered, not hissed.

It was not until *Pioneers* that he succeeded in getting away with his high-style parody of operatic sentiments, his weird blend of melodrama and realism. Until then, I had not been sure whether he was directing and writing this way on purpose. But there were no doubts after that film. Even if there had been, the next two works, *The Merchant of Four Seasons* and *The Bitter Tears of Petra von Kant*, would have dispelled them. By this time what the Germans call his *Thematik* was clear: Fassbinder was primarily concerned with micro-politics, with power relationships between people on the most intimate level.

I once came across a book which purported to present the thirty-five basic plots: my favourite category was Biter-Bit, and that seemed to apply to many of Fassbinder's films. They were sadomasochistic scenarios in which often the exploiter ended up as the exploited. Not all his films fell into this category, but most of the best of them did, which made me begin to wonder a little about Fassbinder's private life. I knew that he claimed to be a proletarian, and he certainly did his best to dress and act the role, but I then discovered that his mother (his doctor father had walked out when Fassbinder was a little boy) was the official German translator for a number of American writers, notably Truman Capote. This didn't sound like a proletarian background.

Fassbinder had been married to one of the stars of his repertory company, Ingrid Caven, but he soon made no secret of his homosexuality. This became clearer with each film: in *Fear Eats the Soul* it was easy to see that the relationship between a much older woman and a Moroccan stud was a metaphor for Fassbinder's sexual relationship with the actor who played the Moroccan. Fassbinder was probably younger than the Moroccan, but he was clearly identifying with the role played by Brigitte Mira. Then, with *Fox*, we had the reverse situation: Fassbinder himself played the role of the working-class boy exploited – after winning a lottery – by his upper-class lover.

Normally one doesn't discuss the private life of film directors, but since Fassbinder himself gave us such a chilling glimpse of that life in his segment of *Germany in Autumn*, presumably he felt that it was significant. The story of his love affair with Armin tells us a lot about Fassbinder's themes; it also may tell us something about his death.

As the Fassbinder entourage explained to me, Armin had been a butcher's boy (see *In a Year with Thirteen Moons*, with its slaughterhouse scenes), and Fassbinder had taken him up – and out of the butcher's shop. They lived together for years, but the difference in their social class created problems. Fassbinder felt (see *Germany in Autumn*) that he was exploiting Armin; but when, after a number of years, he began to grow tired of him, he was tormented with the problem of how to end the affair. After years of *le high-life*, he couldn't send Armin back to the butcher shop with a Dear John letter. Yet that is precisely what he did. During the 1978 Cannes festival he wrote to Armin in Munich that the affair was over and that he didn't want to find him in their flat when he returned. He didn't: neighbours discovered the decaying body first. Armin had committed suicide. The following year Fassbinder made *In a Year with Thirteen Moons*.

My first social encounter with Fassbinder occurred when he finally accepted an invitation to come to New York in 1975 to present *Fox*. A dinner was arranged at a restaurant near Lincoln Center. All through drinks and the first course he refused to look at me, always speaking sideways (and he didn't say much, only responding to direct questions), never looking at me straight on. He was obviously sizing me up, deciding if I was OK (whatever that meant to him). By the time we got to the main course, he had shifted his body round so that he was facing me, and by the time coffee appeared, he was actually talking directly to me. In spite of, or doubtless because of, his outrageous bravado, he was a deeply suspicious and shy man.

Later, when he moved to Paris (an abortive move, for although he bought a flat in Montmartre, and had it decorated by Peer Raben, he hardly lived there and sold it after little more than a year), we saw each other more often. I remember him inviting me, Daniel Schmid, Barbet Schroeder and Bulle Ogier for dinner at the Closerie des Lilas. Perhaps in an attempt to instil self-confidence, Fassbinder had given Armin the money to pay the bill. But Armin was so ill at ease that every time the waiter brought the bill he would say, 'And two more rum and Coca-Colas.' Whereupon the waiter was obliged to take back the bill in order to add on the extra drinks. When he returned, Armin would order more rum and colas, the waiter would take back the bill, and all of us began to wonder whether the dinner was ever going to end. Fassbinder, however, seemed to be enjoying the whole scene.

After Fassbinder had given up his search for the Real Right Place, he settled in Berlin for a few years, and every Berlin festival was enlivened for me by an invitation from him either to dinner or to a private screening of a just finished film. But between dinner and the film, there was always the ritual stop at his flat so that he could cut generous lines of cocaine which were then offered to everyone there. And everyone usually came to at least ten people. The entourage was necessary to Fassbinder's well-being or indeed his self-confidence; cocaine seemed to be part of the daily routine. He was not the only film director who indulged in cocaine, but he was the only one I knew who made a way of life out of it, and the physical signs of this addiction soon became all too apparent.

The last time I saw Fassbinder was after the 1982 Berlin festival screening of *Veronika Voss*, when I told him how much I liked the film. He smiled and said only, 'I, too.' He thought of films like *Maria Braun*, *Lili Marleen* and *Lola* as necessary evils – the films he had to make to pay for the ones closer to his heart and his preoccupations. *Maria Braun* was supposed to pay for the losses incurred by *Thirteen Moons* and *The Third Generation* (and it certainly did). *Lola* and *Lili Marleen* were to pay for a film he was not to live to make: *Cocaine*, an adaptation of a once notorious Italian novel of the 20s. I never got a chance to ask him about what turned out to be his final film, *Querelle de Brest*, an adaptation of Jean Genet's novel.

Fassbinder made more films a year than any important director since the silent days in Hollywood. In the fourteen years of his film-making life, he directed over 38 films – including the 13-hour *Berlin Alexanderplatz*. A good dozen of them count among the best films of the 70s, and his place in film history is secure. He burned his candle at both ends, and it did not last the night; but at his best, he made a lovely light. How satisfying that his last film to be released before his death was a masterpiece like *Veronika Voss*.

SOURCE: 'RAINER WERNER FASSBINDER, BITER BIT', *SIGHT & SOUND*, 51.4, AUTUMN 1982, 288–9

4.10 A PASSION FOR FILMS

[…] And so began a professional relationship and a personal friendship which were to last almost twenty years.[9] In a way, that first meeting summed it all up. Langlois was not an easy person to deal with. He was paranoid; he was bigger than life, not only physically but emotionally. But he had the films I wanted to see, and he did show them to me. The Ophüls films I had come to see had not been preserved by anyone else, because, after *Liebelei*, Ophüls was thought to have dropped to the level of a commercial film-maker. But Langlois, before Bazin, before Truffaut, before Andrew Sarris, was an auteurist.

It is true that most of Ophüls's films of the 1930s were not great – with the dazzling exception of his Italian film *La signora di tutti* – but it is also true that seeing them is essential to an understanding of the path Ophüls followed from *Liebelei* to the last great quartet: *La Ronde*, *Le Plaisir*, *The Earrings of Madame de …*, and *Lola Montès*.

Because of my 'success' with the dreaded Langlois – back in London I found that almost everybody at the BFI had been sure he wouldn't show me anything – the BFI asked me to mount a huge French season the following year at the National Film Theatre, covering the period from 1929 to 1959. Langlois and I had to work out the program together. Everyone said he was impossibly dictatorial, but I did not find this to be true. At least not with the features: he insisted on our showing a few rather odd shorts, made by favorites of his, but that presented no great problem. The only serious discussion I remember was about Grémillon's *Gueule d'amour*, a 1937 film I had seen in a revival house in Paris and liked. 'But that's one of the commercial films he was obliged to make in the late thirties,' said Langlois. 'You can't show that.' I held out, saying it may have been commercial, but it was also damned good, and that it had one of Jean Gabin's best performances. Finally he gave in, with a groan and sneer at my 'English' taste. I was pleased to discover that The Cinémathèque began to screen *Gueule d'amour* regularly a few years later.

On the opening night, when Langlois was to be introduced from the stage of the NFT, he, James Quinn, and I were sitting in the club-room; suddenly Langlois asked if anyone had any black shoe polish. I was surprised, because Langlois never bothered about his shoes; but the assistant manager found some polish. Whereupon Langlois crossed his legs and began applying it to his ankle – to camouflage a rather large hole in his sock.

The season was successful. David Thomson wrote: 'In June 1960, in the third part of a season of French films, the London National Film Theatre showed the best version available of *Lola Montès*. The season itself … is one for which I and some others will always be grateful. Above all, it had placed Renoir in his rightful eminence. But it had introduced me to several other major figures, and because it coincided with the incoming tide of the New Wave it served to stress the abiding themes and vitality of the French cinema.'[10]

Langlois had come to London several times during the course of the preparation of the French season, but he spent most of his time there drawing up a kind of contract between the British Film Institute and the Cinémathèque. He had composed a complicated letter of agreement, which I had to translate. I didn't understand at the time why Langlois attached so much importance to it: later I realised that he must have been preparing for a break with FIAF, which by then had spread round the world, with member archives on six continents. He wanted to make sure that the relationship he had with the British Film Institute would survive.

Langlois's departure from FIAF was a momentous event in the rather recondite story of that organization and its internal battles and power struggles. Did he leave or was he pushed out? The answer is difficult to ascertain. Even harder to determine are the reasons why he would want to leave or why they would want him to go. The several versions of the story contradict each other and are difficult to verify or to reconcile. […][11]

With the end of the Cinémathèque's connection with FIAF, a new era began in Paris, perhaps the most brilliant seven years of the Cinémathèque's history.

My happiest and most rewarding times with Langlois were at restaurants. Talking in his office was difficult: the phone would never stop ringing; there was always some crisis. So I learned that the best way of seeing Langlois whenever I came to Paris was to meet him for lunch.

In the early sixties, we invariably went to a restaurant near the Courcelles offices called Le Vigny. It was a pleasant place, and they were always happy to see Langlois. But there was a ritual: we couldn't go there without first stopping to buy the early edition of *France-Soir*. Langlois, a Scorpio, had to read the daily astrology column. I don't know how completely he believed in it, because although he usually would look up from the paper and crow, 'You see, I knew I was right; there *is* a spy at the Cinémathèque,' sometimes he would put the paper down sadly and say, 'You know, she's losing her grip, that columnist. She hasn't got anything right today.' I think that Langlois used astrology simply to confirm things he already knew or thought he knew. Whether or not one 'believes' in astrological predictions, one can recognize astrological types. Langlois certainly corresponded to the usual descriptions: with an instinctive, imperious nature, volcanic, the Scorpio is essentially a ferocious individualist, rebellious, capable of flying into a rage, irritable, violent.

Once he had decided he liked you, everything changed. He may have harbored suspicions, but by and large, if he accepted you, he was both loyal and generous. And food did calm him. As one can imagine from his size, he ate a lot. But even though in another person obesity like his might have been unpleasant or repulsive, such was the excitement of Langlois's conversation that one simply did not think about how fat he was.

Many theories have been advanced as to why Langlois, formerly so thin, had gradually become fat. W. H. Auden has provided one possible explanation: 'I would say that fatness in the male is the physical expression of a psychological wish to withdraw from sexual competition, and, by combining mother and child in his own person, to become emotionally self-sufficient. The Greeks thought of Narcissus as a slender youth, but I think they were wrong. I see him as a middle-aged man with a corporation, for, however ashamed he may be of displaying it in public, in private a man with a belly loves it dearly; it may be an unprepossessing child to look at, but he has borne it all by himself.'[12] On the other hand, Godfrey Smith, who used this quote from Auden in the *Sunday Times*, 6 April 1980, said that it may be that a certain kind of fat man has, by choosing obesity, deliberately preselected his own death. Some psychologists, however, prefer to think of obesity as being caused by a kind of 'alimentary orgasm': food takes the place of sex.

Over lunch, his first question was, 'Have you any gossips for me?' I don't know what he was like before the FIAF troubles, but afterward, he always wanted to hear what was new at the British Film Institute, and particularly what Ernest Lindgren, his arch-enemy, was doing – or, more important, not doing. These titbits were so important for Langlois that I used to prepare a short list in my head before meeting him, because he would be disappointed if I said, 'Oh well, everything's much the same.'

The purpose of my visits to Paris was usually to ask Langlois for films for a program at the National Film Theatre. But such questions would have to wait until the main course was finished and dessert ordered. It didn't always go smoothly. After he had agreed to help me do a given season, and had worked out in his mental instant retrieval system where the prints were, he became impatient if I tried to pin him down as to when the prints would be sent or how (diplomatic pouch, air shipment, or occasionally sleeping car, thus avoiding, in most cases, the problem of import/export licenses and customs). Although (or maybe because) he knew perfectly well I was American, whenever he wanted to get a dig at me, he would always start with 'You English are so …' whatever. And of course it is true that the National Film Theatre was not run like the Cinémathèque. We had *not* trained our audiences to be surprised if the film announced was the film actually shown. We sent out booklets four or six weeks in advance describing the films, giving the dates, with a booking form for advanced reservations. Langlois refused to take this into account. In Paris, after all, the films were announced only a week at a time, and his audience had been trained to expect anything. The only way I could get him to cooperate was to say, little-boy-like, 'It's not *my* fault; I have to work for them, and I have to do things their way.' That would bring out his latent paternal instincts, and half contemptuously but half reassuringly, he would say, 'Don't worry, you'll get the films on time.' And we did get them – just on time, usually, but nonetheless on time.

If the luncheon ritual never changed, the restaurants did. I remember automatically heading toward the Vigny one day, only to be told by Langlois, 'Oh, we don't go there any more; the restaurant's gone down. Now we go to the Courcelles.' It didn't seem like an improvement to me, and later Kenneth Anger explained to me why Langlois changed restaurants every nine months or so. He never paid on the spot, but charged it to his account; when the bill finally came in, Langlois never had enough money to pay it. The odd thing is that although he eventually paid up, he never went back to the restaurant to which he had owed money. Irrationally, he resented the fact that the bills were so high, or that he had been obliged to scrounge around to pay for meals he had *already* eaten.

He usually walked around without money, as a matter of fact: only if he and I were going somewhere special (where he had no account) would Mary stuff a couple of hundred-franc notes into his breast pocket on the way out of the building. (She would almost never come with us: either she wanted to leave us alone, or she wanted to be alone in the Cinémathèque without Henri.)

Decades Never Start On Time

Henri Langlois

In 1961, a year after the big French season, I arranged a Visconti retrospective in London in the autumn. Most of the prints came from local sources, but I had a problem with *Senso*, because the only print in Britain was the cut, dubbed version called *The Wanton Countess*. Henri came to the rescue. He said, 'We'll fix it all up at the Venice Film Festival with Comencini and the Milan Cinémathèque.' And we did fix it up: to simplify matters for Comencini it was arranged that on my way back to London from Venice I would stay awake until I got to Milan – actually, not even the Central Station, because late at night the Simplon-Orient Express would stop at a suburban station. There at Milano-Lambrate I was to look out the window and be ready to take the cans of film into my sleeping compartment. It seemed to me a highly dubious undertaking: I wasn't sure the print would be there, or that the man carrying it would have enough time to find me while the train made its brief stop. But sure enough, we pulled into the station, I opened the window, and saw on the deserted platform a man with ten cans of film. He hoisted them up to me, I stowed them in the luggage rack, and that's how an original print of *Senso* got to London.

By 1962 we had already gone through two more restaurants and had graduated to La Savoie, a rather better restaurant than the ones we had frequented. It was there that we organized three of the biggest programs I ever did for London: first, a retrospective of the films of Fritz Lang; second, a complete Jean Renoir show; and finally, a more esoteric but fascinating program called 'Dovzhenko and Soviet Cinema of the 30s'. Once again, Langlois's belief in collecting as much as possible proved to be invaluable. One of Dovzhenko's early sound films was called *Ivan* (not to be confused with *Ivan the Terrible* or *The Childhood of*

Ivan). According to the books, it was not successful, but Langlois had got it from the Russians anyhow. And it proved to be a revelation. One could see why people had not liked it at the time – it had plot and structural weaknesses – but it was extremely beautiful. And thanks to Langlois, we (I did the season with the late Robert Vas) did discover some little-known gems from the 1930s – a period in Russian film history that was not highly thought of.

Arranging the Renoir show was the most fun, however, because we had to deal with the legendary Madame Doinel,[13] who looked after Renoir's interests and films in France and who lived in his house on the avenue Frochot. Never has an artist's house and street seemed more suitable than did the avenue Frochot for Renoir. A 'private street', it curled its way in a semicircle up a hill, where it stopped short in a dead end just behind the 'nudie' shows of the place Pigalle. When you were in the little 'street', you seemed miles from Paris in some peaceful provincial town.

Of course, Langlois was not only helping me to program; apart from running the theater on the Rue d'Ulm, he was arranging retrospective shows for other film libraries and for the Cannes and Venice festivals. In 1962 he had shown a small number of unknown early Mizoguchi films at Cannes; for many critics, they were the highlight of the festival.

Langlois also found time to help me do one of my favorite NFT seasons, which I called 'School of Vienna.' The idea was that although Austrian films had never been particularly distinguished, an amazing number of great film directors had been born and brought up in Vienna – Stroheim, Lang, Pabst, and Sternberg, for example – and that furthermore, however individual their talents, all of them shared a common world view: a cynicism born perhaps of the experience of the dying Austro-Hungarian Empire, a fascination for the baroque, the decadent, and at the same time, especially in the cases of Sternberg and Stroheim, a slightly perverse sense of eroticism. Most of the prints were to come from the Cinémathèque, and I was particularly pleased to be able to get the sound-synchronized version of *The Wedding March*, which had never been shown in Britain.

He didn't always approve of the films I wanted to borrow, but after a few slighting references to my 'English' taste, he would agree to let me have them. And he was constantly suggesting films and showing them to me. These screenings didn't always take place on the day planned, and I remember that in the case of the Soviet season Robert Vas and I spent four fruitless days in Paris waiting for the screenings to start. Vas became discouraged and said we ought to go back to London: we were never going to see anything. 'Don't despair,' I said, 'you'll see.' And sure enough, we did get to view everything – but in a two-day marathon, from ten in the morning to nine at night. It would have been so much easier for us and cheaper for Langlois – no overtime for the projectionists – to have spread the screenings over the week, but he just didn't work that way. Like some journalists, he could function only with a deadline hanging over his head. Then the adrenaline would begin to flow, he would get on the phone, and the whole thing would be taken care of.

In the same way, he hardly ever answered letters. First of all, he didn't like to leave written traces that 'could be used against him.' He also had the Italian attitude: if it's really important, they'll send a telegram or phone. Another reason for his reluctance to write letters was that although he dictated them to his secretary, he insisted she take them down in longhand, so that he could constantly look over her shoulder to see what he had said.

In 1962 Langlois did a show of Méliès drawings, sets, and stills at the Louvre. At least that's what Mary kept saying: 'Darling, we're going to be in the Louvre.' Technically she was right; the show was put on in a wing of the Louvre Palace, but it was not the Musée du Louvre, but rather the Musée des Arts Décoratifs, which is also in the Louvre Palace.

The night before the show was to open, I went along to see how things were going. At midnight, Langlois stepped back, looked around the central room, mused, and suddenly declared, 'We've got to start all over again. It's all wrong.' I thought he was crazy; it looked fine to me. The carpenters and other technicians looked grim, realizing that they were going to be working all night. The next morning at eleven the show was opened, and when we entered that central room I realized Langlois had been right: the new arrangement was infinitely more effective than the one I had seen the night before. Art critic Annette Michelson wrote that the exhibition was 'one of the finest I have ever seen. One wandered through the reconstitution of a life-work prodigious in its inventive substance as through a forest alive with apparitions and metamorphoses.'[14] But he couldn't have got it right any sooner: he really did need a deadline. [...][15]

Much as I admired, even loved, Langlois, I realized then that I could never work *for* him. With him, yes. But to work at the Cinémathèque meant that you had to give up any idea of a private life: you had always to be ready if Henri needed you. *He* had no private life; he and Mary lived entirely for the Cinémathèque, and they couldn't understand why anyone else should be any different. Henri must have realized how I felt, or have known that it wouldn't work, for in spite of all he did for me over the years, he never offered me a job.

At least, I don't think he did. Once in the mid-sixties he asked if I minded telling him how much money I earned at the British Film Institute. I told him, and he shook his head, as if dismissing some thought from his mind. Was he at that point going to suggest I come work with him? It's possible: that head shaking only pointed up what I already knew – that although the salaries at the BFI were not lavish, they were much higher than anything Langlois could afford.

Of course, I sometimes had dinner with Langlois, rather than lunch, but then Mary would come along and she tended to dominate the conversation: if Langlois was paternal with me, Mary was maternal with both of us. But from 1962, all such dinners were devoted to discussing a major new development: the approaching opening of a new theater in the Palais de Chaillot. The Rue d'Ulm was to continue, and with a second theater there would be six films a night to program instead of three. Opening shows would have to be found that would impose Chaillot on the Cinémathèque regulars and attract a new and larger audience. Eating seemed to bring out the best in both of them: solutions to old problems were suddenly found; new ideas would come to mind. Everything was subordinated to what Langlois and Mary thought would be the turning point in the history of the Cinémathèque.

SOURCE: 'FRIENDS AND ENEMIES', *A PASSION FOR FILMS: HENRI LANGLOIS AND THE CINÉMATHÈQUE FRANÇAISE* (NEW YORK: VIKING PRESS, 1983), 104–24, © EDITH SMOLENS

4.11 THE FIRST FOREIGN-LANGUAGE FILM I EVER SAW …

The first foreign-language film I ever saw was French. I was fifteen and on a trip from Boston to New York with my father and sister. I cannot remember why I went; it must have been the blurb in *Cue* magazine. The film was Sacha Guitry's *Pearls of the Crown*, and it was playing at the Thalia. I liked it so much that I went to see it again two days later. It was different, different from American films, which were all I had known.

It was, to use an old-fashioned word, risqué, and it was witty, too. I had already seen films like *The Lady Eve*, but here there was a difference. The wit was more sophisticated, more self-conscious; it openly played around with words. I had been studying French in high school for a couple of years, and with the help of the subtitles I was able to follow some of the dialogue. I remember being particularly impressed by a scene that takes place on the grand staircase of the S.S. *Normandie*. Jacqueline Delubac is flirting with Raimu, and Guitry, her jealous husband, forbids her to talk to him again except in adverbs! The answer to every question or remark put to her by Raimu during their long slow walk down that two-deck staircase is answered by an adverb: certainly, surely, probably, absolutely, and so on. Nothing could be more artificial than such a scene, but it was clear to me that it was consciously done for the pure pleasure of playing with words. That kind of language game seemed to me the height of sophistication.

A year passed, once again I was in New York, and this time I went to the 5th Avenue Playhouse to see a double bill of *Mayerling* (the French version) and something called *Bizarre, Bizarre* (*Drôle de drame*, I later discovered). *Mayerling* didn't seem so different from an American film, and I wasn't particularly excited by it. But Marcel Carné's *Bizarre, Bizarre* had many of the qualities that I had enjoyed in *Pearls of the Crown*. It was funny in a surrealist way; and it had sparkling dialogue. I must have been impressed by the fact that, like the Guitry film, it was artificial (not that the Hollywood product I devoured every week was realistic, though it pretended to be). Neither the Guitry nor the Carné film tried to be realistic – they were artificial comedies, and unashamedly so. It was in these two films that I first recognized the absurd or surrealist vein. (The films of the Marx Brothers certainly had surrealist elements in them, but they were 'too close to home' to appear genuinely strange to me then.)

Back in Boston, an art house called the Fine Arts reopened after several years' inactivity; its repertory was largely French. Tucked away behind the old Loew's State Theater on Massachusetts Avenue, it was easy for me to get to, and I got to it very often. One of the excuses I made to myself was that it would 'help my French,' and even the lesser films did that.

In about two years, I was able to see at the Fine Arts many of what I later discovered were the great prewar French classics. The film that impressed me the most was *Port of Shadows* (*Le Quai des brumes*). I can still remember coming out of the theater in a daze, overcome by the beauty of Michèle Morgan's eyes, her sad smile, and her trenchcoat, as well as by the poetic misty quality of the setting of the film and its tragic ending. I thought that this was a film about life as it really is, and that I had never seen anything like it before. (Actually, I had. An old diary reveals that I previously had seen Borzage's *Man's Castle*, and when I saw it again years later, I realized how much it was like *Port of Shadows*, but I had been too young to see this. And, besides, it had a happy ending.)

Later came the revelation of *Grand Illusion*, which was advertised with a quote from President Roosevelt, no less. It, too, impressed me a great deal, but I cannot pretend I liked it as much as *Port of Shadows*. It is difficult to remember the other films I first saw then. I do know that the culmination of my early love affair with the French cinema was *Children of Paradise* (*Les Enfants du paradis*), which I went to several times and decided was the greatest film I had ever seen. It had some of the wit of *Bizarre, Bizarre* (both films were written by Jacques Prévert), and it had the same 'realistic' sadness and some of the same visual qualities as *Port of Shadows* (both films were directed by Marcel Carné).

Looking back on that period of my life, before I had begun to read about the cinema, to acquire some notions of film history, and to learn to recognize the styles of different directors, I often wonder what made me admire French films. How were they different from

Le Quai des brumes (1938)

American films? There was, first, that 'realism,' and that surrealism. Most prewar French films do not look at all realistic now, but they seemed to be so then. They dealt with subjects that the American cinema avoided: people had love affairs and consummated love affairs – indeed most of these films were about sexual passion. Many of them were what is called 'arty', but after a diet of Hollywood films, they seemed to me to be Art. Then, too, these films were an expression of French life, a life, as seen in those films, so very different from life in America that it remained for me endlessly fascinating.

The actresses were elegant – not glamorous, like the Hollywood stars, but sophisticated. I liked the way they talked, their diction. It seemed more like the way people talked in the theater (as indeed it was), and the fact that I could follow some of the French doubtless added to my pleasure. The sound track offered another attraction, too – the music.

All the films, it seemed to me, had the same kind of music. It was reedy, high-pitched, and thin; and compared with the 100-violin type of Hollywood score (which I also liked: Max Steiner's name on the credits was always a plus), it offered a new kind of pleasure, and, I thought, one of a more refined sort.

There were other differences, too, like the fact that nobody ever swore in a Hollywood film — even the Dead End Kids or gangsters never went any further than 'rats'; whereas *merde* was used constantly in French films, and this seemed to me both daring and realistic. And, perhaps more important, many of these French films ended unhappily. American films sometimes contained tragic events, but they generally had upbeat endings. If someone died, the music told you it was a great and noble thing to die. And it was hardly ever the hero who died. Watching the war films, young as I was, I could usually figure out which soldier or airman was going to be killed halfway through. The star, I soon realized, hardly ever died, and he almost always got the girl. But in French films the star could die, or lose the girl, or both. You could not tell in advance, and that seemed right to me.

Then came the revolution of Italian neo-realism, and films like *Open City*, *Shoeshine*, and *Paisan* made me see a different kind of cinema. The fact that these films were shown in America when I was in college, and somewhat more mature, did cast a blight over some of the things I had so liked in the French cinema. But only partially so. There was still the revelation of Gérard Philipe in *Devil in the Flesh* (*Le Diable au corps*); there was the discovery at the University of Wisconsin film society of the comedies of René Clair. And when I went to France on a fellowship in the early 50s, there came two of the greatest discoveries for me: Jean Renoir's *Rules of the Game* (*La Règle du jeu*) and the first Robert Bresson film I saw, *Diary of a Country Priest* (*Le Journal d'un curé de campagne*). These two films made me realize that what I had thought of as 'French films' was only a part of the French cinema — an important part, to be sure. Yet although in the early 50s *Children of Paradise* and *Port of Shadows* lost much of their appeal for me, they regained it later. It was a question of point of view: I had liked them earlier because I thought they were realistic. Then I found they weren't, and was disappointed. But on a third seeing, I discovered that I could enjoy them again, actually because they were not realistic.

It is perhaps as difficult to define what is different about 'the' French cinema as it is to describe 'a' France. To take an example or two, in its cuisine France is divided into three: the north, where lard is the basic fat used for cooking; the centre, where butter reigns, and the south, where olive oil replaces butter. Linguistically, it is divided into two — the north, where langue d'oïl (i.e., French as we know it) is the common language, and the south, where langue d'oc (old Provençal) is still much used in the country. And this is not to count Alsatian (something like Yiddish) or Breton. France is usually considered a Latin country, but in many important ways it is also northern. Politically, it usually divides evenly between Right and Left. And, of course, France is a country of individualists.

There is a feeling nonetheless that we all know what a French film is like. This is partly an illusion founded on the choices of American distributors as to which French films they buy to show us. We do not see all of the best of them either, and we certainly did not see them when they were made. Renoir's *Boudu Saved from Drowning* (*Boudu sauvé des eaux*) was made in 1932; it was released in America thirty-five years later. His *Rules of the Game* was made in 1939; it was not shown in the United States until 1953. Bresson's *Les Dames du Bois de Boulogne* was made in 1945; it was exhibited in New York almost twenty years later on a double bill (badly received by the *Times*) with Renoir's *Le Crime de Monsieur Lange*, shown thirty years after it was made (in 1936). And Bresson's first film, *Les Anges du péché*, made during the Occupation, had its theatrical release in New York in 1980, almost forty years later.

Thus our view of the French cinema has been conditioned as much by what we have *not* seen as by what we have. Among films regularly bought and distributed in America were those of René Clair, Marcel Carné, Jacques Feyder, Marcel Pagnol, and Sacha Guitry, and so it is these directors who have contributed most to our notions of what the French cinema is about. Whether or not critics and audiences actually would have liked those unreleased French films, the fact remains that we were conditioned by what the distributors thought we would like. It is impossible, therefore, to have a precise idea of a nation's cinematic history when so many films have not been seen. The retrospective 'Rediscovering French Film,' on which this book is based, is designed to fill in some of these gaps, and it is hoped that it will modify our view of the French cinema.

Notwithstanding the diversity of France and its cinema, it is useful here to define certain attitudes that I believe are characteristic of French cinema as a whole. First, French directors have been more preoccupied with plastic values than with narrative. The French cinema has been more influenced by the conceptions of the painter than by those of the novelist. Second, their attitude toward realism has been more consciously complex than that of American filmmakers. They believe that art was meant not to copy life but to be a personal interpretation of it, and therefore, inevitably, to be a stylization of it. Even the strong surrealist current in French cinema (a current beginning long before the word was coined or the movement became official, and found in the films of Georges Méliès, Louis Feuillade, and many of the so-called primitives) is also in its way the result of constant meditation on the nature of reality. Third, and perhaps again a concomitant of the painter's approach, is the fact that clarity, supposedly the great French intellectual virtue, is much more a characteristic of American cinema than of French. Narrative clarity usually may be achieved only by ignoring the ambiguities and complexities of reality, and French directors have preferred rendering atmosphere to telling a story neatly. Atmosphere, by definition, cannot be sharply defined. Fourth, the French notion of morality was quite different from that which prevailed for so long in Hollywood. The French had the reputation of producing 'immoral' films. It is, rather, that, recognizing the existence of both sexual passion and evil, the French have not hesitated to portray them in their films. They have also recognized the existence of situations without solutions and of characters who are neither completely good nor bad. French films may not look as realistic as many American films, yet they are often psychologically more so. By and large, the French filmmaker has not told his audience what to think about his characters or his situations; he has presented them as he has seen them and left us to draw our own conclusions.

What I have been saying can be summed up in this way: for the French, a film is a conscious work of art and the director a conscious artist who allows himself a personal interpretation of reality. The American film, until recently, aimed at being 'morally improving.' In the French film, good has not always been rewarded nor evil punished. And, finally, just as the American cinema can be seen as heir to the nineteenth-century Anglo-Saxon novel, so the French cinema can be considered natural heir to the painting of the impressionist period in France.

Comparisons with American films are most useful here, if only because we were all brought up on them and American films are the most widely known. But also because, as Henri Langlois maintained, France and America are the only two countries to have an unbroken continuity of great film-making. (Russian and German cinema did not come into their own before 1919; Swedish cinema was in eclipse throughout the 30s, and so on.) But unlike the

American film industry, the French cinema, at least since the end of World War I, has been largely an aggregate of individual talents working in an artisan-like manner; since 1920 the studio system has almost ceased to exist in France. Since that time, too, the cinema has been recognized by the French as a major art form. In contrast, the studio system was cursed as the bane of American cinema. Yet it worked; and within its limitations, an enormous number of fine films were made. As a result of the studio system, America produced the 'genre' film – the Western, the thriller, the musical comedy. Thanks to the producers, who have been relatively unimportant in France since 1920, the American cinema has had a dynamic quality, a speed and pace, a narrative clarity that the French cinema has not. The American movie, by and large, has been considered entertainment. It is perhaps significant that there is not even a word in French for entertainment (the MGM film *That's Entertainment* thus had as its French title *Once Upon a Time in Hollywood*). This is not to say that the French have not made so-called commercial films since 1920 – they certainly have, but not as effectively as the Americans, perhaps because the people who made them were not proud of them, did not believe in them, unlike the great Hollywood producers and directors who always believed that their films were A Good Thing.

The post-1920 French cinema was not totally free of the 'interfering' producer. Although there was nothing resembling the highly organized Hollywood system, producers sometimes threw their weight around. One example will suffice: Renoir's *La Chienne* was produced by Roger Richebé, and it was he who refused Renoir's choice of leading actress, Catherine Hessling, and imposed instead Janie Marèze, who was under contract to Richebé. After the shooting was finished, Richebé took the film away from Renoir and gave it to Paul Fejos to edit. Unhappy with the results, Richebé then gave it to Denise Batcheff. Renoir protested in vain – although he eventually got the film back, through the influence of a friend of the man who had put up the money for it. Thus, though the 'studio system' as such was much less developed in France after 1920 than it was in America, French films were not completely under the director's control: producers did have their importance. None to better effect, as it happens, then Richebé's partner on *La Chienne*, Pierre Braunberger, who has to his credit an enviable record of discovering and encouraging new talent, a record which began in the late 20s with Luis Buñuel and Renoir and continued down to the first films of the New Wave directors.[16]

SOURCE: 'INTRODUCTION', *REDISCOVERING FRENCH FILM*, MARY LEA BANDY (ED.) (NEW YORK: MUSEUM OF MODERN ART, 1983), 13–36

4.12 MELVILLE

Although he made some of the best French films of the 40s and 50s, and has been universally hailed as the pioneer of those methods of film production and technique generally associated with the New Wave, Jean-Pierre Melville and his films are practically unknown in the United States. This is particularly unfortunate because Melville was a great admirer of America and American cinema. Born in 1917, he was baptized Jean-Pierre Grumbach; it was the reading of *Moby Dick* in a Marseilles hotel room in the early years of the Occupation that made him change his name to Melville. He spent most of the war in England – seeing American movies, among other things – and he began to make films on his return to France in 1945. The first was a short, *Vingt-quatre heures de la vie d'un clown*, a film he later disowned and which hardly anyone has seen.

His first feature, *Le Silence de la mer* (made in 1947 and released in 1949), was an immediate triumph. It was based on a novel by Vercors, written in 1942. Published clandestinely, it had an immediate worldwide success, both as an affirmation of the continuity of French culture and of the spirit of the French Resistance. When Melville decided to film the novel, Vercors told him to go ahead, on one condition: when the film was finished, it was to be submitted to a kind of jury which would decide whether the film was faithful to the spirit of the Resistance movement. The jury voted unanimously in favor of the film.

The novel was a first-person narration of an impossible love between a German officer billeted in the home of the narrator and his young niece. Realizing that the form in which the story was told was as important as the content, Melville preserved the narration in its entirety, with the result that the film has very little dialogue. Far from appearing redundant or 'literary', this commentary rendered the quality of a remembered story. The film takes place almost entirely within the walls of one room, and the intensity gained from the lack of dispersion is increased by the remarkable sobriety of the acting: Nicole Stéphane's tremendously obstinate manner imperceptibly softens as she begins to grow fond of the German, and Howard Vernon gives a distinguished and restrained performance as the officer. In one of the few exterior scenes, Melville achieves a remarkable effect. The girl is walking down a snow-covered lane, and from a distance the officer approaches. The camera alternates angle-reverse-angle shots in the conventional way except that they are tracking shots in *reverse* directions.

At the time the film came out, it was very well received, but there were few who realized what a decisive step Melville had taken. He opened the way to more and more use of narration in the cinema, which meant greater facility in adopting a fixed point of view, something of considerable importance in translating to the screen many modern works of fiction. Even the simultaneous and overlapping dialogue of Marcel Hanoun's *Une Simple Histoire* can be found in embryonic form in *Le Silence de la mer*. The unrealistic use of sound so favored by Bresson is also to be found in the unnaturally loud and portentous ticking of the clock, which emphasizes the silence of the uncle and niece in the scenes where the German's attempts to communicate are completely frustrated. Here is an example of a director who was faithful not only to the spirit but to the letter, the form, of the work on which it was based. The result was, paradoxically, that the film was a highly original work of art.

Melville's next work was also an adaptation: Jean Cocteau's novel *Les Enfants terribles* (1950). Because of Cocteau's reading of the narration, and because the film so effectively translated Cocteau's world into the cinema, many people think of the film as having been directed by Cocteau. The best known of Melville's films outside France, it ironically was attributed to someone else.

Three years later Melville made *Quand tu liras cette lettre* (1953). It is the least known of all his films, not without reason: the script is melodramatic and not terribly believable. Melville himself was unhappy with the film, which has hardly been seen since it first opened. Yet it is not unworthy of attention. What Melville did with Jacques Deval's original script was to try not to cover up its excesses, but rather to emphasize them. Given the story's baroque extravagancies, he chose to carry them to their logical extremes. The musical score for the film is written for piano, organ, harpsichord, and accordion, thus emphasizing the baroque nature of many of the sequences of the film. As the young novice forced to leave the convent after her parents' death to look after her younger sister, Juliette Greco, in counter-point, provides a restraint against which the erotic follies of the other characters are set. In some ways, the film is reminiscent of Stroheim's *Foolish Wives*, not only because of its Riviera setting. The character of Max – brilliantly played by an otherwise indifferent actor, Philippe Lemaire – is an ideal exposition of the slightly sleazy young opportunist who works as a garage mechanic, but who boxes in a nightclub every Tuesday night in order to (as he admits) show off his 'merchandise' to the rich and bored vacationers of the Carlton hotel. His encounter with Thérèse was bound to be stunning, all the more so as Thérèse is revealed to be what her sister always teases her for – Saint Theresa, with all the mixture of piety and passion attributed by Bernini to Theresa of Avila.

The way in which the story is told prefigures to a certain degree that of *Bob le Flambeur*. A group of short, seemingly unrelated sequences dealing with a group of seemingly unconnected characters is gradually seen to coalesce. Thérèse leaving her convent; Max in his garage meeting Irene; Denise in her stationery shop: gradually all the pieces begin to come together as the plot inexorably gets under way. The film is not as successful as Melville's other works, but for those who value the disturbing, the excessive, and the erotic as essentials of art ('Beauty will be convulsive, or it will not *be*,' said André Breton), this may well be Melville's most exciting film.

Bob le Flambeur (released in 1956) begins with a shot of the Sacré Coeur at the top of Montmartre in the early hours of the morning, the twilight that separates the night from the new day: 'The heaven of Montmartre,' says the narrator, and then the camera pans to follow the little funicular railway down, down to 'the hell of Montmartre,' Place Pigalle. There we see the meeting of those who are going to work and those who have been up all night and who never go to work. 'Two lives, two destinies, are going to cross each other,' says the narrator, and we see Anne (Isabelle Corey) sauntering along Place Pigalle, buying a little paper carton of French fries, and accepting the invitation of an American sailor for a ride on his motor scooter. An old man, 'Bob the Gambler,' sees her, shakes his head, and walks on.

The first encounter is over, the first step has been taken. From then on, the story of Bob, Anne, and Bob's 'adopted' son Paulo is told to us in a succession of short scenes. At first viewing one does not always grasp the connection between each scene, and one does not realize for a while what direction the film is going to take, or even what the story is about. For this reason, Melville has been accused by some critics of not knowing how to tell a story. His (original) screenplay is not built according to classic narrative techniques. Each scene is a clue, a hint, and it is only after a certain number of these clues have been presented that we begin to understand how Paulo's meeting with Anne, or Bob's refusal to lend money to a pimp, or the croupier's wife with her dominating manner, all have their place. Bob is a man who believes in chance, in fate, and each scene is a little hint of the impending disaster. Until we see this, we are unable to realize the importance of each event, just as Bob himself is unaware of its importance. But, as in the novels of Faulkner, when we suddenly *do* realize, when we at last catch on, the effect is overwhelming – because it is *we* who discover the pattern behind all the seemingly unrelated incidents. We suddenly understand what fate has in store for Bob. Except that, as in life, there is one final surprise. Everything that we expect to happen does happen, but in a way which we had not expected. Melville went on to make nine more films before his untimely death in 1973, but to this writer he never (unless perhaps in *Le Samourai*) was to surpass the achievement of his early work. *Bob le Flambeur* remains his masterpiece.

SOURCE: 'MELVILLE', *REDISCOVERING FRENCH FILM*, MARY LEA BANDY (ED.)
(NEW YORK: MUSEUM OF MODERN ART, 1983), 161–4

Notes

1. This quotation and those that follow are adapted by Roud from W. H. Auden's 'In Memory of W. B. Yeats' (1939).
2.. Since the time when Roud wrote this text, Bresson's first film, *Les Affaires publiques*, has, in fact, been rediscovered. It dates from 1934, not 1939.
3. We have cut Roud's discussion of *Les Dames du Bois de Boulogne* here, as he discusses this film at length in the earlier 'Novel novel; fable fable?'.
4. We have cut Roud's discussion of *Pickpocket*; see 'Novel novel; fable fable?'.
5. In fact, the film was called *Arrêtez mon chapeau* (Étienne Arnaud, 1905).
6. We have cut the end of this article, in which Roud discusses *La Règle du jeu*; see the earlier text about the film in this collection.
7. On the history of the London Film Festival, see Martyne Auty and Gillian Hartnoll, *Water Under the Bridge: Twenty-Five Years of the London Film Festival* (London: BFI, 1981), 116 pages; Anonymous, 'The London Film Festival', in Allan Eyles (ed.), *NFT 50: A Celebration of Fifty Years at the National Film Theatre* (London: BFI, 2002), 48–52.
8. For contrasting viewpoints on the general history of the New York Film Festival, see Richard Corliss, '70-millimeter Nerves: Richard Roud Interviewed by Richard Corliss', *Film Comment*, 23.5, September–October 1987, 36, 38, 42, 44, 46–7, 50, 52, 54; and Phillip Lopate, 'The New York Film Festival: The First Fifty Years', in Laura Kern, Joanne Koch and Richard Peña (eds), *New York Film Festival Gold: A Fiftieth Anniversary Celebration* (New York: Film Society of Lincoln Center, 2012), 14–41.
9. At the beginning of this chapter, Roud recounts the circumstances of his first meeting with Langlois and Mary Meerson (see Roud's obituary of Langlois, included in this anthology).
10. Roud's note: David Thomson, *Biographical Dictionary of the Cinema* (New York: William Morrow, 1976).
11. Here we have cut a longish sequence in which Roud presents various testimonies of witnesses discussing the different theories as to why Langlois left FIAF.
12. Roud's note: W. H. Auden, *The Dyer's Hand* (New York: Random House, 1963).
13. Roud's note: Truffaut 'adapted' her last name for the character played by Jean-Pierre Léaud in the 'Antoine Doinel' films: *The 400 Blows*, *Stolen Kisses*, etc.
14. Roud's note: Annette Michelson, 'Bodies in space: film as "Carnal Knowledge"', *Artforum*, February 1969.
15. Here we have cut a short passage about Nestor Almendros, the Cuban-born cinematographer.
16. Here we have cut two substantial passages, one on French cinema to the end of World War I, the other on French cinema of the 1920s.

PART 5 1984–9

5.1 DECADES NEVER START ON TIME

NOTE: The following documents are taken from Roud's unfinished autobiographical project, Decades Never Start On Time, *which would have been both a history of the new European cinemas of the 1960s, and a kind of personal memoir about his work as a film critic, especially his experiences of attending film festivals during those years. The archive contains one 'Outline' (4 pages), two 'Proposals' (9 and 7 pages), and two draft chapters (Chapter one, 7 pages, and Chapter four, 11 pages). Evidence from Roud's correspondence in the archive suggests that the idea for* Decades Never Start On Time *goes back to the late 1970s. In a letter from Viking Press, dated 18 April 1977, the editor tells Roud that although they are not interested in publishing a collection of Roud's* Guardian *articles (which Roud must presumably have pitched to Viking), 'a memoir about putting a film festival together' would be a great idea. However, when Roud submitted some draft material to Viking several years later, the proposed book was rejected, the editor (in a letter of 23 March 1984) referring to personnel changes at Viking and arguing that the Langlois biography had not sold as well as anticipated. We do not know if Roud pursued the project any further.*

Decades Never Start on Time – the New Waves and the Film Festivals of the 60s (Book Proposal)

No-one born after World War II can possibly understand why the 60s – which I define as running from 1958 to 1972 – was the most exciting decade in the history of the motion pictures. 'Bliss it was in that dawn to be alive! But to be young was very Heaven!' And it is for them, those who are now 45 or younger, that this book has primarily been written.

1946 was the year that, in America at least, movies made the most money, reached their largest audience. Then the troubles began. It has generally been assumed that the decline of the cinema after 1946 was a result of television, and I continue to believe that this is so. In their book, *The Movie Brats*, Michael Pye and Lynda Miles argue that there were two other more important reasons.[1] One was the divestiture, under the anti-trust act, implemented by President Truman, of the cinemas themselves from ownership by the producers of movies. This accounted for the panics that they say scholars place around 1948, or as late as 1950. Then, with the end of the war, the return of the veterans, the GI Bill of Rights,[2] there came the flight from the inner cities, the movement to the suburbs. Their proof that these last two were more important than the rise of television in diminishing cinema audiences is that some key cities in America: Portland, Oregon; Portland, Maine; Little Rock, Arkansas; Austin, Texas; did not *have* television, and yet film audiences declined.

This may well have had some importance, but it seems to me the clinching argument that it was television that brought about the decline of cinema is that the same thing happened, a few years later, in Europe, where there was no divestiture problem, where there was no flight to the suburbs.

The sign that Hollywood was in crisis was clear, if only from that celebrated advertising campaign 'Movies are better than ever' – the very fact of which proved that a lot of people must have thought they weren't.

Of course, good movies continued to be made for a long time in Hollywood, but fewer than before. And there were fewer new talents. Most serious film-goers were conquered by Italian neo-realism, the first post-war development in cinema that excited everyone: Rossellini's *Open City*, De Sica's *Bicycle Thieves*, et al. But neo-realism collapsed in the early 50s.

Then, suddenly, as it seemed then, the cinema entered a new phase, one entirely different from anything that had come before. Like most European revolutions, this one began in France. W. H. Auden wrote about the Romantic Movement which followed the French revolution of 1789, 'a new aesthetic is always accompanied by and related to religious and political changes, though none can be explained away in terms of another.'

Religion played a part in the aesthetic of the 60s, but politics played a much more important role. Some have claimed that the aesthetic of the New Wave can be summed up in the change from the use of the term movies to that of cinema or film. This is a facetious over-simplification, but it has some truth in it. For the most important thing, I think, about the 60s was not just the new and different kind of films that were made, but in the change in the attitude of those interested in the arts.

Film had become as respectable as literature, painting or music. And indeed, the New Waves were nourished by contemporary literature, painting (to a lesser extent), and music.

There have been several excellent books on the French New Wave (James Monaco, et al.), but they have largely concentrated on the aesthetics of these films. I want to do something different. That is, describe the phenomenon of the New Waves – first in France, then Italy, Czechoslovakia, Germany, etc. How and why did they come into being; in what ways were these directors, producers, scriptwriters, cameramen different from their predecessors? Then, how did they make themselves known, how did their films get to be seen? What was the relationship between the general economic conditions of the 60s and this phenomenon, and finally, of course, why did it end?

Briefly, the rise of the New Wave can be ascribed to several factors. First, I think, it came to fill a vacuum. With the decline of the 'commercial' cinema, the New Wave was first and foremost an attempt to *replace* the almost unbroken string of great films that had gone on since about 1915 to the end of World War II – more than thirty golden years. The directors and technicians of the New Wave were all born after the death of the silent film (Alain Resnais, being perhaps the exception, and it shows). They were the first generation of film directors to study film history. Not in dusty libraries, but in equally dusty cinémathèques, film archives, etc. It was the first generation that was consciously concerned with film history, with the form of film as much as its content. Of course, before them, directors had invented film language, but that was different: these men and women knew the film language of Feuillade, Griffith, Eisenstein and Welles (to choose four names almost at random), and they wanted not only to make a new kind of cinema, but also to effect a renewal of all that they thought was best in the older traditions. Most of these directors, but not all, had been film critics, and this, too, was a new development in the history of cinema.

The cinema had just begun to lose its place as the most popular art form to television. Something had to be done to combat TV, and these directors went back to the past in order to build a future. They were helped enormously by advances in technique; someone once said that the French New Wave would have been impossible without the invention of Kodak Tri-X fast film, because it didn't need as much lighting and made it therefore much cheaper to make films.

The example all of them bore in mind was that of Orson Welles, who was perhaps the first important director to make a great film without having passed through the system, without having been an assistant to an assistant director, and then assistant to the director, etc. Welles – who claims to have had only a crash course of seeing *Stagecoach* 36 times before making *Citizen Kane* – gave them confidence that one could make films without having to go through the often stultifying apprenticeship of the past.

But in some ways the oddest thing about the rise of the New Waves was the fact that they achieved their goals by utilizing (instrumentalizing, as it used to be called in the political sixties) the film festivals.

Film festivals are a relatively recent phenomenon. The very first ever was Venice, which began in 1932. But not until Cannes in 1946 was there a second film festival. Since then, they have of course proliferated, and at the same time changed in their nature. Perhaps because so many of the new directors had been film critics and had therefore attended film festivals they conceived the idea that these 'industry markets' could be useful for the launching of a new kind of product. The best known example was that of François Truffaut, whose violently polemical articles attacking the Cannes Festival in 1958 got him banned 'forever' from Cannes. But the very next year he did go back to Cannes, not as a journalist, but as a contestant – and his film *The 400 Blows* won the Prize for Best Direction. A handsome revenge, to be sure, but also an example that was to be followed by many other directors. It was not the prizes they were after, necessarily – simply the kind of exposure that a film festival can bring. So the growing number of film festivals in the late 50s and the expansion of the number of films shown was not purely coincidental with the rise of the New Cinema. Truffaut proved it could be done in 1959; in 1960 Michelangelo Antonioni, who had already made five feature films (he too had been a critic, by the way) but was almost totally unknown outside Italy, and not very highly regarded even there, suddenly leapt to world fame with the screening of *L'avventura* at Cannes. It didn't matter that the film was almost booed off the screen: it was seen, it was written about, and suddenly Antonioni became a star director of the 60s. He even got a 'special' prize.

By coincidence, I became involved with the New Wave movement in 1958. And when I was appointed director of the London Film Festival in 1960 and of the New York Film Festival in 1963, I became part of the mechanism that made it possible for the New Waves to be known abroad, particularly in the all-important American market.

In the 50s the festivals were almost confidential, private affairs for producers and journalists. Suddenly, they began to have a tremendous influence on what people all over the world were going to see.

Because my job was to attend these festivals, and to choose films from them to show, first in London, and then later in London and New York, I was in a privileged position to follow the progress of the New Waves, to get to know the directors and producers, the scriptwriters and actors. I was in Cannes at that famous screening of *L'avventura*, and at the press conference Antonioni gave the next day. I was in Venice when Alain Resnais won the Grand Prize with *Last Year in Marienbad*, I saw the first Straub feature, the first

Decades Never Start On Time

Fassbinder film at the Berlin festival; the first Pasolini and Bertolucci films in Venice. And of course, when these directors accompanied their films to London and New York one got to know them better. I have no intention of writing a book of 'inside information' in the scandal-sheet sense, but it is indeed a kind of 'inside information'. The world premiere of *Last Tango in Paris* in New York was an event that deserves to be recounted. Eric Rohmer's triumph in Cannes with *My Night with Maud* was an event that deserves to be chronicled.

So in a sense, this will be a book as much about the directors of the New Wave as their films. Of course, one sheds light on the other, the biographical approach has been discredited in recent years as a tool for criticism, but a man's life is not totally separated from his career.

And being present when the events of 1968 closed down the Cannes Film Festival is not only of anecdotal interest. The reasons it was done, the way in which it was done, and the official reaction are an important part of film and social history.

Throughout the period from 1958 to 1972 my job placed me at the very centre of the film scene and I was able to observe many things which, I think, should be remembered.

So this book will have a double thrust: first, the rise and fall of the New Waves, and secondly, the enormous role that the film festivals of the world played. The festivals were the places where interest in the new cinemas was focused; the festivals were also the places where the political and economic factors of the 60s were, so to speak, showcased.

Nothing under the sun is really new, we are told, but there was actually something very new about the New Waves. As Godard put it in his press conference in Venice in September 1983: what the New Wave brought to the cinema that was really new, that had never existed in the history of the cinema, was that he, Truffaut, Rivette and several others had started to love film before they loved women, money, war. They discovered life through the cinema, and not vice versa. And, faced with the challenge of television, they were the first vanguard artists who were after – and sometimes got – a large audience.

Perhaps in this attempt lay the seeds of defeat. Certainly since 1972, although many directors have made excellent films, and there have been some new directors, there has been nothing like the world-wide burst of new talent every year as there was in the 60s. This decade may have marked the twilight of the cinema, the beginning of its end. If so, all the more reason to document it.

I shall concentrate largely on Western European cinema, for it was there that the most important changes took place. And it was also the area of my chief concern. But there was interaction between Europe and America – and largely because of the existence of the New York Film Festival. Or rather, because of the situation which made the New York Film Festival possible. If the first film festival in the world occurred almost 40 years after the world's first film show in 1895, it is significant that New York had to wait another thirty years before it was deemed interesting and/or important to have such an event.

And it is significant that such an event would be presented by Lincoln Center for the Performing Arts. As those who were around during the 60s know, and as those who weren't can hardly believe, film or cinema was suddenly elevated in the consciousness of Americans as well as Europeans.

Film began to receive more coverage in the serious magazines than it ever had before. Before then, intellectuals of course went to the movies, but they went, almost apologetically, as if to a brothel. And what did they go to see? Westerns, thrillers, comedy. They, like ordinary folk, just wanted 'to be taken out of themselves.' All that changed, for a time, during the delirious decade in which movies really did get better. And they were more hooked into world events: the French New Wave would have been unthinkable without the stimulus to fight first the Algerian War, and then later, and more importantly, the war in Vietnam.

Ultimately, perhaps, it may be that the most important thing about the New Waves was that the cinema for the first time in its history was closely connected to politics. Not in a propagandistic way – as with the Soviet directors – but much more personally and intimately. Of course there were plenty of love stories and thrillers, but they were usually set in a context of important contemporary political problems. And that surely is as important as the technical innovations – hand-held cameras, jump cuts, new script structures. Or rather, the two perhaps are part of the same thing. These were movies made for adults, people who wanted to think as well as to feel, to be disturbed as much as to be entertained. And, for better or for worse, it was the period when the director was finally recognized as the ultimate author of a film. And therefore, that a film became a personal statement addressed to a large number of people. Gertrude Stein said it years ago: I write for myself and others.[3]

Decades Never Start on Time – Chapter Four

August 1961 was my first time at the Venice Film Festival. I didn't know what to expect, but I had been told that Venice was somehow more aristocratic, less 'commercial' than the Cannes Film Festival. After all, the first film festival in the world was held in Venice in 1932.

It seems odd now that there had never been a film festival in the 37 years the cinema had existed, but on the other hand, festivals were a relatively new part of the international cultural scene. There had been Bayreuth, but that was special, and devoted entirely to the works of Wagner. Salzburg would, I suppose, count as the first festival devoted to an art form, but it was neither competitive, nor did it often produce new works of music.

Venice, on the other hand, was a contest, and devoted entirely to new films of the year from all over the world. Why Venice? There were several reasons, not the least being the attempt to prolong the summer tourist season into the first week of September. Culture and tourism are often closely linked, and indeed, there exists to this day a 'Ministero della Cultura e del Turismo' in Italy. But there were, of course, other reasons. Mussolini, like Lenin before him, believed very much in the importance of the cinema as a popular art. Then, too, the Biennale of Venice already existed for painting and sculpture, and there was also a festival of poetry and music.

By today's standards the early Venice Festivals were sparsely attended. When *Grand Hotel* was shown in 1932, only 2,000 people were able to see it (today, at Cannes and Venice, 4,000 to 6,000 spectators get to see each film in competition). And the number of countries represented that first year was small, too: France, Germany, Italy, Great Britain, Poland, the Soviet Union and the United States (America was well represented not only by *Grand Hotel*, but also by *Dr Jekyll and Mr Hyde*, Lubitsch's *The Man I Killed*, and [King Vidor's] *The Champ*). At first, the festival was to take place only every other year, like the Biennale, but it proved so popular that it soon became an annual event.

As we have seen in the preceding chapter,[4] the festival changed almost from the moment Hitler took power in 1933, and the festivals of the late 30s were dominated politically by German and Italy. The festival stopped during the war, so my first festival in 1961 was the 22nd 'Exhibition of Cinematographic Art,' to use its official title. And what I had been told was true. It was less 'commercial'; there was not so much hoopla, and there were fewer parties. But there were some: I remember my astonishment at being invited to the official Soviet reception especially when the noted French communist critic and historian, Georges Sadoul, had been forgotten.

The festival took place on the island of the Lido, which set it apart from the city in a way in which Cannes was not. Every morning and early afternoon, there was what called the 'Cultural Section,' which that year was in two parts: a homage to Mack Sennet and a panorama of Czechoslovakian cinema. The later afternoon was devoted to the 'Information Section,' i.e., films considered of importance but not in competition, and than at night, the competition itself. Everything took place in one building, the Palazzo del Cinema, conveniently located across the street form the Hotel Excelsior and alongside the Casino. The Festival Palace was in the purest Fascist style, and was strongly up-staged by the aristocratic Hotel des Bains, a few minutes away. This was the oldest hotel on the Lido and was later used by Visconti in his *Death in Venice*.

When I first arrived at the Palazzo I discovered that everything seemed a little less well organized than at Cannes, but there were compensations, the most important being a splendid woman called Flavia Paulon whose job it was simply to solve people's problems. She told you which hotel you were to stay at, how to get tickets, and all the rest. That first year I was consigned to a rather damp little hotel called the Dardanelles, hidden in a wooded section of the narrow sandbar called the Lido, so I walked to the festival each day along a twisting tree-lined road.

Opening night was Kurosawa's *Yojimbo*, later remade in this country under the title *A Fistful of Dollars*. It was at Venice, of course, that the world had discovered Japanese cinema when Kurosawa's *Rashomon* won the Grand Prize in 1951. His new film, though not as great, was an event.

But *Yojimbo* was followed by many disappointing works, now long forgotten. Who, indeed, remembers Autant-Lara's *Thou Shalt Not Kill*, Albicocco's *La Fille aux yeux d'or*, Wajda's *Samson*, Peter Glenville's *Summer and Smoke*, not to mention Basil Dearden's *Victim*? There was, however, one extraordinary film, Alain Resnais's second film *Last Year at Marienbad*.

Even before the film was completed rumor had begun to circulate that *L'Année dernière à Marienbad* was a strange, difficult work – one that would make *Hiroshima* look like a Jerry Wald Fox production.[5] It was up before the Cannes Festival selection committee, but it was reportedly rejected by André Malraux himself, who is supposed to have said 'It's *too* good for Cannes.' Understandably annoyed, the producers refused to show it out of festival, and kept it under wraps all summer long hoping for Venice and the Lion of Saint Mark.

It was a long shot, but it paid off. *Marienbad* was chosen for Venice, and the 22nd Mostra Internazionale d'Arte Cinematografica will be long remembered as the festival that gave it the Golden Lion, in the face of strong opposition.

At the gala first screening, most of the audience sat trembling in apprehension waiting for the film to begin – would they *understand* it? The blame for this atmosphere of dread lay partly with its scriptwriter Alain Robbe-Grillet: his interviews and press statements had the unfortunate effect of making *Marienbad* sound like a pure essay in the higher reaches of non-Euclidean geometry. And perhaps it is that, too. But novelists' critical theories have often been harder to understand than their novels, and *Marienbad* turned out to be remarkably easy to 'take.'

Everyone admitted it was visually an extremely beautiful film – and Delphine Seyrig was instantly hailed as a great new face. The contributions of Robbe-Grillet were more controversial, but the film could be taken as a puzzle, epitomized by that match game (a variation on 'Nim's Game') that everyone was trying out for himself on the café tables for days following the film's premiere.

L'Année dernière à Marienbad (1961)

It is difficult now to imagine such a difficult film winning the grand prize and exciting so much attention; of course the film had its detractors, but by and large it was the very fact of its being a 'difficult' film that fascinated most people. It was difficult (though not impossible) to identify with a woman called 'A' or two men called 'X' and 'M'. And Resnais's treatment of his rococo Grand Hotel setting left one in no doubt that this was a different world from that of *Grand Hotel* shown 30 years earlier at the very first Venice Festival.

Resnais and Robbe-Grillet had developed a technique briefly used in *Hiroshima, mon amour* – there is no past, no present; neither future nor conditional. Or so it seems, until one realizes with shock half-way through the film, that one is not even sure *when* the film is taking place. Are the events of this year and last already over, or are this year's events happening now, or are we at the still point of the turning world?

> Time past and time future
> What might have been and what has been
> Point to one end, which is always present.[6]

No-one dared deny the perfection with which Resnais directed *Marienbad*; its formal beauty and its rigorous composition. Image, sound, dialogue, music, camera movements are all autonomous, interacting one with another to create patterns of extreme complexity and brilliance.

Decades Never Start On Time

But even more important, perhaps, is the fact that it is the culmination of a whole series of films – a new kind of film in which the story is not the most important element. A kind of film in which the director deliberately chooses a thin, fable-like story in order to be freer to express himself and his view of life, his interpretation of life. *Last Year at Marienbad* deals with some of the most important subjects … love, memory, freedom, but it does so in a completely integrated fashion.

I met Alain Resnais for the first time on the Excelsior beach, and learned to my surprise that this was not the first time I had seen Delphine Seyrig. She had appeared in an 'underground' American featurette called *Pull My Daisy* (1959), directed by [Robert Frank and] Alfred Leslie. But although she was living in America at that time and married to the artist Jack Youngerman, for some reason she did not use her own name, appearing on the credits as Beltiane. I also learned that Resnais had wanted to make the film in some kind of large, anonymous and faintly run-down hotel like the Strand Palace in London where he had often stayed. His producers talked him into using the far more acceptably glamorous setting in Bavaria.

But the real excitement of a festival in those days was the discovery of new talent, and, for that, one had to look in the 'Information Section,' where two new Italian directors were making their debuts: Ermanno Olmi, with *Il posto/The Sound of Trumpets/The Job*, and Pier Paolo Pasolini with *Accattone*. Although *Il posto* was presented as Olmi's first film, I later learned that he had made a featurette called *Time Stood Still* for the Edison-Volta electric company, but it had been seen by very few people. *Il posto* told the story of a young man looking for his first job with a large company in Milan. It was both funny and touching because although he gets the job, we see, if he does not, what a dreary kind of life he is going to have. The strange thing was that when I went to find the producer of the film to invite it to the London Film Festival, he almost didn't want to give it to me, because he was convinced that the film could only be understood by people who knew Milan. Even the Romans, he feared, wouldn't get it. I had to explain to him that although I knew practically nothing of Milan (except for *The Last Supper*, the Cathedral, and La Scala), I had thoroughly enjoyed the film, and that it could be appreciated by anyone who had ever worked in an office job of any sort in almost any country. 'Really?' he kept asking me, amazed, 'really?' Yes, I assured him, really.

The Italians at Venice, however, did not much appreciate the Olmi film and they absolutely hated the Pasolini. This was the first time I had come across that strange phenomenon, not unique to Italy, but very strong there, of not appreciating their own local talent until it had been 'consecrated' by foreign approval. *The Bicycle Thief*, for example, had run for only two weeks in Milan – nobody had wanted to see it until the news filtered back from America that it was considered a masterpiece. Then, and only then, was it possible to re-release the film to good audiences. This systematic undervaluing of everything Italian was not new: even Pirandello had not been considered a great playwright by the Italians until after the success of *Six Characters in Search of an Author* in Paris. And the same was true of Pasolini. *Accattone* was booed and hissed. I didn't realize at the time that this was partly because of Pasolini's Communist Party affiliations and partly because of his homosexuality, something which he never bothered to try to keep secret. But it seemed to me, and to most of the other foreign critics, that here was a new voice which was saying something about the Roman sub-proletariat that had never been said before. Its producer, too, was surprised that I should want the film for the London Film Festival, but he was very pleased.

Pasolini did not come to London for the screenings, but a woman suddenly turned up at the National Film Theatre claiming to be the star of *Accattone* and Pasolini's representative.

I saw this lady before hearing her name properly, and I was convinced she must be some kind of fraud, for the 'stars' of the film were all young people and this lady, though attractive, was not young. But the mystery was soon solved: the woman was Laura Betti, who only played a small role in the film but who was indeed Pasolini's closest friend and a well-known stage actress and 'intellectual cabaret' singer. She was not easily mollified, for she thought (or pretended to think) that everyone must know who she was and so why had I pretended not to know her?

The second and last time I attended the Venice Festival was the following year. This time I knew the ropes and had less need to call upon the services of Signora Paulon. I was at a better hotel, the Villa Otello, but it was further from the festival palace, so I ended up renting a bicycle to get back and forth. That was the year I also made the discovery of a drink unique to Venice, the Bellini, which turned out to be a heavenly combination of fresh peach juice and champagne.

But there were more important discoveries that I made that year, for the Information Section presented Bernardo Bertolucci's first film, *La commare secca*, and Godard's *Vivre sa vie* (*My Life to Live*) was in competition. On paper, the competition films had looked formidable: we had been promised Joseph Losey's *Eva* and Orson Welles's adaptation of Kafka's *The Trial*. But *Eva* was suddenly pulled by its producers, the Hakim Brothers. This, we were subsequently to learn was but the first stage in the attempted destruction of the film. It was cut, re-edited, and many of the songs by Billie Holliday were also removed. These songs punctuated the film, and as Edgardo Cozarinsky has pointed out, Holliday's myth was a larger-than-life projection of the film's heroine (played by Jeanne Moreau), who is seen reading *Lady Sings the Blues* as a clue to her own character and in ironical contrast to the clean bourgeois business girl (Virna Lisi) who displays a copy of T. S. Eliot. In fact, the only complete print that ever came to light was the one with Finnish subtitles! Somehow, the Finnish distributor had gotten hold of a print before the producers had decided to begin their hatchet job. If more people had been able to see the film as Losey had made it, they would have been less surprised by the mastery of his following film, *The Servant*. *The Trial* never arrived, supposedly because Welles was not satisfied with the music for the film. This was a needless disappointment. When I eventually went to see *The Trial* in Paris that winter, I could hear, from the lobby, the end titles music being played, and to my horror, it turned out to be the then notorious arrangement of the Albinoni Adagio – not a very *recherché* piece of music.

Kubrick's *Lolita* was also shown in competition, and it may have been an historical event, because the festival newspaper made the strange announcement that, from the next day on, *Lolita* was to be considered a British, not an American film. Of course the film had been almost entirely shot in Britain. And after long calculations (an important item being the laboratory where the film was developed and printed), it had turned out to be more 'British' than 'American' in spite of the nationality of its director and its putative setting. From that day on, the nationality of a film became more a financial calculation than anything else.

Like *Accattone* and *Il posto* the previous year, the Italians all seemed to hate the Bertolucci film – perhaps because it was based on a screenplay by Pasolini. In fact, Pasolini had expected to direct his own script, but other projects took more of his time than he had expected, and he asked his assistant, Bertolucci, to direct the film instead. The two men had met because Bertolucci's father, Attilio, a well-known poet, was a friend of Pasolini and he actually lived in the same apartment house. Bertolucci was then only twenty-one, but he handled the story of the murder of a young prostitute with great skill. It was a kind of episode film in the sense that the police round up five suspects, each of whom tells his story. And each one lies. But the point of the film was not the impossibility of determining the truth; rather the lies of each suspect are the means by which the director reveals his characters to us. What is extraordinary is the way in which Bertolucci managed to communicate his excitement in making the film. Here, I thought, was a man who knew how to use film not only to tell a story but also to express his own personality. His muscular technique and nervous style instantly commanded attention.

Vivre sa vie was the first film by Godard that convinced me that he was one of the great directors. I had seen *Breathless*, *Le Petit Soldat* and *Une Femme est une femme*, but interesting as each was, it was nevertheless his fourth film that completely won me over. In a way this is less strange than it may appear, for there were many who loved *Breathless* and considered all the films following it to be of less interest, which must mean, I suppose, that there was something essentially *non*-Godardian about that first film.

Vivre sa vie told the story of the life and death of a young prostitute, but it was also a tribute by Godard to Dreyer, Bresson, and his actress wife Anna Karina, and he did well by all three. Extremely objective — existential, even — the film nevertheless communicated great emotion, partly through his use of Dreyerian close-ups: almost everything was in the faces. Godard was not afraid to let us compare Anna Karina with Falconetti (an extract from Dreyer's *Jeanne d'Arc* is cut into the film), and Miss Karina was far from being annihilated by the comparison. In moments such as her solo dance around a pool table she achieved not only the intensity of a Falconetti, but the compelling fascination of a Louise Brooks. But for all the references to Dreyer, and Godard's own statement that he wanted to do for prostitution what Bresson had done for the world of thieves in *Pickpocket*, *Vivre sa vie* remained defiantly original. In its enormous reliance on close-ups and its comparatively long takes, it was quite different from his earlier films. Nonetheless one could not mistake his style, a compound of sloth, nervous energy and a will to abstraction. The intermittent use of silence and the camera movements can only be explained by purely formal necessities.

Both the Godard film and the Bertolucci film were invited to London, and a month later, both directors came. It was a difficult period — the festival took place during the Cuban missile crisis, and everyone was nervous. It was the first time I had really met Godard (we had been introduced at one of Agnès Varda and Jacques Demy's New Year parties), and he surprised me by not wanting to stay around the NFT during the screening of his film but rather asked if I could take him to see the first James Bond movie which was showing at the London pavilion, but had not yet opened in Paris. I was surprised because I had never thought that he would like seeing this kind of film, but off to *Doctor No* we went. I was in for a bigger surprise afterwards. He expressed a desire to visit one of London's strip clubs and so off we went, only to discover that it was a pitifully sordid spot. The thing that tickled us most about the event was that the club was so cheap that the strippers had to exit from the minuscule stage to turn over the phonograph record that was accompanying the number. I did not get to know Godard well on that occasion, and indeed I never got to know him well.

Bertolucci arrived in London with his girlfriend, the actress Adriana Asti, and the three of us became friends. Bernardo was nervous about how his film would be received, especially after the way it had been treated in Venice. It was his first time in London and he and Adriana wanted to do everything. Most of all, they wanted to eat a 'typically English' meal. I wasn't up for roast beef and Yorkshire pudding, so I took them to Wheeler's, the fish restaurant. Bernardo wolfed down a dozen oysters with great gusto, although I was to find out shortly thereafter that he had never before eaten them. When I took them back to the Mayfair Hotel, where the Festival had put them, we bumped into Godard, also at the same hotel. Bertolucci had a great admiration for Godard who, with Rossellini, he considered the director who had influenced him most and whose work he admired more than any of his contemporaries. But what with the missile crisis, and every one of us apocalyptically expecting to be blown up any minute, and the dozen oysters, Bernardo got sick. It turned out later that it was the meeting with Godard, however, that had shaken him up the most, and he began by throwing up over Godard's shoes in the lobby of the hotel. I quickly got him into the men's room, and he emerged ten minutes later, pale, but purged. This was to be a continually repeated pattern. Not that he literally vomited over his father figures, but he did have a compulsion to reject those he had admired the most. Godard was the first 'victim' but there were to be others.

The London Festival over (and the missile crisis, too), I set off for a short vacation in Paris. Agnès Varda had been in London for the commercial opening on her film *Cleo from Five to Seven*, and so we travelled to Paris by train together. After crossing the channel, Agnès suddenly suggested we get off at Boulogne because her friend Alain Resnais was shooting *Muriel* there. 'But how will we find them?' I asked her. 'Don't worry,' she said, 'it's easy. We'll just stop the first person we meet on the street and ask him where the film people are. It's a small city, and, you'll see, they'll know.' I had doubts, but she proved right. Unfortunately, it was late in the afternoon so we didn't get to see any of the shooting of the film, and because the shooting was suspended for a day or two, we ended up going back to Paris with Resnais and Delphine Seyrig. There was a dining car on the train, so the four of us had dinner together. Resnais didn't get a chance to say much, because Agnès was inveighing against Anatole Dauman, the producer of *Muriel*. She had had some problems with him over a short she had made, and in her usual aggressive manner, she was telling us what she was going to do to Dauman when she got hold of him. Madame Seyrig, speaking in that wonderful breathy voice of hers, kept insisting that it must surely be some kind of mistake which would be cleared up with little difficulty. 'Mistake,' replied Agnès, 'mistake my ass.' 'But Agnès,' Seyrig continued, 'surely this can all be patched up amicably.' 'Patched up,' shouted Agnès, 'he's the one that's going to have to be patched up.' All the while Resnais said nothing, but contented himself with eating and smiling. So my great chance to talk to him about *Muriel*, a film about which I was intensely curious was lost. Still, the dialogue between Varda and Seyrig made it almost worth it.

SOURCE: 'DECADES NEVER START ON TIME', ARCHIVE DOCUMENT, 1983–4, RICHARD ROUD COLLECTION, HOWARD GOTLIEB ARCHIVAL RESEARCH CENTER, BOSTON, BOX ONE, F.9, ITEMS A–H (EXTRACTS: 'BOOK PROPOSAL', 9 PAGES; 'CHAPTER FOUR', 11 PAGES)

5.2 THE MORAL TASTE OF LOTTE EISNER

'Richard, Richard, we must be very, *very* careful crossing the Kurfürstendamm. I was born in this horrible city, but I don't want to die here.' And indeed, on 5 March 1896, Charlotte Henrietta Eisner was born not far from the Ku-damm in the fashionable Tiergarten area of Berlin. When she was a young girl, her father wouldn't let her go near the

Kurfürstendamm: if it is now the centre of West Berlin, it was then the vice centre of all Berlin, the street down which Sally Bowles used to walk with Herr Issyvoo.

Lotte was born into a well-to-do Jewish family that had converted to Protestantism and, as she told me, she never particularly thought of herself as Jewish. Others were to take care of that later. She studied archaeology and art history and wrote her PhD dissertation in 1924 on 'The Images on Greek Vases'. Two years later she began to write articles, book reviews and interviews for the *Literarische Welt*. In 1927, she joined the staff of *Film Kurier*, a cinema and theatre daily newspaper, for which she reviewed both plays and films.

Then came 1933 and, more prescient than many, Lotte realised it was time to leave. Her brother assured her that all this 'Nazi nonsense' would soon blow over. She knew better, and she told him, 'I'm leaving now, but with all my books and belongings. One day you'll leave, too, but you'll only be able to take out an overnight bag.' Sure enough, one day in 1938 there was a knock on Lotte's door in Paris and there was her brother – with a small suitcase. She chose Paris because her sister had married a Frenchman, Eugène van der Meersch, so she would not be entirely alone in her exile. Although, as she cryptically told me, 'I didn't get on with my sister. She played bridge.'

Once in Paris, she made her living writing for a German-language Czech publication called *Internationale Film Schau* – until Hitler invaded Prague. She became for a time the Paris correspondent of *World Film News*, the periodical of the British documentary film movement. Meanwhile, something important had happened: in 1934, she had read in the French trade weekly *La Cinématographie Française* (now defunct) that two young men, Henri Langlois and Georges Franju, had set about saving silent films from destruction. That caught her interest because she had been brought up on silent films, and for her those films had an atmosphere, a certain mystery, even, which was different from that of the sound film. So she wrote to the magazine, and arranged a rendezvous with the two men at the Café Wepler, Place de Clichy: each of them was to carry a copy of the *Cinémato* (as it was called) under his (or her) arm. Langlois was only twenty years old, half Lotte's age, but the three of them hit it off immediately, and although she did not accompany them in their search for prints she did help them sort and classify stills, programmes, posters and scripts.

When the war came, like all Germans – Nazi or anti-Nazi – she was interned in the camp at Gurs in the Pyrenees. Because her brother-in-law was a colonel in the French army, she got out after three months; but as a result of the inadequate rations, she told me, she left behind four teeth – victims of malnutrition. Later she found her way to Montpellier in the Unoccupied Zone, where Langlois came to visit her from time to time. When he heard that the Germans were about to cross the demarcation line between Occupied and Unoccupied France, he wrote to her to leave. By the time she got the letter, however, it was too late: the Germans were already in Montpellier. And her money was all gone. She happened to meet a young man she had known in Berlin, who told her to go to the local rabbi for help. But since she had been brought up as a Protestant, she felt foolish going to see a rabbi. What could she say to him? Another friend suggested that she get in touch with Pastor Exbrayat, a Protestant minister, who found her 'an interesting case' and gave her some money. But she soon realised she would have to move on. Langlois had suggested Nice, but she preferred to hole up in a smaller town. She was right in her instincts: a few weeks later, the German troops took over Nice.

Under the *nom de guerre* of Louise Escoffier, and with the help of Exbrayat, she got a job cooking in a girls' school. That didn't work out; she was, in spite of her choice of alias, not a good cook, and when she was sacked, she went to Figeac, where she was taken in by the aunt of Georges Sadoul, the film critic and historian. She spent the rest of the Occupation there, taking time out only to visit the nearby Château de Béduer, where Langlois had stored some films: she felt she must check on their condition.

Sleeping Cars

When the war ended, she was fetched by Langlois, and now that the Cinémathèque Française was receiving a government subsidy and had a permanent home, she became its Curator-in-Chief, a job she held for thirty years. As Langlois would always say, two-thirds of the objects (costumes, sets, maquettes, etc.) in the Museum of the Cinema were obtained by Lotte. She was also Langlois's 'Madonna of the Sleeping Cars', for often it was she who, to avoid officialdom and paperwork, would transport films – even nitrate prints – under her sleeping-car berth from one country to another. And she would either precede or accompany Langlois on his visits to the Cannes, Berlin and Venice Film Festivals.

But unlike Mary Meerson and Langlois himself, Lotte Eisner had a professional life outside the Cinémathèque. In 1948 she published an important article on the German films of Fritz Lang in the *Penguin Film Review*. Then in 1952 appeared the work that was to make her famous: *L'Ecran démoniaque* (*The Haunted Screen*). It has been called by many critics perhaps the finest single book of film criticism, and that may well be true. Unlike Siegfried Kracauer, who specialised in 20/20 hindsight and *ex post facto* judgments, Lotte Eisner knew that *Caligari* led to more than Hitler. Equally important was her knowledge of the German theatre, which she related to the development of films. Expressionism, yes, of course, but she also made us see the importance of *Kammerspiel*, a style of chamber acting developed by Max Reinhardt; she explained the importance of the German *Stimmung* (atmosphere, mood); she was the first to insist on the unique quality of Louise Brooks, whom she first met on the set of *Diary of a Lost Girl* poring over a volume of Schopenhauer. Aha, she thought, this is Pabst's idea to make everyone think his American discovery is an intellectual. Then she discovered that Louise Brooks was indeed an intellectual. The two women didn't see each other for years, but when Louise Brooks came to Paris for her triumphant retrospective in 1958, she spent most of her time there with Lotte.

Her definitive study of Murnau appeared first in Paris in 1964, and then in a revised and enlarged edition in London in 1973. The last book she published was *Fritz Lang* (London, 1976; New York, 1977). As she noted in her preface, it was more difficult for her to write about Lang than about Murnau because she had never actually met Murnau (he left Germany in 1927). And, as she said, 'For my own part, I do not claim to have produced a definitive study.' The book is soon to be published in its original French. How she found time to write these books while working more than full time for the Cinémathèque is a mystery. She retired in 1975 – at the age of 79 – and then only because she had had her first heart attack. Until then, she was constantly enriching the collection with new films, scripts, costumes, artefacts. It was she who was able to persuade the 80-year-old art director Hermann Warm to supervise the reconstruction – by his original sculptor, Walter Schultze Mittendorff – of the robot from *Metropolis* for the new Museum of the Cinema.

But what was most amazing – and laudable – about Lotte was that, although she was essentially a film historian, a film archaeologist, even, she never lost interest in contemporary cinema, particularly German cinema. She may have 'hated' Berlin, and indeed, it was always somewhat embarrassing being there with her, because she would hiss – in English, to be sure, but that language is not unknown there – 'Look at those faces. They must have been Nazis. I'm sure of it.' And people *would* understand, would turn round, would stare. She loved Berlin, too, especially its own brand of humour. One of the funniest – and most chilling – examples was the story she told me of a middle-aged Jew who took a taxi from Tempelhof airport into town. On the way, he kept commenting, in perfect German and even with a Berlin accent, on how this building had disappeared, how that street had changed. Finally, the driver, a man of the same age, turned to his passenger, and said, 'I guess you haven't been here for a while.' 'Not since 1933,' replied the Jew a little ostentatiously. 'Hmm,' said the driver, 'Well, you didn't miss much.'

Lotte was always able to distinguish between Nazis and Germans, and she was one of the first to recognise the existence in the 1960s of a new German cinema; to hail Werner Herzog, in particular, as a worthy successor to the German cinema of her time. Her only blind spot was Leni Riefenstahl, whom she loathed, but whose films she couldn't bring her-self to dismiss. She used to pretend to think that anything that was good about them *must* have been due to the influence of the editor Walter Ruttmann, or the genius of the cam-eraman Hans Ertl. Her appreciation of the younger German film directors was much appreciated by them, and it is well known that when Lotte was ill a few years ago Werner Herzog set off in the dead of winter to *walk* from Munich to Paris in the hope that somehow this would help Lotte recover. And, for whatever reason, she did recover.

Nostalgia

Lotte Eisner had taken French nationality in 1952, but when she died in the suburbs of Paris on 25 November 1983, a friend who was in Cologne at the time told me that her death was one of the chief items on the 11pm West German television news programme, a fact that I somehow feel would have pleased her enormously. Like many 'assimilated' German Jews she was as much (if not more) German than Jewish. 'I wrote my books out of longing for German culture and nostalgia for the 1920s,' she said in 1982, when she received the first Helmut Käutner prize endowed by the city of Düsseldorf.

When I last saw her in her flat in Neuilly (paid for by the 'reparations' the German gov-ernment made for her having been obliged to leave Germany), she was noticeably fading, but she was working away on a book of memoirs, helped by Werner Herzog's wife Maartje. I hope enough had been written for it to be published one day.

François Truffaut once described Lotte as the 'angel' of the Cinémathèque; she may have been an angel, but she was no saint. She could be very witty indeed at the expense of those she considered unworthy, and she had high standards. Her death, in the same month as that of Herman G. Weinberg in New York, marks the end of an era, of a certain kind of film historian who had seen the great silent classics as they came out. And she had one other, supremely rare distinction. Lotte was small, frail, yet indomitable. She had about her a dignity born of (justified) intellectual and moral self-confidence that made her the one person whom Henri Langlois, known for his towering rages, never yelled at, never even raised his voice to. Like Hannah Arendt, who had also been interned at Gurs, she possessed that greatest of qualities, what Arendt called 'moral taste'.

To have met Lotte Eisner was a privilege; to have known her was to have known a representative of the best of German intelligence, wit and warmth.

SOURCE: 'THE MORAL TASTE OF LOTTE EISNER', *SIGHT & SOUND*, 53.3, SUMMER 1984, 139–40

5.3 REMEMBERING LOSEY

Montpelier Square

My first meeting with Joe Losey came about in 1960, as the result of a review of *The Criminal* I had written for this magazine. Although I had seen several of his earlier films, this was the first one to convince me that he was one of the important film-makers of our time. I had admired some of his American work, but this seemed to be his first European film which really fulfilled the promise of *The Prowler* and *The Dividing Line* (*The Lawless*), probably because the subject he had been offered was more congenial to his temperament and his interests: power relationships, or what the French call *rapports de force*. Although the film was called *The Criminal*, its most remarkable characterisation was that of the prison warder (played with unusually controlled viciousness by Patrick Magee), and the film powerfully rendered all the ambivalent oneness between the keeper and the kept, the murderer and the victim, the judge and the judged.

To my surprise and pleasure, I got a letter from Losey, beautifully typed on the best quality notepaper (he was very particular about such details) in which he thanked me for the review. The letter ended with an invitation to come round for a drink. He was then living with his third wife, the actress Dorothy Bromiley, in Montpelier Square, in that picturesque corner of London between Harrods and Hyde Park: one could not imagine a more English setting.

We took an instant liking to each other. Although there was a twenty-year gap in our ages, we were both Americans living in London, and there was enough of a generation overlap to allow him to talk to me about his past without, as it were, having to supply footnotes. When he first mentioned his work in New York with the Living Newspaper, he was surprised and pleased to discover that I knew what it was. He had been born in Wisconsin and come east to Dartmouth College; I had been born in Boston and gone to the University of Wisconsin.

Losey had come to Britain because of the McCarthy blacklisting. I don't know if Joe was or ever had been a member of the Communist Party, but he was certainly a man of the Left. He had directed the world première of Brecht's *Galileo* (with Charles Laughton) and most of his best friends were either Communist or Communist-sympathisers. Even in Europe his first three films had to be released under what the French so aptly (in this case, at least) call a *nom de guerre*. For it was indeed a war between Joe and not only the American government but also that government's representatives and sympathisers in Western Europe and Britain.

His first Hollywood movie had been a short made for MGM in 1945, *A Gun in His Hand*, for which he received an Oscar nomination. He was then already 36. True, he had made three commissioned shorts already, but it was still a late start in films. Joe didn't believe in astrology, but he was nevertheless a little upset when, in the late 1930s, just before the première of his first stage production, a friend took him to an astrologer who told him that, as a Capricorn, he should expect neither fame nor success until he was at least 50. Oddly enough. *The Servant*, which most people would call his first real success, came when he was 54.

Markham Street

After that first meeting, and the retrospective season of his work which I organised at the National Film Theatre shortly thereafter, I lost sight of Joe for nearly two years. One reason was that he was abroad making *Eva*; another was that his domestic situation was changing.

Joseph Losey, Harold Pinter

After his divorce from Dorothy, he met Patricia Tolusso (née Mohan) in Rome, where they were introduced by Hugo Butler, one of the scriptwriters for *Eva*. They fell in love, she divorced Signor Tolusso, and the next time we met Joe had married Patricia and they had rented a house in Markham Street.

When Joe had finished *The Servant*, his first film scripted by Harold Pinter, he invited me to a private screening in Audley Square. It was the first film, I think, that he had ever made without any outside interference, and I thought it was a truly remarkable work. Losey had told me only that the script was based on a short novel by Robin Maugham, and that it was a kind of Faust-film. But it was a lot more than that. Like *The Criminal* (indeed, one is tempted to say like all his films before and after), it was about power relationships. In this case it dealt with the destruction of a weak man by a stronger one, and perhaps also the destruction of an obsolete upper class by a ruthless but more realistic rising middle class. Dirk Bogarde gave what I still think was perhaps his greatest performance as the servant who preyed on his young master's weaknesses in order to take over the household.

That year I was programming the first New York Film Festival. I wanted the film for New York and I wanted Joe to come over to present it; and heaven knows he wanted to go back to America, where he hadn't been since 1951. He was worried, however, that there might be trouble with the immigration authorities. I assured him that the then Secretary of the Lincoln Center for the Performing Arts, John Mazzola, had made certain that there would be no trouble at Kennedy Airport, so Joe agreed to come.

As it turned out, there was no trouble at all – no questions, nothing. When we met in the city, Joe seemed almost disappointed at the ease with which the exile had been allowed to return. At first I thought he was just being perverse, quirky. But thinking it over, I realised that the fact that there had been no trouble, that no one in the government cared one way or the other, was almost an affront. Joe had been self-exiled for over ten years, forced to start a new life abroad, and the issues that had made him feel he *had* to leave were so dead that it seemed retroactively to devalue all his sacrifices.

The Servant was well received in America, and this pleased Joe a great deal, for he never lost his feeling that he was an American, and his dearest wish in his last years was to return to the States to make at least one film there 'before I die'. There were several projects (among them the James Kennaway novel *Silence*), but they all came to nothing.

The following year brought *King and Country*, again with Dirk Bogarde, which was as classical in style as *The Servant* had been baroque (a word Joe hated to hear applied to his work, by the way). Again it was the story of the conflict between two men (the other being Tom Courtenay who, partly thanks to Bogarde's restrained and supportive performance, was overwhelming as the World War I deserter). Then, two years later, *Modesty Blaise*, a film I did not like very much. (Nor did Penelope Houston, who encapsulated its essential impermanence by calling it Losey's Paper Handkerchief.) Joe was not pleased with my displeasure, and I thought this was the end of our relationship. But no. The following year I got a note from him announcing a screening of *Accident*, again scripted by Pinter. He said I would find him 'back at the old stand again'. This was typical of Joe: his opinions of his own films often changed, and he now seemed to think that I might not have been completely wrong about *Modesty Blaise*.

There were some fans who didn't admire *Accident*. I seem to remember Susan Sontag and Elliott Stein coming out of it in London saying it was 'contrived'. And of course it was. Edgardo Cozarinsky has pointed out the remarkable cross-cutting between 'sequences which, in story development, are neither simultaneous nor associated by flashback but plainly contiguous'. The film was further distinguished by its use of non-synchronised dialogue (who can forget the soundless sequence with Delphine Seyrig and Dirk Bogarde as seen through the window of Nick's Diner?) and by the near-surrealist scene of indoor rugby.

Losey's career was strewn with unrealised projects. It was during the period of *Accident* that he first spoke of his desire to make a film of *Under the Volcano*, with Richard Burton as the Consul. I still think *Under the Volcano* is an unfilmable book, but Joe might have done a better job than John Huston eventually did. At least he would probably have been able to find visual equivalents for the baroque style of Lowry's writing, and while Joe was no alcoholic, he was acquainted with vodka, if not with tequila. It was also around this time that, through Sonia Orwell, he met Marguerite Duras. He was eager to film her *Sailor from Gibraltar*. She was enthusiastic, too, but of course it was Tony Richardson who finally made the film.

Royal Avenue

After leaving Markham Street, the Loseys lived for a time in flats lent them by Robin Maugham and then Tom Courtenay. Finally, they borrowed money from Joe's sister Mary to buy a house. Faithful to Chelsea, he and Patricia settled in Royal Avenue, the very street on which *The Servant* had been set. It is a beautiful avenue, lined with eighteenth century houses separated by a wide tree-lined centre strip. It had been intended to go from Wren's Palladian Royal Hospital as far as Kensington Palace, a long French-style street-picture perspective, but for some reason it only got as far as the King's Road (one block, in fact). The house meant a lot to Joe; as is evident from his films, decor was important to him.

Joe and Patricia were abroad for the next year or so during the shooting of *Boom* and *Figures in a Landscape*. Then came his finest achievement: *The Go-Between*. In adapting L. P. Hartley's full-length novel (both *The Servant* and *Accident* were fairly short novels), Pinter and Losey reduced the story to its essence, and then Losey's job was in a sense to blow it up again, to restore the novelistic density, the texture, the life by cinematic means.

For example, the novel has a prologue and an epilogue: both are discarded, and instead there is a double articulation of time. As the story of one Edwardian summer runs along, it is interrupted, at first only by occasional flashes, later by longer scenes, of Colston (the boy go-between) arriving in Norwich forty years later. The effect of this playing with time is even more intense than in *Accident*. And although, like so many of Losey's films, this one is about the self-destructive male, it also contains his most dramatic study of a battle of wills between two women, the mother (Margaret Leighton) and daughter (Julie Christie). The battle is the more gripping because it is expressed only in guarded looks, conversational gambits and raised eyebrows. More than in his previous films, Losey achieved here an almost palpable sense of reality, which gives the moral force of the film a greater intensity. You can feel the clothes, you can smell the heat; and because all these sensual details are so physically realised, you end up hearing the unsaid, seeing the unseen.

The next step in Losey's career would ideally have been Proust's *Remembrance of Things Past*. Producer Nicole Stéphane, who owned the rights, had decided she wanted Joe to direct it, and he asked Harold Pinter to script it. All she needed was the money. So, in the meantime, Joe made four more films: *The Assassination of Trotsky*, *Galileo*, *A Doll's House* and *The Romantic Englishwoman*. They were not among his best work, partly, I think, because he was obsessed with the Proust project. But there were other reasons. He had waited too long to do *Galileo*; not through choice, of course, but projects can go stale. And that other theatrical adaptation, *A Doll's House*, seemed to be not really a subject to which Joe could contribute much. *The Romantic Englishwoman*, too, for different reasons, did not seem to cry out for his talents. The Trotsky film was the best of the four, but there was still something not quite right about it – perhaps because of Joe's ambivalent attitude towards Trotsky.

In between his sojourns abroad, life went on much the same at Royal Avenue. Except when Joe went through one of his periodic self-enforced bouts of teetotalism. He could be difficult without a little vodka to smooth things over. Nor was he always in good health: his asthma never stopped troubling him, and there were other functional disorders. He was also often pained by what he considered to be a lack of appreciation from American and British audiences and critics. This may have been an exaggeration, but it is true that he was more highly thought of in France and Italy. And, more important, Joe was appreciated more by his peers on the continent than in Britain. Resnais and Bertolucci admired him greatly – in particular his direction of actors. Indeed, this was one of the most important things about his films – the actors he chose and how he directed them, how he was able to let them contribute to the film.

Joe was no one-man band. Not only were his actors important to him, but there were also his collaborators: Reginald Beck, who edited most of his films: Gerry Fisher, who shot most of them; Richard MacDonald, who not only did the sets but also worked out the 'storyboards' with Joe. The secret of his success with actors (and of course I mean actresses as well) lay in the fact that he really liked them. He could, however, be amused by their foibles. I remember him telling me that after the shooting of *Boom*, Elizabeth Taylor approached Richard MacDonald and asked if he would agree to do the decor for the private jet plane she and Richard Burton had just bought. MacDonald said he would be happy to oblige, but could she give him some idea of what style she had in mind. When she replied without hesitation 'Regency', he, unfazed, simply said, 'Where am I going to put the fireplace?'

Rue du Dragon

I never fully understood the state of Joe's finances – except that it always seemed to be either boom or bust. Only now that his estate has been published in *The Times* do I realise just how bad things were, for all Joe left behind him was £1,600. During a year in which he made no film, he had to borrow money. But when, as in 1972, he made both *Galileo* and *The Romantic Englishwoman* in the same tax year, he had not only to pay back the debts of the previous year but also to pay the tax on the earnings from two films. It was for this reason that Joe's accountants told him he had to leave England for several years at least. But where to go? Since the Proust project was still a possibility, he chose Paris.

Once more, Joe and Patricia found a nice place to live, though it was really too small for any couple, let alone for a man who worked a great deal at home. Joe was not happy in Paris. True, he was recognised by taxi drivers, butchers and bakers (and I can bear witness to this), but he didn't speak French very well, and he felt cut off. In 1976 he made his first French film, *Monsieur Klein*. Many critics count it as one of his finest, and indeed it ought to have been, for the subject was congenial, the actors good. Somehow, however, I felt that it didn't quite work. Perhaps because it was too perfect a 'Losey subject', perhaps because Alain Delon was not the right type of actor for the part – not obsessive enough. And then the Proust film finally fell through, as did *Under the Volcano*, *Nostromo* and *Voss*. Losey's next French film, *Les Routes du Sud*, had an uninspiring script and was wrongly cast. I don't know what Joe himself thought of it, but he never once said a word about it to me, even though I was seeing him quite regularly.

Vicenza

It was Daniel Toscan du Plantier of Gaumont who pulled Joe out of his depression by asking him to make a film of *Don Giovanni*. Joe hesitated, but not for long. He liked the opera, and thought he could do something special with it. Rather than shoot the film in Spain, he chose to do it in and around Vicenza, using almost exclusively villas and other buildings by Palladio.

We hadn't seen each other for a while, and when I was invited by Gaumont to the shooting of the film in November 1978, Joe hadn't been told. That day they were in Palladio's Teatro Olimpico, so it was there I went. I settled down unobtrusively in a seat in the theatre, while Joe was directing a scene on stage. Then, during a break, he looked over the footlights and caught sight of me. 'Well,' he said, 'I thought you were dead.' Joe knew that I had not really liked his preceding three or four films, and he was very susceptible to slights. But he was soon his genial self again. He invited me that night to dinner and we spent a pleasant evening in the nearby villa where he and Patricia were staying.

After the success of *Don Giovanni*, Joe was able to pay off his British taxes, and he wanted to return to London. But he made one more film before leaving France, *La Truite*, based on a novel by Roger Vailland which he had wanted to do for years. In some ways, it was his most rewardingly complex film. It dealt with the relations between power and sex – all kinds of power and all kinds of sex. The heroine, herself as slippery as a trout, is a ferociously independent young woman who begins her life working on a trout farm and ends up owning one. This 'naive' peasant girl is more than a match for the three rich businessmen who find her attractive: the one man she really loves is her homosexual husband – perhaps because their marriage has never been consummated. The film was not generally well received, and I never quite understood why. Perhaps the plot-lines were too complex, perhaps there was too much incident, perhaps the novel was no longer as interesting to Joe as it once had been. But one thing it did prove (although *Eva* and *Secret Ceremony* ought to have done that years ago): Joe was not only a great director of actors, but also of actresses. In *The Trout*, Isabelle Huppert, Jeanne Moreau and Alexis Smith were all superb.

Royal Avenue

Once Joe got back to the Royal Avenue house, plans began to materialise. There was to be a new film with a Pinter script: an adaptation of William Trevor's *Fools of Fortune*. The money was there, and the contracts were ready for signing. But the first project to be realised was Patricia Losey's adaptation of Nell Dunn's play *Steaming*, still to be released, and which I have not yet been able to see.

The last time I saw Joe was at his 75th birthday party in January 1984. He was in good spirits and seemed genuinely to be enjoying himself, for that very day he had succeeded in getting Vanessa Redgrave to play in *Steaming*. I was in London again in April, but when I phoned, Patricia said Joe wasn't feeling too well and that we had better wait until I came back to London after Cannes in June. For some reason I didn't phone then, and it was only when I arrived in New York that I discovered that Joe had died on 22 June while I was on the high seas. This made me remember all the more fondly the trip we had taken together on the old S.S. *France* in 1970, when Joe was coming over for the commercial opening of *The Go-Between*. Joe had liked the idea of crossing by ship (Conrad was one of his favourite writers) and he was treated like a king by the staff and crew of the French Line. But he grew impatient after a day or two as he always did when he was not working. Then, too, this royal treatment was in too great a contrast to what he wanted from Americans (and Britons). But, of course, directors aren't superstars in either Britain or America, and this is something Joe ought to have realised.

The most important reason for his discontent was, as always, the fact that he could not make as many movies as he wanted to. And that he was often obliged to make films he would have preferred not to make. Joe could not content himself with the great body of work he did accomplish. He always wanted to do more. Be patient, people would tell him, but Joe was not a patient man. His driving sense of urgency is what made him so stimulating to be with, and what gave his films their excitement and their power.

SOURCE: 'REMEMBERING LOSEY', *SIGHT & SOUND*, 54.1, WINTER 1984–5, 40–3

5.4 AN UNTITLED BIOGRAPHY OF TRUFFAUT

NOTE: The following extracts are taken from the draft manuscript of Roud's biography of François Truffaut. The manuscript comprises some 115 pages and around 50,000 words. It covers Truffaut's life from beginning to end and discusses all of his films. Evidence from Roud's correspondence in the archive suggests that he got the idea of writing the biography shortly after Truffaut's death in October 1984. Contact was established with Truffaut's family, notably his wife Madeleine Morgenstern, who approved the project via their representative, and Truffaut's business manager, Maurice Berbert (December 1984). Furthermore, Roud contacted Roland Truffaut, the film-maker's father, who sent him some personal letters and photographs (December 1984–January 1985). In researching the biography, for which he had a contract with Alfred A. Knopf by the summer of 1985, Roud also conducted many interviews with people who had known Truffaut (Nestor Almendros, Fanny Ardant, Janine Bazin, Catherine Deneuve, Claude de Givray, Marie de Poncheville, Suzanne Schiffman, Helen Scott and others). He was equally able to draw on the interviews that he had done himself with the film-maker, as well as on their personal friendship, which dated back some twenty-five years. Much of Roud's research material can be found in the Boston archive. Parts of the text from which we have taken the following extracts are dated 1988–9, which suggests that Roud had continued working on the biography almost up to the time of his death. However, the publishers with whom Roud had a contract for the book, Alfred A. Knopf, decided not to publish it posthumously.

Prologue

On the closing night of the 12th Cannes Film Festival in 1959, three men in tuxedos walked down the grand staircase of the old art-deco Palais du Cinema. *Les 400 Coups* (*The 400 Blows*) had just won its director, 27-year-old François Truffaut, the prize for Best Direction.[7] Truffaut was accompanied by his 14-year-old star, Jean-Pierre Léaud. With them was their guardian angel, Jean Cocteau, twice president of the Jury at Cannes and its lifetime honorary president. Cocteau was heard to whisper to Léaud, 'Keep your head held high, don't look at your feet; smile now at that blond woman on your left – she's France Roche (then the most important French movie columnist); now look to your right, don't walk too fast, and *don't look at your feet.*'

The two younger men looked nervous but triumphant. Truffaut had made only one previous film, the 23-minute *Les Mistons*. He earned his living as a journalist, and only two years before had denounced the Cannes Film Festival. He called it a den, if not of iniquity, then at least, of intrigue; he accused the jury of deal-making; and he indicted the director of the festival, the Robert Favre le Bret, for corruption and stupidity. 'Dominated by schemes, false manoeuvres, and compromises, the Cannes Film festival was an undeniable failure ... a failure because too many diplomatic and industrial considerations have determined the prizes' (*Arts*, May 22, 1957). The Grand Prize had gone that year to *The Friendly Persuasion*, William Wyler's high-minded saga of a Quaker family disrupted by the Civil War. Truffaut wrote that far better films, like Wajda's *Kanal* and Bergman's *The Seventh Seal*, had been fobbed off with a shared 'Special Jury Prize'. Bresson received a Best Director prize for the body of his work, rather than for the film actually shown that year, *A Man Escaped*, which was only mentioned in the citation as an afterthought. Furthermore, Truffaut accused Favre le Bret of having sabotaged the Bresson film by

Les Quatre Cents Coups (1959)

showing it only in the afternoon. Given that the president of the jury in 1957 was Jean Cocteau, and that the jury included such distinguished directors as Marcel Pagnol and Michael Powell, and such important writers as Jules Romains and André Maurois, the young Truffaut could only conclude that the jury had somehow been influenced, cajoled, or in some subtle way bribed, to have made such choices.

His attacks on Cannes (appearing in a weekly called *Arts-Spectacles*) were so violent that in the following year, the festival had refused Truffaut the customary bed and board accorded to all journalists of any importance. He was not, however, 'banned', even though his newspaper printed after his by-line 'only French journalist excluded from the film festival'. He was 'accredited', which meant that he had free access to all the press screenings. His newspaper was glad to pay for his hotel room and meals because of the great public interest in Truffaut's incendiary articles.

Needless to say, the articles in 1958 were no more favorable than they had been the preceding year. Nonetheless, when *The 400 Blows*, shot between November 1958 and January 1959, was finished, Truffaut had the nerve to propose the film to Robert Favre le Bret, the man he had so violently attacked, as an official French entry at Cannes. Years later, when a reporter asked how he had felt about the festival's taking his film after all he had said, Truffaut coolly replied, 'Well, that showed proof of their objectivity.' Favre le Bret, when asked the same question in reverse, remarked that Truffaut's submitting the film meant that he couldn't really have thought the festival was such a corrupt enterprise.

But more important, said Favre le Bret, was the fact that he had found the film extremely moving, innovative, and sure to attract attention to a new talent, which was one of the chief functions of a film festival.

There was one more hurdle before the film could represent France officially. Favre le Bret's decision had to be ratified by two representatives of the French government: Philippe Erlanger, representing the Quai d'Orsay [Ministry of Foreign Affairs] and André Malraux, Minister of Cultural Affairs under the newly established de Gaulle government. How the decision was made was described by Jean-Luc Godard in an article in *Arts-Spectacles*: 'As soon as the screening was over, the lights came up in the tiny screening room. There was silence for a few moments. Then Erlanger leaned over to Malraux, and asked, "Is this film really going to represent France at the Cannes Festival?" "Mais oui, mais oui," replied Malraux.' Perhaps Erlanger was worried because, as former Minister of Education, he found Truffaut's depiction of the French elementary school system un-flattering.

And so the film did go to Cannes, and it was a success, not only there but all over the world – in spite of its ridiculously mistranslated title. Few people questioned what '400 Blows' meant. 'Les 400 coups' is a French idiom for getting into all kinds of trouble, generally used about boys or young men. But if no one was particularly curious about its title, everyone did want to know how autobiographical the film was. Truffaut's answer varied over the years. At first he said it was mostly autobiographical, which caused his parents much grief. Later, he maintained that he had been misquoted, that journalists had exaggerated, that it was not really his own story, and that he was not the film's hero, Antoine Doinel. But if he was not Antoine Doinel, who was he?

Chapter 1

On 6 February 1932, an un-married, sixteen year old girl, Janine de Montferrand, gave birth in Paris to a boy who was christened François. Janine Truffaut, as she later became, died over twenty years ago and the only survivor who knows her story is her husband, Roland Truffaut. What follows is based in part on what he told me.

Janine came from an aristocratic family, but, as Roland put it, with a lower-case *a*. Her father worked for *L'Illustration*, the most important pre-war weekly magazine. He was also a captain in the reserve army, and very military-minded. Her mother was born 'de Saint Martin'. Who François's biological father was, no one knows. Roland thinks he was a student of dentistry who often came to Janine's home and took her out on dates. When it was discovered that Janine was pregnant, he was barred from the house and never heard of again. There have been unconfirmed rumors that he is living somewhere in eastern France. There is also the rumor that he was Jewish, which might explain why the Montferrand family never tried to make him marry Janine. It is a rumour that pleased François greatly because of his Jewish wife and the large number of Jews he counted as friends and collaborators.

In the extremely bourgeois milieu of Janine's family – the so-called 'petite aristocracie' is often more bourgeois than the bourgeoisie – an illegitimate child had to be hidden, even from the rest of the family. When Janine's pregnancy became apparent, she was sent to live in a religious institution that cared for un-wed mothers until they gave birth. This 'home' was not a convent, but it was directed by nuns, and during Janine's stay there, she and the other women were treated every morning to sermons about their sin, and were constantly reminded of how bad they had been. 'I am sure,' Roland added, 'that this influenced my wife's feelings about François a great deal. All of those girls had *something* against the child they were to bear.'

In such a milieu, it was understandable that Janine sent her baby to an establishment in the suburbs of Paris called 'La Petite Etoile' which took in illegitimate children. Through her father's influence, Janine got a job at *L'Illustration*, and, it seems, she did her best to think as little as possible about the 'fruit of her sin'.

François was about a year old when Roland met Janine. He was by trade an architectural draughtsman, but his hobby was mountain climbing, as was Janine's. In the forest of Fontainebleau, not far from Paris, there was (and still is) a mountain-climbing camp. The forest is not in the mountains, but it does have some impressive out-croppings on which one can practice *l'alpinisme*. Roland met Janine there and soon fell in love with her. When he declared his feelings and asked her to marry him, she said she must refuse because of her blemished past. 'It didn't take me long to make up my mind,' said Roland. 'I loved her very much and I didn't mind taking on the child.' Roland and Janine were avid film-goers, and a year before they met he had been very much struck, he said, by *Angèle*, a film by Marcel Pagnol, in which a young man wants to marry an unmarried mother. The girl's father is reluctant to give his permission because he does not think it would be right − sin must be punished. But the young man only replies that the girl's child has all the more need for a father. Roland was much impressed by such noble conduct and proceeded to do the same thing. François's life was thus transformed, and by a film whose director he was later to esteem highly.[8]

Janine and Roland were married on 9 November 1933. Roland legally 'recognized' François as his own child, and so François de Montferrand became François Truffaut. But he did not come to live with Janine and Roland until 1942 when he was ten years old. His early years were spent shifting between his grandmother's homes. Roland says that it was from Janine's mother that François acquired his love of literature. She had been a school-teacher, and she didn't just make François read − she got him to analyze what he had read.

Why the young François did not live with his parents was a question I tried to put, as tactfully as possible, to Roland. He replied that since both he and his wife had to work, they were not in a position to take care of a child. But, he added, François's maternal grandmother lived only a few houses away, so they did see François on Saturday and Sunday. 'We had always gone to see him as often as possible when he was at La Petite Etoile, but you couldn't say we *raised* him. When my mother died, in August 1942, we took him in. She had told me that we were going to have a lot of trouble with him, and she proved to be right. François felt himself to be an unwanted child.' And, given the circumstances of his conception and birth, perhaps he was. 'Janine,' Roland said, 'had inherited from her father a very strict, even severe, nature, and she and François had some terrible battles. She knew he resented her lack of love for him, but she could do nothing about it. It made her very unhappy, but that didn't stop her from being tougher on him than I was.'

Did François know he was illegitimate, and, if so, from what age? 'His mother and I had decided we would tell him when he was eighteen. But I had the misfortune of keeping diaries. They were always locked away, in an *armoire*, the same one we used for keeping other valuables, like sugar.' Sugar? 'Oh yes. During the Occupation, sugar was very valuable. Now, François knew where we kept the sugar, and one day when we were away, he managed to pry open the *armoire* to get some − (one of his 4,000, not 400, *coups*) − and he must have found the diaries, read them, and discovered the truth. That was in 1944, when he was twelve. He didn't tell me or his mother. I only found out thanks to that episode of the stolen typewriter you saw in *The 400 Blows*. Because he did steal a typewriter − that was one of the things in the film that was absolutely true. I saw the typewriter in the apartment, and asked him where he got it, but he said he had found it in the street, whereas he had actually stolen it to sell it. Well, I didn't know what to do. I asked my brother-in-law, who lived next door, and he warned me that if I didn't take it to the police, I could be considered as receiver of stolen goods, a fence. So I went with François and that damned typewriter to the local police station, and there I discovered that it had been stolen from an office where François worked part-time. A complaint had been registered, and the serial numbers tallied. The commissioner was interrogating François, and I was waiting in the corridor outside, where I could hear everything. François told the policeman that I was not his father, that he had been only recognized by me. So that's how I found out that he knew the truth.'

'But François never mentioned it to me – never, never. And I don't think he ever talked to his mother about it. It was just one more of those many secrets he kept locked up within himself. Many, many years later, we finally discussed it, and he said that he wanted to know something about "his origins", as he put it. So then I told him as much as I knew, that is to say, as much as his mother had told me. I don't know who his real father was.'

It is possible that François suspected something before the age of twelve. In an unfinished taped 'autobiography', made during the last year of his life with his old friend Claude de Givray, Truffaut begins by telling a story of his childhood. Someone had offered him a French translation of *David Copperfield* when he was seven or eight, and he was very much struck by a couple of lines at the beginning of the book: 'I was a posthumous child. My father's eyes had closed upon the light of this world six months when mine opened on it. There is something strange to me, even now, in the reflection that he never saw me.'

If these lines struck the young François so deeply that he remembered them forty-odd years later, this could mean, perhaps, that he had some intuition that Roland was not his real father. Or it could simply mean that, like many unhappy children, he wanted to believe it. In any case, he was fascinated by what he called 'the mystery of birth.' Of course, it is also possible that this childhood memory did not go as far back as he remembered four decades later. What is clear is that he was haunted by the circumstances of his birth. They were forever dramatically present in his mind and they profoundly influenced his life and his films.

'François, as a child,' said Roland Truffaut, 'was always lying and cheating – perhaps because he felt he had been lied to, had been cheated of a 'real' father, and of a mother's love. He was always stealing, too; but he was never violent or brutal. Never having enough money to go to the movies as often as he wanted to, he would steal the money in one way or another. At one point, François kindly offered to run downstairs to get the morning paper for us – a nice gesture, I thought. But then one day I passed by the kiosk and the newsstand dealer said, "Monsieur Truffaut, it's been four months since you last paid me." "But I always gave François the money every morning," I replied. "Oh," said the dealer, "he always told me you'd settle up the bill later."'

'But our life together wasn't all bad. Janine and I liked going to the movies, and whenever we thought a film was suitable for a child, we would take him, too.' François's first memory of seeing a movie alone goes back to 1939, a few months before the French surrendered to the Germans. The cinema was the Gaieté Rochechouart, and the film Abel Gance's *Paradis perdu* (*Paradise Lost*) starring Micheline Presle and Fernand Gravey, a film which dealt principally with World War I and its aftermath. 'The theatre,' he later wrote,[9] 'was full of soldiers on furlough with their wives and girlfriends … and the resemblance between the situation of the characters of the film and the members of the audience was so great the whole theater was in tears, with hundreds of handkerchiefs dotting the darkness of the cinema with white specks. I was never again to feel such an emotional unanimity at the screening of a film.'

'We went to the theatre, too, sometimes,' added Roland. 'Where we lived, halfway up Montmartre, you could find cinemas and theatres within three hundred yards. The neighborhood has changed a lot since those days. Place Blanche, Place Clichy, even Place Pigalle were different then. Of course, there were nightclubs and some disreputable people then, but not many. We went to Place Blanche for the Moulin Rouge (Toulouse-Lautrec's old music-hall had been changed into a cinema which is still there) and to Place Clichy for the Gaumont Palace (then the largest cinema in Europe, now destroyed). Those big cinemas had organs and stage shows and they weren't very much more expensive than the ordinary ones.'

'And we even gave François his first acting part in movies! Of course, it was an amateur film, 16mm, no sound, made with an old Bell and Howell camera. It was a kind of parody of Marcel Carné's *Les Visiteurs du soir* (*The Devil's Envoys*) which we called *Les Visiteurs du samedi soir*, and we made it out in Fontainebleau about people like us who came every Saturday night to practice our mountain-climbing. François must have been about fifteen then. I know it must sound strange to you to think of the father and son of *The 400 Blows* making a movie together, but it's true. As I said before, Janine and I were real film buffs, and she even wrote some reviews for a magazine that printed amateur criticism.'

What Roland didn't realize was that François hated nature and sports, and so their shared interests were strictly limited. He often refused to go with Roland and Janine on their outings.[10] François hated school, too, and he always said that he had never even gotten his *Certificat d'études* (an elementary school diploma), let alone the indispensable baccalauréat. But a few years after his death, Madeleine Morgenstern, his ex-wife, did, in fact, find among Truffaut's papers his *Certificat d'études*, a copy of which she gave me. A minor surprise was that he had somehow acquired a middle name – it was made out to François Roland Truffaut.

One can only conjecture about why Truffaut should have said he never got his certificate. He was largely self-taught and may have unconsciously decided to forget about his one diploma. Madeleine Morgenstern said that she thought he actually did want to go on to a lycée, but with his constant moving between Paris and Juvisy in the suburbs where his paternal grandparents lived,[11] his parents didn't, or weren't able to, get him into one. She also said that François didn't take well to religious education. He did sign up to study his catechism for a year, but never wanted to go to class, which was on Thursday afternoon, the only afternoon he could go to the *Cinéac-Italiens*, a movie house that showed newsreels and cartoons. He got so far behind that he never took his second communion.

Roland Truffaut says that when François left school at the age of fifteen,[12] he asked him what he wanted to do with his life. 'I told him that if he really wanted to go into the cinema, I didn't mind, although I didn't really like the idea because I thought it would be too hard for him to make a living that way. But when I asked him if he wanted to enter *L'IDHEC* (*L'Institut des Hautes Etudes Cinématographiques*, then the official government film school), he threw up his hands and said, "No, God, no. I wouldn't be any more studious at *L'IDHEC* than I have been anywhere else. No, I want to become a director all by myself."'

Feeling deprived of affection at home, the young François found it with his school-mates. Roland Truffaut confided that he had never even met François's best friend, Robert Lachenay. The two boys first met in 1943 at school in the Rue Milton when François was eleven and Robert, who was repeating a year, was twelve. As Truffaut remembered the encounter, Lachenay took one look at him and said, 'You, there. I bet you steal money from your parents.' François just looked at him in amazement, too astonished to reply. But soon they started to walk each other home. Robert had problems with his parents too: his mother drank too much, and his father was a compulsive gambler. So it was natural for the two boys to form their own 'family'. (Goethe's novel *Kindred by Choice*, also translated as *Elective Affinities*, was later to become one of François's favorites).

Their teacher, a certain Monsieur Ducornet, shrewdly sized up the two boys, and told Robert to sit next to his new friend. 'You two are just right for each other.' Sure enough, one of them was always the worst in the class, the other second worst, the order changing occasionally.

They soon became inseparable. When François was expelled from school in the Rue Milton and sent to another one nearby, Robert quickly found a way of making the same transfer. And when François got thrown out of the new school, they again found themselves together, this time at the 'commercial' school in the Rue Condorcet.

Both boys were compulsive readers. François had already discovered what the local municipal library had to offer, but he wanted to *own* books, so he managed somehow to find the money to buy – over a period of time – the complete *Les Classiques Fayard*, a cheap but good series of paper-bound classics. He began to read them in the alphabetical order of the authors' names, skipping Aristophanes in order to get straight to Balzac. Lachenay enjoyed more popular authors like Pierre Loti, Paul de Kock, and Paul Bourget, but François finally convinced him of the superiority of Balzac, whose works he had already begun to read under the influence of his maternal grandmother. François was also influenced by his favorite aunt, Monique, his mother's sister, but her interests were chiefly musical – she was a violinist.

François and Robert's greatest shared interest, however, was movies. Robert's mother often took her son to the cinema. And François had already begun to take movies seriously. In an interview in 1976, he recalled: 'It happened in several stages, of course. First I was a film fan: I liked to see lots of movies. The next stage was to want to see the film I liked several times. The third stage was to try to figure out what lay behind the film. And then there came the time when I began to write down the name of a director when I came out of a film I liked.' As a matter of fact the first film he saw twice was Marcel Carné's *Les Visiteurs du soir*. He had skipped school one afternoon to see it, but when he got home he found his aunt Monique there: she was planning to go that evening to see *Les Visiteurs du soir*, and asked young François to go with her. He didn't dare admit he had just seen it, so off they went.

He then began to put together film files, classified by director, filling them with articles cut from newspapers and magazines. The hardest part, although perhaps the most fun, was finding stills to complete the files. François and Robert worked as a team on this: they would go out after midnight, usually on a Saturday when their parents were away. Armed with a screwdriver, they undid the showcase in front of movie theatres, and made off with the stills.

In his taped autobiography, Truffaut told Claude de Givray, 'Robert didn't have much judgment; he had a kind of authority instead. He was very certain of what he liked, but it was often his political and historical views that made him admire a film. As for me, I didn't know where my preferences lay: I liked music (Aunt Monique's influence?), and I liked a certain sense of religious mysticism. That was one of the reasons I adored Robert Bresson's *Les Dames du Bois de Boulogne* when half the audience was making fun of it. My favorite film for a while – I saw it a dozen times – was Henri-Georges Clouzot's *Le Corbeau* (*The Raven*). It was tough to sit through, and at first there were some words I didn't understand, but later I was able to recite whole sections of the dialogue, particularly those abominable poison-pen letters which were the subject of the film.'

Throughout the German Occupation, which began when François was eight and ended when he was twelve, American and British films could not be shown. So François's taste was formed almost entirely by French films. He did go once or twice to see a dubbed German film: he liked *The Golden City* because it was salacious and he also remembered 'that film about the Boer War (*Ohm Krüger*) in which the great German actor, Heinrich George, played President Kruger.' Fortunately for Truffaut, the Occupation era (1940-1944) was one of the golden ages of French cinema. There is no paradox here. People went to cinemas and theaters in droves because they were better heated than their homes, and provided an escape from the drudgery of life under the Occupation. The lack of American films, always the main competition for French audiences since World War I, stimulated the production of French films. Many important pre-war directors – Jean Renoir, René Clair, Julien Duvivier, and Max Ophüls – had fled to America because they were Jewish, or had Jewish wives, or for political reasons. Their absence made it easier for new talents to emerge.

When Truffaut presented *The Last Metro* at the New York Film Festival in 1980, people asked him how it had been possible for patriotic French actors and directors to put on plays (as in *The Last Metro*) or to make films during the Occupation. Truffaut reminded them that until about 1943, no one in France could be sure that the Allies were going to win the war, and to stop working then could have meant no work ever again. He also reminded them that, of all the films made in France during the Occupation, not one could be construed as giving aid and comfort to the Germans.[13] Furthermore, many of these films were made by actors and technicians who hid the fact that they were Jewish behind names which they borrowed from friendly Aryans. (It is true that after the Liberation, Truffaut's favourite *Le Corbeau* almost got its director into serious trouble. It was claimed that the film had been commissioned by the Germans, and that it had been shown in Germany during the war under the title of *A Little French Town* in order to demonstrate that the behavior of its admittedly repulsive characters was typical. But it was soon discovered that the film had never been shown in Germany under any title, and that the so-called 'demoralizing' script by Louis Chavance dated back to 1937, thus disposing of the charge that the film had been 'made to order' for the occupying forces.)

François's exclusive diet of French films determined his standards. When American films began to be shown, they came to him with a force of revelation that it is hard for us to understand. The first he remembers seeing were the documentary series, *Why We Fight*, supervised by Frank Capra, and Gregory Ratoff's 1941 *Adam Had Four Sons*, which made a strong impression. It was Truffaut's discovery of *une vraie vedette* (a real star), Ingrid Bergman. And then, there was *Citizen Kane*, made in 1940, and released in France in 1946, when François was fourteen.

Meanwhile, François's files grew so large that his parents threatened to throw them out of their small apartment. He took them to the Lachenay's flat, which was larger, but they still took up half of Robert's room. François kept adding to them, and that cost money, so the two boys compiled weekly hand-written programs of the neighborhood cinemas, and sold them.

Neighborhood (third run) cinemas, in those days, changed their bills once a week on Wednesdays. And because of the paper shortages, there was not much room in regular newspapers for the full details of films that were on. The boys also took various part-time jobs to make enough money to keep collecting – and to keep on going to the movies.

François worked as a welder, he got a job working for a grain and seed merchant: he took anything he could get.

Besides Robert Lachenay, Truffaut had another close friend, Claude Thibaudat (later to become the pop star singer Claude Véga).[14] Claude's mother was the concierge of a building on the Rue de Martyrs where it crossed the street on which Truffaut lived, the Rue Navarin. François shared Claude's passion for popular songs and music-halls (a taste he was never to lose). Claude had been drafted into preparing with Robert and François their weekly film programs. Claude had his own room, which, because it had sliding doors, could be made bigger. There, he and François and three other 'recruits' occasionally put on 'poetic evenings', when each would recite a poem or a speech from a play.

The immediate post-war period in Paris was the great age of the ciné-clubs, and by the time he was sixteen François belonged to almost all of them. The only problem was that most clubs had their screenings on Tuesday night – the commercial cinema houses, which they rented, were usually closed Tuesday night because it was the least popular night of the week. So François and Robert decided to have their own ciné-club with screenings on Sunday mornings (then, as now, commercial houses never opened before noon on Sundays). François was the artistic director of the club, which they called the *Club Cinémane* (The Film Maniacs' Club), but Robert had to be the director because he, at eighteen, was legally of age. They obtained the use of a well-situated theater in the heart of the Latin Quarter, the Cluny Palace, but the life of the club was brief because they did not have enough money to advertise it properly. There were other problems too. Their first session was almost a disaster because the film they had been promised, and paid for, didn't arrive. Catastrophe was barely averted when François discovered that the film that had been showing in the cinema the previous week was still there, so they put that on instead. It was no real solution, but it kept the audience quiet. On another occasion, Lachenay remembers, Truffaut had (for the first time) written to Henri Langlois, co-founder and director of the Cinémathèque Française, asking him to lend them three avant-garde French films, including Jean Cocteau's *Le Sang d'un poète* (*The Blood of a Poet*). Langlois had replied that they could have René Clair's *Entr'acte* and Buñuel/Dalí's *Un Chien andalou*, but that he could not supply them with the Cocteau film. Unfortunately they had already announced a screening of *Le Sang d'un poète* 'in the presence of the director', but in the event neither showed up.

The Cinémathèque was to play an important part in Truffaut's life. Founded in 1936 by Henri Langlois (1914–1977) and Georges Franju (1912–1988), it was the first film archive that was as interested in showing films as in preserving them. By 1948, when Truffaut began to frequent it, the Cinémathèque was located on the Avenue Messine in a residential district on the Right Bank. The theatre was not large, but it showed three films a night – at 6:30, 8:30, and 10:30. It was not only the number of films that could be seen there in a week, but also the way in which they were programmed that was important. By juxtaposing films which appeared to have little in common, Langlois often made his audiences see subtle connections between seemingly disparate works.

Truffaut's first encounter with the Cinémathèque was not, however, at the Avenue de Messine screening room, but at a screening put on by the Cinémathèque one Sunday afternoon at the Lycée Montaigne, he told Claude de Givray. 'I must have seen an ad for it in *L'Ecran Français* (*The French Screen*, a Communist weekly on film) – that's the only way I could have known about it. I seem to remember it was a screening of some shorts by D. W. Griffith – *The New York Hat*, for example. I even think that that was the first time I ever saw André Bazin. But I can't be sure – there were so many things happening at once then.'

'As for the regular Avenue de Messine screenings, I started going there around 1948, and it was there that we all met – (Jacques) Rivette, Jean-Luc (Godard), a Polish-born girl called Liliane, and Suzanne Schiffman. We always met there. My first surprise at Avenue de Messine was that sometimes the screenings ended very late, after the last metro, so I had to walk home. I would go see a film called *Birth of a Nation* without knowing how long it was.'

'The Cinémathèque was really a haven for us then, a refuge, our home, everything. There were only about fifty seats, and we had the habit of not sitting, but of lying on the floor in front of the first row of seats – especially for the popular films. I must admit now that, looking back, I used to behave quite badly at Avenue de Messine. I used to try to get in without paying; I used to smoke during the screenings; and I used to try to see three screenings for the price of one. In those days judgment of films was very fluctuating, so I depended a lot on Rivette,[15] who had a great influence on me. I was impressed by everything I saw in those early days – the films were like a drug for me. And seeing silent films for the first time was a great shock. The first films I remember really liking sincerely were those of Jean Vigo. I didn't need anyone's advice or persuasion for them, whereas I never in those days had a very precise judgment on silent films.'

A greater influence than Langlois on the young Truffaut was André Bazin. He was the most important film critic of his time, and he also ran a ciné-club on Sunday mornings. One Sunday, as Dudley Andrews put it, 'a brash teenager appeared and after the screening engaged in several hours of conversation with Bazin.'[16] Truffaut had come to complain that Bazin's ciné-club with its discussion sessions was cutting into his potential audience at the *Cercle Cinémane*. But the two men were so taken with each other, in spite of their difference in age (Bazin was thirty, Truffaut sixteen) that François ended up by asking Bazin to come to speak at his club on the following Sunday.

Bazin had started from fairly humble beginnings, working for left-Catholic organizations like *La Maison des Lettres*, *Jeunesses Cinématographiques*, and *Travail et Culture*. By the time Truffaut met him, he was an extremely influential critic, especially because of the enormous amount of writing he did. He was film critic for a popular daily newspaper, *Le Parisien Libéré* (now defunct); two weeklies, *L'Observateur* (now *Le Nouvel Observateur*) and *Radio-Cinéma-Télévision* (now called *Télérama*); and two monthlies, *Esprit* and, most important of all, *La Revue de Cinéma* (predecessor of *Les Cahiers du Cinéma*). Bazin was so impressed with the enthusiasm and knowledge of this youngster that he was prepared not only to talk to him but, eventually, almost to adopt him.

The demise of the *Cercle Cinémane* was inevitable, but the way in which it happened is unclear. One story has it that Roland Truffaut, upon discovering what his 'delinquent' son was up to, after seeing his name on an ad for the *Cercle Cinémane*, had found him. Roland, however, does not remember it this way. According to him, it was he who, at François's request, had designed the poster for the *Cercle Cinémane* (he was, it will be remembered, an industrial draughtsman), so he perfectly well knew the whereabouts of François. In any case, it was Roland who had to pay up the club's arrears in rent and repay the members their subscription fees when it became clear that the club could no longer continue. As the legal parent of a minor, he was responsible under French law for the boy's debts. It was this, no doubt, that made Roland take such a drastic step as sending the boy to a reform school. 'The terrible thing is that everyone has his reasons' was Truffaut's favorite line from Jean Renoir's *Rules of the Game*. Bazin, whose only child was yet to be conceived, saw in the young Truffaut a boy who may have needed supervision but not a reform school. He set out to get François out, promising the authorities that he would henceforth make himself responsible for him. He would arrange for François's legal 'emancipation' from his family, so that Roland and Janine would no longer bear responsibility for his debts, etc. Bazin was to become Truffaut's 'real' father, and it was he who encouraged Truffaut, first to write about films, and later to make them.

His first job as a freelance writer came about by a chance meeting with the literary director of the magazine *Elle* at an extraordinary institution called *Le Club du Faubourg* (The Neighbourhood Club) and since it was in François's neighborhood, he started going to the weekly meetings. Anyone was allowed admission, and some quite distinguished people attended, including the man from *Elle*. François, brashly adolescent, used to speak up boldly whenever the subject was movies, and his age and assurance called attention to him. Hence the freelance job with *Elle*, but the magazine's regular employees made sure that he didn't get too much of a toe-hold there.

After Bazin got François out of [the reform school at] Villejuif, he gave him a job at *Travail et Culture* and François continued to do some freelance work as well. Bazin's friendship got him an invitation in July 1949 to the first Biarritz Film Festival (of which there would only be two). This event was conceived as a kind of anti-Cannes festival under the leadership of Jean Cocteau, who was also president of the jury. Other jury members included Henri Langlois, Robert Bresson, Alexandre Astruc, Roger Leenhardt, Jean Grémillon, Jean-George Auriol, François Mauriac, and Raymond Queneau. Its point was to show films that had not and would not otherwise be seen in France. According to Dudley Andrew, the *Festival du Film Maudit* (Festival of the Cursed Film) had a great impact on film criticism in France, and might be said to have been the first step toward the personal cinema of *auteurs* which would culminate in the New Wave ten years later.

The choice of films was eclectic: Bresson's *Les Dames du Bois de Boulogne* (1945), Grémillon's war-time *Lumière d'été* (1943), John Ford's *The Long Voyage Home* (1940), and the first screening of a restored complete version of Jean Vigo's *L'Atalante* (1934). But there were some new films, too: Jacques Tati's *Jour de fête*, and Orson Welles's *The Lady from Shanghai*. Apart from Bazin, Truffaut hardly knew any of the dignitaries, and was there, as it were, on sufferance, but seeing all these films he did not know made it one of the most exciting film events of his adolescence.

By 1950 Truffaut's freelance activities had increased. He continued to write un-signed (and therefore un-attributable) pieces for *Elle* and in July, he went to northern France to report on the shooting of Bresson's newest film, *The Diary of a Country Priest*, an adaptation of the novel by Georges Bernanos. He stayed for some time on the shoot, planning to get five articles out of this visit, but found it difficult to ring so many variations about the same subject.

By now, Robert had been called up for military service in the army – fortunately he drew West Germany rather than Indochina. François, already a great letter-writer, corresponded regularly with Robert. They had begun writing to each other in 1945 when Truffaut was only thirteen and bored with the summer camp to which he had been sent. As anyone who has ever seen *The 400 Blows* will remember, the great annual problem was 'What are we going to do with the kid over the summer vacation?' The early letters, from Binic, a seaside resort in Brittany, are not very interesting: 'Send me books, bread, dried bananas.' And, conversely, 'did you get the chocolate I sent? Was it good? What movies have you seen lately?' But with the extended separation and the growing maturity of the two boys, their letters became more and more interesting.

These were critical years – François had left his parents and was more or less fending for himself. He kept on going assiduously to the Cinémathèque. Although he did not know it, a director he was soon to admire greatly, Ingmar Bergman, was also spending time there in 1949. In *Bergman on Bergman*,[17] the Swedish director, when asked if he had been influenced by the Russian silent films or the early American cinema, replied, 'No, not until 1949, when I first went abroad. I was in Paris for a couple of months and was always running to the Cinémathèque in the Avenue de Messine. That was when I seriously began to study cinema. I'd never seen any old films before, only our Swedish silents.' It was there that he discovered films of Méliès, Feuillade, and *Pages from Satan's Book* by the great Danish director, Carl Dreyer. For him, as for the young Frenchmen, it was an uninterrupted parade of discoveries, whetting an insatiable appetite.

The Cinémathèque was also a place for social encounters. It was there that François met the first love of his life, a woman whose privacy Truffaut always respected (as shall we) by calling her 'Colette', as he did in his episode *Antoine et Colette* in *Love at 20*, and then later in *Stolen Kisses* and *Love on the Run*. This does not mean that he had not had any sexual encounters before. Initials of female names run all through the letters to Lachenay, and given his propensity for seeking out prostitutes, it is likely that his relationship with 'Colette' was not the first in a physical sense. But she was his first girlfriend.

In *Love at 20*, they meet at a concert for young people. As in the film, François then moved to a furnished flat on the same street where 'Colette' lived with her parents, who liked him very much. She, however, seemed to be interested in older boys. Nevertheless they were happy for a time, and the euphoria made François consider making his first movie. He planned to begin shooting in October 1950. Truffaut had twenty-five reels of blank 16mm stock, which would come to a hundred minutes of screening time, but planned on a running time of forty-five minutes, and so there was plenty of margin for error. It was going to be a documentary on first communions, but as Truffaut was never particularly interested in documentary, he planned to use, with modifications, a script he had already written about one girl ('Colette'?) taking her first communion. The film, however, was never made, for reasons which remain unclear.

Meanwhile André Bazin was laid up with tuberculosis in a sanatorium, and Truffaut went to visit him. They made plans to work together on a biography and filmography of Jean Renoir, with Bazin writing the text and Truffaut doing the necessary research. Truffaut also continued to write for *Elle* magazine, and all seemed to be going fairly well.

Then, in July 1950, he went off the rails. 'Colette' had not succeeded in passing her baccalauréat, and François, as a kind of compensation, had organized a surprise party for her birthday, July 21. He invited forty people from what he called the journalistic and 16mm milieus of Paris. It was a disaster. There was not enough to drink and some party crashers' unwelcome presence made others leave. And worse was to follow. As Truffaut described the evening in film terms in his letter to Lachenay, it was very much like Renoir's *Rules of the Game*, with Colette playing the part of the flirtatious Nora Gregor, going from one man to another while François moped about watching her − and watching doors close in his face.

François arrived home at seven o'clock the next morning, totally distraught. The 'great love affair of his life' had ended. 'I got into bed,' he wrote Lachenay, 'and slashed my wrists.' A few hours later, at eleven o'clock, Colette came to see him. She saw blood on the sheets and the floor and 'concluded that I had fainted.' But he was only asleep. 'I hadn't lost enough blood to faint. She looked after me, with terrifying calm, boiling water, making compresses and bandages. I stayed in bed two days with a fever. Now I've got a sling on my arm, and I tell people that I sprained it.'[18] Colette then went off to Monte Carlo without leaving François her address, or even a note. He felt very much alone, and being alone at eighteen is pretty frightening. He could not console himself with a visit to her parents, for she had told them what he had done, and they could no longer look on him favorably. He was despondent for several weeks. He would not go out alone. In an effort to 'cure' himself, he went out with friends, but he was only eighteen and the 'cure' didn't work.

In emotional and financial despair, he made two drastic decisions. He sold most of Lachenay's books to pay his debts. And he decided not to wait to be drafted for military service. In mid-October 1950 he volunteered for the army, asking to be sent, not to Vietnam, but to Germany. By the grace of God, he got what he asked for.

Chapter 2

Before enlisting, Truffaut asked Langlois if he could exchange his film files for free admission to the Cinémathèque's screenings after he got back from the army. Langlois agreed and so Truffaut rented a cart and brought all his 'treasures' to the Cinémathèque. His next step was to enlist. As he wrote to Lachenay: 'On October 29, 1950, I went to the barracks at Reuilly-Diderot to enlist; from there they sent me to the Rue St Dominique; from there to the Palace of Justice to get a copy of my police file. I won't get that for six or seven days. Then I went [to the town hall of the seventeenth arrondissement] to get a copy of my birth certificate. I'm to go back to the Rue St Dominique, and I think I'll be off in two weeks … Of course, I'm asking to be sent to West Germany.'[19]

Truffaut had wanted to join the army for only two years – then the usual period for military service – but since the war in Indochina was going badly, he was obliged to sign on for three. At least, he was assigned to the French Occupying forces in West Germany – less far away and much less dangerous. As one might imagine, his army career was nasty, brutish, and as short as he could make it.

One of his first letters from Germany was to Eric Rohmer, his friend from the Cinémathèque days. Writing from Wittlich in the French zone, he described the life as 'hell – incredible discipline and exhausting work – forced marches with thirty-two kilograms on my back, and classes in topography and trigonometry.' He told Rohmer he wanted to escape from Wittlich by becoming an editor of *The Information Magazine of the Occupying Troops in Germany*, which had offices in Baden-Baden. The job would pay 30,000 (old) francs a month and he would be automatically promoted; he would be able to have as much sex as he wanted and smoke whenever he wanted. To get the job, he needed a letter from Rohmer attesting to the fact that he had been an editor of Rohmer's bi-monthly magazine *La Gazette du Cinéma* from May to December in 1950, and giving a good report of his work on that periodical. He also had written to *Elle* magazine, he said, asking for a similar recommendation. He ended dramatically, saying that if Rohmer didn't send the letter and he died in Indochina, it would be Rohmer's fault.

As much as he hated the army, Truffaut did write to Lachenay that despite all that crawling around in the snow, the army did have a certain profound meaning – 'a real value' – of which the NCOs were unaware. Of course, he also tried to explain that he was able to pay his Paris hotel bills only by selling all his own books and Lachenay's as well: the hotel had lodged a complaint with the police. He also urged Lachenay to start reading Proust, whom François declared the equal of Balzac. We also learn that the 'faithless' Colette was taking care of any letters François received in Paris. In spite of all that had happened, she and François also exchanged letters.

Unfortunately, François's officers thought very highly of him because he had signed up for the army voluntarily. Determined to make an NCO out of him, they gave him responsibility for an artillery regiment. Although this relieved him of a lot of drudgery, Truffaut just didn't have the voice for it. When he shouted 'Forward, march!', nobody moved. His superiors gave him yelling lessons and generally kept a careful eye on him, which was for his own good, they said. It seemed, after all, that Truffaut was going to be sent to Indochina and they didn't want him to get shot down the first day he arrived.

There was still no news from the army magazine in Baden-Baden, and Truffaut was beginning to resign himself to a prompt departure for the Far East. He still had some hope. Film director Alain Resnais (who had just won an Oscar for his short film on Van Gogh) was trying to pull strings, as was André Bazin. François told Lachenay he was looking forward to a four-day furlough, during which he hoped they could meet up in Baden-Baden (Lachenay was also in the army in Germany).

By February 1951 basic training was over. But even during that period Truffaut managed to see Joseph Mankiewicz's *House of Strangers*, which he liked; Cocteau's *Orphée*, which, surprisingly, he didn't like – 'too flat, too cold, too glacial'; and *Rebel Without a Cause*, which he recommended highly to Lachenay. Truffaut also had the pleasure of seeing a twenty-page article of his on *The Rules of the Game* published in the special Jean Renoir issue of the luxurious new film magazine, *Raccords*. 'Printed on glossy paper,' he adds proudly in a letter to Robert.

And neither did Truffaut's sex life languish. He wrote to Lachenay about sleeping with 'G', but only as a 'more or less unconscious' way of getting even with Colette.

By June 1951, Truffaut had come to the decision that he would refuse to go to Indochina. He had more or less made up his mind to desert. His plan was to go to Cannes, where someone he knew would hide him in a villa. As it happened, he went to Paris, where film-maker Chris Marker (whom he had met at *Travail et Culture*) saw him wandering around St Germain des Prés in a pitiable state. Marker phoned Resnais, who immediately got in touch with Bazin, and François was driven to Bazin's house. On 15 August 1951, he wrote to Robert that he had gone to the Ministry of the Army, accompanied by André and Janine Bazin – and Colette – where it was decided that he was not technically a deserter, only absent without leave, because the period of his desertion was eight hours short of the specified time. He was to spend a week at a disciplinary barracks in Paris. Then he was to be admitted to a military hospital for a month and a half, all preparatory to a psychiatric examination at the chief military hospital, the Val de Grâce. A medical discharge did seem possible.

François, however, once he got out of the first military hospital, went into hiding for four days. He was arrested this time, and sent back to Germany, where his head was shaved and he was put in military prison for twelve days. Then they decided to send him to a hospital. Finally he was declared 'unfit for colonial service'. He wrote to Lachenay that the head doctor wanted to propose his military discharge for 'psychic troubles and nervous crises resulting from hereditary syphilis.' A regimen of penicillin was begun. By the middle of October he was out of military prison, and his hair was growing back.

Two months later he was sure that he would be out of the army in another two months. His enlistment would be annulled for technical reasons. He had not admitted to having syphilis and, indeed, he seemed to have been unaware of his condition. There had also been a misunderstanding about what corps he was enlisting for. And, of course, there was the medical report which stated that he was 'unfit for colonial service'.

Truffaut's syphilis was finally cured, and on January 3, 1952, he was given a medical discharge, the main stated reason being 'psychological instability'. The psychiatrist had concluded that letting him out of the army was as desirable from its point of view as it was from Truffaut's. Besides confirming his hatred of all things military (and curing him of syphilis), the army did Truffaut one great disservice: his hearing was permanently damaged as a result of that stint in the artillery.

Truffaut's departure from the army was not the same as that of his alter ego, Antoine Doinel, in *Stolen Kisses*. François was demobilized in Coblenz, not in Paris, so the quick trip to the brothel near the Place Clichy did not take place in real life – at least not immediately. Nor did the visit to Colette's parents, as far as we know.

We do know that on his return to Paris, Truffaut went to live with André and Janine Bazin, who by now had a two-year-old boy, Florent. As we have seen, Bazin had fallen ill in January 1950, and after spending six months in a hospital, he went to a sanatorium to recuperate. According to Janine Bazin, François came to live with them in their house in suburban Bry-sur-Marne early in 1952, although she admits she is not certain of her dates: 'I never thought I'd be talking about his life. I thought he would outlive me.'

The Bazins had a third-floor apartment in a run-down bourgeois building: three rooms, a kitchen, and a 'maid's room,' which was where François was installed. They were happy days. François at last had a family he liked and who liked him, and he enjoyed playing the role of Florent Bazin's older brother. The Bazins were not rich. When André went to Cannes in 1953 on behalf of a daily newspaper, there wasn't enough money to take François along.

If André Bazin, sixteen years older than François, was a father-figure for him, and Janine something like a big sister, Janine herself maintains that 'Truffaut did as much for us as we did for him'. Bazin had not had an unhappy childhood – he just found his parents boring. He had never had many friends, and so with François he discovered for the first time a real pal. Of course, it didn't stop them from arguing about films all the time – their tastes were not identical. Truffaut liked Hitchcock and Howard Hawks, for example, more than Bazin did. Too often for Janine, their discussions took place when André, never a good driver, was behind the wheel of the family car, and this used to make her nervous.

Bazin was an enormous help to Truffaut professionally. What was to become the most important and prestigious film magazine in France – and in the world, many would say – *Les Cahiers du Cinéma* (literally, *Cinema Notebooks*) had first appeared in April 1951, and Bazin was one of its founders. In March 1953, in the 21st issue of the magazine, he published Truffaut's first piece for the magazine. It was a review of David Miller's *Sudden Fear*, a psychological thriller starring Joan Crawford. As one of the co-editors of *Les Cahiers* later said, 'We should have known from that piece just how subversive François was already, for in that review there were a few cracks against the tradition of the French *cinéma de qualité* and praise for the American cinema, including a declaration of love to Gloria Grahame. He also managed to slip in his admiration for Renoir, Bresson, Leenhardt, and Cocteau.'

Writing for magazines like *Cahiers* did not bring in enough money to live on, even though Truffaut now occupied a cheap one-room apartment on the Rue des Martyrs, in the same neighborhood in which he had grown up. He found a job for several months in 1953 working for the Cinema Services of the Ministry of Agriculture. And in 1954 he started writing for a weekly called *Arts-Spectacles*. Originally devoted to painting and sculpture (it was then called *Arts*) it began to include movies, music and the theatre. *Arts-Spectacles* had a larger circulation than *Cahiers*, so Truffaut became better known. And yet it was an article for *Cahiers* that really made him a figure to contend with. Called 'A Certain Tendency of the French Cinema', it appeared in March, 1954.

The 'tendency' in question was so-called 'psychological realism', which Truffaut considered to be neither psychological nor realistic. In the first paragraph he sketched out its limitations. A quiet enough beginning, but then came an attack on such popular and highly regarded directors as Jean Delannoy, Claude Autant-Lara and Yves Allégret as all too dependent on their script-writers. They were not, Truffaut charged, essentially film-makers because they depended too much on finding what they considered good scripts. Then he launched into a violent attack against the writers – Jean Aurenche, Pierre Bost, Jacques Sigurd, and others – who claimed to have faithfully adapted for the screen such novels as André Gide's *Symphonie pastorale*, Raymond Radiguet's *Devil in the Flesh*, and Colette's *Le Blé en herbe*. Finally, Truffaut launched his battle cry; what the French cinema needed was not its 'tradition of quality' but a cinema of *auteurs* (authors). This was, I believe, the first use of the word '*auteur*' in association with the cinema. It did not necessarily mean that the director of a film had actually to write original scripts, but rather that the director should be the person responsible for a film. A good director could transcend a bad script because he did not simply film it; he put himself into his work regardless of how the script originated.

Today these ideas have penetrated the whole world of film criticism. At the time, they aroused an enormous outcry. Bazin himself was not in total agreement with Truffaut, but he made sure the article got published, and it made Truffaut famous – or infamous. The language of the piece was violent, and the article was violently attacked.

When Truffaut collected his selected film criticism in 1975 in *Les Films de ma vie* (*The Films of My Life*),[20] to many people's disappointment, he did not include this article. (It was posthumously re-published in 1988.) He said his reason was that so much time had passed that many of the people he had attacked were no longer working, and little purpose would be served by publishing diatribes against forgotten films.

1954 was a productive year for Truffaut: he wrote the original treatment of *Breathless*, based on a news item, which he was later to give to Jean-Luc Godard who, with many changes (Truffaut's hero is not killed at the end, for example), made from it his first feature film.[21] Truffaut also made his first film that year, a 19-minute silent short, filmed in 16mm, called *Une Visite*. Jacques Rivette was the cameraman, and it was shot in the apartment of Jacques Doniol-Valcroze (a film-maker and editor of *Cahiers du Cinéma*), and featured his young daughter. Truffaut had no story when he started, just two actors and one actress, plus the little girl. So he had to improvise, which, he later admitted, was madness for a newcomer.

Although Alain Resnais is usually credited as the editor of this film, he says that he only made a few suggestions, at Truffaut's request. The film has a story of sorts, about a young man who is using the classified ads to find a room. After some phone calls he goes to visit the flat of a young lady – and takes the room. Her brother-in-law brings her his daughter to look after for the weekend. The brother-in-law flirts with the girl, and so does the new lodger. But she rebuffs them, and the young man packs his bags and leaves with the brother-in-law.

Truffaut always claimed that the film had no interest whatsoever and denied everyone's request to see it. Indeed, for a long time, it seems to have been lost, but Robert Lachenay found a print in the early 80s. Although Truffaut still didn't want anyone to see the film, he nevertheless went through the administrative procedure of getting what is called a *visa de contrôle* on March 12, 1982, thus giving the film a legal existence. He even had it blown up into 35mm because some Japanese admirers wanted to see it, and the film was duly sent to Tokyo for a screening.

That same year Truffaut wrote a short story which appeared in the May 1955 issue of a literary monthly called *La Parisienne*. It was called, significantly, *Antoine et l'orphéline* (*Antoine and the Orphan Girl*). Its hero was not yet Truffaut's alter ego, but this Antoine does have a friend called René, as in *The 400 Blows*, and his parents live in a suburb called J., like Juvisy. Antoine has also gotten out of a centre for juvenile delinquents, and enlisted in the army to avoid being drafted. The other elements of the story are less auto-biographical, but there are little details, like a rhapsody on women's stockings, which antic-ipates those on women's legs in *The Man Who Loved Women* many years later.

1954 was also the year in which Truffaut first met Roberto Rossellini. This meeting in Paris came about as a result of a letter the *Cahiers* group wrote to Rossellini (who was shooting *Fear* in Germany) to ask him to protest against the badly dubbed version of *Viaggio in Italia* (*Strangers*) which was then circulating in Paris under the title of *That Naples Divorcée*. As a result of the letter, and Rossellini's reactions to it, the dubbed version was withdrawn and the original subtitled version was shown in the art houses of Paris. Truffaut and the others later met Rossellini at the Hotel Raphael, where he always stayed while in Paris. Rossellini soon became another father-figure for Truffaut, and a director who may have had as much influence on his films as Hitchcock did.

As it happens, Truffaut also met Hitchcock in 1954. According to Claude Chabrol, Hitchcock was working at the suburban Billancourt studios on *To Catch a Thief* and Truffaut, along with Chabrol, went out there to tape an interview with him. The interview apparently went well but somehow, on their way out of the studio, the two young men fell into a swimming pool, tape-recorder and all. They were fished out and given a dressing room in the studio in which to dry off. François said, 'This tape recorder is all wet, we'll have to dry it out.' So he plugged it into the wall, and it caused a terrifying short-circuit, which destroyed the machine.

Truffaut remembered the incident somewhat differently: he says it took place in Joinville, where Hitchcock was post-synching *To Catch a Thief* in a darkened auditorium. They intro-duced themselves to Monsieur Hitchcock, who asked them to wait for him in the bar on the other side of the courtyard. The two came out of the darkened auditorium, their eyes momentarily blinded by the bright daylight, and made for the bar which was only fifteen yards away. Without noticing, they walked onto a frozen pool of water. The ice broke, and they found themselves up to their chests in icy water. Chabrol raised the dripping tape-recorder. 'As in a Hitchcock film,' Truffaut said, 'there was no way out.' The pool was curved inward and every time they got to the edge, they slipped back in again. Finally someone helped them out. And the rest of the story is as Chabrol described it. Hitchcock looked at these two wet journalists, but made no comment on their state. He simply suggested that they postpone the interview until that evening, at the bar of the Hotel Plaza Athénée.

The unreliability of reminiscence, the plague of the biographer, is further underlined by Hitchcock's own version of the story. According to Truffaut, once back in Hollywood, Hitchcock told his friends that Chabrol had been dressed as a priest and Truffaut as a policeman. The following year, when Hitchcock came back to Paris, he picked Truffaut and Chabrol out of a group of journalists and said, 'Gentlemen, I think of you every time I see ice cubes clinking against each other in a glass of whisky.'

Truffaut saw Rossellini whenever he came to Paris, and became his assistant for nearly two years starting in 1956. Rossellini had just come out of the turbulent period of his life with Ingrid Bergman, when the films they made together were considered by most to have been disastrous. Today, films like *Viaggio in Italia*, *Europa '51*, *L'amore*, and *Angst*, are often successfully revived. But neither of the two projects that Truffaut worked on with Rossellini, *Carmen* and *Le Destin d'Isa*, ever got made for reasons that still remain obscure.

Rossellini, Truffaut later said, took over from Bazin as his mentor. He helped Truffaut to straighten out his ideas on cinema. Rossellini was all for clarity, simplicity, a coherent and logical discourse. He also helped Truffaut to look at American films with a little more objectivity, and impressed the young man with his hatred of clever credit titles, pre-credit sequences, flashbacks: in other words, everything that was merely decorative and did not serve the idea of the film or the nature of its characters. Truffaut once said that *The 400 Blows* owed much to Rossellini's film about an orphaned young boy: *Germany, Year Zero*.

Rossellini could also be considered the father of the New Wave movement – he was the first to read and comment on the scripts of Chabrol's *Le Beau Serge* and Truffaut's *The 400 Blows* and he gave advice and help to Jean Rouch, Godard, Rohmer, and Rivette.

Truffaut did not, however, work full-time for Rossellini. He continued his journalistic work, and in September 1956, he went to the Venice Film Festival to report on it for *Cahiers* and *Arts*. There, on the beach at the Lido, a distinguished French producer, Pierre Braunberger, introduced Truffaut to Madeleine Morgenstern. What happened was not, as Braunberger has said, *le coup de foudre*, love at first sight, but love it was.

Madeleine, a warm and beautiful young woman, had been brought up in the world of the cinema. Her father, Ignace Morgenstern, was of Hungarian-Jewish origin; he had emigrated to France before World War II, and, after the difficult period of the Occupation (when the family hid out in a small town near Lyon), he became the head of Cocinor, the third most important film distributor in France. He was also head of seven or eight production companies. Soon Truffaut and Madeleine were talking about marriage. Morgenstern at first was not happy with their relationship – after all, Truffaut had harshly criticised many of the films he had produced. But on further acquaintance, he grew to like him – so much so that he posed only one condition for his acceptance of the marriage: he, Ignace Morgenstern, was to be the man to produce Truffaut's first feature film, *The 400 Blows*. Truffaut had already written the first script and Morgenstern liked it.

When François let it be known to Madeleine that he wanted to make a short film, *Les Mistons*, first, Morgenstern said to his associate, Marcel Berbert, 'François wants to make a film: we must create a company for him.' François chose Les Films du Carosse as the name for his company because Renoir's *Le Carosse d'or* (*The Golden Coach*) was one of his favorite films. When François proposed going to a bank that specialized in lending money for films, Berbert, unknown to him, phoned ahead of time and told the bank manager to lend Truffaut the 20,000 francs he needed, saying that Berbert (and therefore Morgenstern) couldn't put it on paper but would stand as guarantor for the money. Robert Lachenay, who had just inherited some money from his grandmother, also invested in the film.

In May of 1957, at the Cannes Festival, Louis Malle introduced Truffaut to Jeanne Moreau, whom he directed in *Ascenseur pour l'échafaud* (*Elevator to the Gallows*, also known as *Frantic*). Truffaut was immediately fascinated with her, and their friendship was to last, with a few bad patches, the rest of his life. Of course, we cannot know precisely what his feelings were when they first met. In any case, he was engaged to Madeleine, and Jeanne Moreau's ball card was, and would remain, quite full for a long time.

Madeleine and François were married on October 29, 1957. Bazin and Rossellini were their two witnesses, and it was at the wedding that Madeleine met François's parents for the first time. Roland and Janine Truffaut were not happy about the ceremony. It wasn't in a church, and there seemed to be more talk about movies than there ought to have been.

It is quite possible that Roland was unhappy about not being one of François's witnesses.

Before making *Les Mistons* there was another project in Truffaut's mind: a short film about the Eiffel Tower. It was to run twenty-five minutes: a story about a young man from the country who longs to visit the Eiffel Tower, but has some difficulty in finding it – it's easy to see from a distance, but he keeps taking the wrong streets the closer he gets to it. There is a young girl, too, and they are eventually to meet at the top of the Tower. The film was never made (Braunberger says Truffaut just lost interest in it), but shots of the Eiffel Tower were to begin Truffaut's first feature, and it would appear in many of his films. Truffaut, brought up almost in the shadow of the Sacré Coeur, and except for a brief period of two years always living on the Right Bank, was obsessed with the Eiffel Tower (which is, of course, on the Left Bank). In the attic of the building where Les Films du Carosse is located, there is a room full of Eiffel Towers – models, souvenirs, photographs, engravings. All of his intimates were aware of this obsession, but none of them was able to explain it. Once he could afford it, he always succeeded in living in a house that had a view of the Tower.

The shooting of *Les Mistons* had begun in the Provençal city of Nîmes in August 1957. The film was based on an eponymous short story from a collection by Maurice Pons called *Virginales*. The plot was quite simple: a gang of young 'mischief-makers' (amateurs, recruited by an advertisement in a local newspaper), prompted, no doubt, by an unconscious desire for the heroine of the film (the young and perky Bernadette Laffont), follow her and her boyfriend (Gérard Blain) everywhere they go, plaguing them as much as possible. The boyfriend is accidentally killed while mountain climbing, and the gang of kids, seeing how much Bernadette is suffering, realize contritely what brats they had been.

Truffaut had already chosen Gérard Blain when he met Blain's fiancée, Bernadette, and he wanted to have her in the film, too. Blain was not keen on the idea; he thought that the cinema was not the proper milieu for a young lady. But Truffaut (and Bernadette) insisted, and *Les Mistons* was the beginning of a long film career for Laffont.

Robert Lachenay was director of production, and Claude de Givray was one of the two assistant directors. As we have seen, Truffaut had met Givray, who was to become one of his best friends and one of his most important collaborators, by chance at the Ciné-Club du Quartier Latin. Givray later said that he noticed Truffaut because in the debates following the film he was so aggressive. Givray had come to love movies because he was a school friend of Michel Perez (now arguably the best film critic in France), and the two of them started going every Tuesday night to the Studio Parnasse, an art house in Montparnasse. Tuesday nights were special, because a movie quiz was held by J. L. Chiray, the director of the theatre, and those who won got free admission the following week. One Tuesday night in 1952, Givray had plucked up his courage and spoke to Truffaut, alone that night (Chabrol was doing his military service, and Jacques Rivette had gone home to Rouen to recuperate after an illness). They talked, and, since Givray had a car, he drove François back to the Place Clichy.

Short as *Les Mistons* was, it did not pass un-noticed: it won Truffaut a director's prize at the 1958 Brussels Film Festival, and a gold medal at the Mannheim (West Germany) festival.

That same year, Truffaut's friendship with Givray was further cemented. On his return from military service in Algeria, Givray found that his girlfriend, Lucette Deuss, was working as Truffaut's assistant. They had first met the year before when Givray was working with Philippe de Broca on Claude Chabrol's first film, *Le Beau Serge*. Born in Java, Lucette was of Dutch origin, but since her father, a tea planter, had been transferred to the company's

Decades Never Start On Time

head office in Paris, she arrived in Paris at the age of four. She had experience as a make-up person and secretary, so de Broca hired her to work on the Chabrol film. Truffaut, then preparing *The 400 Blows*, had asked de Broca if he knew of a good secretary, and he suggested Lucette. (She stayed on until Truffaut's death.) Givray and Lucette married in 1963, and Truffaut, who adored this kind of coincidental situation – introducing a friend to a girl with whom he was already in love – was godfather to their first son, Georges.[22]

In the early spring of 1958, some of the suburbs of Paris were flooded. Truffaut had already been fascinated with floods; he liked seeing them in newsreels, except that he had always said to himself, 'What a shame there are never any actors in such sequences.' He went to producer Pierre Braunberger and said, 'I can get (actor) Jean-Claude Brialy and a girl (Caroline Dim); give me a little raw film stock and we can improvise a film.' Braunberger agreed, and, borrowing Chabrol's car, off they went to the suburbs. But by that time, Truffaut said later, 'there wasn't much floodwater left, and we didn't have the heart to shoot much film. It wasn't, after all, so very funny and we were ashamed of making a comic film with all those people. Still, we did shoot the 2400 feet of film we had, and went back to Paris.' Truffaut was convinced the whole thing had been a mistake and asked Braunberger to let him abandon the idea.

In the meantime, however, Godard had somehow seen the rushes, and said he would like to do something with the material as long as he could ignore Truffaut's original conception. He worked quickly in order to keep the costs down, writing the commentary and choosing the music himself. When Truffaut saw the finished product, he thought it was entertaining, but didn't want his name on the credits. Finally, they agreed to co-sign the film, *Histoire d'eau*.

Most people didn't find the result amusing, but it was significant in its revelation of Godard's attitude towards filmed reality as something to be played with, re-created, re-formed by the process of editing – an attitude completely different from that of Truffaut. Furthermore, it displayed Godard's interest in the kind of commentary that doesn't actually comment on what we are seeing, but acts rather in counterpoint to it. The music Godard had chosen was a mélange of 18th-century rococo, jazz, and some *put-put* drums which appropriately gave the feeling of both motorboats and pumping machines. The circumstances of the filming had made the recording of direct sound difficult, so Godard dubbed Brialy's voice. No one remembers why. Perhaps because Brialy was otherwise occupied, or perhaps just to save time.

As Truffaut later declared, *Histoire d'eau* was neither his nor Godard's best film. (The title, of course, was a pun on the contemporary 'scandalous' novel *Histoire d'O ... – The Story of O ...*).[23]

Three films released in 1959–60, Truffaut's *The 400 Blows*, Chabrol's *Le Beau Serge*, and Alain Resnais's *Hiroshima mon amour* launched *la nouvelle vague* ('The New Wave'). The term 'New Wave' is commonly thought to have been launched by the journalist Françoise Giroud, in the weekly magazine *L'Express*. But Truffaut's Japanese translator Koichi Yamada wrote to him in 1976 pointing out that he had dug up back issues of *L'Express* and discovered that although Madame Giroud had indeed used that phrase in 1957, it had nothing to do with the film-makers of the period.

I have already mentioned the influence of the Cinémathèque Française, where the 'New Wave' directors had met, and where they were exposed to the great films of the past, films that were no longer to be seen anywhere else in France. But there is more to it than that. Because their films were made on lower budgets and with smaller crews, and also because

Kodak had just launched Triple X, a 'faster' film which required less artificial lighting, the 'New Wave' was also an economic revolution that had been foreshadowed more than a decade before, in 1947, by Jean-Pierre Melville's first film, based on the Vercors novel *Le Silence de la mer* (*The Silence of the Sea*). It was, as Tom Milne has written, 'entirely an outlaw production, since Melville had no union card, or authorization to buy film stock, and no rights to the Vercors novel.'[24]

And, in 1948, Alexandre Astruc wrote an influential article in *L'Ecran Français* called 'La caméra-stylo' ('The Camera Fountain Pen') in which he argued that films could be made just as personally as an author writes with pen and ink. He maintained that the whole apparatus of film production was unnecessary, and even harmful, and went so far as to say that one could make a film out of anything, even, he suggested (perhaps playfully) Montesquieu's *L'Esprit des lois*.[25]

Then, in 1955, Agnès Varda made her first feature, *La Pointe Courte*. It, too, was an independent – even wildcat – production, and as it was not a full-length feature, it opened at the Studio Parnasse along with Jean Vigo's first film, another wildcat production from 1929, *À propos de Nice*. From Truffaut's review (reprinted in *The Films in my Life*), one gets the impression that he did not like the film unreservedly: 'The main fault with this film … is that it is loosely directed. I am not speaking of the technique, which is surprisingly mature for a first film, but about the completely slack direction of the actors.' Nevertheless, he thought that it showed that one could make a film outside the industry.

The 400 Blows, however, was made within the norms of the industry. It was produced by his company, with the help of a distributor guarantee from Cocinor, Morgenstern's company. It was not expensive, but Truffaut was shrewd enough to realize that as he had to shoot it in black-and-white, he could make it more 'spectacular' by making it in Dyaliscope, the French version of the wide-screen anamorphic process.

The main problem was finding someone to play the role of a thirteen-year-old boy, whom he named Antoine Doinel. (When asked at the time where he had gotten the name Doinel, Truffaut couldn't remember; only later did he recall that Renoir's assistant and Girl Friday in Paris – she lived in his house – was a splendid woman called Ginette Doinel. And he had, of course, already used Antoine in the short story called *Antoine and the Orphan Girl*.)

He did not use the system of advertising in the newspapers; instead, the important movie columnist France Roche included a note about Truffaut's search for a thirteen-year-old boy in her column in the daily *France-Soir*, and Truffaut received two hundred letters of application. First, he eliminated systematically all letters from outside Paris, for he did not want to oblige these kids to make the trip to Paris. That still left one hundred to be given screen tests. By far the best was Jean-Pierre Léaud who had made his entrance by announcing brashly, 'I hear you want a kid who shoots his mouth off a lot.'

Léaud had already played a bit part two years earlier in a film called *La Tour, prends garde*, and he had also done a bit of dubbing. He was, as Truffaut wrote,[26] 'a difficult child who was studying in a prep school for kids who had been thrown out of other schools. The shooting of the film did him a lot of good, because he was more at ease with adults than with kids his own age … He was terrific in the film, but he was so frightened that he was going to appear unlikeable that he would smile all the time. For three whole months I stopped him from smiling on camera … and I'm sure I was right to do so.' Another problem was that of the setting. Truffaut would have preferred to set the film in the period in which this, at least semi-autobiography, took place: during the Occupation. But that would have made it too expensive. They would have had to get old automobiles and period clothes, avoid TV antennas, and all the rest. Furthermore, he felt that the clothes of that period would look too ridiculous now, so he decided to update the story to 1959. The shooting began on November 10, 1958.

On the next day, André Bazin, long ill, died. Truffaut, naturally, was devastated, but now that all the actors and technicians had been hired, he had to go on. He would dedicate the film to Bazin, who, one can be almost certain, would not have wanted Truffaut to stop work on it.

None of the shooting (the lighting cameraman was Henri Decaë) was done in studio, and the crew was as small as the unions would allow. And the film was almost entirely post-synchronized, except for the scene with the psychologist, which worked out wonderfully, and the scenes in the school which are so noisy they are hard to understand.

The shooting ended on January 3, 1959. Truffaut's first child, Laura, was born on January 22. For years, people thought that his first two children, Laura and Eva, were named after the films by Otto Preminger and Joseph Losey. Not true — he and Madeleine just liked the names. It is, however, perhaps significant that the usual forms for these names in France were Laure and Eve.

The 400 Blows was ready for the Cannes Festival in May. With his first child and his first film appearing the same year, 27-year-old Truffaut was no longer a boy, no longer without a family, no longer someone who went to Cannes to write about other people's films. This time he went to Cannes to compete with films by directors from all over the world, most of whom were much older than himself. And winning the Best Director prize catapulted him to world-wide fame.

SOURCE: 'DRAFT MANUSCRIPT: AN UNTITLED BIOGRAPHY OF TRUFFAUT', ARCHIVE DOCUMENT, 1988–9, PRIVATE COLLECTION, EDITH & KAREN SMOLENS, 115 PAGES (EXTRACTS: 'PROLOGUE', 2 PAGES; 'CHAPTER ONE', 14 PAGES; 'CHAPTER TWO', 13 PAGES)

Notes

1. Michael Pye and Lynda Miles, *The Movie Brats: How the Movie Generation Took Over Hollywood* (New York: Holt, Rinehart and Winston, 1979).
2. Roud is referring to the postwar legislation in the USA that gave certain rights to soldiers returning from World War II, among which were assistance with mortgage loans and university tuition fees.
3. The quotation should be 'I write for myself and strangers', Gertrude Stein, *The Making of Americans* (1925).
4. Chapter three is sketched out in the 'Outline' document but it does not appear to have been written; at least, we do not have a copy of it.
5. Jerry Wald (1911–1962), writer, director and producer, working in the 1950s as an independent producer of films distributed by 20th Century-Fox.
6. Lines from 'Burnt Norton', T. S. Eliot, 1936.
7. Roud's note: Not the Palme d'or, the Grand Prize, which went to the late Marcel Camus for his forgettable, and forgotten, *Orfeu Negro*.
8. Roud's note: On checking dates, I discovered that *Angèle* had come out only in 1934, the year after Roland and Janine got married. Of course, it is possible that Roland had read the Jean Giono story *Un de Baumugnes* on which Pagnol based the film, or he may have been simply conflating two memories.

9. Roud's note: In his 1975 preface to André Bazin's book, *The Cinema of the Occupation* (Paris: UGE, 1975). But in the intervening years, his memory must have played a trick on him, for *Paradis perdu* only came out in September 1940, several months after the French capitulated to the Germans and the war was, for them, over.

10. Roud's note: Many years later Truffaut told Claude de Givray that he didn't have the strength or the courage for mountain climbing.

11. Roud's note: François's paternal grandfather was a stone-cutter, and his principal occupation was carving tomb-stones. François would sometimes spend the day with him in cemeteries.

12. Roud's note: In a statement made in 1968 about the student uprising, Truffaut said he left school at the age of 14.

13. Roud's note: Alain Resnais, however, recalls one 45-minute pro-Nazi documentary.

14. Claude Véga was best known as an impersonator, especially of French female stars and singers. He appears in Truffaut's *Domicile conjugal* (1970) as the strange neighbour who turns out to be a television performer (doing an impersonation of Delphine Seyrig in *L'Année dernière à Marienbad*!).

15. Roud's note: Truffaut was later to co-produce Jacques Rivette's first feature, *Paris nous appartient* (*Paris Belongs to Us*) and gossip had it that he used to court Rivette's sister, a pharmacist, but whose main interest for him was said to have been the mere fact that she was Rivette's sister.

16. Roud's note: Dudley Andrew, *André Bazin* (New York: OUP, 1978), 150.

17. Roud's note: *Bergman on Bergman*, interviews with Ingmar Bergman by Stig Bjorkman, Torsten Manns, and Jonas Sims (London and New York: Secker & Warburg, 1973).

18. Roud's note: *François Truffaut: Correspondence* (Paris: Hatier, 1988), 42–3.

19. Roud's note: *François Truffaut: Correspondence*, 50.

20. Roud's note: *Les Films de ma vie* (Paris: Flammarion, 1975); *The Films in My Life* (New York: Simon & Schuster, 1978).

21. Roud's note: Truffaut's treatment was published later in *L'Avant-Scène du Cinéma*, 79, March 1968.

22. Roud's note: Georges de Givray, under the name of Georges Demonceaux was later to play the kid in Truffaut's *Small Change* [*Argent de poche*] (1976) who falls in love with his best friend's mother.

23. Pauline Réage, *Histoire d'O* (Paris: Jean-Jacques Pauvert, 1954).

24. Roud's note: see Richard Roud (ed.), *Cinema: A Critical Dictionary* (London: Secker & Warburg, and New York: Viking Press, 1980), 682.

25. In fact Astruc says that, if the seventeenth-century philosopher René Descartes were alive today, he would be writing his philosophy on film. In the same article he quotes Jacques Feyder saying that he could make a film from any material, even Montesquieu's treatise in political philosophy, *L'Esprit des lois* (1748).

26. Roud's note: In an interview in *Cinéma 59*, June 1959.

BIBLIOGRAPHY

Bibliographical references for material by Roud included in the anthology

'Britain in America', *Sight & Sound*, 26.3, Winter 1956–7, 119–23.

Max Ophüls: An Index (London: BFI, 1958), 3–6.

'Face to face: James Agee', *Sight & Sound*, 28.2, Spring 1959, 98–100.

'Face to face: André Bazin', *Sight & Sound*, 28.3, Summer 1959, 176–9.

'How to see a movie (in the USA)', archive document, 1959, Richard Roud collection, Howard Gotlieb Archival Research Center, Boston, box 1, F8, item j.30, 13 pages.

'Novel novel; fable fable?', *Sight & Sound*, 30.1, Spring 1962, 84–8.

'NFT 10th anniversary: the first ten years', brochure, National Film Theatre, October 1962, 8 pages.

'The Left Bank: Marker, Varda, Resnais', *Sight & Sound*, 32.1, Winter 1962–3, 24–7.

'Festival at the Lincoln Center', *Guardian*, 10 October 1963, 8.

'End of Bardolotry', *Guardian*, 31 October 1963, 7.

'Muriel observed', *Guardian*, 20 March 1964, 13.

'Cannes ho!', *Guardian*, 30 April 1964, 8.

'Rondo Galant: the world of Jacques Demy', *Sight & Sound*, 33.3, Summer 1964, 136–9.

'*The Red Desert*', *Sight & Sound*, 34.2, Spring 1965, 76–80.

'Object lesson', *Guardian*, 8 April 1965, 9.

'Anguish: *Alphaville*', *Sight & Sound*, 34.4, Autumn 1965, 164–6.

'New films', *Guardian*, 15 April 1966, 11.

'Film criticism in Britain', archive document, May 1967, Richard Roud collection, Howard Gotlieb Archival Research Center, Boston, box 1, F8, item j.27, 8 pages.

'*Masculin féminin*', *Guardian*, 22 June 1967, 5.

'*Far from Vietnam*', *Guardian*, 20 December 1967, 5.

'A Langlois unto himself', *Guardian*, 23 February 1968, 8.

'Weekend in Paris', *Guardian*, 2 April 1968, 8.

'The end of the Cannes party', *Guardian*, 25 May 1968, 7.

'Minimal cinema: *Chronicle of Anna Magdalena Bach*', *Sight & Sound*, 37.3, Summer 1968, 134–5.

'The Cossacks go in at Pesaro', *Guardian*, 6 June 1968, 6.

'If with no buts', *Guardian*, 19 December 1968, 6.

'*Le Gai Savoir*', *Sight & Sound*, 38.4, Autumn 1969, 210–11.

'The varieties of tyranny', *Guardian*, 4 July 1970, 8.

'Films to change the world?', *Guardian*, 26 October 1970, 8.

'Fathers and Sons', Sight & Sound, 40.2, Spring 1971, 60–4.

'Look back in shame', *Guardian*, 4 May 1971, 8.

'Going Between', *Sight & Sound*, 40.3, Summer 1971, 158–9.

'The international gravy train', *Guardian*, 11 December 1971, 8.

'Visconti misses the gondola', *Guardian*, 22 December 1971, 8.

Jean-Marie Straub (London: Secker & Warburg; New York: Viking Press, 1971), 'Introduction' and 'Background', 6–27.

'Daddy of 'em all', *Guardian*, 6 April 1972, 10.

'The dragon and despair', *Guardian*, 1 August 1972, 10.

'It takes two to tango', *Guardian*, 20 November 1972, 8.

'How can we know the dancer from the dance?', programme, Film Society of Lincoln Center gala in honour of Fred Astaire, 30 April 1973.

'Hollywood embers', *Guardian*, 29 October 1973, 10.

'Apple pie bedlam', *Guardian*, 27 November 1973, 14.

'*The Rules of the Game*', in Philip Nobile (ed.), *Favorite Movies: Critics' Choice* (New York: Macmillan, 1973), 97–104.

'Hold the front page', *Guardian*, 19 February 1974, 10.

'*The Passenger*', *Sight & Sound*, 44.3, Summer 1975, 134–7.

'Film of the century', *Guardian*, 7 January 1976, 8.

'Memorandum on processes of prospection and selection', archive document, 16 December 1976, Richard Roud collection, Howard Gotlieb Archival Research Center, Boston, box 1, F17, item b (also: box 3, F10, 1971–6), 6 pages.

'Movies versus Motion Pictures', archive document, 1976, Richard Roud collection, Howard Gotlieb Archival Research Center, Boston, box 1, F8, item j.28, 3 pages.

'Henri Langlois', *Sight & Sound*, 46.2, Spring 1977, 119.

'The Left Bank revisited', *Sight & Sound*, 46.3, Summer 1977, 143–5.

'The baggy-trousered philanthropist', *Guardian*, 28 December 1977, 8.

Cinema: A Critical Dictionary: The Major Film-makers, Richard Roud (ed.), (New York: Viking Press; London: Martin Secker & Warburg, 1980), 'Robert Bresson', 141–53, 'Louis Feuillade and the serial', 348–59, 'Jean Renoir: to 1939', 835–45.

'London and New York', *Sight & Sound*, 50.4, Autumn 1981, 233–6.

'Gross can be beautiful', *Guardian*, 15 July 1982, 9.

'Rainer Werner Fassbinder, biter bit', *Sight & Sound*, 51.4, Autumn 1982, 288–9.

A Passion for Films: Henri Langlois and the Cinémathèque Française (New York: Viking Press, 1983), 'Friends and enemies', 104–24.

Rediscovering French Film, Mary Lea Bandy (ed.), (New York: Museum of Modern Art, 1983), 'Introduction', 13–36, 'Melville', 161–4.

'Decades Never Start On Time', archive document, 1983–4, Richard Roud collection, Howard Gotlieb Archival Research Center, Boston, box one, F.9, items a–h, 40 pages.

'The moral taste of Lotte Eisner', *Sight & Sound*, 53.3, Summer 1984, 139–40.

'Remembering Losey', *Sight & Sound*, 54.1, Winter 1984–5, 40–3.

'Draft Manuscript: An Untitled Biography of Truffaut', archive document, 1988–9, private collection, Edith & Karen Smolens, 115 pages.

Bibliographical references for Roud material mentioned but not included in the anthology

'*The Man in the Grey Flannel Suit*', *Sight & Sound*, 26.2, Autumn 1956, 97.

'*The empty streets*', *Sight & Sound*, 26.4, Spring 1957, 191–5.

The early work of Robert Bresson', *Film Culture*, number 20, 1959, 44–52.

'Two cents on the rouble', *Sight & Sound*, 27.5, Summer 1958, 245–7.

'The naturalness of Renoir', in William Whitebait (ed.), *International Film Annual*, number 3 (London: John Calder, 1959), 105–15.

'The French line', *Sight & Sound*, 29.4, Autumn 1960, 166–71.

'Five films', *Sight & Sound*, 30.1, Winter 1960–1, 8–11.

'Rogopag', *Guardian*, 28 March 1963, 8.

'Film art's new frame', *New York Herald Tribune*, 25 August 1963.

'*Les Vampires*', *Sight & Sound*, 33.2, Spring 1964, 96–7.

'Prestige through print', *Guardian*, 9 April 1964, 8 .

'New York Film Festival', *Guardian*, 5 October 1964, 7.

'A proposal for a Lincoln Center Film Institute', document co-written with Amos Vogel, Richard
     Roud collection, Howard Gotlieb Archival Research Center, Boston, dated November 1964,
     box 21, F4, item D.1.3, 23 pages.

'Playing the festival game', *Sunday Times* magazine, 3 July 1966, 30–2.

Jean-Luc Godard, London: Secker & Warburg, 1967, 176 pages; second edition, London:
     Thames & Hudson, 1970, 192 pages; third edition, London: BFI/Palgrave Macmillan, 2010,
     190 pages.

'André Bazin: his fall and rise', *Sight & Sound*, 37.2, Spring 1968, 94–6.

'Richard Roud at Cannes', *Guardian*, 14 May 1968, 6.

'Festival films', *Guardian*, 22 June 1968, 7.

'Celluloid renaissance', *Guardian*, 1 July 1968, 6.

'Verse against Vespas', *Guardian*, 11 February 1970, 8.

'Cable TV and the arts', report for Sloan Commission, 15 March 1971, Richard Roud collection,
     Howard Gotlieb Archival Research Center, Boston, box 21, F4, item D.1.3; also box 23, F13,
     item 3, 37 pages.

'Citizen Bogdanovich', *Guardian*, 6 November 1971, 10.

'Frontiersman', *Guardian*, 21 March 1972, 12.

'London Journal', *Film Comment*, 8.1, March–April 1972, 2, 4, 6.

'Godard is Dead, Long Live Godard-Gorin, Tout va bien!', *Sight & Sound*, 41.3, Summer 1972,
     122–4.

'Cannes Journal', *Film Comment*, 8.3, September–October 1972, 2, 4.

'Cordon Buñuel', *Guardian*, 11 November 1972, 10.

'London Journal', *Film Comment*, 9.2, March–April 1973, 2, 4.

'SLON', *Sight & Sound*, 42.2, Spring 1973, 82–3.

'Melodrama in realistic setting', *Guardian*, 5 July 1973, 10.

'Berlin Journal', *Film Comment*, 9.5, September–October 1973, 2, 64, 66.

'People We Like: Janet Gaynor', *Film Comment*, 10.1, January–February 1974, 37.

'In Broad Daylight', programme, Film Society of Lincoln Center gala in honour of 'London
     Journal', *Film Comment*, 10.2, March–April 1974, 2, 4.

'Alfred Hitchcock', 29 April 1974; reprinted in *Film Comment*, 10.4, July–August 1974, 36.

'The Phantom of Liberty', *Guardian*, 27 September 1974, 12.

'Berlin Journal', *Film Comment*, 10.5, September–October 1974, 4.

'Golden bull', *Guardian*, 26 February 1975, 10.

'Knokke Journal', *Film Comment*, 11.2, March–April 1975, 4, 64.

'Rotterdam Journal', *Film Comment*, 11.3, May–June 1975, 2, 62.

'[Sonimage]', *Guardian*, 31 July 1975, 8.

'Scatological dilemmas', *Guardian*, 27 January 1976, 10.

'Berlin Journal', *Film Comment*, 12.5, September–October 1976, 4, 69.

'Coming home', programme, Film Society of Lincoln Center gala for Martin Scorsese, world
     premiere of *New York, New York*, 21 June 1977.

'Rotterdam Journal', *Film Comment*, 13.4, July–August 1977, 6.

'Berlin Journal', *Film Comment*, 13.5, September–October 1977, 4.

'The redemption of despair', *Film Comment*, 13.5, September–October 1977, 23–4.

'Talk of the Devil', *Guardian*, 17 January 1978, 9.

'Turning points: Ruiz/Truffaut', *Sight & Sound*, 47.3, Summer 1978, 163–6.

'Alain Resnais', in Richard Roud (ed.), *Cinema: A Critical Dictionary: The Major Film-makers* (New York: Viking Press; London: Martin Secker & Warburg, 1980), 854–66.

'You're never alone on the strand', *Guardian*, 23 May 1980, 13.

'Rivette's punch goes home', *Guardian*, 4 February 1982, 11.

'Cheerful pessimist with the Spartan touch', *Guardian*, 23 June 1983, 11.

'At last! Proust the movie', *Tatler*, 279.3, March 1984, 76, 84.

'Freedom of the city forty years on', *Guardian*, 15 May 1986, 13.

'Letters from Truffaut', *Film Comment*, 24.5, September–October 1988, 76, 78.

'Malle x 4', *Sight & Sound*, 58.2, Spring 1989, 125–7.

Bibliographical references for other works cited

Anonymous, 'The London Film Festival', in Allan Eyles (ed.), *NFT 50: A Celebration of Fifty Years at the National Film Theatre* (London: BFI, 2002), 48–52.

Auty, Martyne, and Gillian Hartnoll, *Water Under the Bridge: Twenty-Five Years of the London Film Festival* (London: BFI, 1981), 116 pages.

Corliss, Richard, '70-millimeter nerves: Richard Roud interviewed by Richard Corliss', *Film Comment*, 23.5, September–October 1987, 36, 38, 42, 44, 46–7, 50, 52, 54.

Haberski, Raymond J., 'The first New York Film Festival and the heroic age of moviegoing', *It's Only a Movie! Films and Critics in American Movie Culture* (Lexington: University of Kentucky Press, 2001), 144–64.

Langlois, Georges, and Glenn Myrent, *Henri Langlois, premier citoyen du cinéma* (Paris: Editions Denoël, 1986), 445 pages.

Lopate, Phillip, 'The New York Film Festival: the first fifty years', in Laura Kern, Joanne Koch, and Richard Peña (eds), *New York Film Festival Gold: A Fiftieth Anniversary Celebration* (New York: Film Society of Lincoln Center, 2012), 14–41.

Mannoni, Laurent, *Histoire de la Cinémathèque française* (Paris: Gallimard, 2006), 507 pages

Nowell-Smith, Geoffrey, 'The *Sight & Sound* story, 1932–1992', in Christophe Dupin and Geoffrey Nowell-Smith (eds), *The British Film Institute, the Government and Film Culture, 1933–2000* (Manchester: Manchester University Press, 2012), 237–51.

Paletz, Robert Elliot, '*The New York Film Festival 1963–1966*', unpublished Master of Arts thesis, University of Wisconsin, 1969, 230 pages.

Rosenbaum, Jonathan, *Moving Places: A Life at the Movies* (New York: Harper and Row, 1980), 280 pages.

INDEX

Page numbers in italics denote illustrations.

FILM INDEX

Decades Never Start On Time

Decades Never Start On Time

Decades Never Start On Time

List of Illustrations

While considerable effort has been made to correctly identify the copyright holders, this has not been possible in all cases. We apologise for any apparent negligence, and any omissions or corrections brought to our attention will be remedied in any future editions.

The Thirty-Nine Steps, Gaumont–British Picture Corporation; Les Dames du Bois de Boulogne, FIlms Raoul Ploquin; Momma Don't Allow, British Film Institute Experimental Film Fund; Lola, Rome–Paris Films/Euro International Films; Il deserto rosso, Film Duemila/Francoriz; Une Femme mariée, Anouchka Films/Orsay Films; Alphaville, Chaumaine Productions/Filmstudio; If …., © Paramount Pictures Corporation; Il conformista, © Mars Film S.p.A.; The Godfather, © Paramount Pictures Corporation; The Sky's the Limit, RKO Radio Pictures; Badlands, © Pressman-Williams-Badlands Ltd; La Règle du jeu, Nouvelle Edition Française; Professione: reporter, © Compagnia Cinematografica Champion; Singin' in the Rain, © Loew's Incorporated; Pickpocket, Agnès Delahaie Productions; Les Vampires, Film Gaumont; La Grande Illusion, Réalisations d'Art Cinématographique; E.T. the Extra-Terrestrial, © Universal City Studios Inc.; Le Quai des brumes, Ciné-Alliance; L'Année dernière à Marienbad, Terra-Film/Société Nouvelle des Films Cormoran/Précitel/Como-Films/Argos-Films/Les Films Tamara/Cinétel/Silver-Films/Cineriz; Les Quatre Cents Coups, © Les Films du Carrosse.